Method in Madness: Case Studies in Cognitive Neuropsychiatry

edited by

Peter W. Halligan and John C. Marshall

Neuropsychology Unit,
University Department of Clinical Neurology,
Radcliffe Infirmary,
Oxford, UK

Psychology Press

An imprint of Erlbaum (UK) Taylor & Francis

© 1996 by Psychology Press, an imprint of
Erlbaum (UK) Taylor & Francis Ltd

Psychology Press
27 Church Road
Hove
East Sussex, BN3 2FA
U.K.

British Library Cataloguing in Publication Data

A catalogue record for this book is available from the British Library.

ISBN 0-86377-441-5 (hbk)
ISBN 0-86377-442-3 (pbk)

The cover illustration is taken from a
sculpture by Tom Greenshields after his stroke in 1989.

Cover design by Peter Richards
Subject Index by Dr Campbell Purton
Typeset by DP Photosetting, Aylesbury, Bucks.
Printed and bound in the United Kingdom by BPC Wheatons Ltd., Exeter

Contents

Preface

Though this be madness, yet there is method in it – Hamlet

Since cognitive processes are a manifestation of brain functioning, it would be surprising if we could understand the nature of mental illness following the effects of brain disease without considering the nature of the cognitive disorders involved. As the Decade of the Brain moves beyond the halfway mark, understanding the behaviour and subjective experiences of people who suffer from mental disorders remains a major challenge for medical science.

In the past, explanations of mental disorders at the biological and cognitive levels were often so different from each other that the potential for productive cross fertilisation was missed. Over the last decade, however, we have witnessed the fruitful application of cognitive neuropsychological models to the understanding of several psychiatric disorders. The success of this convergence has already given rise to a new hybrid term within neuroscience which emphasises the cognitive dimension when attempting to deconstruct the traditional syndromes of clinical psychiatry. Evidence of the growing interest in the explanation of the signs and symptoms *per se* can be seen from the growing number of relevant publications, together with the launch, earlier this year, of the new journal *Cognitive Neuropsychiatry*. We hope that this book will demonstrate some of the productive links that have been forged between cognitive neuropsychology and psychiatry over the past few years.

Following a general introduction, the book is divided into four sections, each of which deals with the breakdown of a specific kind of knowledge.

The aim of the book is to introduce the reader to a series of case studies which exemplify some of the best current developments in the new field of cognitive neuropsychiatry. The role of the single case, the emphasis on symptoms and signs, and the testing of explicit hypotheses (as in cognitive neuropsychology) is seen as paramount and has already contributed to considerable initial progress. A second aim of the book is to bring to life the essence and character of the patient's experience and behaviour, so often lost in third-person 'academic descriptions'. Unlike previous accounts, the chapters in this book attempt to reduce the discrepancy between formal presentation of the psychiatric illness and the experience of the actual patient struggling to make sense of the consequences of their illness.

The final version of the book was greatly improved by helpful reviews by John Morton, Simon Fleminger and Tony David. We would also like to thank Sonia Sharma and Paul Dukes at Psychology Press for their efficient editorial and production skills in guiding the book to completion. We are likewise grateful to Valerie Berry and Perdy Dobson for their considerable help in preparing, typing and collating the final manuscript. Finally, we must remember the many patients whose personal struggle to cope with, and understand, the consequences of their brain damage provided the inspiration for this research enterprise.

Peter W. Halligan and John C. Marshall
Oxford, September 1996

List of Contributors

Nick Alderman Kemsley Brain Injury Rehabilitation Unit, St Andrews Hospital, Northampton, NN1 5DG, UK.

Doreen Baxter Kemsley Brain Injury Rehabilitation Unit, St Andrews Hospital, Northampton, NN1 5DG, UK.

Paul W. Burgess Department of Psychology, University College London, Gower Street, London, WC1E 6BT, UK.

Connie Cahill Department of Psychology, University of Sheffield, Psychology Building, Western Bank, Sheffield, S10 2TP, UK.

Anthony David Institute of Psychiatry, De Crespigny Park, Denmark Hill, London, SE5 8AF, UK.

Sergio Della Sala Department of Psychology, University of Aberdeen, Aberdeen, AB24 2UB, UK.

Hadyn Ellis School of Psychology, University of Wales, Cardiff, PO Box 901, Cardiff, CF1 3YG, UK.

Thomas Fahy Maudsley Hospital, Denmark Hill, London, SE5 8AZ, UK.

Roberto Freschi Reparto di Neurologia, Ospedale di Legnano, Italy.

Christopher Frith Wellcome Department of Cognitive Neurology, Institute of Neurology, Queen Square, London, WC1N 3BG, UK.

Peter W. Halligan University Department of Clinical Neurology, Neuropsychology Unit, Radcliffe Infirmary, and Rivermead Rehabilitation Centre, Abingdon Road, Oxford, OX1 4XD, UK.

Roisin Kemp Department of Psychological Medicine, Institute of Psychiatry, London, SE5 8AF, UK.

Keith Laws Department of Experimental Psychology, University of Cambridge, Cambridge, UK.

Kate M. Leafhead   MRC Applied Psychology Unit, 15 Chaucer Road, Cambridge, Cambridge, CB2 2EF, UK.

Federica Lucchelli   Reparto di Neurologia, Ospedale S. Carlo Borromeo, Milan, Italy.

Claudio Luzzatti   Istituto di Psicologia della Facoltà Medica, Università di Milano, Italy.

John C. Marshall   University Department of Clinical Neurology, Neuropsychology Unit, Radcliffe Infirmary, Oxford, UK.

A. Paula McKay   Psychiatric Rehabilitation Service, Fulbourn Hospital, Cambridge, CB1 5EF, UK.

Peter J. McKenna   Psychiatric Rehabilitation Service, Fulbourn Hospital, Cambridge, CB1 5EF, UK.

Silvia Muggia   Clinica Neurologica III, Ospedale S. Paolo, University of Milan, Italy.

Alan Parkin   Experimental Psychology, University of Sussex, Brighton, BN1 9QG, UK.

Martyn Rose   Kemsley Brain Injury Rehabilitation Unit, St Andrews Hospital, Northampton, NN1 5DG, UK.

Ladé Smith   Maudsley Hospital, Denmark Hill, London, SE5 8AZ, UK.

Hans Spinnlerr   Clinica Neurologica III, Ospedale S. Paolo, University of Milan, Italy.

T. Krystyna Szulecka   Department of Psychiatry, Roundhay Wing, St. James's University Hospital, Leeds, LS9 7TF, UK.

Ruggero Verga   SRRF, Ospedale di Rho-Passirana, USSL 68 (Milano), Italy.

Edwin A. Weinstein   Laboratory of Neuroscience, National Institute on Aging, Bldg 10, 6C, 414. Bethesda, MD 20892, USA.

Andrew Young   MRC Applied Psychology Unit, 15 Chaucer Road, Cambridge, CB2 2EF, UK.

Section A

INTRODUCTION

1

Towards a Cognitive Neuropsychiatry

John C. Marshall and Peter W. Halligan
University Department of Clinical Neurology, Neuropsychology Unit, Radcliffe Infirmary, Oxford, UK

Controversy and disagreement are always at the heart of scientific advance. The enterprise is driven by Karl Popper's mixture of bold conjectures followed by rigorous attempts at falsification; competition in the world of ideas may be the best (perhaps the only) example of how a free market can produce (not the perfect theory but at least) successive approximations to the Truth. Discord, then, is healthy. And yet ... and yet ... there are some areas where one does begin to wish for somewhat more solid ground.

One of the most obvious examples is the study of "mental illness", the topic of *Method in Madness: Case Studies in Cognitive Neuropsychiatry*. It would be odd to put "physical illness" in scare quotes: Few people will disagree that stomach cancer or the mere common cold are regrettably real (and unhealthy) conditions. But the sheer range of opinion in psychiatry seems almost to demand that the concept of mental illness should not be taken at face value. In other branches of medicine, the incidence of different illnesses can vary substantially over time as a function of factors that raise no conceptual problems: heart attacks rise with a fatty diet and too little exercise; poliomyelitis falls as vaccination programmes become widespread. But in psychiatry, it seems, comparable fluctuations in incidence are often the result of diagnostic decisions determined by "the sociocultural fads and fashions of the day" (McHugh, 1995, p.110).

For example: Neurasthenia decimated the middle-class populations of the late 19th century (Beard, 1869; Gosling, 1987), disappeared in the early years of the 20th, and has (perhaps) re-emerged as ME (chronic fatigue syndrome) as the millennium draws nigh (Wessely, 1990). Likewise, multiple personality disorder (MPD) "has of late taken on epidemic proportions particularly in certain treatment centres" (McHugh, 1995, p.113). McHugh (1995) notes that the "diagnosis was reported less than 200 times from a variety of supposed causes prior to 1970", but "has been applied to more than 20,000 people in the last decade and largely attributed to sexual abuse" (p.113). McHugh then argues that the increase of MPD is "a remarkable example of manufactured artifactual behaviour" that is "bolstered by an invented view of its cause that fits a cultural pattern". Needless to say, McHugh's view is not without its critics (Powell, 1995), or indeed its ironies.

McHugh (1995) pours scorn upon the psychiatric profession for manufacturing the phenomenon of MPD, but he is then equally scathing of Thomas Szasz's claim that "Psychiatry creates schizophrenia" (Szasz, 1976). It is at this point that one really begins to worry. What, one asks, would count as empirical evidence (or theoretical argument) for or against the validity of a psychiatric diagnosis such as multiple personality disorder (Morton, 1994)? Or indeed *any* diagnostic category in psychiatry. The discipline seems to have bypassed Popper's rational falsificationalism in favour of Paul Feyerabend's Maoist anarchism (Let a thousand diagnoses flourish!). We are, for example, not entirely sure whether the authors of "Exorcism-resistant ghost possession treated with Clopenthixol" (Hale & Pinninti, 1994) really (truly, sincerely, hand-on-heart) believe in "genuine possession". Not the least of the problems posed by their fascinating paper is that the ghost in question was seen not merely by the "patient" but also by the prison chaplain and numerous "frightened cellmates". Strangely enough, neither the chaplain nor the cellmates were treated with Clopenthixol.

None of the chapters in *Method in Madness: Case Studies in Cognitive Neuropsychiatry* discusses these conundrums head on. None the less, issues of what kind of discipline psychiatry should be, what kinds of evidence are relevant to diagnosis, and what kinds of theoretical interpretation of positive and negative symptoms are possible and plausible, do form the background to all the studies reported here.

In terms of style, we asked the contributors to paint pictures of individual people. One reason for this request is well-expressed by Chadwick (1992, p.xii): "The essence and character of the psychotic subject is so easily lost or obscured in the, usually, rather dry pages of the experimental psychopathology literature—a fact that cannot help researchers and practitioners in this field to relate their conceptual knowledge to the flesh-and-blood people they deal with daily." But, as befits an investigation of psychopathology, our request was multiply determined. Study of single cases (or case series) over the last quarter of a century has led to a very considerable deepening of inquiry in the related discipline of cognitive neuropsychology; the study of disorders of language, memory, perception, and praxis consequent upon acquired brain damage began to flourish (again) once the notion of clinical syndromes ceased to be the primary "unit of analysis". The versatility of the single case approach is amply demonstrated throughout the current book. In one form, an illustrative case is described using interviews, standardised tests and neurological findings. Another variant involves theoretical discussion of particular symptoms as they emerge in the case presentation. Finally, a third approach describes the relatively "raw" phenomenology encountered by the examiners before the patient's condition is classified in terms of current neuropathology and psychopathology.

There is every chance that neuropsychiatry will be invigorated by concentration upon the signs and symptoms shown by individual patients (Shallice, Burgess, & Frith, 1991) just as a similar emphasis led to a renaissance in neuropsychology over the last quarter century. One problem common to earlier clinical studies in both neuropsychology and neuropsychiatry is that all definitions of major syndromes are polytypic (Schwartz, 1984). Patients are assigned a diagnostic label on the basis of a variable collection of features. There is thus no guarantee that patients within a particular taxonomic category have anything in common with each other, other than the diagnostic label itself. As Bedford and Foulds (1975, p.209) remark, in addition to the multiple primary signs and symptoms of illness diagnostic criteria in psychiatry have often also included "putative personality, aetiological, course of illness, situational, demographic and other such variables". The likelihood that any group of patients of purported type X will actually be homogenous at any useful theoretical level is not great. It is well known that the *Diagnostic and Statistical Manual of Mental Disorders* (*DSM*) of the American Psychiatric Association (and many comparable classification schemes) are intellectually vitiated by this fact. Yet, despite widespread acknowledgement of the limitations of unprincipled classificatory systems, mainstream psychiatry has shown little interest in moving beyond polytypic labelling; successive revisions of the *DSM* seem to have been more concerned with reliability than validity. This lack of concern with scientific justification can have seriously detrimental knock-on effects: For example, so-called "biological psychiatry" has often attempted to move directly from clinical label to biochemical deficit without paying much (if any) attention to the systemic level of analysis that could mediate between behaviour and material substrate (Marshall & Halligan, 1995). The danger, of course, is that this strategy will lead to extensive (and expensive) searches for the biological substrate of non-existent entities.

By contrast, modern neuropsychology has concentrated on the acquisition of empirical data that would support or disconfirm a theoretical position about the form and organisation of mental functions. The underlying construct is thus a model of normal performance in some cognitive domain or other. Such models of normal sentence comprehension, or face recognition, or long-term memory then provide the theoretical constraints on how the system can fractionate after brain damage. There is no need to attempt generalisation about "Wernicke's aphasia" (for example); there is no such entity (except as clinical shorthand). Rather, the patterns of impaired and preserved performance in individual cases (who may or may not have been assigned that taxonomic label) can be assessed for compatibility with normal models of psychological functioning. Those latter accounts can in turn be revised when data from pathology cannot be accommodated by the current version of the model.

This route to a genuinely scientific cognitive neuropsychology should be equally applicable to cognitive neuropsychiatry. As Persons (1986, p.1252) reflected, there are considerable advantages to "studying psychological phenomena rather than psychiatric diagnoses". Similarly, Bentall, Jackson, and Pilgrim (1988) have argued that the ever-controversial topic of "schizophrenia" should be approached from the standpoint of particular symptoms rather than syndromic classification. It is thus not surprising that, so far, many of the most detailed and insightful contributions of the cognitive approach have concentrated on such relatively rare but precise psychiatric conditions as the Capgras, Frégoli, and Cotard delusions. None the less, there is a very considerable literature on aspects of "schizophrenic" and "paranoid" disorder where inquiry has been guided by models that are already reasonably well-established in normal cognitive psychology (Bentall, 1990; Chadwick, 1992; David, 1994a; Frith, 1992). Likewise, there is theoretically motivated work on delusional memories (Kopelman, Guinan, & Lewis, 1995) and on psychogenic amnesias (Kopelman, Christensen, Puffett, & Stanhope, 1994). Whether the cognitive stance will throw significant light on conditions such as the affective psychosis and the more common neuroses (anxiety neurosis, phobias, and obsessive-compulsive conditions) remains to be seen. The interpretation of some forms of major depression in terms of the theory of learned helplessness (Peterson, Maier, & Seligman, 1993) is one encouraging example of the potential breadth of the approach. "Personality disorder", including psychopathy, is undoubtedly another area ripe for investigation; Blair (1995) suggests that the cognitive approach to "moral" (or forensic) disorders holds very considerable promise.

One further emphasis: We have no doubt that a *neuro*psychiatry is possible, despite the fact that many (or perhaps most) psychiatric conditions remain as yet "functional". The current chapters provide illustrations of psychopathology for which the underlying biological substrate is either unknown or highly controversial, and also cases where the disorder has been provoked (in part) by structural brain damage that is visible to such "old-fashioned" techniques as CT imaging. As Starr and Sporty (1994, p.977) note, the disciplines of neurology and psychiatry seem to be investigating "similar disorders viewed with different perspectives". It will be a major challenge, they write, to reconcile those perspectives. They (p.980) "recommend that efforts be made to bridge the gaps separating psychiatry and neurology, even to the point where the two specialities might become one" (as indeed they were in the 19th century). That bridge may have to be built from both sides, for, as Ron (1994) notes in her paper on somatisation, many of the physical symptoms seen in neurological practice have no "adequate physiological explanation". How much of a gap will always separate the two disciplines is debatable. Likewise, the extent to which the gap can be bridged by *in vivo* functional brain imaging is likely to remain highly controversial for some time to come (Silbersweig, Stern, Frith, Cahill, Holmes, & Grootoonk, 1995).

Irrespective of individual differences in the biological substrate of cognition, a further reason for concentrating on individual people ("cases") in the current volume is that it allows one to give due emphasis to the phenomenology of "mental illness". That the thoughts and feelings of these people have a neuronal bias is not in dispute here: None of our authors are Cartesian dualists (to our knowledge at least). None would deny that genetic, psychopharmacological and neurophysiological inquiries may be highly pertinent to the study of psychiatric phenomena. Nevertheless, the interpretation of pathological thoughts, feelings and beliefs (by both "patient" and "doctor") is as much a hermeneutic enterprise as it is a neuropharmacological one. Although we have not included full-scale self-reports in the current volume, we do note that what patients say (during or after their illness) has a significance over and above the status of verbal signs and symptoms (Chadwick, 1993; Sutherland, 1976). A unicausal medical model that adopts a reductionist attitude is not helpful (Graham, 1977). Concentration upon individuals and their individual symptoms enables their (and our) search for "meaning in experience" (Graham, 1977, p.78) to assume a significance at least as great as the search for the responsible anatomic or chemical lesion. Many of the patients reported here suffer hallucinations and delusions. To the individuals concerned, the content of their percepts and thoughts may be more important than their form. For some individuals, hallucination and delusion may even be an adaptive response to otherwise intolerable situations (Roberts, 1991). The investigator who wishes to understand the role that hallucinations and delusions play in the patient's life may likewise have to concede that content is at least as important as any formal thought disorder that may be present (Cutting, 1990).

More perhaps than in any other branch of medicine or psychology, psychiatry cannot avoid discussing the place of value in a world of facts (Köhler, 1938). Subsequent to the purported death of dualism, the mere fact that a particular psychological state is associated with a statistically atypical brain state (either morphological or physiological) does not licence the inference that the psychological state is "diseased". That there may be a morphological correlate of same-sex sexual orientation (LeVay, 1993) has no logical implications whatsoever concerning whether particular societies will regard homosexuality as a mental disease or as an acceptable way of life in a culturally diverse world. Frances (1994) has reported that more than 100 "new mental disorders" were proposed for inclusion in *DSM-IV*. Some of these "seem to have been suggested as a way of stigmatising undesirable behaviours by labelling them as an aspect of mental disorder", writes Frances, p.vii, giving as an example "Racist Personality Disorder". Would one be any more inclined to regard racism as a "mental illness" if the condition was (to some degree) heritable and was associated with a smaller than average thalamus?

This emphasis upon content and value leads straight to the psychological core of many mental illnesses: "The patient is deluded." A concern with "beliefs" is central to psychiatry but irrelevant to many of the conditions typically described in texts of behavioural neurology or cognitive neuropsychology. We say "many", not all, because some of the "frontal lobe syndromes" and some of the confabulatory behaviour seen after organic memory-loss fall into a hazy overlapping area of neurology and psychiatry that is concerned with conceptual content and appropriate action (Scheerer & Goldstein, 1966).

Discussion of delusions recurs in many of the following chapters, and we have intentionally spread the topic across different sections. We did not wish to imply that there was only one problem of "delusion": It is unlikely that a unified theory of delusions will be forthcoming and we have accordingly categorised the "pathological" beliefs reported here primarily by content. One would none the less hope that theories of normal belief-formation will eventually cast light on both the content of delusions and on the processes whereby the beliefs came to be held (and how they might be changed for the better). Current diagnostic criteria in psychiatry often imply that one can distinguish in a principled fashion between delusion and false belief (but see Berrios, 1991; Spitzer, 1990). An account of mental states that did not do so would seem to leave the entire population of the world in cognitive limbo, or worse still, subject to the protean forces of ideology: The belief that life in the USA is preferable to life in the USSR may (or may not) have been true, but to hold the opinion that it was better, hardly seems to qualify one for the diagnosis of paranoid schizophrenia (Podrabinek, 1980). None the less, as Chadwick (1992) writes, "the stock textbook image" of the deluded patient "invariantly and rigidly holding on to a certain belief has been challenged" in recent years. Indeed, some scholars have even denied that delusions are appropriately conceptualised as beliefs (see Garety & Hemsley, 1995). The notion that there is a continuum from normal to "delusional" thinking should come as a relief to many scholars. In a recent review of a book of interviews with highly eminent cognitive scientists, Sutherland (1995, p.223) has reflected that "It is interesting to observe the reluctance of the great to change their minds and to note the ways in which their arguments pass one another by."

Even within the more strictly psychiatric literature, Winters and Neale (1983, p.227) have observed that there are two broad classes of interpretations of delusions. The defect theme, they write, "argues that delusional thinking results from some fundamental cognitive-attentional deficit". By contrast, the motivational theme "assumes that the individual develops the delusion either to explain unusual perceptual experiences or to reduce uncomfortable psychic states". In the extreme case, some patients have found that it is their delusional belief system that gives meaning to their life (Roberts, 1991). One suspects that it is not only patients to whom this applies. The notion that delusions are maladaptive must be argued, not assumed. As Lyon, Kaney, and Bentall (1994) note, persecutory delusions may have a useful defensive function.

We cannot emphasise too strongly, however, that normal information-processing systems are the domain over which any disorder of psychological function must be defined. The elucidation of a disorder of reasoning presupposes an account of how normal reasoning takes place (Garety & Hemsley, 1995). The (correct) description of failures of reality testing presupposes a theory of normal reality-monitoring (Johnson, 1991). The (correct) description of hallucinations presupposes adequate theories of veridical perception (Halligan, Marshall, & Ramachandran, 1994). There are already many instances where explicit information-processing models, derived from cognitive psychology and neuropsychology, have been used to explain psychiatric symptoms. Well-known examples include delusional misidentification (Young, Reid, Wright, et al., 1993), alien control (Frith & Done, 1989), thought echo (David, 1994b) and aspects of autistic disorder (Baron-Cohen, Ring, Moriarty, et al., 1994). Some of these conditions (and many more) are exposed in the chapters that follow.

Although this volume stresses the "cognitive" in cognitive neuropsychiatry, it is apparent that there is significant variation in the extent to which the contributors are currently able (or willing) to provide a cognitive interpretation for all the presenting symptoms that they discuss. None the less, however disparate in content and however diverse in the specifics of their approach, all the chapters are firmly linked by the constraint that David (1993, p.4) stated in an earlier introduction to cognitive neuropsychiatry: "The only way to understand psychological phenomena is in terms of psychology."

Many of the psychiatric conditions that have recently exercised the imagination of cognitive neuroscientists are summarised in the following introductory chapter by Edwin Weinstein, a pioneer explorer of the border zone between neurology and psychiatry.

ACKNOWLEDGEMENTS

We acknowledge the support of our own work provided by the Medical Research Council. We are also very grateful to Val Berry and Perdy Dobson for administrative support.

REFERENCES

Baron-Cohen, S., Ring, H., Moriarty, J., Schmitz B., Costa, D., & Ell, P. (1994). Recognition of mental state terms: Clinical findings in children with autism and a functional neuroimaging study of normal adults. *British Journal of Psychiatry, 165*, 640–649.

Beard, G.M. (1869). Neurasthenia, or nervous exhaustion. *Boston Medical and Surgical Journal, 3*, 217–221.

Bedford, A., & Foulds, G.A. (1975). Humpty Dumpty and psychiatric diagnosis. *Bulletin of the British Psychological Society, 28*, 208–211.

Bentall, R.P. (Ed.). (1990). *Reconstructing schizophrenia*. London: Routledge.

Bentall, R.P., Jackson, H.F., & Pilgrim, D. (1988). Abandoning the concept of schizophrenia: Some implications of validity arguments for psychological research into psychotic phenomena. *British Journal of Clinical Psychology, 27*, 303–324.

Berrios, G.E. (1991). Delusions as "wrong beliefs": A conceptual history. *British Journal of Psychiatry, 159* (suppl. 14), 6–13.

Blair, R.J.R. (1995). A cognitive developmental approach to morality: Investigating the psychopath. *Cognition, 57*, 1–29.

Chadwick, P.K. (1992). *Borderline: A psychological study of paranoia and delusional thinking*. London: Routledge.

Chadwick, P.K. (1993). The stepladder to the impossible: A first hand phenomenological account of a schizoaffective psychotic crisis. *Journal of Mental Health, 2*, 239–250.

Cutting, J. (1990). *The right cerebral hemisphere and psychiatric disorders*. Oxford: Oxford University Press.

David, A.S. (1993). Cognitive neuropsychiatry. *Psychological Medicine, 23*, 1–5.

David, A.S. (1994a). Dysmodularity: A neurocognitive model for schizophrenia. *Schizophrenic Bulletin, 20*, 249–255.

David, A.S. (1994b). Thought echo reflects the activity of the phonological loop. *British Journal of Clinical Psychology, 33*, 81–83.

Frances, A.J. (1994). Foreword. In J.Z. Sadler, O.P. Wiggins, & M.A. Schwartz (Eds.), *Philosophical perspectives on psychiatric diagnostic classification*. Baltimore, Md.: The Johns Hopkins University Press.

Frith, C.D. (1992). *The cognitive neuropsychology of schizophrenia*. Hove, UK: Lawrence Erlbaum Associates Ltd.

Frith, C.D., & Done, J.D. (1989). Experiences of alien control in schizophrenics reflect a disorder in the central monitoring of action. *Psychological Medicine, 19*, 359–363.

Garety, P.A., & Hemsley, D.R. (1995). *Delusions: Investigations into the psychology of delusional reasoning*. Oxford: Oxford University Press.

Gosling, F.G. (1987). *Before Freud: Neurasthenia and the American medical community, 1870–1910*. Urbana, Ill.: University of Illinois Press.

Graham, P. (1977). Psychology and psychiatry—Relations and overlap. *Bulletin of the British Psychological Society, 30*, 76–79.

Hale, A.S., & Pinninti, N.R. (1994). Exorcism-resistant ghost possession treated with clopenthixol. *British Journal of Psychiatry, 165*, 386–388.

Halligan, P.W., Marshall, J.C., & Ramachandran, V.S. (1994). Ghosts in the machine: A case description of visual and haptic hallucinations after right hemisphere stroke. *Cognitive Neuropsychology, 11*, 459–477.

Johnson, M.K. (1991). Reality monitoring: Evidence from confabulation in organic brain disease patients. In G.P. Prigatano & D.L. Schacter (Eds.), *Awareness of deficit after brain injury.* New York: Oxford University Press.

Köhler, W. (1938). *The place of value in a world of facts.* New York: Liveright Publishing Corporation.

Kopelman, M.D., Christensen, H., Puffett, A., & Stanhope, N. (1994). The great escape: A neuropsychological study of psychogenic amnesia. *Neuropsychologia, 32,* 675–691.

Kopelman, M.D., Guinan, F.M., & Lewis, P.D.R. (1995). Delusional memory, confabulation and frontal lobe dysfunction: A case study of De Clérambault's syndrome. *Neurocase, 1,* 71–77.

LeVay, S. (1993). *The sexual brain.* Cambridge, Mass.: MIT Press.

Lyon, H.M., Kaney, S., & Bentall, R.P. (1994). The defensive function of persecutory delusions: Evidence from attribution tasks. *British Journal of Psychiatry, 164,* 637–646.

Marshall, J.C., & Halligan, P.W. (1995). Method in madness. *British Journal of Psychiatry, 167,* 157–158.

McHugh, P.R. (1995). Witches, multiple personalities, and other psychiatric artefacts. *Nature Medicine, 1,* 110–114.

Morton, J. (1994). Cognitive perspectives on memory recovery. *Applied Cognitive Psychology, 8,* 389–398.

Persons, J.B. (1986). The advantages of studying psychological phenomena rather than psychiatric diagnoses. *American Psychologist, 41,* 1252–1260.

Peterson, C., Maier, S.F., & Seligman, M.E.P. (1993). *Learned helplessness.* Oxford: Oxford University Press.

Podrabinek, A. (1980). *Punitive medicine.* Ann Arbor, Mich.: Karoma.

Powell, B.R. (1995). Psychiatry disabused. *Nature Medicine, 1,* 491–492.

Roberts, G. (1991). Delusional belief systems and meaning in life: A preferred reality? *British Journal of Psychiatry, 159* (suppl. 14), 19–28.

Ron, M. (1994). Somatisation in neurological practice. *Journal of Neurology, Neurosurgery, and Psychiatry, 57,* 1161–1164.

Scheerer, M., & Goldstein, G. (1966). Denial and selective amnesia following brain damage: A case study. *Neuropsychologia, 4,* 357–363.

Schwartz, M.F. (1984). What the classical aphasia categories can't do for us, and why. *Brain and Language, 21,* 3–8.

Shallice, T., Burgess, P.W., & Frith, C.D. (1991). Can the neuropsychological case-study approach be applied to schizophrenia? *Psychological Medicine, 21,* 661–673.

Silbersweig, D.A., Stern, E., Frith, C., Cahill, C., Holmes, A., Grootoonk, S., Seaward, J., McKenna, P., Chua, S.E., Schnorr, L., Jones, T., & Frackowiak, R.S.J. (1995). A functional neuroanatomy of hallucinations in schizophrenia. *Nature, 378,* 176–179.

Spitzer, M. (1990). On defining delusions. *Comprehensive Psychiatry, 31,* 377–397.

Starr, A., & Sporty, L.D. (1994). Similar disorders viewed with different perspectives: A challenge for neurology and psychiatry. *Archives of Neurology, 51,* 977–980.

Sutherland, S. (1976). *Breakdown.* London: Weidenfeld.

Sutherland, S. (1995). Optimistic mumblings. *Nature, 376,* 222–223.

Szasz, T. (1976). *Schizophrenia: The sacred symbol of psychiatry.* New York: Basic Books.

Wessely, S. (1990). Old wine in new bottles: Neurasthenia and "ME". *Psychological Medicine, 20,* 35–53.

Winters, K.C., & Neale, J.M. (1983). Delusions and delusional thinking in psychotics: A review of the literature. *Clinical Psychology Review, 3,* 227–253.

Young, A.W., Reid, I., Wright, S., & Hellawell, D.J. (1993). Face-processing impairments and the Capgras delusion. *British Journal of Psychiatry, 162,* 695–698.

2 Reduplicative Misidentification Syndromes

Edwin A. Weinstein
Laboratory of Neuroscience, National Institute on Aging, and National Institute of Health, Bethesda, Maryland, USA

INTRODUCTION

Reduplicative misidentifications include reduplicative paramnesia, other reduplicative phenomena, a number of the eponymic delusions such as those of Capgras, Frégoli, and Cotard, the illusion of intermetamorphosis and enchantment, and autoscopic experiences. These occur in many neurological and psychiatric diseases and have in common the idea of doubles, duplicates and substitutes—the term "reduplication" is used because there may be more than one double. The conditions have been usually grouped under the rubric of "delusional misidentification syndromes" (DMS), but the terms "reduplicative misidentification syndromes" (RMS) and "reduplicative phenomena" (RP) are used here to emphasise the theme of reduplication and because patients may or may not recognise the irrational quality of their beliefs. Moreover, not only delusions but hallucinations and altered feeling states are involved. For didactic purposes I refer to neurological and psychiatric patients: by neurological, I mean a patient admitted to hospital for symptoms suggestive of a central nervous system lesion; by psychiatric I mean a patient admitted to hospital for disturbances of behaviour even though investigation reveals evidence of brain damage.

TYPES OF REDUPLICATION

Reduplicative phenomena occur in the modalities of place, person, time and event, objects, parts of the body, and the self.

13

Environmental Reduplication

This is the belief that there are two or more places of the same name although only one actually exists. The first case was described in 1903 by Arnold Pick under the title, "reduplicative paramnesia". Pick's patient was a 67-year-old woman with senile dementia who stated that there were two clinics in Prague, each headed by a Professor Pick, a "town" clinic and a "suburb" clinic, at times an "old" clinic and a "new" one, and that she knew one of the patients and one of the assistants from the "old" clinic. Pick commented that "by her dignified demeanor and a certain wit she was able to deceive one as to her mental state" (Pick, 1903).

Henry Head (1926) reported the case of a British soldier who sustained a frontal missile wound in World War I. The man believed that there were two towns of Boulogne in France, one which he went through on his way to the front, and the other through which he passed on his way home to England on leave. Head remarked that the man was rational in all other respects except that he wrote letters to his mother, even though he knew that she had been dead for years.

FIG. 2.1.   Arnold Pick, 1851–1924.

Paterson and Zangwill (1944) reported the case of a New Zealander who sustained a head wound in World War II. The soldier stated that according to the map he was in Scotland (his actual location) but that he was really in Auckland. It is not uncommon for patients to say that they are in a "branch" or "annex" of the main hospital, or that one part is a hospital and another something else. An occasional patient may claim that he or she is in more than one location, as in the case of a woman reported by Ruff and Volpe (1981) who commented that it was kind that the New York Hospital had constructed an annex in her home. A patient may state that the hospital was formerly a non-medical facility, such as a restaurant.

Reduplication of Person

This is the belief that a single person has more than one identity or that a person has been replaced by an identical or almost identical other. For example, a man with Alzheimer's disease claimed that he had two wives each named Mary (Weinstein, Friedland, & Wagner, 1994), and a woman recovering from a subarachnoid haemorrhage believed that her physician was also her insurance agent (Weinstein, Kahn, & Sugarman, 1952). Affected patients have also be known to add to the number of their children.

Capgras syndrome, described by Joseph Capgras in 1923, is the delusion that a person, usually a close relative, has been replaced by a double or near

FIG. 2.2.   Joseph Capgras, 1873–1950. (*Source:* Jean-Pierre Luauté.)

double. Capgras' first patient was a 53-year-old woman with delusions of grandeur and persecution who believed that her husband was an impostor (Capgras & Reboul-Lachaux, 1923). His second patient was a 30-year-old woman who thought that her boyfriend had left her and been replaced by several doubles (Capgras, Lucchini, & Schiff, 1924).

The Frégoli delusion, named for a popular stage impersonator, is the false belief that a person, often a persecutor, has disguised himself as someone known to the patient. The first case, described by Courbon and Fail (1927), was that of a young would-be actress who believed that she was being persecuted by the famous French actresses, Robine and Sarah Bernhardt who, while impersonating her relatives, tormented her and caused her to have erotic feelings. Capgras and Frégoli may be difficult to distinguish as in a case in which a patient thinks that other men are her husband in disguise (Bland, 1970).

The rare illusion of intermetamorphosis, initially described by Courbon and Tusques in 1932, differs from Frégoli in that a person is thought to have been physically transformed "body and soul" into another. Their patient was a 49-year-old woman with paranoid and depressive features, and feelings of unreality and depersonalisation, who believed that certain people could change themselves bodily into others. The distinction between Frégoli and intermetamorphosis is sometimes not clear, as in beliefs that people have been disguised or transformed by plastic surgery or organ transplants. Young (1993) comments that while cases of delusional misidentification are often discussed as if they fall into distinct syndromes, in practice the recognised variants may shade into or accompany one another.

Temporal Reduplication

This is the belief that an ongoing event or period of time has also occurred in the past; an enduring *déjà fait*, *déjà vecu*, or *déjà vu* experience. A patient admitted to hospital for a head injury after a car accident may state that he has been in several recent automobile accidents, and on entering for surgery may claim that he has had the operation previously. A patient with a severe head injury studied by Staton, Brumback, and Wilson (1982) expressed the belief that the eight years of disability which had elapsed since his injury had also occurred in the more remote past. Patients may believe that particular events or states may be occurring elsewhere, as in the belief that other people have the same illness. One patient, following a head injury, wondered whether it was also 15th March on other planets (Weinstein & Burnham, 1991). It may be very difficult to separate temporal reduplication from other forms, as in the case of a man with Alzheimer's disease who insisted that his examining physician had performed the same procedures a year earlier (Weinstein et al., 1994).

Reduplication of Objects

This involves both inanimate and animate objects, and is almost always limited to things "belonging" to the patient. These have included reduplication of an automobile in a case of encephalitis (Weinstein, Linn, & Kahn, 1955), binoculars and paint brushes in a patient with a pituitary tumour (Anderson, 1988), a hospital bed in a patient with a spinal cord tumour receiving electroconvulsive therapy (ECT) for depression and intractable pain (Weinstein, Linn, & Kahn, 1952), household objects in a woman with episodes of anxiety and depression (Abed & Fewtrell, 1990), and the patient's pet cat in a case of head injury (Staton et al., 1982).

Reduplication of Parts of the Body

This is the belief that one has an additional part or parts of the body, or that a member has been replaced. Such "phantom" organs have since included both left and right arms and legs, eyes and ears (Critchley, 1953; Halligan, Marshall, & Wade, 1993; Weinstein, Kahn, Malitz, & Rozanski, 1954). The patient states, however, that he has only one self.

Reduplication of the Self

This is the belief that one has another self, or that the original self has been replaced. Capgras' original patient believed that there were doubles of herself as well as of her husband and children, plotting to steal her inheritance (Capgras, 1923). A variant is the belief by the patient that he is himself an impostor or an impersonator of his "real" self. A patient with Alzheimer's disease may believe that his reflection in the mirror is that of another person. Autoscopic phenomena are transient reduplicative phenomena in that a person sees or otherwise senses the presence of someone who looks and acts exactly, or almost exactly, like himself.

Cotard's syndrome is the delusion that one is dead or does not exist, or that others are dead or do not exist, or that one's body has been replaced by a corpse. It occurs in severely depressed neurological and psychiatric patients and is not uncommon. Described under the heading of "nihilistic delusions" by Jules Cotard in 1882, the first reported case may have been that of Charles Bonnet in 1769 (Förstl & Beats, 1992). Bonnet's patient was a 70-year-old woman, who, following a stroke which paralysed one side of her body, lay as dead for four days. She then insisted that she was dead and should be dressed in a shroud, placed in a coffin, and buried. Bonnet comments that she was of otherwise sound reason, and that even in death could not abstain from her female habit of beautifying herself, arranging her shroud and complaining about the whiteness of the linen.

INCIDENCE AND DISTRIBUTION

As the examples indicate, reduplicative misidentification syndromes (RMS) occur in a wide variety of neurological and psychiatric conditions. The incidence is difficult to state because reduplicative phenomena (RP) may not be distinguished from other delusions or confabulations or may be regarded as manifestations of memory loss or confusion. Also, patients may be reluctant to voice their reduplicative experiences and feelings of unreality for fear of being thought psychotic. Systematic questioning of the patient is only rarely done, and is especially important because one form of reduplication is so often associated with another. An investigation of RP should including the following questions:

- Have you ever been here before?
- How many hospitals of this name are there?
- Have you seen or met me before?
- Have you known any of the people here previously?
- How many recent accidents (operations) have you had?
- How many children (other relatives) do you have?
- Have any of your possessions been replaced?
- Do you know of anyone else with your illness?
- How many arms (legs, etc.) do you have?
- Do you or other people feel unreal?

RMS are common after severe closed head injuries. A study of 100 patients seen at the Walter Reed Army Medical Center after a loss of consciousness of at least eight hours showed that when aphasic and severely withdrawn patients were excluded, 90% expressed some form of reduplication at some stage in the course of recovery (Weinstein & Lyerly, 1968). Estimates of delusional misidentification syndromes (DMS) in Alzheimer's disease run from 18 to 35% depending on whether such phenomena as phantom boarders and mistaking television performers for people in the room are included (Förstl, Burns, Jacoby, & Levy, 1991; Rubin, Drevetz, & Burke, 1988). RMS have been reported after ruptured aneurysms of the circle of Willis (Bouckoms, Martuza, & Henderson, 1986; Weinstein, Kahn, & Sugarman, 1952); with tumours of the third ventricle, basal frontal lobes, and other midline structures (Weinstein & Kahn, 1955); and with lateralised neoplasms, haematomas and infarcts, more frequently in the right than the left hemisphere (Leiguarda, 1983; Levine, Calvanio, & Rinn, 1991; Ruff & Volpe, 1981; Todd, Dewhurst, & Wallis, 1981). Capgras, Frégoli, and other RP have been noted in epilepsy (Christodoulou, 1976; Drake, 1987; Lewis, 1987); in two cases of migraine (Bhatia, 1990; MacCallum, 1973); and sporadically in a large number of infectious, metabolic, endocrinological, and drug-related disorders (Förstl, Almeida, Owen, Burns, & Howard,

1991). RMS have also been reported in several patients receiving electroconvulsive therapy (Hay, 1986; Weinstein, Linn, et al., 1952). Existing RMS may also clear as the result of ECT. Among psychiatric patients, paranoid schizophrenia and depression have been the most frequent diagnoses. A study of consecutive admissions of 195 patients meeting criteria for functional psychoses showed a prevalence of full definite DMS of 3.6% (Lewis, 1993).

CLINICAL FEATURES

Despite the many types and different etiologies, and whether or not patients are considered psychotic or delusional, RMS have to some degree a number of features in common. These are: selectivity, the coexistence of one form with another, dissociation and implicit knowledge, feelings of unreality, symbolic aspects, and associated behavioural disorders.

Selectivity

As a rule, only one or a few people, places, objects, or parts of the body are involved in the reduplicative process. The Capgras patient may misidentify only a spouse, a few close relatives, or a single doctor or nurse. Environmental reduplication is limited to the hospital and patient's home or, in one case, home city (Thompson, Silk, & Hover, 1980). Reduplication of objects includes only personal possessions. The patient who sees his or her double in a mirror identifies the mirror images of other people correctly. Patients only reduplicate a part of the body, the function of which is impaired in some way: an arm on the side of a hemiplegia, a head which has been the site of a craniotomy.

Situational factors may be a determinant. One of our patients (Weinstein et al., 1954) with an "extra" arm would brush away the phantom during interviews, but was not observed to do so on other occasions. MacCallum (1984) described the behaviour of three elderly women who accepted their daughters as they were when the daughters were engaged in caring for them, but who addressed them as different women with the same names when the daughters were engaged in other duties.

Coexistence of Types

One form of reduplication is frequently associated with another. The patient who says that there are three Walter Reed Hospitals may claim that he has been in several accidents, and the one who believes that he has an extra hand may think that other patients are old friends and relatives. About half the patients with reduplication of body parts reported in the literature have had other forms of reduplication or feelings of depersonalisation. Capgras,

Frégoli, and Cotard may be associated, and the rare illusion of metamorphosis and enchantment has invariably been coupled with other RP.

The eponymic delusions may also be associated with environmental reduplication. After the patient described by Charles Bonnet no longer believed that she was dead, she thought that she was in Norway rather than in her home in Copenhagen (Förstl & Beats, 1992). A review of the literature by Signer (1987) showed an approximate 3:2 ratio of single to multiple forms, but the incidence of coexistence is difficult to state because of differences in methods of study and classification.

Dissociation and Implicit Knowledge

Capgras observed that while a patient misidentified her spouse, she recognised him in that she did not mistake him for any known person, did not mistake someone else for him, or give the impostor a name. She might say that the double looked exactly or almost exactly like the real spouse but that she felt that he was different. It was because sensorium, memory, and perception were intact that Capgras rejected an organic aetiology, although some of his cases had evidence of brain damage. He concluded, rather, that the behaviour was an affective conflict of psychological origin (Luauté, 1986). Although a neurological patient may say that a nurse is a former girlfriend from his home town, he does not talk to her about the old days, and relates to her strictly in her professional role.

Feelings of Unreality

Feelings of unreality and unfamiliarity are a common component of RMS. Depersonalisation and derealisation were prominent in Capgras' second case (Capgras et al., 1924). The patient was a 30-year-old dancer with general paresis who was admitted to hospital for sensations of being electrocuted and auditory hallucinations. She complained of a feeling of strangeness about herself and the world around her: "It seems to me that it is not I who lived my previous life, and I remember very well my life as a dancer in the balls of Menilmontant. I remember everything exactly." As noted she went on to develop the delusion of doubles. Capgras believed that the delusion served to combat the threat of depersonalisation.

Cotard's syndrome, the delusion of nihilism, may be the ultimate expression of depersonalisation—derealisation. Such patients not only claim that they are dead or non-existent and that their bodies have been replaced by corpses, but they may also act dead. They may be mute or speak in sepulchral tones. Along with saying that they have no feelings, they may not respond to noxious stimuli and threatening gestures, showing the phenomenon of pain asymbolia (Weinstein, Kahn, & Slote, 1955). They are akinetic and often refuse to eat. While most are severely depressed, some are paranoid with ideas of torture and body dismemberment, and others show no affect at all.

Other forms of reduplication are frequently present. A study of 22 cases with Cotard symptomatology and neoplastic, vascular, and encephalopathic lesions found that 14 patients had associated environmental, personal, or temporal reduplication (Weinstein, Kahn, & Slote 1955). In a case reported by Greenberg, Hochberg, and Murray (1984), the patient following a craniotomy for a right frontal malignant astrocytoma had the feeling that he was dead and in two places at once. The authors note that he was oriented to place and had excellent insight and judgement. A young woman with a diagnosis of schizophrenia studied by Enoch and Trethowan (1979) had Capgras and Cotard syndromes, reduplication of an inanimate object (the Bible), and a feeling that strangers were old acquaintances.

Symbolic Aspects

The actual and the other or fictitious persons, places, objects, events, periods of time, parts of the body, and selves are not identical but almost always differ in some respect germane to the patient's own experiences, feelings, and problems. With feelings of unreality, a patient may find some trivial physical difference to support his or her conviction that the "other" person is not who he or she claims to be. Among neurological patients, the "other" may be a personification or other symbolic representation of the disability. For example, a man with a craniopharyngioma filling his third ventricle and a visual defect thought that his special nurse had a daughter who took care of him on alternate days. He said that the two women looked exactly alike except that the daughter wore glasses (Weinstein & Kahn, 1955, pp.49 & 132, and Case 10). Depressed and paranoid patients preoccupied with ideas of death and violence may claim that the person who has been replaced by a double has been murdered, tortured, abducted, or imprisoned. Patients with sexual problems may feel that the "real" spouse was more sexy, and elderly patients who feel neglected may believe that the "real" spouse was more affectionate and caring.

In environmental reduplication, the "other" hospital is frequently located in the patient's home town or even in his or her home. A patient who had sustained multiple injuries in a car accident claimed that there were three Walter Reed Hospitals, one for head injuries, one for fractures, and one for plastic surgery (Weinstein, Salazar, & Jones, 1995). In the instance of temporal reduplication described by Staton et al. (1982), the patient who thought that the eight years that had elapsed since his head injury had occurred in the more remote past believed that the earlier period had resulted in complete recovery. In the case of reduplication of objects reported by Anderson (1988), the patient, a 73-year-old married man with a pituitary tumour, a visual field defect, and a history of probable sexual impotence, claimed that the replaced paint brushes had fewer bristles and the replaced binoculars had more worn threads than the originals. A hemiplegic patient with an "extra" left hand may state that there is nothing wrong with his own hand. In reduplication of the self an Alzheimer's patient may see her double in the mirror as looking older and more haggard.

Associated Behaviour

Reduplicative phenomena following severe head injury with loss of consciousness may occur along with retrograde amnesia, confabulation, anosognosia, and environmental disorientation and are apt to persist after these disturbances have cleared. In some patients, RP do not appear until these states are no longer present, sometimes weeks, months, and even years after the trauma, and the patient seems relatively normal. In two stroke patients well studied by Gilliatt and Pratt (1952) and Halligan et al. (1993) a phantom limb did not develop until several months after anosognosia for hemiplegia. In the case reported by Staton et al. (1982) the patient had had feelings of unreality since the first months after his head injury but *déjà vu* experiences did not appear until four years later. Subsequently, he came to believe that his parents and siblings, the family farm, and his pet cat were not really his but were slightly different look-alikes.

In other patients, some with a history of brain impairment, RMS have been precipitated by some stressful event. Capgras syndrome has been reported following a drug overdose in a patient with complex partial seizures (Lewis, 1987), during a migraine attack (Bhatia, 1990; MacCallum, 1973), with a bout of fever in depression (Christodoulou, 1976), and after an emotional crisis in a man with ideas of persecution and a history of a skull fracture and a febrile seizure in childhood (Lansky, 1974). In the schizophrenic and affective psychoses, RP are less apt to appear as an initial manifestation than they are after a period of agitation, hallucinations, and other delusions. A literature review of Capgras syndrome in psychoses showed RP as an initial symptom in only one-third of cases, and late onset, up to 10 years after initial symptoms in the remainder (Kimura, 1986). With multiple hospital admissions a patient may have RP in one episode and not another. Retrograde amnesia, confabulation, anosognosia, and environmental disorientation not only occur along with RMS or precede them, but also share some features with them. These include feelings of unreality, evidence of implicit knowledge, and selective and symbolic aspects.

Retrograde Amnesia following head injuries may be associated with depersonalisation and derealisation (Weinstein, Marvin, & Keller, 1962). A patient may not only not recall his accident but may not believe that it actually occurred, despite having been told many times by his doctor and family, and in the face of such evidence as side rails on his bed and a cast on his leg. There is often implicit knowledge of what one does not consciously remember. The soldier who does not recall if he has been in the military still talks in army slang, and is capable of carrying out service procedures. Similarly, a patient who cannot remember if he is married may be able to describe his wife and recognise her when he sees her.

Confabulations following brain injury are of several types. They may be fantastic or banal, spontaneous or elicited, related or not related to the patient's experience. Most confabulations after brain damage are elicited in response to questions about the accident, injury, disability, or hospitalisation. While such fictitious narrations are ostensible references to past events they may also be allegorical or metaphorical representations of current experiences and problems. (Weinstein, Kahn, & Malitz, 1967). For example, a patient with an oculomotor nerve palsy after rupture of an aneurysm confabulated that he had been punched in the eye in a fight over a girl (Weinstein, 1991). Initially, confabulations may be multiple, evanescent, and changeable, but, later in the course of recovery, there may be only a single consistent story. The content is determined by the nature of the trauma and disability, those themes which have been important sources of identity and elements in patterns of social relatedness such as work and family, and popular topics in the news like Communism and nuclear warfare during the Cold War. For example, an officer who had undergone a painful carotid angiogram confabulated that he had presided over the hanging of an American World War II deserter, in which "his neck was stretched at least several inches" (Weinstein & Lyerly, 1968). The execution was the subject of a best seller at the time. The patient also believed that an "extra" child had been killed in the car accident.

Anosognosia for hemiplegia—and other disabilities—has features of depersonalisation and derealisation. Alienation is also expressed in *anosodiaphoria*, a lack of emotional concern for the disability. A patient may not feel that his arm is paralysed or even that it belongs to him. He may refer to it as an inanimate or even an animate object, and talk of it, and also himself, in the third person, as "he", "she", or "it" (Weinstein & Kahn, 1955). Implicit knowledge of what the patient does not consciously perceive or remember is often evident. A patient may admit that his arm does not move but deny that he is paralysed, and some awareness is indicated in such pejorative characterisations of the limb as "dead wood". A series of 16 patients with RP showed denial of various disabilities to be present in 12 cases (Weinstein, Kahn, et al., 1962). From the standpoint of classification it may be hard to separate anosognosia for hemiplegia from reduplication of body parts, as in the case of a woman who said that her arm felt so strange that it must, in fact, belong to her dead husband (Ullman, Ashenhurst, Hurwitz & Gruen, 1960).

Environmental Disorientation   also has positive, symbolic aspects in that the misdesignations of the hospital or its location may represent the patient's experiences, problems and relationships, and help impart feelings of familiarity. As in reduplication, the patient's errors persist despite cues, clues and corrections. Environmental disorientation may precede environmental reduplication. A patient initially maintained that Mount Sinai Hospital in Manhattan was situated close to her home in the Bronx even though she recognised Central Park from her windows (Weinstein & Burnham, 1991). She solved her dilemma by deciding that there were two Mount Sinais, one in Manhattan and the other in the Bronx. Similarly, the paradox that one is in two places at the same time may be resolved by the reduplication.

CASE REPORTS

Case 1

The first case illustrates the ocurrence of reduplication in an amnestic-confabulatory state, the way "other" places and events may symbolise the patient's feelings and experiences, and the association of RP with feelings of unreality.

A 43-year-old field grade military officer was admitted to the Walter Reed Army Medical Center because of four days of intense headache. Papilloedema was found and ventriculography and angiography showed dilatation of the lateral ventricles and a mass in the third ventricle. Through a right frontal approach a colloid cyst, 3–4cm in diameter, arising from the anterior roof of the third ventricle was removed. The column of the right fornix stretched over the tumour was sectioned during the procedure. The patient had a stormy post-operative course, with confusion, disorientation, and memory loss. While he appeared rational he variously stated that he was at Fort Smith, Virginia (where he had been commander), or at Fort Meade in Maryland, and that Fort Smith had been moved to Germany. He made a good physical recovery and was allowed to go on convalescent leave. At home, however, he became agitated and sexually aggressive and, after threatening his wife, was admitted to the psychiatric service of the hospital.

The patient was initially interviewed four weeks after his operation. When asked why he had come to the hospital he went into a long, rambling, garbled partly confabulatory account of his military career, citing the assignments he had been given, the posts in which he had served, and the technical training which he had received. When the question was repeated he confabulated that he had been evacuated from Vietnam (where he had not served) for psychiatric difficulties. He did not deny that his memory was impaired but did not bring up the subject. When asked about the craniotomy scar, he claimed that he had been operated upon in Germany (where he had served) for his mental problem. He was disoriented for date but stated correctly that he was in Walter Reed Hospital. Several days later, however, he offered a confabulated journey stating that he had spent the weekend at Fort Smith.

The first RP appeared six weeks following surgery. He expressed the belief that the examiner had brought him from Fort Smith to Walter Reed for his memory problems. He also advanced the idea that this was his second admission to Psychiatry. He thought that he had been hospitalised several years previously with a similar problem for which he had been given ECT successfully and had returned to duty. He also believed that he had had two tours of duty at Fort Smith, one as commander and the other as a patient. There were, moreover, two Fort Smiths, one in Virginia and one in Germany. There was also reduplication of his operation. He claimed that he had two craniotomies, one for a benign tumour and the other to learn whether there had been a recurrence.

Over the next three weeks there was much less confabulation and more mention of his memory loss. He maintained, however, that there were two Walter Reed Hospitals, a branch for psychiatry located in Virginia, and a main hospital in Washington. By the end of the third post-operative month he was completely oriented and not confabulating or reduplicating. His EEG had returned to a normal rhythm after a period of diffuse slow wave acuity. He had a verbal IQ of 124, performance IQ of 104, and a full-scale IQ of 119. Memory quotient was 72.

It was at this point that the officer began to speak of his feelings of unreality, which he had had for some time but which had become more marked recently.

> Some of the things I do it's like it was in a dream. I remember having talked with you a lot but it doesn't seem real. I know that you two are real because I can reach out and touch your bodies. I thought I saw my mother on the ward. I know that can't be because she has been dead for 20 years. Sometimes I feel that this hospitalisation is just a figment of my imagination. I know that I had only one operation but the feeling that I had two is still there.

He was interviewed six months after his operation. Memory had improved and he gave an accurate review of his military career. He had not, however, been motivated to work, had not taken up former interests and had not had any sexual desire. He did not express any confabulation or reduplication, but remarked that he still had the feeling that he had known the examiner prior to entering the hospital.

Case 2

The second case includes reduplication of both the hospital and the patient's car accident, denial of both memory loss and the death of a fellow passenger, the appearance of depression with the giving up of the denial and reduplication, and a suggestion of a Cotard's syndrome.

A 20-year-old enlisted man was admitted to the Bethesda Naval Hospital on 3rd June, 1986, nine days after having sustained a closed head injury. He had been a passenger in a car in which the occupants had been drinking and the driver (the patient's nephew and close friend) had been killed. He had first been taken to a hospital in the Pittsburgh area in coma and transferred to another Pittsburgh hospital. There a needle had been inserted into the right lateral ventricle to monitor intracranial pressure. CT revealed bilateral frontal and temporal lobe contusions and diminished ventricle size compatible with brain swelling. Patient also had incurred a left acromial clavicular joint separation.

In an interview on 4th June, the patient was in a euphoric mood particularly in giving his reduplicative delusion. He stated that he had been in three automobile accidents, two while going to hospitals in Pittsburgh and the other while travelling from the airport in Maryland to Bethesda. He said that he had been injured in only one of the accidents. He also said that he was in "Bethesda Naval Hospital where the President goes". (President Reagan had recently been hospitalised there.) When questioned further, he claimed that there were two other Bethesda Naval Hospitals, the regular one, and one in a state beginning with a K. He did not reduplicate any of the hospital personnel and showed significant memory loss. He was vague about events in the months preceding his injury, could not remember what he had eaten that day, and could not retain three items for three minutes. He, however, denied any memory loss while admitting the injury to his shoulder. Although he had been told by his family and physicians about his nephew's death, he denied it and confabulated that his nephew had visited him.

The patient's memory improved over the next two weeks but he continued to reduplicate. He stated that he had been in seven car accidents all within the 10-day span preceding his actual injury. These, he said, had occurred while driving with various members of his family. He also claimed, falsely, that each of six brothers had been in a serious car accident, some of them involving alcohol. He still believed that his nephew had only suffered a few cuts and abrasions.

The patient began the interview of the 25th June by stating that his mother had told him of his nephew's death, and that he himself had died twice of cardiac stress. He no longer believed that he had been in multiple accidents. When asked about the hospital, he said that, while it was for the President, it was known officially as Bethesda Naval Hospital. He was mildly depressed and concerned that his family would blame him for the accident because of his drinking. He returned to duty and when interviewed again five months after the accident he said that he could recall only little beyond what he had been told. There was no reduplication.

Case 3

The next case illustrates the association of environmental and personal reduplication and the way in which the misidentification serves to assert the patient's own identity.

A 30-year-old naval electrical engineer officer was admitted to Bethesda Naval Hospital because of a week of headache, fatigue, confusion, and memory loss following a brief febrile illness. Neurological examination showed an unsteady gait and an inconstant left Babinski reflex. He appeared to lack affect, answered slowly, and had difficulty with recent memory. Lumbar puncture yielded spinal fluids with total proteins of 127 and 184mg/100ml without cells; electroencephalogram (EEG) showed diffuse slow waves more marked posteriorly; and magnetic resonance imaging (MRI) demonstrated multiple lesions, subcortically and in the periventricular regions, cerebellum, and brain stem. A diagnosis of post-infectious limbic encephalitis was made and the patient placed on steroids.

In the initial interview, the patient stated that he was in the Institute of Electrical Engineering situated in the Upper Peninsula of Michigan (where he had been on vacation the previous summer) and that he had come to fix the phone. When asked if he were ill, he said he had come for a radio licence, but that it wasn't contagious. Several days later he was more coherent. He said that his memory had not been up to snuff for some time. He was, he stated, in the Naval Hospital in Bethesda, having flown down the previous day from a branch of the hospital in Iron Mountain, Michigan. When the examiner expressed doubt, he offered to open his closet to show the labels on his clothes. He recalled having seen the examiner in the hospital and also thought that the examiner had been head of the Department of Electrical Engineering at his university. When the examiner thought it was unlikely that anyone could be both a professor of neurology and engineering, he commented that it wasn't unusual for medical people to have two degrees. He admitted to having some memory impairment but did not believe that it amounted to anything.

By the beginning of February the patient had made marked improvement. He was aware of his memory loss, could date its onset and did well on psychological testing. He realised that there was only one Bethesda hospital even though he had thought that he had been transferred from a branch on the Upper Peninsula. He recognised me as a nerve doctor but still believed that he had seen me in the electrical engineering department of the university. The patient returned to work successfully and in later interviews had little recollection of the events of the hospital stay.

Case 4

The next case illustrates the coexistence of reduplication and denial, implicit knowledge of memory loss, and, as in the patient described by Head (1926), the idea that a relative can be both dead and alive.

A 75-year-old widow began to have word-finding difficulty in 1984, and in the following year had several hallucinations concerning her deceased husband. On examination she was anxious and concerned over her condition. She could not spell "world" backwards or state how many dollars there were in 60 nickels. The face/hand test of double simultaneous tactile stimulation was positive with extinction and displacement.

Because of the patient's progressive memory loss she was admitted to the National Institute on Aging in Bethesda, Maryland for study. She scored 20 out of 30 on the Mini Mental Status Questionnaire. She knew that she was in a hospital in Bethesda and was oriented for date and time of day. She was unable to draw a clock and place the hands to a designated time. EEG showed runs of diffuse slowing with left hemisphere predominance. Computerised tomography (CT) showed moderate dilatation of the left ventricle, slight dilatation of the third ventricle, prominent cortical sulci over the convexities, and reduced density in periventricular white matter. MRI was reported as showing increased signal intensities in the periventricular areas, and in the corona radiata and centrum semiovale bilaterally. On returning to her room after a procedure she thought that she had been brought to a different room because her old room was larger and airier. She also denied that her memory impairment was any worse than that of other people her age.

On her return home she thought that she was in an apartment, different from the one which she had left. She said that she owned both apartments, that they had the same designer furniture, and that they were located at the same address. At times she located one of the apartments in another part of the city. They were different in that there were more people about in the one which she was presently occupying (she now had round the clock attendants). She spoke of her husband as if he were alive but would admit that he was dead. She continued to deny her memory loss while complaining on other occasions of her addled brain. The denial and environmental reduplication persisted for a year, after which time she was depressed and withdrawn.

Case 5

The final case illustrates how confabulations can be symbolic representations of the patient's feelings, problems, and experiences; how premorbid behaviour may be a determinant of content; and the association of

reduplication with a Frégoli syndrome and delusions of intermetamorphosis.

A 30-year-old unmarried factory worker was admitted to The Mount
Sinai Hospital with an eight-month history of uncontrolled head and trunk
movements and pain in her neck. Examination disclosed dystonic turning of
her head to the left and hypertrophy of the right sternomastoid muscle and a
diagnosis of dystonia musculorum deformans was made. Because of the
pain and associated depression she was given a course of 18 ECTs over a six-
week period. Shocks were given in the morning after intravenous
administration of sodium amytal, and the patient was interviewed after
each treatment and on intervening days.

The patient was completely oriented on admission and distressed about
her pain and involuntary movements. On the day of her third ECT she
expressed transient reduplication stating that there were two Mount Sinai
Hospitals, one at its correct location and another in a suburb. In addition,
she offered a confabulated journey, saying that she had visited a hospital
where she had formerly been a patient on the previous evening. She was also
disoriented for month and time of day. She was in a euphoric mood, had no
pain, and claimed that the movements were much improved although there
was no objective change. Following the seventh ECT, she had environmental disorientation or reduplication even on days on which she had not
had a treatment She also thought that she had met two of the doctors prior
to coming to hospital. Memory loss was mild.

On the morning of the day after her 10th ECT, the patient reported
that two men had entered her room during the night. One of them had
hit her on the head while the other had tried to put her to sleep with an
injection in the arm, so that he could have sex with her and prove that
there were no good girls left. She went on to develop delusions about two
women on the floor who were wearing cervical collars after laminectomy.
She claimed that one of the women was a man in disguise, that the other
had been changed from a man into a woman by the operation, and that
both were pursuing her sexually. Whereas previously she had remained in
her room because of embarrassment about the dystonic movements, she
now walked about freely, swinging her hips in a sexy fashion, and claimed
that the other patients were looking at her because they were sexually
interested. She also provided an explanation of the involuntary movements. She said that she had fallen in love with the foreman in her shop,
and would turn her head to look at him only to remember that he was
married with two children. She would then avert her head and eyes, only
to repeat the movements a few minutes later. During the period of her
sexual delusions the patient did not complain of pain. EEG which had
been normal prior to ECT showed a moderate amount of 6–7 CPS
activity.

By the beginning of the last week of treatments the patient was well oriented and did not reduplicate. The sexual delusions, however, persisted for another three weeks. She thought that some of the women patients acting seductively towards her were men wearing wigs, and asked the nurses to have them examined to determine their gender. When interviewed a month after the completion of her ECT she was no longer delusional. The patient came from a patriarchal, religiously orthodox Eastern European family. Her sisters described her as extremely conscientious, devoted to her parents, sexually prudish, and afraid of men.

BRAIN DYSFUNCTION

The question of localisation of dysfunction in RMS is a difficult one because of the diversity of diseases and the paucity of controlled studies. Most reports of structural pathology have been in patients with either (1) closed head injuries in which there is predominant damage to the tips and bases of the frontal lobes, the tips, bases, and lateral surfaces of the temporal lobes and underlying white matter, or (2) Alzheimer's disease in which there is extensive involvement of parietal and temporal cortical association areas, and, in some instances, frontal and paralimbic and limbic involvement. One of the few controlled studies was carried out by Joseph, O'Leary, and Wheeler (1990) on patients hospitalised with a diagnosis of paranoid schizophrenia. They found more frontal and temporal lobe atrophy in patients with Capgras syndrome than in those without the delusion.

Among patients with more lateralised and focal pathology, RMS have been found more frequently with right than with left hemisphere lesions. Capgras syndrome has been attributed to prosopagnosia (Hayman & Abrams, 1977), environmental reduplication to spatial and topographical disorientation (Ruff & Volpe, 1981), and other RP to disturbances in the sense of familiarity said to be localised in the right temporal lobe (Feinberg & Shapiro, 1989). However, there are no reported cases of prosopagnosia with RP and prosopagnosic patients can identify people by voice, gesture, posture and gait. Nor do most patients with topographical disorientation have RP, and if it does play a role it must be in conjunction with other processes.

The idea of a right temporal localisation is based on the work of Mullan and Penfield (1959) who reported that electrical stimulation of the temporal lobes in epileptic patients produced disturbances in the sense of familiarity principally in the right hemisphere. Subsequent studies, however, have found no significant asymmetry. Halgren, Walter, Cherlow, and Crandall (1978) in their stimulations reported no hemisphere difference in the elicitation of *déjà vu* and *jamais vu* phenomena. Similarly a study of 19 patients in whom feelings of unreality, strangeness, and *déjà vu* occurred spontaneously showed no predilection for either hemisphere (Ardila, Botero, Gomez, & Quijano, 1988).

While the right hemisphere plays a specialised role, RP cannot be localised in it in the sense that aphasia is localised in the left hemisphere. Moreover, RP have not occurred following right hemispherectomy (Sergent & Villemure, 1989; Smith, 1969). A review of the right hemisphere lesions reported in the literature of RMS indicates that focal infarcts or atrophy in the absence of generalised cortical atrophy or bifrontal involvement are rare, and that haematomas, haemorrhages, and neoplasms with more widespread effects are far more common (Hayman & Abrams, 1977; Kapur, Turner, & King, 1988; Leiguarda, 1982; Levine & Grek, 1984; Ruff & Volpe, 1981; Todd et al., 1981; Weinstein & Kahn, 1955). There must also be altered function of the left hemisphere to allow for the symbolic representation of feelings and experiences (Förstl, Burns, et al., 1991; Levine & Grek, 1984; Weinstein, Cole, Mitchell, & Lyerly, 1964). On the basis of bifrontal and right temporal lobe pathology, Alexander, Stuss, and Benson (1979) proposed a temporolimbic frontal disconnexion. The data indicate that the neural substrate of RMS involves widely spaced networks and interaction of both hemispheres.

The networks in the brain most relevant to coping in the environment, validating experience, and defining the self are those pathways which interconnect the frontal, parietal, and temporal multimodal cortical association areas with one another, with paralimbic association areas on the mesial and undersurfaces of the hemispheres, and with primary limbic structures in the mesial temporal lobes and diencephalon. These systems are responsive to the emotional relevance of stimuli, with particular relevance to those necessary to survival (Mesulam, 1985; Pandya & Seltzer, 1982), to what Paul Broca called the pleasures of food and the suffering of pain. When these systems are interrupted, the person perceives the stimulus but not its emotional significance and relevance to the self. For example, in pain asymbolia caused by a lesion involving the connections of the parietal association areas and the paralimbic insula, the patient feels the sharpness of a pinprick but not the noxious quality (Mesulam, 1985). In anosognosia for hemiplegia, the patient may admit that his arm is motionless, but deny that it is paralysed, or even belongs to him. In the Capgras syndrome the patient recognises his spouse, but does not feel that she is really his wife and "belongs" to him.

PET Studies

Positron-emission tomography (PET) data support the view that the neural substrate of DMS includes an interruption of connections between multimodal cortical association areas and paralimbic and limbic structures causing a perceptual-affective dissonance. A study of patients with Alzheimer's disease (dementia of the Alzheimer type; DAT) compared the clinical behaviour, neuropsychological test results, and regional metabolic rates of glucose in DAT patients with and without RP (Mentis et al., 1995). Because the nine RMS patients had 17 reduplicative delusions among them (person = 9; place = 4; event = 4) and only one subject had reduplication in only a single modality, it was not feasible to assign each subject to a group based on reduplicative modality.

Seven of the nine DAT patients with RP denied memory loss, whereas only two of the 15 without RP did so. An extensive battery of neuropsychological tests did not differentiate the groups. Both the DAT groups, as compared to age-matched controls, showed typical hypometabolism in parietal and temporal association areas bilaterally. Compared to each other, however, the DAT group with RP had significantly reduced metabolism in the orbitofrontal and anterior and posterior cingulate areas bilaterally, and in the left caudate and lenticular nuclei, and in the left posterior mesial temporal lobe. The DAT group with RP also showed a relative hypermetabolism in a wide cortical band which included the sensory association cortices (superior temporal and inferior parietal) and precuneus bilaterally. There was also bilateral dorsolateral frontal hypometabolism in both DAT groups compared to normal controls, which, while greater in the group with RP, did not reach statistical significance ($P = 0.53$ left, $P = 0.77$ right).

While PET studies in other diseases are necessary, the clinical observations, psychological test results, and metabolic data suggest that a perceptual-affective dissonance is a basic neural mechanism. While the prefrontal hypometabolism did not significantly distinguish between the two DAT groups, such frontal involvement appears relevant to the patient's failure to resolve the dissonance in other than delusional fashion.

There is some evidence of discrete localisation of individual reduplicative modalities. Environmental reduplication and reduplication of body parts occur more often with lesions limited to the right hemisphere than do person, object, temporal and self-reduplication, which are less lateralised (Feinberg & Shapiro, 1989; Förstl, Burns, et al., 1991). However, the coexistence of one form of reduplication with another in a degree so far above chance, the clinical features shared by the different forms, and the finding of common metabolic abnormalities argue for a core neural mechanism, with individual variations.

Adaptive Processes

The perceptual-affective dissonance, however, even with the additional cognitive loss, does not account for the positive, adaptive symbolic aspects of RMS. Thus, most patients following anterior communicating artery aneurysm rupture with orbitofrontal and cingulate damage have some combination of confabulation, denial, and reduplication, but a number do not have reduplication although there is apathy, amnesia, and anosodiaphoria. It is useful to think of the loss of the feeling of reality, and the breakdown of the unities of time and space, as negative symptoms in the Jacksonian sense, and misidentifications, delusions, and confabulations as positive ones. RMS are adaptive in that they follow periods of agitation, combat feelings of unreality, and provide solutions to incongruous information.

Adaptive mechanisms depend not only on what parts of the brain are destroyed but on those which are preserved. The retention of left hemisphere function allows for the use of metaphorical speech and the representation of the patient's feelings and experiences in personification and other tropes in the various reduplicative modalities. Such metaphor, as in poetry, slang, and humour, impart a more vivid and vibrant feeling of reality than would a more referential or veridical statement. A metaphor also may give unity to what would otherwise be masses of disparate and conflicting data. These are reasons why patients persist in their false identifications despite evidence of implicit knowledge. The neural basis of adaptive processes is not understood but the nature of the patient's problems, premorbid experience, and the existence of prior brain damage are important determinants of what patterns of synaptic connectivity are activated in stressful situations.

CONCLUSION

While RMS in disease of various etiologies have features in common, there are differences. Neurological patients, who on the whole do not have a history of mental illness, tend to reduplicate nurses, doctors, and the hospital because these are connected with their physical disabilities. Psychiatric patients are more likely to have reduplicative delusions and misidentifications about close relatives with whom relationships are apt to have been stressful. Also, patients with a background of emotional difficulties or mental illness are more apt to have ideas of persecution, imposture and deception.

Reduplication phenomena are not limited to patient with brain damage and psychoses, but occur under conditions of emotional stress and when people are in search of meaning and reality in their lives. Feelings of unreality coupled with *déjà vu* phenomena, a sense of suspended time, and out of body experiences are common in life threatening situations (Noyes & Kletti, 1976). Belief in ghosts may be a form of reduplication. Almost universally, reduplicative themes appear in religion, myth, folklore, literature, and drama.

REFERENCES

Abed, R.T., & Fewtrell, W.D. (1990). Delusional misidentification of familiar inanimate objects. *British Journal of Psychiatry, 157,* 915–917.

Alexander, M.P., Stuss, D.T., & Benson, D.F. (1979). Capgras syndrome: A reduplicative phenomenon. *Neurology, 29,* 334–339.

Anderson, D.N. (1988). The delusion of inanimate doubles. *British Journal of Psychiatry, 15,* 334–339.

Ardila, A., Botero, M., Gomez, J., & Quijano, C. (1988). Partial cognitive-dysmnesic seizures as a model for studying psychoses. *International Journal of Neuroscience, 38,* 11–20.

Bhatia, M.S. (1990). Capgras syndrome in a patient with migraine. *British Journal of Psychiatry, 157,* 917–918.

Bland, R.C. (1970). Capgras' syndrome. *Canadian Psychiatric Association Journal, 16,* 369–371.

Bouckoms, A., Martuza R., & Henderson M. (1986). Capgras syndrome with subarachnoid hemorrhage. *Journal of Nervous and Mental Disease, 174,* 484–488.

Capgras J., Lucchini, P., & Schiff, P. (1924). Du sentiment d'étrangeté a l'illusion des sosies. *Bulletin de la Société Clinique Médecine Mentale, 121,* 210–217.

Capgras, J., & Reboul-Lachaux, J. (1923). L'illusion des "sosies" dans un délire systématisé chronique. *Bulletin de la Société Clinique Médecine Mentale, 11,* 6–16.

Christodoulou, G.N. (1976). Delusional hyperidentification of the Frégoli type. *Acta Psychiatrica Scandanavica, 54,* 305–314.

Cotard, J. (1882). Du delire des negations. *Archives of Neurology Paris, 4*(132), 170, 282–296.

Courbon, P., & Fail, G. (1927). Syndrome d'illusion de Frégoli et schizophrenie. *Bulletin de la Société Clinique Médecine Mentale, 15,* 121–125.

Courbon, P., & Tusques, J. (1932). Illusion d'intermetamorphose et de charme. *Annales Medico Psychologiques, 1,* 401–406.

Critchley, M. (1953). *The parietal lobes.* New York: Hafner.

Drake, M.E. (1987). Postictal Capgras syndrome. *Clinical Neurology and Neurosurgery, 89,* 271–274.

Enoch, M.D., & Trethowan, W.H. (1979). *Uncommon psychiatric syndromes* (pp. 125–126). Bristol, UK: John Wright & Sons.

Feinberg, T.E., & Shapiro, R.M. (1989). Misidentification—reduplication and the right hemisphere. *Neuropsychiatry, Neuropsychology and Behavioral Neurology, 2,* 19–48.

Förstl, H., Almeida, O.P., Owen, A.M., Burns, A., & Howard, R. (1991). Psychiatric, neurological and medical aspects of misidentification syndromes: A review of 200 cases. *Psychological Medicine, 21,* 905–910.

Förstl, H., & Beats, B. (1992). Charles Bonnet's description of Cotard's delusion and reduplicative paramnesia in an elderly patient (1788). *British Journal of Psychiatry, 160,* 416–418.

Förstl, H., Burns, A., Jacoby, R., & Levy, R. (1991). Neuroanatomical correlates of clinical misidentifications and misperception in senile dementia of the Alzheimer type. *Journal of Clinical Psychiatry, 52,* 268–271.

Gilliatt, R., & Pratt, R. (1952). Disorders of perception and performance in a case of right-sided cerebral thrombosis. *Journal of Neurology, Neurosurgery and Psychiatry, 15,* 264–271.

Greenberg, D.B., Hochberg, F.H., & Murray, G.B. (1984). The theme of death in complex partial seizures. *American Journal of Psychiatry, 141,* 1587–1589.

Haigren, E., Walter, R.D., Cherlow, D.G., & Crandall, P.H. (1978). Mental phenomena evoked by electrical stimulation of the human hippocampal formation and amygdala. *Brain, 101,* 83–117.

Halligan, P.W., Marshall, J.C., & Wade, D.T. (1993). Three arms: A case study of supernumerary phantom limb after right hemisphere stroke. *Journal of Neurology, Neurosurgery and Psychiatry, 56,* 159–166.

Hay, G.G. (1986). Electroconvulsive therapy as a contribution to the production of delusional misidentification syndrome. *British Journal of Psychiatry, 148,* 667–669.

Hayman, M.A., & Abrams R. (1977). Capgras' syndrome and cerebral dysfunction. *British Journal of Psychiatry, 130,* 68–71.

Head, H. (1926). *Aphasia and kindred disorders.* Cambridge, UK: Cambridge University Press.

Joseph, A.B., O'Leary, D.H., & Wheeler, H.G. (1990). Bilateral atrophy of the frontal and temporal lobes in schizophrenic patients with Capgras syndrome: A case control study using computed tomography. *Journal of Clinical Psychiatry, 51,* 322–325.

Kapur, N., Turner, A., & King, C. (1988). Reduplicative paramnesia: Possible anatomical and neuropsychological mechanisms. *Journal of Neurology, Neurosurgery and Psychiatry, 51,* 579–581.

Kimura, S. (1986). Review of 100 cases with the syndrome of Capgras. *Bibliotheca Psychiatrica, 164,* 121–130.

Lansky, M.R. (1974). Delusions in a patient with Capgras' syndrome. *Bulletin Menninger Clinic, 38,* 360–364.

Leiguarda, R.C. (1983). Environmental reduplication associated with a right thalamic hemorrhage. *Journal of Neurology, Neurosurgery and Psychiatry, 46,* 1154.

Levine, D.N., Calvanio, R., & Rinn, W.E. (1991). The pathogenesis of anosognosia for hemiplegia. *Neurology, 41,* 1770–1781.

Levine, D.N., & Grek, A. (1984). The anatomic bases of delusions after right hemisphere infarction. *Neurology, 34,* 577–582.

Lewis, S.W. (1987). Brain imaging in a case of Capgras syndrome. *British Journal of Psychiatry, 150,* 117–121.

Lewis, S. (1993). *Prevalence of delusional misidentification.* Paper presented at the First International Conference on Delusional Misidentification Syndromes. Paris, France, 21–22 July, 1993.

Luaute, J.P. (1986). Joseph Capgras and his syndrome. *Bibliotheca psychiatrica, 164,* 9–21.

MacCallum, W.A.G. (1973). Capgras syndrome with an organic basis. *British Journal of Psychiatry, 123,* 639–642.

MacCallum, W.A.G. (1984). A syndrome of misinterpreting changes as changes of person. *British Journal of Psychiatry, 144,* 649–650.

Mentis, M.J., Weinstein, E.A., Horowitz, B., McIntosh, A.R., Pietrini, P., Alexander, G.E., Furey, M., & Murphy, D.G.M. (1995). Abnormal glucose metabolism in the delusional misidentification syndromes: A positron emission tomography study of Alzheimer disease. *Biological Psychiatry, 38,* 438–449.

Mesulam, M.-M. (1985). *Principles of behavioral neurology.* Philadelphia, Pa.: Davis.

Mullan, S., & Penfield, W. (1959). Illusions of comparative interpretation and emotion. *American Medical Association Archives of Neurology and Psychiatry, 81,* 269–284.

Noyes, R., & Kletti, R. (1976). Depersonalization in the face of life-threatening danger. *Psychiatry, 30,* 19–27.

Pandya, D.P., & Seltzer, B. (1982). Association areas of the cerebral cortex. *Trends in Neurosciences, 53,* 386–390.

Paterson, A., & Zangwill, O.L. (1944). Recovery of spatial orientation in the post-traumatic confusional state. *Brain, 67,* 54–58.

Pick, A. (1903). On reduplicative paramnesia. *Brain, 36,* 260–267.

Rubin, E.H., Drevetz, W.C., & Burke, W.J. (1988). The nature of psychotic symptoms in senile dementia of the Alzheimer type. *Journal of Geriatric Psychiatry and Neurology, 1,* 16–21.

Ruff, R.L., & Volpe, B.T. (1981). Environmental reduplication with right frontal and parietal injury. *Journal of Neurology, Neurosurgery and Psychiatry, 44*, 382–386.

Sergent, J., & Villemure, J.G (1989). Prosopagnosia in a right hemispherectomized patient. *Brain, 112*, 975–995.

Signer, S.F. (1987). Capgras' syndrome: The delusion of substitution. *Journal of Clinical Psychiatry, 48*, 147–150.

Smith, A. (1969). Non-dominant hemispherectomy. *Neurology, 19*, 442–445.

Staton, R.D., Brumback, R.A., & Wilson, H. (1982). Reduplicative paramnesia: A disconnection syndrome of memory. *Cortex, 18*, 23–36.

Thompson, M.I., Silk, K.R., & Hover, G.L. (1980). Misidentification of a city: Delimiting criteria for Capgras syndrome. *American Journal of Psychiatry, 137*, 1270–1271.

Todd, J., Dewhurst, K., & Wallis, G. (1981). The syndrome of Capgras. *British Journal of Psychiatry, 139*, 319–327.

Ullman, M., Ashenhurst, E.M., Hurwitz, L.S., & Gruen, A. (1960). Motivational and structural factors in the denial of hemiplegia. *Archives of Neurology, 3*, 78–88.

Weinstein, E.A. (1991). Anosognosia and denial of illness. In G.P. Prigitano & D.L. Schacter (Eds.), *Awareness of deficit after brain injury* (p.244). New York: Oxford University Press.

Weinstein, E.A., & Burnham, D.L. (1991). Reduplication and the syndrome of Capgras. *Psychiatry, 54*, 78–88.

Weinstein, E.A., Cole, M., Mitchell, M., & Lyerly, O.G. (1964). Anosognosia and aphasia. *Archives of Neurology, 10*, 376–386.

Weinstein, E.A., Friedland, R.P., & Wagner, E.E. (1994). Denial/unawareness of impairment and symbolic behaviour in Alzheimer's disease. *Neuropsychiatry, Neuropsychology, and Behavioural Neurology, 7*, 176–184.

Weinstein, E.A., & Kahn, R.L. (1955). *Denial of illness: Symbolic and physiological aspects.* Springfield, Ill.: Charles C. Thomas.

Weinstein, E.A., Kahn, R.L., & Malitz S. (1967). Confabulation as a social process. *Psychiatry, 19*, 383–396.

Weinstein, E.A., Kahn, R.L., Malitz, S., & Rozanski, J. (1954). Delusional reduplication of parts of the body. *Brain, 77*, 45–60.

Weinstein, E.A., Kahn, R.L., & Slote, W. (1955). Withdrawal, inattention and pain asymbolia. *American Medical Association Archives of Neurology and Psychiatry, 74*, 235–246.

Weinstein, E.A., Kahn, R.L., & Sugarman, L.A. (1952). Phenomenon of reduplication. *American Medical Association Archives of Neurology and Psychiatry, 67*, 808–814.

Weinstein, E.A., Linn, L., & Kahn, R.L. (1952). Psychosis during electroshock therapy: Its relation to the theory of shock therapy. *American Journal of Psychiatry, 109*, 22–26.

Weinstein, E.A., Linn, L., & Kahn, R.L. (1955). Encephalitis with a clinical picture of schizophrenia. *Journal of the Mount Sinai Hospital, 21*, 341–354.

Weinstein, E.A., & Lyerly, O.G. (1968). Confabulation following brain injury. *Archives of General Psychiatry, 18*, 348–354.

Weinstein, E.A., Marvin, S.L., & Keller, N.U.A. (1962). Amnesia as a language pattern. *Archives of General Psychiatry, 6*, 259–270.

Weinstein, E.A., Salazar, A.M., & Jones, F.D. (1995). Behavioral consequences of traumatic brain injury. In F.D. Jones & L. Sparacino (Eds.), *Textbook of Military Medicine: Part 1. War Psychiatry.* Washington, DC: US Government Printing Office.

Young, A. (1993). *The Capgras and Cotard delusions.* Paper presented at the First International Conference on Delusional Misidentification Syndromes. Paris, France, 20–22 July, 1993.

Section B

WHO ARE YOU?

To exist as a hermit or stylite is an option that few people nowadays achieve or even desire. For better or for worse, life is with people. As social beings we must recognise ("in a flash") our friends and enemies, lovers and colleagues, children and parents, milkman and bank manager. In modern societies, these people need to be recognised in a wide variety of locations and costumes. Furthermore, current mobility is such that we must often try to recognise people that we have not seen for considerable periods of time.

The importance of *facial* recognition is (and always has been) such that it would be plausible to conjecture that a dedicated brain module is devoted to the task. There is considerable (albeit still controversial) evidence for such a module. Within the mainstream neurological literature, the primary disorders of this system are the prosopagnosias. In these conditions, patients may, for example, have problems in recognising that two views of an unknown face are indeed views of the same person. Alternatively, they may fail to learn new faces. Or they may fail to recognise by sight people who are extremely well known to them; in the extreme case, prosopagnosic patients may even fail to recognise themselves in a mirror.

Although these conditions are obviously annoying and sometimes disabling, they do not usually cause a major catastrophe in the life of the patients or their relatives and friends. There is, however, a set of conditions in which the patient systematically *mis*identifies significant others. Intuitively, it seems obvious that misunderstandings of this nature will be likely to provoke a serious breakdown in the web of interpersonal relationships in which the patient is involved. If I cannot be sure who you are, how should I behave towards you? If you think I'm someone else, how can I continue in *my* role? If you believe I'm disguising myself in order to fool you, how can any of our social interactions be normal?

The two chapters by Ellis and Szulecka and by Burgess, Baxter, Rose, and Alderman concern a range of conditions in which the patient's beliefs about the *personal identity* of others seem, at the very least, to be bizarre. By contrast, the patient with Asperger's syndrome studied by Ellis and Leafhead shows a more generalised impairment of social skills. None the less, the presenting symptoms include extremely poor ability to recognise people either by face or by voice. One might accordingly speculate that *some* of the impairments of social judgement in this case could be secondary to prosopagnosia: If I cannot be sure that I have recognised you, how can I learn what are the roles appropriate to you?

3

The Disguised Lover:
A Case of Frégoli Delusion

Hadyn D. Ellis and T. Krystyna Szulecka
School of Psychology, University of Wales, Cardiff, UK

Betty is the youngest of six children, born in a Midlands mining family. Her education was disrupted by rheumatic fever at the age of 10 and subsequently she was mainly employed as a domestic help, duties which she always carried out conscientiously. Her husband worked in a foundry during the early years of their marriage. However, he soon gave up regular employment and spent his time drinking in public houses or fishing. He treated Betty as a housekeeper, becoming violent when he ran out of money and cigarettes. After eight years of marriage he left her for another woman and died shortly afterwards. Betty devoted herself to looking after an aunt who was ill with cancer. While residing there, a cousin, Mr C showed her an interest and affection which she had never experienced before. She became pregnant by him but the convention of the day demanded that their child be fostered by her married sister. Betty and Mr C continued their clandestine relationship for over 10 years, even after he had married someone else. If she was not at home, he would leave traces of his visit in the form of an item he was selling for his company. She put an end to his visits when he started coming late at night as she did not wish to be seen as a "fancy woman". From then on her life revolved around her siblings, daughter, grandchildren and housework.

Between 1955 and 1983 Betty consulted a psychiatrist on four occasions as an outpatient for anxiety and depression. One episode, two months after a hysterectomy at the age of 47, was marked by dreams concerning her late husband, a preoccupation with her married lover and a longing for the affection of her daughter. She remained secretive about her private life and was easily angered if her personal space was invaded. She did not mix socially outside the family circle but kept close contact with her relatives, whom she visited at regular intervals, seeing at least one of them every day. She was the only member of the family who had a history of psychiatric consultations and was well accepted and supported at times of distress and illness.

In November, 1983, at the age of 64, Betty suffered a sudden, transient bout of dizziness with blurred vision, headache, slurred speech, and disorientation. She was treated for hypertension but a year later experienced a similar episode, this time accompanied by impaired memory. Although her cognitive deficits completely resolved after a month, she became convinced that Mr C had left his wife and moved into a neighbouring house with a lady friend, Mrs W. Betty believed she was kept under constant surveillance by them to prevent her from disclosing their affair to other members of the family.

> They have to follow me to keep an eye on me... They keep changing their clothes and their hairstyles but I know it's them... They follow the bus when I get into it... They watch me lock my door. At night I cannot sleep because they drive their cars outside my house and shine the headlights at my bedroom windows and keep me awake.

With time it became evident to her that the only way they could have access to so many cars was by using stolen vehicles, perhaps with the co-operation of other residents from her neighbourhood. Mr C and Mrs W not only changed clothes and hairstyles but also disguised themselves with make-up, wigs, dark glasses, and false beards. Mr C would call at her flat, pretending to be a gas man or a salesman, or watch her from the street. The couple not only changed their appearances but also altered their ages and gender. One minute, Mrs W looked like a teenage girl walking casually from school with her rucksack slung over her shoulder, and the next she was wearing expensive, fashionable outfits, of a sort that Betty herself had never been able to afford; and sometimes she pretended to be an old man with a walking stick or a dog.

Cars circled around the complex of flats where Betty lived, disappearing into nearby streets and emerging from entirely different exits shortly afterwards. When she took the initiative to follow them, sometimes for long distances, she witnessed the vehicles being driven into garages only to appear minutes later, different in make or colour. Betty allowed herself little time either to sleep or eat: Instead she constantly watched the street, noting the time and the number plates of passing cars. She sometimes confronted the drivers, demanding that they reveal their true identities and intentions. Oblivious to the cold and snow, she visited waste grounds, and when she observed men transferring things from their cars, she began to suspect that her cousin was dealing in contraband as well. At one stage she noticed that the waste ground had changed in appearance, becoming much flatter than usual, and concluded that it was because the stolen goods, which the milkman distributed on his rounds, had been hidden underneath. On her way home Betty took complicated routes to shake off Mr C, even reporting him to the police. She found little comfort in their reassurance that private detectives were keeping an eye on the area.

In March, 1985, following a referral by her general practitioner, Betty presented to her local psychiatric outpatient department. She arrived an hour late because she had made a long detour around the town and hospital to lose her pursuers. Agitated and unable to relax, she described in minute detail the activities of Mr C. She admitted that other people, including members of her family, were unable to discern the subtle clues whereby she recognised the true identities of her disguised cousin and his lady friend, such as their gait, voices, and the way they held their heads. "They want a medal for doing it so well. It's like an actor and actress preparing for different scenes", she exclaimed. On departing from the clinic she rushed into the waiting area, convinced that she had seen someone familiar and only calmed down after people had been introduced to her and their identities confirmed by the staff.

Betty was compulsorily admitted to hospital and treated with trifluoperazine, following which she reported that:

> They have gone now. I did see the woman in town and she was going to see her husband. I think he [her cousin] must have gone back to his wife. They aren't bothering me with the cars any more. I can go in and out of the house without bothering about them. The police made them clear their cars away, you know. They were always under my nose. I know I've got to change and ignore them if I see them again. I realised if they are stupid enough to do that sort of thing, then that's their problem. It'll all come out in the open one day and get sorted out. I am absolutely sure I am not making it up. It's really going on you know.

Five months later, two months after she had discontinued her medication, Betty reported that Mr C and Mrs W had returned to plague her again. They moved into a recently sold house, using numerous garages and cars as before. After she had gone to the post office to check the name of the new resident, Betty concluded that Mr C was using a false name. Her neighbours stopped talking to her after she had approached them about Mr C and had confronted people who were waiting in a van near her flat. In public she believed she had recognised Mrs W, disguised as an elderly woman, and her cousin by his gait. When being driven in a relative's car she thought that people in two cars kept an eye on her movements by driving in opposite directions to ensure that they did not lose sight of her in case her car turned round. At that time she decided to go ahead with a planned holiday to Spain. Her companion later reported that although she had difficulties finding her way she had been free of her worries about Mr C as she believed "It was too far for them to follow." Upon her return, however, she remained symptom free for only a week before noticing that she was still under constant observation. On one occasion, in an attempt to confront Mrs W, Betty ran out of her house, barefoot, fell badly and injured her leg. On another, she saw Mrs W while waiting for a bus. Betty deliberately did not catch the bus to test the woman's intentions, her suspicions being confirmed when she stayed behind as well.

Although Mr C and Mrs W never entered Betty's house, she knew that "they are all around". People who walked their dogs in the morning kept an eye on her too. Her daughter observed her in town running from one car park to another taking down number plates, particularly red cars. The milkman reported to her family that she could be found outside her house at the crack of dawn, examining the contents of cars parked nearby or looking through people's windows. As a result of those investigations, Betty again believed that she had discovered concrete evidence of Mr C's activities. In her search she had come across a house with wigs and dummy heads which she believed he and Mrs W were using. Later, to her horror, she saw one of the dummy faces pressed against the window of a passing car, the faces of the driver and passenger covered by masks with penetrating, artificial eyes. "They are dressing up to show that I am out of my mind because they know I am coming here [to the psychiatric outpatient clinic]." With time, however, she realised that "these were not masks but their own faces".

Betty grew concerned that Mr C's wife would hold her responsible for his long absences from his family, when, in fact, he was devoting his time to Mrs W. However, she understood why he would look for comfort elsewhere, explaining that his wife was "a professional woman", who made him take responsibility for the home and stay with the children when they became ill—"She is not much of a wife to him." In an attempt to confront him Betty stalked the neighbourhood of her cousin's marital home and became such a nuisance to his family that she was assaulted by his daughter and threatened with an injunction. When subsequently seen in the clinic Betty was so agitated it was impossible to comfort or reassure her. Compulsory detention in hospital for treatment again became unavoidable.

Treatment with a combination of carbamazepine, an anticonvulsant, and pimozide, often used to treat delusions, was unsuccessful and Betty only recovered after the reintroduction of trifluoperazine, a moderately strong tranquilliser, which was eventually reduced to a maintenance dose of 1mg/ day. Other drugs such as chlorpromazine could have adversely affected her already high blood pressure, while a stronger agent such as haloperidol could have caused unacceptable side-effects. As before, however, she did not gain full insight and her beliefs regarding her cousin recurred sporadically, e.g. triggered off by bereavement in the family, albeit not causing the same degree of distress. At the age of 72, Betty complained that one of her neighbours was replacing the ant powder, which she had placed in their common utility room, with flour. She insisted that she was able to tell the difference as the ant powder was much finer and more expensive. She became very distressed and even planned to report the events to the police. In her personal contact with the neighbour and her warden she was aggressive and suspicious. She recovered fully within a week after the dose of her trifluoperazine had been increased to 10mg/day, but without gaining full insight into her erroneous beliefs.

THE FRÉGOLI DELUSION

The symptoms displayed by Betty were first described in detail by Courbon and Fail, who, on 17th January, 1927, presented to the Societé Clinique de Médecine Mentale the case of a 27-year-old woman with unusual persecutory beliefs. A full rendering of their paper is given in Ellis, Whitley, and Luauté's (1994) translations of the three classical French papers on delusional misidentifications (DMI). Here we shall simply highlight certain aspects of the case.

Although from a disadvantaged background and working as a domestic servant, the patient of Courbon and Fail loved the theatre, which she visited whenever possible. It was this passion, however, that in an ironic way caused her such anxiety, for she developed the belief that the then famous actresses Robine and Sarah Bernhardt were disguising themselves in order to persecute her. Moreover, her tormentors could influence her thoughts, preventing her carrying out certain things and forcing her to commits acts such as masturbation.

Courbon and Fail chose to label this delusion the "syndrome d'illusion de Frégoli" in honour of Léopoldo Frégoli, the Italian mimic who at the time was very popular in French music halls. The essence of the delusion is that the patient believes that significant others are able to disguise themselves to look like anyone they wish in order to achieve some influence—usually, but not invariably, malign. In Betty's case, the negative intention is salient and one of us (HDE), with Angela Quayle, recently examined the case of a young woman for whom a whole family appeared to disguise themselves in order to keep a benign eye on her and ensure she came to no harm.

Ellis, Luauté, and Retterstøl (1994) have recently compared the four main delusions of misidentification. The other three are:

- the Capgras delusion (Capgras & Reboul-Lachaux, 1923)—a belief that others often, but not exclusively, close to the patient have been replaced by near-identical others
- the delusion of intermetamorphosis (Courbon & Tusques, 1932)—the belief that others can change their identity and appearance so that they become almost exactly like someone else
- and the delusion of subjective doubles (Christodoulou, 1978)—in which the patient either sees others who seem identical to him or her, or believes that there are such (unseen) doubles in existence.

The Frégoli delusion differs from these in at least one important respect. It involves a belief either that people can alter their appearance without changing their personality in order to influence the patient or that they can disguise themselves as others: It does not entail any alteration in the appearance of other people.

One of the additional features of the Frégoli delusion mentioned by Courbon and Fail (1927) was their patient's erotomania—here simply indicated by the sexual connotations of her delusions. For Betty, too, there is an obvious sexual aspect of her delusion: Her cousin, the persecutor, is also the father of her only child. Wright, Young, and Hellawell (1993) described a case of Frégoli delusion with true erotomania, which usually involves the belief that someone (usually of higher social status) is in love with a patient. UH, a 35-year-old woman, developed the belief that she was the girlfriend of the American actor Erik Estrada and that he visited her regularly disguised sometimes as her present boyfriend.

The neurological component to this case is significant: There was a history of epilepsy in this patient and some degree of EEG abnormality still present. In a study of 10 similar cases, Joseph and O'Leary (1987) found obvious signs of brain atrophy in most of them. Betty herself had a history of depression with anxiety, but her Frégoli delusion did not appear until after a series of transient ischaemic attacks that eventually resulted in an infarct situated in the right posterior temporoparietal area (de Pauw, Szulecka, & Pollock, 1987). This was apparent in the CAT scan, taken after her second ischaemic episode in 1984, which also revealed a moderate degree of cortical atrophy.

Given this obvious association between structural brain pathology and the Frégoli delusion, it is not surprising to learn that a more transient form of the delusion has been reported in a patient with acute toxic psychosis, induced by cannabis (Eva & Perry, 1993). This patient, a 19-year-old man with no previous psychiatric history, had a urine cannabinoid level of 160mg/litre. He asserted that two nurses, one male one female, were his father. When it was pointed out that he identified two people as being his father he replied that his father was "very clever". Ten days later when the cannabinoid level had dropped to less than a third of the admission level, he was entirely free of the delusion. Thus, as with other DMI symptoms, the Frégoli delusion can be precipitated by toxic-metabolic states and may resolve once those conditions are reversed (Ellis & de Pauw, 1994).

That is not to deny any interaction between neurological and psychological factors. Previous history and experiences may well play a significant role in determining the form of a DMI (Fleminger, 1994) but the association with neurological, structural, or toxic-metabolic factors, cannot now be dismissed. Betty, for example, had had an affair with the cousin she accused of persecuting her in the guise of others and it would be foolish to ignore the psychological impact that this man, the father of her illegitimate daughter, must have had upon her psyche. But, equally, it would be derelict of us not to note that the onset of the Frégoli delusion symptoms followed a stroke resulting in a substantial infarct.

NEUROPSYCHOLOGICAL TESTING

In order to explore the extent of Betty's problems in person recognition, Young, Ellis, Szulecka, and de Pauw (1990) gave her a battery of face-processing tests and compared her responses to those of controls matched for age. These tests were designed to examine her abilities to recognise facial expressions, identify famous faces, match unfamiliar faces, and recognise unfamiliar faces and words.

Recognition of Emotional Facial Expressions

A task involving labelling emotional facial expressions was given. This used 24 facial expression photographs from the Ekman and Friesen (1976) series, with four of these corresponding to each of the emotions: happiness, sadness, surprise, fear, anger, and disgust. The photographs were presented one at a time, along with a list of the six possible emotion labels printed below each face, in random order. The task involved choosing the correct emotion label for each face. Six practice trials were given at the start of the task, using photographs which did not appear in the main series of trials. Control data for Betty were taken from a group of 34 normal subjects of comparable age.

Identification of Familiar Faces

To test Betty's ability to identify familiar faces, she was given a face recognition test consisting of 60 face photographs; 20 of highly familiar people (Margaret Thatcher, the Queen Mother, Jimmy Saville, etc.), 20 less familiar people (Max Bygraves, David Attenborough, Dora Bryan, etc.), and 20 unfamiliar people (minor celebrities and local politicians from two towns in north-west England). There were also 14 practice faces.

She was shown each face photograph one at a time, and asked whether or not it was a familiar person and, if so, his or her occupation and name. From her responses, scores were derived for the number of high familiarity faces given a correct occupation, and the number correctly named. A score for the number of unfamiliar faces correctly rejected as unfamiliar was also calculated, to give some idea of the rate at which details were confabulated.

Unfamiliar Face Matching

Two separate tests of unfamiliar face matching were used. First, the Benton Test of Facial Recognition (Benton, Hamsher, Varney, & Spreen, 1983), which is a standard test in neurological assessments of face-processing difficulties. In this test, subjects have to choose which of six simultaneously presented photographs of unfamiliar faces are pictures of the same person as in a simultaneously presented target face photograph. The test includes items involving choice of identical photographs, or transformations of orientation and lighting, but these are pooled into an overall composite score. The patients' performances were evaluated by reference to the test's norms (Benton et al., 1983).

The second unfamiliar face-matching test examined ability to match disguised faces. Tzavaras, Hécaen, and Le Bras (1970) had included items of this type in their unfamiliar face-matching battery, and it seemed a particularly interesting test for Betty, given her misidentification signs.

The disguise task involved faces of eight unfamiliar people, each of whom was photographed in undisguised form, and then wearing a variety of paraphernalia (spectacles, false beards, moustaches, and wigs). Two separate test sheets were made, on each of which there was one version of each face in the top row, and then a 3 × 4 matrix below, where each of the four people from the top row appeared in three further disguised or undisguised forms. Subjects were asked to pick out the photographs from the matrix which showed each of the four people in the top row. Each test sheet was given to Betty, leading to an overall score out of a maximum of 24 possible correct choices on this disguise test. Control data for Betty were assembled by testing 10 women of comparable age (range 63–75 years).

Memory for Faces of Unfamiliar People

Memory for face of unfamiliar people was tested with the Recognition Memory Test (RMT) produced by Warrington (1984). This involves the presentation of 50 photographs of faces of unfamiliar people for three seconds each, while the subject performs an orienting task of deciding whether each face is "pleasant" or "unpleasant". Recognition memory for the faces is then measured immediately by working through a booklet of 50 pairs of face photographs, each pair containing one member from the original series.

A parallel version of the RMT using printed words as stimuli is also available, and was given to the patients in this study. Betty's performance of the face and word components of the RMT was evaluated by reference to the test's norms (Warrington, 1984).

FACE PROCESSING AND THE FRÉGOLI DELUSION

Betty's performance of the face-processing tasks is summarised in Table 3.1, which shows she was able to label facial expressions without difficulty, and she was unimpaired on the Benton unfamiliar face-matching test. On the Warrington RMT her score for faces (36/50 correct) was at the low end of the normal range (7th percentile). Her recognition memory for words was good (47/50 correct), and there was a significant discrepancy between her relatively poor and good recognition memory for faces and words respectively.

TABLE 3.1
Performance of Frégoli Patient Betty on Face-processing Tasks

	Frégoli Patient	Controls	
	Betty	Mean	SD
Facial Expressions			
Labelling	20/24	21.1	1.7
Faces Line-up			
High familiarity faces			
Occupation	15/20*	18.86	1.15
Name	5/20*	16.25	2.81
Unfamiliar faces			
Correct rejections	20/20		
Unfamiliar Face Matching			
Benton test	42/54		
"Disguise" task	13/24**	22.30	2.16
Recognition Memory Test			
Faces	36/50***	42.26	3.44
Words	47/50***	42.63	5.21

Means and standard deviations are for control subjects of comparable age; * more than 2.5SDs below control mean; ** = more than 4.0SDs below control mean; *** significant discrepancy between faces and words RMT scores (< 5th percentile).

Betty showed impaired ability to identify familiar faces, with poor scores both on giving occupations and for naming the high familiarity faces. She did correctly reject all the unfamiliar faces, however, showing that she did not confabulate. In particular, she did not suggest that any of the faces might be her cousin, or his friend, in disguise or otherwise.

Betty's most marked impairment, however, was on the "disguise" task. She found this quite exceptionally difficult, and was very slow and hesitant in her choices. Her performance was above chance level (chance = 6/24 correct), but was very poor in relation to controls (4.31 SDs below the control mean).

OVERVIEW

Betty, then, presents the classic symptoms of the Frégoli delusion. Her belief that she was being persecuted by a cousin, a former lover of hers, and his present partner, each able to disguise themselves as others, is paradigmatic. The association of her delusions with structural brain pathology may be coincidental but, given her abnormal performance on the battery of face-processing tasks, it seems more likely that her symptoms result from the organic changes. That is not to deny the psychological factor underlying the specific nature of Betty's delusions: Clearly her relationship with her cousin was important to her and his significance determined the details of her Frégoli delusion.

Ellis and Young (1990) offered a cognitive neuropsychiatric explanation for her Frégoli delusion, which is compatible both with the psychological and the neurological factors that seem to combine in the case of Betty. They employed an information-processing model of face recognition which deconstructs the operation into three essential stages: (1) an initial structural encoding, followed by (2) the excitation of units sensitive to the unique characteristics of each known face, and finally (3) the link to other multi-modal nodes that access biographical/episodic information about people (Bruce & Young, 1986; Ellis, 1986; Hay & Young, 1982). It is in that last stage that Ellis and Young (1990) suggest lies the genesis of the Frégoli delusion. If any person nodes are particularly easy to activate, they argue, then they may be triggered inappropriately by a variety of people. In the case of Betty the person node accessing information to her cousin may be hyperactive, firing in the presence of other people. His partner's node, by association, would also be triggered inappropriately.

The advantage of interpreting psychiatric phenomena within models of normal cognitive processes is attractive (David, 1993; Ellis, 1991), but the explanation for the Frégoli delusion offered by Ellis and Young (1990) is incomplete. Even if one accepts their suggestion of hyperactive person nodes it still does not account for the fact that Betty accepted the anomalous experience of seeing a stranger and believing him to be her cousin. Ellis and

Young (in press) have argued that delusional behaviour arises from dysfunctioning at two levels: a perceptual/cognitive level (such as the person node, just described); and a subsequent decision-making stage where beliefs are monitored and, if very unusual, illogical, etc., are discarded. Betty remains convinced that her cousin and his partner did disguise themselves to "mither" her and, although with medication she is no longer made anxious by their perceived activities, she is unable to accept that the incidents she complained about did not occur. Ellis and Young (in press) suggest that for this intransigence to occur there must be a failure at a higher level where self beliefs are monitored. Betty's behaviour resulting from her Frégoli delusion is testimony to the certainty with which she held these beliefs. It is, perhaps, the conviction and lack of insight shown by her and by patients with other kinds of delusions that merits the greatest efforts in future research.

ACKNOWLEDGEMENTS

We should like to acknowledge Dr Karel de Pauw and Dr Andy Young for their help with the preparation of this chapter.

REFERENCES

Benton, A.L., Hamsher, K. de S., Varney, N., & Spreen, O. (1983). *Contributions to neuropsychological assessment: A clinical manual.* Oxford: Oxford University Press.

Bruce, V., & Young, A. (1986). Understanding face recognition. *British Journal of Psychology*, 77, 305–327.

Capgras, J., & Reboul-Lachaux, J. (1923). L'illusion des "sosies" dans un délire systématisé chronique. *Bulletin de la Société Clinique de Médecine Mentale, 1,* 6–16.

Christodoulou, G.N. (1978). Syndrome of subjective doubles. *American Journal of Psychiatry, 135,* 249–251.

Courbon, P., & Fail, G. (1927). Syndrome d' "illusion de Frégoli" et schizophrénie. *Bulletin de la Société Clinique de Médecine Mentale, 15,* 121–125.

Courbon, P., & Tusques, J. (1932). Illusions d'intermetamorphose et de charme. *Annales Medico-Psychologiques, 14,* 401–406.

David, A.S. (1993). Cognitive neuropsychiatry? Editorial. *Psychological Medicine, 23,* 1–5.

de Pauw, K.W., Szulecka, T.K., & Pollock, T.L. (1987). Frégoli syndrome after cerebral infarction. *Journal of Nervous and Mental Disease, 175,* 433–438.

Ekman, P., & Friesen, W. (1976). *Pictures of facial affect.* Palo Alto, Calif.: Consulting Psychologists Press.

Ellis, H.D. (1986). Processes underlying face recognition. In R. Bruyer (Ed.), *The neuropsychology of face perception and facial expression.* Hillsdale, NJ: Lawrence Erlbaum Associates Inc.

Ellis, H.D. (1991). *Delusional misidentification syndromes—a cognitive neuropsychiatric approach.* Paper presented at the International Symposium on the Neuropsychology of Schizophrenia, Institute of Psychiatry, London, October 1991.

Ellis, H.D., & de Pauw, K.W. (1994). The cognitive neuropsychiatric origins of the Capgras delusion. In A. David, & J. Cutting (Eds.), *Cognitive neuropsychology of schizophrenia.* Hove, UK: Lawrence Erlbaum Associates Ltd.

Ellis, H.D., Luauté, J.-P., & Retterstøl, N. (1994). Delusional misidentification syndromes. *Psychopathology*, *27*, 117–120.

Ellis, H.D., Whitley, J., & Luauté, J.-P. (1994). Delusional misidentifications: The three original papers on the Capgras, Frégoli and Intermetamorphosis delusions. *History of Psychiatry*, 117–146.

Ellis, H.D., & Young, A.W. (1990). Accounting for delusional misidentification. *British Journal of Psychiatry*, *156*, 239–248.

Ellis, H.D., & Young, A.W. (in press). Problems of person perception in schizophrenia. In C. Pantelis, H.E. Nelson, & T.R.E. Barnes (Eds.), *Neuropsychology of schizophrenia*. Chichester, UK: John Wiley & Sons Ltd.

Eva, F.J., & Perry, D. (1993). The Frégoli syndrome and cannabis delusional disorder. *British Journal of Psychological Medicine*, *10*, 87–88.

Fleminger, S. (1994). Delusional misidentification: An exemplary symptom illustrating an interaction between organic brain disease and psychological processes. *Psychopathology*, *27*, 161–167.

Hay, D.C., & Young, A.W. (1982). The human face. In A.W. Ellis (Ed.), *Normality and pathology in cognitive functions*. London: Academic Press.

Joseph, A.B., & O'Leary, D.H. (1987). Anterior cortical atrophy in Frégoli syndrome. *Journal of Clinical Psychiatry*, *48*, 409–411.

Tzavaras, A., Hécaen, H., & Le Bras, H. (1970). Le problème de la specificité du déficit de la reconnaissance du visage humain lors des lésions hémisphériques unilatérales. *Neuropsychologia*, *8*, 403–416.

Warrington, E.K. (1984). *Recognition memory test*. Windsor, UK: NFER-Nelson.

Wright, S., Young, A.W., & Hellawell, D.J. (1993). Frégoli delusion and erotomania. *Journal of Neurology, Neurosurgery and Psychiatry*, *56*, 322–323.

Young, A.W., Ellis, H.D., Szulecka, K. & de Pauw, K.W. (1990). Face processing impairments and delusional misidentification. *Behavioural Neurology*, *3*, 153–168.

4 Delusional Paramnesic Misidentification

Paul W. Burgess
Department of Psychology, University College London, London, UK

Doreen Baxter, Martyn Rose, and Nick Alderman
Kemsley Brain Injury Rehabilitation Unit, St Andrews Hospital, Northampton, UK

INTRODUCTION

Imagine that one day a friend or relative visits you, and after observing them carefully, you begin to realise that this person is not actually who they claimed to be but is in reality a double, who is now acting as the original. Or perhaps you begin to suspect that an apparently unfamiliar person you keep seeing is actually someone you know in disguise.

These experiences are most commonly reported as symptoms of psychiatric disorders (Berson, 1983); perhaps more surprisingly, however, they are also sometimes seen in patients who have suffered neurological problems (Signer, 1992). Such delusions about the identity of others have a long history: The belief that someone is a double acting as the original was first described by Capgras and Reboul-Lachaux in 1923, and has come to be known as the Capgras syndrome. Enoch (1963) points out that Capgras himself called the phenomenon "L'illusion des Sosies", meaning the illusion of doubles, where the word "Sosie" derives from Plautus's play *Amphytreon*. In this play, the god Mercury assumes the appearance of Sosia, the servant of Amphytreon.

The second belief—that the apparently unfamiliar person you keep seeing is actually someone you know in disguise, also has a long history. Courbon and Fail (1927) called this delusion "The Illusion of Frégoli" after the Italian actor, Leopoldo Frégoli, who was a famous impersonator.

Even more spectacular delusions about identity also exist: for instance "intermetamophosis" (Bick, 1984; Joseph, 1985), where the patient believes

51

that an individual has been transformed both physically and psychologically into another person; "subjective doubles", where the belief is that another has turned into a being physically identical to yourself, and even role changes are misinterpreted as changes of person (MacCallum, 1984)—where a relative, for instance, is believed to be different people according to what they are doing at any specific moment.

At approximately the same time as cases of Capgras syndrome were being reported in the psychiatric medical journals, neurologists were noticing some strange phenomena in patients with brain damage or disease. Pick (1903) described the case of a woman, probably with senile dementia, who believed that she had been in two identical clinics, each headed by a professor who shared the same name. Pick called this disorder "reduplicative paramnesia", where "paramnesia" means "false reminiscence" (Whitty & Zangwill, 1966), and "reduplicative" refers to the type of error made; in this case that items are duplicated.

Sub-types of reduplicative paramnesia also exist. For instance, the belief that there are two identical environments (Benson, Gardner, & Meadows, 1976; Weinstein, Kahn, & Sugarman, 1952)—for example that your hospital is in fact an identical image of another (real) hospital located in a different place—has been termed "environmental reduplication" (e.g. Leiguarda, 1983). However, cases have also been described documenting reduplication for people, objects, time, and events, or even for the patient themselves (Fialkov & Robins, 1978; Weinstein, 1969; see also Ruff & Volpe, 1981).

Pick (1903) originally called these reduplications "paramnesia" because he thought that the central problem for these patients lay in a disturbance of memory. In fact, a patient reported by Staton, Brumback, and Wilson (1982) was described as suffering from "déjà vu" by his consultants, and the patient himself seemed to acknowledge the role of memory in his disorder: This 31-year-old man, who had suffered a brain injury in a car accident, complained that his friends and relatives, including his parents and siblings, were not "real" but were slightly different "look-alikes" or doubles. He recognised these people as duplicates through differences between their current behaviour or appearance and how he remembered them. For instance, he believed that his cat was not real because of a new scar on one ear.

Other types of disturbance of memory are less specific. Some patients will talk about events which they think have happened, but in fact are completely false (known as "confabulations"). Often these confabulations are quite bizarre and fantastic in content. For instance Damasio, Graff-Radford, Eslinger, Damasio, and Kassell's (1985) patient thought that he was a spaceship commander or a "space pirate", and the case reported by Shallice, Burgess, Schon, and Baxter (1989) told his doctor that he had met Harold Wilson (the former British Prime Minister) the day before and discussed a building job they were both working on.

It might be tempting to think that these patients are lying, or are poking fun at their doctors. However, we know that they believe their confabulations because they sometimes act on them (even when they don't know they are being observed). Baddeley and Wilson (1986, 1988) described a confabulating man (patient RJ) who, on a weekend visit home from hospital where he was being treated for a head injury, turned to his wife in bed and asked why she kept telling people they were married. His wife insisted that they were married, and produced their wedding photographs as evidence. RJ replied "that chap certainly looks like me, but it's not me!"

A number of patients suffering from Capgras syndrome and related disorders have also acted on their delusions. A particularly sad tale is related by Blount (1986) who reports that a patient in a psychiatric facility in Missouri State who had accused his stepfather of being a robot— subsequently decapitated him to look for batteries and microfilm in his head.

Recently a number of researchers have attempted to identify the factors which contribute to the development or maintenance of these syndromes and to speculate about the structures in the brain which are malfunctioning in these people (e.g. Filley & Jarvis, 1987; Marciniak & Luchins, 1981; Walter-Ryan, 1986). The debate particularly involves the question of whether patients with reduplication have normal abilities to perceive objects visually or to recognise faces, and exactly which memory mechanisms may be damaged. We report the case study of a patient who might provide evidence for this debate. Our patient, PD, developed a selective delusional misidentification following brain trauma. His delusion is unique in so far as it appears to incorporate elements of both the Capgras syndrome and paramnesic reduplication for both a person and an object, but does not fall clearly into any of the previously described categories. PD misidentified one person for another he had previously known, and a delusional system was formed around this person. The structure of the delusional misidentification is clearly of a paramnesic nature (i.e. involves a memory disturbance). This chapter will attempt to explain how the cognitive deficits PD suffers have contributed to his delusion, and the final section will describe his treatment and progress in rehabilitation.

CASE REPORT

PD, a 27-year-old recently married engineer, fell somewhere between 40 and 70 metres in an accident in America, shortly after he had moved to the country with his new wife. He remained unconscious for three months. At the time of his accident, brain scans showed generalised brain swelling with widespread bruising, especially in the right parietal area. Eleven months after his accident he was flown to England and transferred to a rehabilitation ward.

At this time it was noted that he had marked difficulty recognising peoples' faces although he became competent at recognising people by their stature, hair, and clothes. He called all females by his wife's name and would often confabulate, usually about imagined sexual misdemeanours committed by the male staff. It was at this time that his selective delusion fully manifested itself (described later). He was transferred to a second rehabilitation unit in England after 10 months (his recovery and progress in this unit is described at the end of this chapter).

Paramnesic Misidentification

During the first month of PD's illness, his wife and friends organised an almost 24-hour rota to ensure that someone he knew was with him at all times. At this time PD was nursed by Ian, a tall, dark, bearded nurse with a smiling face. This nurse took a special interest in PD and continued to visit him when he was transferred to the rehabilitation ward. On occasions Ian brought his own wife to meet PD and his wife. By coincidence, both wives had the same first name (Jane).

After his initial period in intensive care, PD was transferred to a rehabilitation ward, where he was nursed by a young friendly male auxiliary nurse called Jamie, described as tall and clean-shaven with mousy hair. PD saw this nurse as a threat to his relationship with his wife, and at about this time his wife describes the beginning of a delusion that she was having an affair with this nurse auxiliary. Attempts to convince PD of the fallacy of his delusion only made matters worse. Prior to the accident PD had never been possessive or jealous, their recent marriage had been extremely happy, and there had never been any foundation for the delusion.

Three weeks after his admission to the first rehabilitation unit in England (approximately 12 months post-accident), PD had a very heated argument with a patient called Jake with whom he had disagreed on a number of previous occasions. Over the next few weeks PD developed the delusion that Jake was actually the male nurse who had looked after him in intensive care in America, who was having an affair with his wife. The delusion became a preoccupation and many times each day PD would start shouting stereotyped phrases in respect to Jake and his wife. At these times he would get very upset and angry. He would threaten staff and other patients and was in such despair that he would shout repeatedly for staff to bring him a shotgun so he could take his own life.

A key role in the delusion was played by a watch that PD saw the patient wearing. Part of PD's "proof" that the patient was in fact the nurse from America was that the patient was wearing his (i.e. PD's) watch. PD had been given a rectangular stainless-steel Seiko watch by his brother for his 21st birthday which was engraved and was of great sentimental value to him. His wife keeps it at home for safety. The watch that the patient PD believes the nurse has stolen from him is indeed a Seiko watch, but is of a different colour and shape.

PD was able to talk rationally about subjects other than those that form the content of his delusion. He was able to appreciate the improbability of the delusion but never failed to rate his belief in the delusion as 100%, as the following transcription of a taped interview with the patient demonstrates:

PWB (Examiner)	Now tell me about this Jamie character—where did he come into all this?
PD	He was a bloke [at the rehabilitation unit] called Jamie [surname] ... he was a Dutch Welshman.
E	So what about him?
PD	I went into [the rehabilitation unit]. Jamie was one of the nurses who looked after me when I had my head injury. I couldn't believe it, he was identical ... he was the identical bloke that looked after me when I had my head injury. I couldn't believe it.
E	He was the identical bloke to the one who looked after you ... in America?
PD	Yeah, in [hospital name] in America. That's where I was admitted for my head injury. And Jamie was the male nurse who was looking after me. I know it makes me a bit of a bastard to ... he saved my life ... Jamie, he's knocking off my missus, but he was the male nurse who looked after me.
E	The chap in America—were they the same guy or different people?
PD	No, no, the bloke at [the first rehabilitation unit in Britain] was the male nurse.
E	So he must have come over from America?
PD	Yeah, that's what I would...
E	What was his name when he was in America then? Was he Jamie or somebody else?
PD	I can't remember his name. You don't forget a face like Jamie—red face, beard, mousy coloured hair and a Seiko watch on his wrist. The watch that Jamie had on his wrist was mine. Definitely was mine. No doubt about it. He said ... he gave me the usual story that mum and dad bought it for him...

| E | But how do you know he's having an affair with your wife? |
| PD | Its all a bit too coincidental ... like, he's here when I'm doing my rehabilitation. I know I'm a bit ... completely non-trustful of my wife. Yet I can't get the face of Jamie out of my system. |

Investigations Into the Causes of PD's Misidentification

To the experienced clinician, there are a number of obvious questions that arise on meeting a patient who shows a paramnesic misidentification. First, some neurological patients may show isolated deficits in recognising people's faces ("prosopagnosia"). In a number of cases this deficit can be so severe that patients are unable to recognise members of their own family (e.g. Hécaen and Angelergues, 1962). Sometimes this recognition deficit is accompanied by other problems with recognition. For instance, Bornstein, Sroka, and Munitz's (1969) patient, who was a farmer, was unable to recognise people or his livestock, who he used to be able to recognise as individuals. However, it seems that in some cases the deficit in recognition can be restricted only to human faces; McNeil and Warrington's (1993) patient, also a farmer, was unable to recognise his family, but was still able to recognise his sheep! An obvious question to ask about PD, then, is whether his ability to recognise people is intact; if it is not, this may contribute to the misidentification of his fellow patient as the nurse from America.

A second question to ask is whether PD's memory functions are intact. If he had a deficit in his ability to remember clearly events surrounding his recovery in America it is easy to see how he could become confused about the two "Janes"; the first his wife, and the second Ian's (the nurse) wife. If it were the case that PD suffered from a confabulation-style memory problem in addition to a face-recognition problem, it is easy to imagine how he might become confused about which Jane was which, and who had accompanied whom at any one time. The following sections of this chapter will concentrate on the investigations carried out to try understand better the types of cognitive difficulties experienced by PD, and explain how these problems might have contributed to his delusion that the fellow patient in his rehabilitation ward was the nurse from America, whom he believed was having an affair with his wife.

Brain Scan

The first investigation to be carried out on PD was a magnetic resonance imaging (MRI) brain scan. This is a particularly accurate method of gaining a "picture" of damage to the brain, which relies upon measuring weak radio-frequency signals emitted by protons after they have been made to resonate (vibrate) by a very strong magnetic field.

PD's MRI, taken three years after his injury, showed evidence of widespread brain damage, with damage most marked in the occipital lobes (the "back" of the brain) and frontal lobes (the foremost area of the brain). For those who have specific knowledge about brain anatomy, the details were as follows: The scan showed dilation of the right lateral ventricle involving the anterior and temporal horns and the trigone. The size of the left lateral ventricle was within normal limits. The third ventricle was moderately enlarged whereas the aqueduct and fourth ventricle and the subarachnoid space were all normal. There was some enlargement of the brain stem cisterns and the right cerebellar sulci. Areas of hyperdensity in the white matter of the right frontal lobe, both occipital lobes, and a rim of hyperdensity around the bodies of the lateral ventricles were noted. No abnormality was seen in the basal ganglia. An electro encephalogram (EEG) showed evidence of mild instability and localised neuronal hyperexcitability in the right temporal region but no gross structural focal disturbance.

Although the results of PD's brain scan show widespread brain damage, it is interesting that the primary focus of his damage was in the occipital and frontal lobes. Bilateral damage to the occipital lobes has been long associated with impairments in the visual analysis of faces (e.g. Efron, 1968; Warrington, 1986), and the ability to recognise faces (Warrington & James, 1967).

As regards the effects of damage to the frontal lobes, these have long been associated with memory disorders involving paramnesia and confabulation. Table 4.1 details the results of a literature search showing (albeit very roughly) the areas of the brain damaged in patients with confabulatory, paramnesic, or delusional disorders, where damage has been detected by radiological or other techniques. (Patients who show these syndromes do not necessarily have structural brain damage, but this can occur in a wide range of patients, including those with psychotic disorders—Christodoulou, 1978; dementia—Kumar, 1987; or even those with endocrine disorders—Hay, Jolley, & Jones, 1974 and Madakasira & Hall, 1981.)

The striking finding from Table 4.1 is the prevalence of damage to the frontal lobes in the right hemisphere. It is generally accepted these days that damage to the frontal lobes is often implicated in memory disorders such as confabulation, and that where the symptoms appear to be delusory in nature (i.e. the patients cannot be convinced of the falsehood of their beliefs—typically in confabulation this is not the case), this damage is accompanied by more extensive damage to the right hemisphere of the brain (see Fleminger & Burns, 1993; Signer, 1992 for reviews).

In summary, we can see from an examination of this literature that the areas of PD's brain that were damaged in his fall are broadly the same as

TABLE 4.1

Primary Locus of Lesions in Cases of Confabulation, Paramnesias, Reduplicative Phenomena, Capgras Syndrome, Frégoli Syndrome, and Related Delusions with Known Neurological Pathology[1]

Study	Sex	Age	Occipital	Parietal	Temporal	Frontal
			Left			
Stuss et al. (1978)	m	42				*
	m	53				*
	m	54				
	m	45	*	*		
	m	57				
Kapur & Coughlan (1980)	m	48				*
Shapiro et al. (1981)	m	54				*
	m	46				
	m	31				*
	m	45				
	m	64				*
	m	57				
Alexander & Freedman (1984)	m	43				*
Damasio et al. (1985)	m	55			*	*
Baddeley & Wilson (1986)	m	42				*
	m	41				*
Parkin, Leng, Stanhope, & Smith (1988)	m	42				*
Moscovitch (1989)	m	61				*
Delbecq-Derouesne, Beavois, & Shallice (1990)	m	53				*
Benson et al. (1976)	m	49				*
Ruff & Volpe (1981)	f	64				
	f	23				
	m	29				
	f	60				
Leiguarda (1983)	m	74				
Staton, Brumback, & Wilson (1982)	m	31				*
Marshall, Halligan, & Wade (1995)	m	69				*
Hayman & Abrams (1977)	m	37				
Alexander, Stuss, & Benson (1979)	m	44				*
Lewis (1987)	f	19	*			*
De Pauw, Szulecka, & Pollock (1987)	f	66				
Levine & Grek (1984)	f	67				
	m	64				
	m	74				
	f	82				
	m	66				
	m	75				
	f	80				
	f	75				
Greenberg (1988)	f	75			*	*
Young, Robertson, Hellawell, de Pauw, & Pentland (1992)	m	28				*

[1] A number of cases in the literature with medical complications (e.g. marked hydrocephalus, history of alcohol abuse or previous trauma) are not included here.

Occipital	Parietal	Temporal	Frontal	Specifically Thalamic	Diffuse Bilateral	Form	Cause
			Right	Left	Right		
			*			Confabulation	Trauma
			*			Confabulation	Infarction
			*			Confabulation	Anterior communicating artery aneurysm
		*	*			Confabulation	Trauma
			*			Confabulation	Anterior communicating artery aneurysm
			*			Confabulation	Subarachnoid haemorrhage
			*			Confabulation	Posterior cerebral artery aneurysm
			*			Confabulation	Anterior communicating artery aneurysm
		*				Confabulation	Trauma
			*			Confabulation	Trauma
			*			Confabulation	Trauma
			*			Confabulation	Trauma
						Confabulation	AVM
		*	*		*	Confabulation	HSE
			*			Confabulation	Trauma
			*			Confabulation	Anterior communicating artery aneurysm
						Confabulation	Anterior communicating artery aneurysm
			*			Confabulation	Subarachnoid haemorrhage
			*			Confabulation	Anterior communicating artery aneurysm
			*			Environmental reduplication	Trauma
	*		*			Environmental reduplication	Space occupying lesion
	*		*			Environmental reduplication	AVM
	*		*			Environmental reduplication	Meningioma
			*			Environmental reduplication	Trauma
				*	*	Environmental reduplication	Haematoma
*	*	*	*			Reduplicative paramnesia	Trauma
			*			Reduplicative paramnesia	Trauma
	*		*			Capgras	Aneurysm
		*	*			Capgras	Subdural haematoma
*			*			Capgras	Devel
	*	*			*	Frégoli	Middle cerebral artery aneurysm
	*	*	*			Delusions[2]	Infarction
			*			Delusions[2]	Infarction
		*	*			Delusions[2]	Infarction
		*	*			Delusions[2]	Infarction
		*	*			Delusions[2]	Infarction
*		*	*			Delusions[2]	Infarction
*	*	*				Delusions[2]	Infarction
			*			Delusions[2]	Infarction
			*			Delusions[2]	Meningioma
	*	*	*			Delusions[2]	Trauma

[2] Complex delusions which include reduplications, Capgras, etc.
AVM = Arteriovenous malformation
HSE = Herpes simplex encephalitis
Devel = Developmental abnormality

those in other patients who show similar types of symptoms. But what is it that these areas do? For this we need to examine PD's neuropsychological status.

Neuropsychological Assessment

A detailed investigation of PD's cognitive functions was carried out. Tables 4.2, 4.3, and 4.4 present summaries of the results for those readers with specialised knowledge. They broadly indicate the following: PD has most impairment in those abilities which are generally associated with the non-dominant (i.e. right, in right-handed people) hemisphere of the brain. Particularly relevant to his misidentification delusion is the fact that his visual perceptual abilities have been impaired by his accident, and he can no

TABLE 4.2
Summary of PD's Performance on Tests of
General Intelligence, Perception, and
Literacy Skills

General Intelligence: WAIS[1]
Verbal IQ 92
Performance IQ 56
Raven's Matrices IQ = 55[2]

Visuospatial Skills
Figure Detection: X: 50%ile[6]
                                 O: < 5%ile
Dot Centre: 50%ile[5]
Dot Counting: < 5%ile[5]

Perceptual Integration
Degraded Letters: < 5%ile[9], [7]
Silhouettes: < 5%ile[6]
Unusual Views: < 5%ile[5]
Usual Views: < 5%ile[5]

Literacy Skills
Reading, NART quotient = 100[3]
Spelling, GAST = 50%ile[4]

Naming
Graded Naming Test[8]
Scaled Score = 10 (oral and visual presentation)

---

[1] Wechsler (1955); [2] Raven, Court, and Raven (1977); [3] Nelson and O'Connell (1978); [4] Baxter (1987); [5] McKenna and Warrington (1983); [6] Warrington and Taylor (1973); [7] Warrington and James (1988); [8] Warrington (1982); [9] Degraded Letters (Warrington, 1985).

TABLE 4.3
PD's Performance on Tests of Memory

Forced Choice Recognition
Forced Choice Words: SS < 3)[1]
Forced Choice Faces: SS < 3)[1]
3 Choice Photographs: < 5%ile[2]
Famous Face Triplets[3]
Old Faces = 4/15
Recent Faces 5/15

Paired Associate Learning[7]
Easy, Hard
5, 2; 5, 2; 5, 1

Free Recall
Recall of Short Stories (× 4)
Immediate: range 5.5–11.5/20[7]
30-minute delay: range 5.5–12/20
Coughlan and Hollows Story[8]
Immediate Recall: < 10%ile
Rey-Osterreith Figure[9]
  Copy = 16.5/36
  30-minute delay = 3/36
Famous Faces 1/12 (impaired)[10]

Cued Recall
Fragmented Words: < 5%ile[4]
Gollins Pictures: < 5%ile[5]
Prompt and Recognition Test[6]
  Prompted Recall: < 5%ile
  Recognition: < 5%ile

[1] Warrington (1984); [2] Warrington (personal communication); [3] Warrington and McCarthy (1988); [4] Warrington and Weiskrantz (1968, 1970); [5] Gollin (1960), Warrington and Weiskrantz (1968); [6] Warrington and Weiskrantz (1974); [7] Stone and Wechsler (1946), Wechsler (1945); [8] Coughlan and Hollows (1985); [9] Osterreith and Rey (1944), Taylor (1958); [10] Warrington and James (1967), Whiteley and Warrington (1977).

longer perceive complex (and especially ambiguous) material accurately (Table 4.2). Unsurprisingly, given that faces are very complex things indeed from a perceptual point of view, his performance on a memory test which requires identifying faces which were recently presented (Warrington's RMT faces, Table 4.3) was extremely poor indeed.

In addition, the results of the neuropsychological examination show that PD has a severe problem with his memory. As with the patient reported by

TABLE 4.4
PD's Performance on Tests of Executive Functions

Test	Score	Comment
Alternation Task[1] (trial of last error)	27	Impaired [2]
Cognitive Estimates[3]	2	Mean of posterior lesion group = 4.9 (N = 51)
Money's Road-Map Test (errors)[5]	15	Mean of left frontal group = 11.9; normals = 1.7
Personal Orientation Test[5]	19	Max possible errors = 34
Proverb Interpretation	—	Very concrete
Self-Ordered Memory: representational pictures (errors)[6]	28	> 3 SD below mean of a lesion control group[7]
Tower of London (score)[8]	1	Controls mean = 24.9; SD = 4.5
Trail Making (time)[9]	84	PD also made 12 errors on this performance. Controls mean time = 29.6 seconds (SD = 4.5)[2]
Verbal Fluency[10] FAS 60 seconds	19	Controls mean = 34.8; SD = 14.3 (N = 30)
Wisconsin (MWCST)[11] Categories	1	Controls mean = 5; SD = 1.6; N = 46; mean age = 45; SD = 14

[1] Chorover and Cole (1966); [2] Non-lesion patient controls (N = 24; FSIQ = 114.9; SD = 12.7) Shallice, Warrington, & Watson, unpublished data; [3] Shallice and Evans (1978); [4] Butters, Soeldner, and Fedio (1972); [5] Semmes, Weinstein, Ghent, and Teuber (1963); [6] Petrides and Milner (1982); [7] Eight right posterior lesion patients (mean FSIQ = 107.1; SD = 8.9), Shallice and Burgess (1991); [8] Shallice and McCarthy, see Shallice (1982); [9] Reitan (1958); [10] Miller (1984); [11] Nelson (1976).

Young and De Haan (1988), the severity of PD's impairment on formal memory tests was surprising, since in everyday functioning he is oriented in time and place and can converse about recent personal events (although it is clear that he does have some memory difficulties). We also noticed, however, that his performance on memory tests is highly variable, with his ability to remember short stories, for instance, appearing quite normal one minute, but being really quite impaired the next. Some have claimed that this variability reflects damage to the frontal lobes in certain patients (Burgess & Shallice, 1996), and, indeed, PD had great difficulty with a range of executive function tests which are thought to be sensitive to frontal lobe involvement (see Table 4.4).

For instance, on Shallice and Evans's (1978) Cognitive Estimates test, where patients are asked to estimate the answers to questions to which they are unlikely to know the answer, PD estimated that racehorses gallop at 80mph (which is far too fast), that the oldest person in Britain today is 75 (which is far too young), and when he was asked what he thought was the largest object normally found in a house, he replied "a vacuum cleaner". The kinds of abstract reasoning, planning, and strategy use involved in performing such tests can be compromised in patients with frontal lobe damage, and it would appear that PD has great difficulty in this area. Of course if PD has difficulty in examining the plausibility of his answers to simple questions such as these, one might expect it to be equally difficult for him to examine the likelihood of a nurse coming over from America in order to masquerade as a patient on his rehabilitation ward.

PD's Face Recognition Abilities

In order to further investigate PD's difficulties with recognising faces, a selection of 18 currently famous TV and sports personalities were administered either auditorily or visually (ABBA design). PD was able to identify only 1/18 of the personalities from their photograph but named the occupations of 12/18 from their names. Examples of his errors in face identification included the following: Martina Navratilova was named as John McEnroe, Fatima Whitbread the javelin thrower was named as (perhaps significantly) a nurse in a previous rehabilitation unit, and Maradona was named as the rugby player, Gareth Edwards.

PD's Ability to Recognise Watches

In view of the role a Seiko watch played in confirming his delusional belief about his fellow patient whom he mistook for the nurse from America, PD's ability to discriminate accurately between watches was also tested.

He was first asked to identify his own watch amongst 15 unfamiliar watches borrowed from the staff on his rehabilitation ward. He identified three as possible candidates, one of which was his own. He had no degree of certainty about his own watch, merely saying that it might be his. His mistakes included a watch of the same make but a different colour, showing the date (his did not include the date), and one which was of a different make and colour, also showing the date. This latter watch was also a digital watch which his was not.

PD was then shown a watch (randomly chosen) for 10 seconds, and then immediately asked to identify it when it was presented on the table along with four other watches. He was successful on only 3/6 occasions. Once again his errors were not just small mistakes. For instance, a man's large black analogue watch with a date was mistaken for a woman's small silver analogue watch without a date, and a hexagonal man's silver watch was mistaken for a man's rectangular gold watch.

DISCUSSION

PD's delusion proved to be his greatest problem in rehabilitation. Several times each day he became preoccupied with it, and at such times he was extremely agitated and was destructive, aggressive, and abusive (described later). Such outbursts came without provocation and also subsided without intervention, although on occasions he could be coaxed out of them. The content of this delusion remained static for several years (see later).

Explaining the Contribution of PD's Cognitive Deficits to his Delusional Misidentification

The investigations of PD's neurological and neuropsychological state have confirmed a number of factors which can help us to understand how PD came to suffer from his delusion. First, the brain-scanning results and review of the literature have confirmed that PD has sustained trauma to the areas of the brain damaged in other patients who have suffered similar problems (such as the Capgras syndrome). Second, neuropsychological testing has shown that PD has problems with his memory, and also has many features of prosopagnosia (the inability to recognise the identity of people by their faces). PD had great difficulty in recognising staff on his ward, and would do so by using clues such as the colour or style of someone's hair, or the sound of their voice. This meant that sometimes if someone he knew well came onto the ward having just had a haircut, he would often have difficulty working out who they were. At these times you could see him wait until the person spoke before greeting them.

His memory problems also showed themselves in his day-to-day routine. In traditional, severe, amnesia, patients will often not be able to remember what has happened to them only a few minutes before. One patient, GAS, reported by Alderman and Burgess (1994) had such a poor memory that if one of his therapists left the room for a couple of minutes in the middle of a session, when they returned he would not remember having seen them at all that day.

PD's memory problem was not like this. Most often he would be able to remember the outline of events that had happened to him, but often certain details would be inaccurate, and he would recall things out of their correct time sequence, for instance thinking that things that had happened a week ago had happened yesterday. In addition in the early stages of his recovery, he would confabulate about engineering projects that he was currently working on. In fact he would often annoy other patients by talking about these details, which the other patients knew to be false, although he was convinced were true.

Such problems with memory, combined with a face-recognition problem, might contribute to PD's delusional misidentification.

Contribution of Memory Factors

We will be arguing that PD's delusion has been constructed from a number of memories which have been recalled inaccurately and without proper context, and that these memories have been conflated to form one new robust whole. How might this happen?

It is generally accepted by memory theorists that remembering something acts as a learning trial for subsequent retrieval; in other words, the more you've thought about something, the more likely you are to remember it in the future (whether correct or not). PD would ruminate about his delusion many times a day, and so it is quite likely that the memories relevant to PD's delusion have now fixed, long-term characteristics. In other words, they are unlikely to be susceptible to change.

Patterson and Mack (1985, p. 120) assert that one of the problems which accounts for paramnesic syndromes is that there exists "an integration problem, not restricted to memory, which lead poorly perceived stimuli held in poorly operating memory systems [to be] particularly likely to be improperly associated with [one] another". Certainly, PD did show these sorts of integration difficulties in everyday life. As already mentioned, PD would get confused about the temporal order of events. For instance, on one occasion when PD was asked what he had for lunch that day, he gave an accurate description of a lunch he had eaten two days before with his parents. What he remembered was actually correct, but was out of context and was not the information required. PD's recall in this instance bears close parallels with the disordered recall of a confabulating patient described by Delbecq-Derouesne et al. (1990) who recalled details of a shopping trip correctly, but had the order of the events confused, and showed a transposition of details from one situation into another.

It would seem that PD's account of the characteristics of the nurse (Jake) is a conflation of information about two people who shared similar roles and who he met and knew at similar times. One of the nurses (Jamie) had a similar name to the patient that PD later misidentified (Jake). In addition the wife of one of the nurses had the same name as his own wife, and in view of PD's perceptual and prosopagnosic difficulties this must have made it difficult to be clear about whom it was that this nurse was referring to when both wives were present (and indeed this is reported by PD's wife). The patient that PD later mistook for Jake had similar facial characteristics to an amalgam of both nurses in terms of colour of beard, hair, and so forth, but PD's wife reports that the patient actually looked nothing like either of them. It appears that PD was using the same mechanisms of person identification as he does with staff around him: He will try to work out who a person is by his verbal semantic knowledge of people's hair colour, stature, and so forth. Key evidence for PD was the fact that this patient was wearing what he mistook as his watch. As has been demonstrated by testing, PD is not able to recognise watches accurately, and (as he does with people) relies upon verbal semantic information when trying to distinguish his watch from others. PD used his (correct) knowledge that both watches were of a particular make and incorrectly concluded that therefore the patient's watch was his.

It is well accepted now that remembering things that have happened to us is not a simple case of retrieving a set "memory". Instead, it requires an active reconstructive process (see e.g. Conway, 1992). Burgess and Shallice (1996) have shown that ordinary people make many errors initially when recalling events, which are however usually corrected. Correction requires the operation of a series of control processes which guide remembering, and a series of verification and problem-solving processes to help when recall fails or some aspect of what has been remembered doesn't fit with others. Thus the memory is "constructed" rather than just recalled. Burgess and Shallice (1996) have argued that it is the operation of these control processes which is damaged in people who confabulate. PD's conflation of events surrounding his recovery would seem to be evidence that these control processes have been affected by his brain damage.

Perceptual Factors and Prosopagnosia

A number of authors have emphasised the role of perceptual factors, particularly symptoms such as prosopagnosia in cases of reduplicative paramnesia and delusional misidentification (Lewis, 1987; Shraberg & Weitzel, 1979; Synodinou, Christodoulou, & Tzavaras, 1977). PD's perceptual discrimination is certainly markedly defective, and one might expect that impoverished perceptual input could increase the propensity for the development of false beliefs since one would lack disconfirming evidence. For instance, we have all had the experience of seeing someone on the street whom we think we recognise, but feel that it can't really be the person we know, perhaps because we know that they are unlikely to be in that particular place at that time. In these circumstances, one usually looks even more carefully at that person, trying to find some feature which aids you to be convinced that the person you see just looks like the person you know, rather than actually being them. However, if those processes which are involved in perceiving faces were impaired, it would obviously be harder for you to perform this "disconfirming" routine.

Indeed, it is possible that, in patients generally, the nature of the perceptual deficit may determine the specific form and content of the delusion, explaining the apparent specificity of paramnesic symptoms (see, for example, Ellis & de Pauw, 1994). Such category-specific deficits might explain why Ruff and Volpe's (1981) patient, for instance, who had right frontal and parietal damage, exhibited selective reduplication for environ-ment. Similarly, PD showed reduplication for a person and an object but never for environment.

Although perceptual deficits and agnosia might increase the probability of a delusional system developing, this cannot be the complete picture. Patients with gross perceptual deficits, memory deficits or prosopagnosia do not generally show reduplicative syndromes. Clearly an additional deficit must be postulated to account for the formation of such symptoms.

Accounting for the Delusional Aspects of PD's Misidentification

Not all neurological patients exhibiting delusions show the selective symptoms of reduplicative paramnesia. We have already shown that, where a patient is suffering from paramnesia, it is most often the case that there is evidence of damage to the frontal lobes. But, as we have seen, paramnesias do not have to be delusional in form. For instance, confabulators are often willing to accept that they are wrong about what they are misremembering, and they will misremember different things from day to day. This appears to be different from a patient with a fixed delusion, where the patient is convinced against all contrary evidence that what they believe is true, and where they may hold the same belief for many years (as in the case of PD). Moreover, some patients suffer from delusions where it seems unlikely that a fault in the remembering process can be involved. For instance, one of the (schizophrenic) patients (HE) reported by Shallice, Burgess, and Frith (1991) believed that he was being sent messages from "the Planet H". As far as were can be aware, he had never been in contact with a Planet H, and we have not yet found references to a Planet H in literature or films (indeed he claimed he was the only person aware of its existence). So it seems unlikely that he is misremembering events that have actually happened to him. Instead it seems likely that this type of false belief (delusion) and misremembering as in confabulation are two different syndromes.

HE's belief in Planet H raises an interesting possible source for erroneous beliefs. If his belief is not a "false reminiscence", where does the belief come from? One possibility is that delusions may reflect preoccupations within particular cultures: Much of HE's description of his beliefs seemed to have details which were derived from popular mythology about extra-terrestrial beings. More direct evidence for culture-specific delusions comes from the study of one particular delusion known as "Koro" (which means "head of turtle"). This is the name for a symptom characterised by the belief that one's penis is shrinking, and that, once it has disappeared altogether into the abdomen, death will follow (Berrios & Morley, 1984). This delusion, obviously only held by men, was originally thought only to exist in Chinese subjects, and was therefore a "culture-bound syndrome" (Yap, 1965a), although more recently other cases have been found from outside China (e.g. Berrios & Morley, 1984; Cremona, 1981; Oyebode et al., 1986; Yap, 1965b). People with this delusion become very agitated, and their false belief (although see Oyebode, Jamieson, Mullaney, & Davison, 1986) causes them great suffering. One man (Oyebode et al., 1986) was so worried that his penis would disappear altogether that his wife hung onto it in order to prevent its total disappearance! Whilst it is clear now that it is not only Chinese men who can show this delusion, Koro is evidence that some false beliefs are apparently more common in certain groups of people, perhaps reflecting particular issues prevalent within that culture.

Given then that some delusions do not seem to have aspects of "misremembering", whilst others are clearly just this, one might argue for the existence of three categories of disorder: (1) paramnesic without delusion (e.g. confabulation); (2) delusion without paramnesia (e.g. HE's disorder— Planet H); and (3) delusion with paramnesia (PD's disorder).

Such a possibility would seem to be supported by the radiological literature in the sense that where a disorder, delusional or otherwise, involves paramnesia (misremembering), there is usually evidence of frontal lobe involvement (Table 4.4). On the other hand, there are cases of delusions without paramnesia where there is no evidence of frontal lobe damage. Levine and Finkelstein (1982) report eight such patients with generalised delusional systems following right temporoparietal stroke or trauma, and Peroutka, Sohmer, Kumar, Folstein, and Robinson (1982) also report a 72-year-old woman who exhibited delusions of a more generalised and unstable nature following a right temporo-parieto-occipital infarction. Similarly, Pakalnis, Drake, and Kellum's (1987) non-paramnesic case (a right parieto-occipital infarction) suffered delusions not markedly paramnesic in content.

In contrast, Levine and Grek (1984) report nine cases of patients with delusions following right cerebral infarction, many of whom (p. 579) included reduplication "as a prominent feature" and whose delusions "were distortions or condensations of actual events". Seven of their nine patients showed clear evidence of frontal, in addition to more posterior, involvement. It therefore seems likely that both frontal and more posterior non-dominant hemisphere involvement is present in most patients who exhibit paramnesic delusions; in other words where their delusions are not based on misremembering. (One caveat here: a number of these non-paramnesic delusional cases suffered hallucinations, and it is possible that the hallucinations were significant contributers to their delusions; see Halligan, Marshall, & Ramachandran, 1994, for discussion of this point.)

So far, this chapter has focused on a theoretical explanation of how the cognitive deficits PD suffered in his fall might explain some of his delusional symptoms. We will now describe his progress in rehabilitation and our (not always successful) attempts at treatment.

REHABILITATION

On his admission to the second rehabilitation unit in England, PD's ruminative delusional talk was monitored by recording it as absent or present at 15-minute intervals during the day. During this initial stage of his admission, he spent more than 50 hours in such talk in just one week alone (222 15-minute recordings)!

PD was also extremely disruptive in rehabilitation sessions and at these times he was escorted to his room. With the exception of some improvements in his personal hygiene, PD did not respond well to behavioural treatment, and a programme where he was rewarded every 15 minutes of the day if he was doing what he was supposed to be doing at that time had to be dropped as his response to the reinforcement was totally unpredictable. A second programme where he was awarded time doing his favoured activity (using an exercise bicycle) if he was behaving appropriately also proved ineffective. The unit, however, managed to contain his physical aggression and the frequency of such incidents reduced to a minimal level over 1.5 years (see Figure 4.1).

PD remained at the unit (Kemsley Brain Injury Division, St Andrews Hospital, Northampton, UK) as his potentially dangerous and disruptive

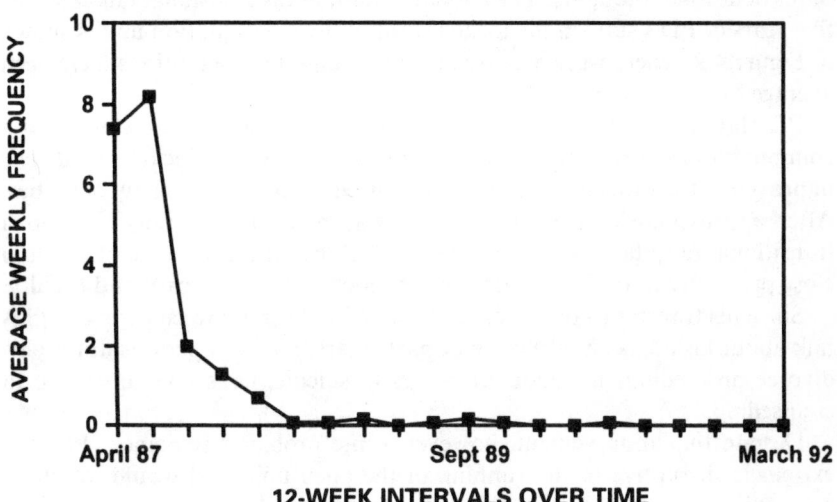

FIG. 4.1.   Episodes of physical aggression over five years.

behaviour could not be managed elsewhere at the time. However, he did not actively take part in rehabilitation, and few expectations were made of him. At this time he was in a very emotional state, and he frequently needed constant observation; he made 14 parasuicidal attempts (superficial self-inflicted cuts to his wrists) during the first year of his admission, with five occurring in the first month.

Although there was an overall trend towards a reduction of his delusional talk (i.e. ruminating about his wife's infidelity with the patient he believed was the nurse from America), it was not until his wife visited America for three months that staff noticed improvement. During her visit abroad, PD was unable to continue with his usual daily routine of phoning his wife at frequent intervals. It is possible that this disruption in his routine, with thoughts continually focused on his wife, may have interrupted his ruminative thinking.

On her return from America, PD's wife decided to start divorce proceedings. There was an increase in his talk about his delusion, but not to its previous level. However, there was an increase in his parasuicidal attempts, which were more serious, with some cuts requiring stitches. He would sometimes talk calmly and rationally about making a new future for himself following the divorce, but at other times he said he felt that life was not worth living.

Perhaps surprisingly, PD's behaviour started to get better, and he started taking part in ward activities and began a intensive physical fitness programme. Some time later he described how at this time he made a decision that he would get himself better, and would exercise to rid himself of his delusional thoughts. The overall pattern of his delusional talk over the five years of PD's stay on the locked ward of the rehabilitation unit is shown in Figure 4.2, where weekly frequency of 15-minute observations have been averaged over 12-week periods.

PD showed steady improvement, so he was eventually transferred to a community-based rehabilitation programme on another locked ward. His improvement continued, and he was allowed to choose his daily activities. After approximately seven months he was ready to be transferred to a transitional hospital-based open hostel which has the advantage of being in close proximity to back-up staff from the locked wards, in case of difficulty.

Since his transfer to this open unit, there has been no re-emergence of his talk about his delusion; although at particularly stressful periods during his divorce proceedings he made references to suicide, he is now amenable to counselling.

Despite this improvement, however, some problems remained. PD was extremely disruptive to the running of the open unit, and would interfere, aggressively, with the rehabilitation activities of other patients. This behaviour started to increase in frequency, and although counselling and

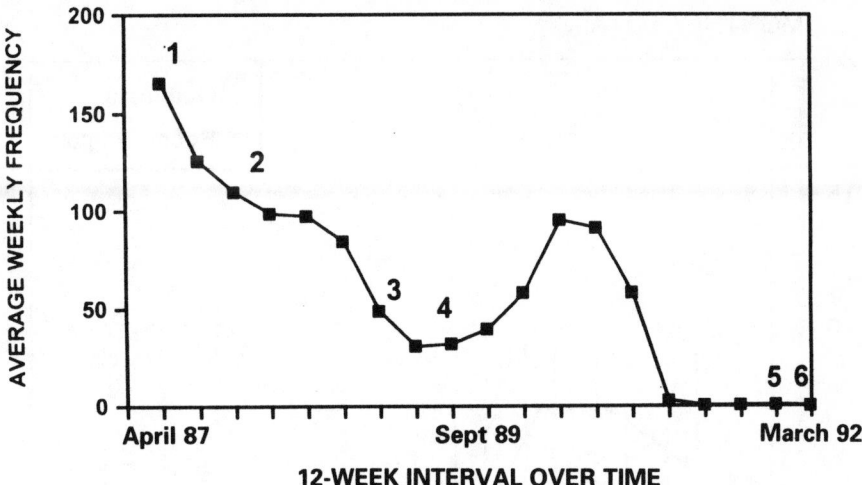

FIG. 4.2. Delusional talk over five years (15-minute weekly recordings).

[1] Tokens stopped after 2 months; [2] Bicycle programme: 10.12.87; [3] Wife in America: Jan–March 89; [4] Told of divorce proceedings: 10.6.89; [5] Kemsley West: 19.8.91; [6] Kemsley Annexe: 16.3.92.

cognitive therapy had been tried before when PD was on the locked wards, it was judged that he may now have improved sufficiently to give it another try. Weekly cognitive sessions were instigated by the consultant neuro-psychologist (DB) which focused on anger management and the use of alternative coping strategies and problem solving. In addition, when his behaviour was poor, staff would give him a brief prompt as a signal that he should stop and go to his room to calm down.

The incidence of PD's aggressive outbursts was baselined (i.e. observed without intervention) for one month. Part of his problem, however, was that when staff were talking to him about his outbursts—which may have happened a few days ago—PD was unable to remember clearly the event himself. He was aware that he often got events confused in his mind, and two weeks into therapy he accepted the idea that staff would provide him with written descriptions of these incidents at his weekly session, to help him remember them. In addition, staff gave brief daily feedback about his behaviour. The number of prompts recorded in the baseline and treatment periods is given in Figure 4.3.

PD made good progress, and nine months later we were able to tackle one of PD's most irritating habits, "food talk". His conversation by this time centred almost entirely on food, every meal and every cup of tea being described as "this is the best … I've ever had", and he would repeat the same comment many times. At one meal, staff recorded a 20-minute conversation about the merits of the hospital gravy! Attempts to encourage

MONTHLY TOTALS

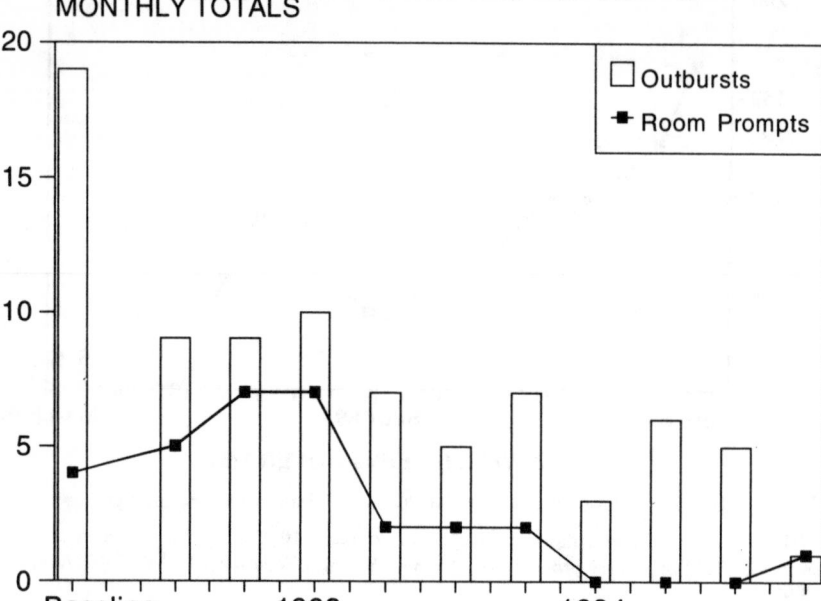

FIG. 4.3.   Effect of feedback on outbursts.

Baseline from 1.6.92 to 28.6.92; Feedback from 29.6.92.

alternative conversation with cue cards failed miserably, and it appeared that PD, rather than talking repeatedly about his delusion, now had another theme—food.

The programme that did work, however, was quite simple. A mini flip-chart with increasing numbers on each page was placed on the window-sill by PD's meal-table. Every time he started inappropriate talk about food, a page was turned, revealing a higher number. This enabled PD to monitor his own behaviour. The results of the programme are given in Figure 4.4. Within a relatively short space of time, PD was even beginning to ask for alternative topics of conversation to practise. The monitoring procedure was stopped after eight months, and PD has continued to maintain his progress. Following the success of this programme, we were able subsequently to increase his time keeping and use of a timetable using similar methods of monitoring and feedback.

PD's progress has been a learning experience for all concerned. In particular, cases such as PD emphasise the importance of carefully controlling the choice of staff, grading expectations, and involving the patient in decisions (see Turkat & Behner, 1989). PD was unresponsive to cognitive therapy in the early stages of his recovery, and it was not until his

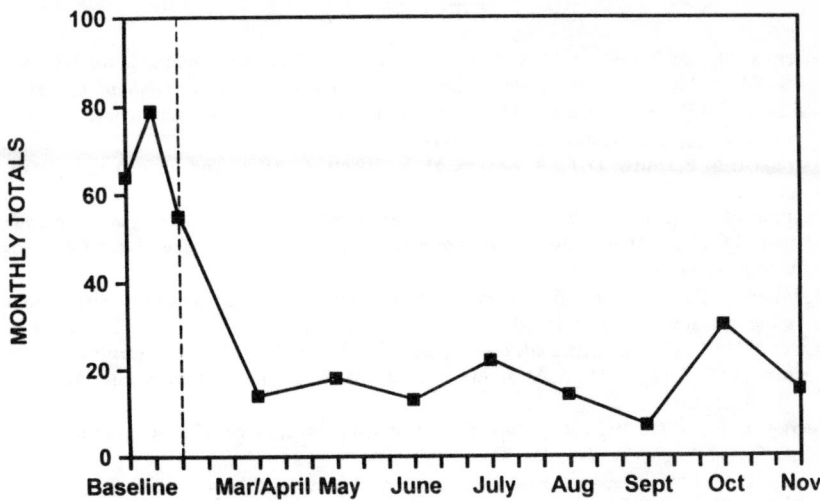

FIG. 4.4   Effect of feedback on frequency of "food talk".

Baseline recordings from 6.1.93 to 28.3.93; Feedback from 29.3.93 to 18.11.93.

delusion had subsided that progress could be made. The case of PD guards against hasty decisions about the failure of individuals to respond to rehabilitation methods in the early stages of recovery from a brain injury. It also emphasises the need for appropriate methods designed around the individual at the appropriate time in recovery. This may occur many years after the injury.

The Future for PD

At the current time, PD would be able to transfer into a community setting with staff appropriately trained. However, because of his wife's divorce and legal complications which have prevented a settlement, the local authorities withdrew funding for his rehabilitation two years ago. He remains as a charity patient at the Kemsley Unit as no local authority will accept responsibility for his care.

ACKNOWLEDGEMENTS

We would like to thank the very considerable amount of help we received from Mrs Mary Lees, Senior Social Worker at St Andrews Hospital, in dealing with and detailing this case. Thanks also to Ms Rajul Ved for help with this study. This work was supported by MRC grant number SPG8920199 and Wellcome Trust grant number 38964/Z/93/Z/1.5.

REFERENCES

Alderman, N., & Burgess, P.W. (1994). A comparison of treatment methods for behaviour disorder following Herpes Simplex Encephalitis. *Neuropsychological Rehabilitation, 4*, 31–48.

Alexander, M.P., & Freedman, M. (1984). Amnesia after anterior communicating artery aneurysm rupture. *Neurology, 34*, 752–757.

Alexander, M.P., Stuss, D.T., & Benson, D. F. (1979). Capgras syndrome: A reduplicative phenomenon. *Neurology, 29*, 334–339.

Baddeley, A.D., & Wilson, B.A. (1986). Amnesia, autobiographical memory, and confabulation. In D.C. Rubin (Ed.), *Autobiographical Memory*. Cambridge, UK: Cambridge University Press.

Baddeley, A.D., & Wilson, B.A. (1988). Frontal amnesia and the dysexecutive syndrome. *Brain and Cognition, 7*, 212–230.

Baxter, D.M. (1987). *The graded adult spelling test.* Unpublished PhD Thesis, University of London.

Benson, D.F., Gardner, H., & Meadows, J.C. (1976). Reduplicative paramnesia. *Neurology, 26*, 147–151.

Berrios, G.E., & Morley, S.J. (1984). Koro-like symptom in a non-Chinese subject. *British Journal of Psychiatry, 145*, 331–334.

Berson, R.J. (1983). Capgras' syndrome. *American Journal of Psychiatry, 140*, 969–978.

Bick, P.A. (1984). The syndrome of intermetamorphosis. *American Journal of Psychiatry, 141*, 588–589.

Blount, G. (1986). Dangerousness of patients with Capgras syndrome. *Nebraska Medical Journal, 71*, 207.

Bornstein, B., Sroka, M., & Munitz, H. (1969). Prosopagnosia with animal face agnosia. *Cortex, 5*, 164–169.

Burgess, P.W., & Shallice, T. (1996). Confabulation and the control of recollection. *Memory, 4*, 359–411.

Butters, N., Soeldner, C., & Fedio, P. (1972). Comparison of parietal and frontal lobe spatial deficits in man: Extrapersonal vs personal (egocentric) space. *Perceptual and Motor Skills, 34*, 27–34.

Capgras, J., & Reboul-Lachaux, J. (1923). L'illusion des "sosies" dans un délire systématisé chronique. *Bulletin de Société Clinique de Médicine Mentale, 11*, 6–16.

Chorover, S.L., & Cole, M. (1966). Delayed alternation performance in patients with cerebral lesions. *Neuropsychologia, 4*, 1–7.

Christodoulou, G.N. (1978). Syndrome of subjective doubles. *American Journal of Psychiatry, 135*, 249–251.

Conway, M.A. (1992). A structural model of autobiographical memory. In M.A. Conway, D.C. Rubin, H. Spinnler, & W.A. Wagenaar (Eds.), *Theoretical perspectives on autobiographical memory* (pp. 167–193). Netherlands: Kluwer Academic.

Coughlan, A.K., & Hollows, S.E. (1985). *The adult memory and information processing battery.* Leeds, UK: St. James's University Hospital.

Courbon, P., & Fail, G. (1927). Illusion de Frégoli. *Bulletin de la Société Clinique de Médecine Mentale, 15*, 121–124.

Cremona, A. (1981). Another case of Koro in a Briton. *British Journal of Psychiatry, 138*, 180–181.

Damasio, A.R., Graff-Radford, N.R., Eslinger, P.J., Damasio, H., & Kassell, N. (1985). Amnesia following basal forebrain lesions. *Archives of Neurology, 42*, 252–259.

Delbecq-Derouesne, J., Beauvois, MF., & Shallice, T. (1990). Preserved recall versus impaired recognition: A case study. *Brain, 113*, 1045–1074.

De Pauw, K.W., Szulecka, T.K., & Poltock, T.L. (1987). Frégoli syndrome after cerebral infarction. *Journal of Nervous and Mental Disease, 175*, 433–438.

Efron, R. (1968). What is perception? In R.S. Cohen & M. Wartofsky (Eds.), *Boston studies in the philosophy of science* (Vol. 4, pp. 137–173). New York: Humanities Press.

Ellis, H.D., & de Pauw, K.W. (1994). The cognitive neuropsychiatric origins of the Capgras delusion. In A.S. David & J.C. Cutting (Eds.), *The neuropsychology of schizophrenia*. Hove, UK: Lawrence Erlbaum Associates Ltd.

Enoch, M.D. (1963). The Capgras syndrome. *Acta Psychiatrica Scandanavica, 39,* 437–462.

Fialkov, M.J., & Robins, A.H. (1978). An unusual case of the Capgras syndrome. *British Journal of Psychiatry, 132,* 403–404.

Filley, C.M., & Jarvis, P.E. (1987). Delayed reduplicative paramnesia. *Neurology, 37,* 701–703.

Fleminger, S., & Burns, A. (1993). The delusional misidentification syndromes in patients with and without evidence of organic cerebral disorder: A structured review of case reports. *Biological Psychiatry, 33,* 22–32.

Gollin, E.S. (1960). Developmental studies of visual recognition of incomplete objects. *Perceptual and Motor Skills, 11,* 289–298.

Greenberg, L.B. (1988). Prospective electroconvulsive therapy in a delusional depressed patient with a frontal meningioma. *British Journal of Psychiatry, 153,* 105–107.

Halligan, P.W., Marshall, J.C., & Ramachandran, V.S. (1994). Ghosts in the machine: A case description of visual and haptic hallucinations after right hemisphere stroke. *Cognitive Neuropsychology, 11,* 459–477.

Hay, G.G., Jolley, D.J., & Jones, R.G. (1974). A case of the Capgras syndrome in association with pseudo-hyperthyroidism. *Acta Psychiatrica Scandanavica, 50,* 73–77.

Hayman, M.A., & Abrams, R. (1977). Capgras syndrome and cerebral dysfunction. *British Journal of Psychiatry, 130,* 68–71.

Hécaen, H., & Angelergues, R. (1962). Agnosia for faces. *Archives of Neurology, 7,* 92–100.

Joseph, A.B. (1985). Bitemporal atrophy in a patient with Frégoli syndrome, syndrome of intermetamorphosis, and reduplicative paramnesia. *American Journal of Psychiatry, 142,* 146–147.

Kapur, N., & Coughlan, A.K. (1980). Confabulation and frontal lobe dysfunction. *Journal of Neurology, Neurosurgery, and Psychiatry, 43,* 461–463.

Kumar, V. (1987). Capgras syndrome in a patient with dementia. *British Journal of Psychiatry, 150,* 251.

Leiguarda, R.C. (1983). Environmental reduplication associated with a right thalamic haemorrhage. *Journal of Neurology, Neurosurgery, and Psychiatry, 46,* 1154.

Levine, D.N., & Finkelstein, S. (1982). Delayed psychosis after right temporoparietal stroke or trauma: Relation to epilepsy. *Neurology, 32,* 267–273.

Levine, D.N., & Grek, A. (1984). The anatomic basis of delusions after right cerebral infarction. *Neurology, 34,* 577–582.

Lewis, S.W. (1987). Brain imaging in a case of Capgras' syndrome. *British Journal of Psychiatry, 150,* 117–121.

MacCallum, W.A.G. (1984). A syndrome of misinterpreting role changes as changes of person. *British Journal of Psychiatry, 144,* 649–650.

Madakasira, S., & Hall, T.B. (1981). Capgras syndrome in a patient with myxedema. *American Journal of Psychiatry, 138,* 1506–1508.

Marciniak, R.D., & Luchins, D.J. (1981). Neuropsychologic deficits and Capgras syndrome. *American Journal of Psychiatry, 138,* 856–857.

Marshall, J.C., Halligan, P.W., & Wade, D.T. (1995). Reduplication of an event after head injury? A cautionary case report. *Cortex, 31,* 183–190.

McKenna, P., & Warrington, E.K. (1983). *The graded naming test.* Windsor, UK: NFER-Nelson.

McNeil, J., & Warrington, E.K. (1993). Prosopagnosia: A face-specific disorder. *Quarterly Journal of Experimental Psychology, 46*(A), 1–10.

Miller, E. (1984). Verbal fluency as a function of a measure of verbal intelligence and in relation to different types of cerebral pathology. *British Journal of Clinical Psychology, 23,* 53–57.

Moscovitch, M. (1989). Confabulation and the frontal systems: Strategic versus associative retrieval in neuropsychological theories of memory. In H.L. Roediger, III and F.I.M. Craik (Eds.), *Varieties of memory and consciousness: Essays in honour of Endel Tulving* (pp. 133–160). Hillsdale, NJ: Lawrence Erlbaum Associates Inc.

Nelson, H.E. (1976). A modified card sorting task sensitive to frontal lobe defects. *Cortex, 12,* 313–324.

Nelson, H.E., & O'Connell, A. (1978). Dementia: The estimation of pre-morbid intelligence levels using the new adult reading test. *Cortex, 14,* 234–244.

Osterreith, P., & Rey, A. (1944). Le test de copie d'une figure complexe. *Archives de Psychologie, 30,* 206–356.

Oyebode, F., Jamieson, R., Mullaney, J., & Davison, K. (1986). Koro—A psychophysiological dysfunction? *British Journal of Psychiatry, 148,* 212–214.

Pakalnis, A., Drake, M.E., & Kellum, J.B. (1987). Right parieto-occipital lacunar infarction with agitation, hallucinations and delusions. *Psychosomatics, 28,* 95–96.

Parkin, A., Leng, N.R.C., Stanhope, N., & Smith, A.P. (1988). Memory impairment following ruptured aneurysm of the anterior communicating artery. *Brain and Cognition, 7,* 231–243.

Patterson, M.B., & Mack, J.L. (1985). Neuropsychological analysis of a case of reduplicative paramnesia. *Journal of Clinical and Experimental Neuropsychology, 7,* 111–121.

Peroutka, S.J., Sohmer, B.H., Kumar, A.J., Folstein, M., & Robinson, R.G. (1982). Hallucinations and delusions following a right temporo-parieto-occipital infarction. *Johns Hopkins Medical Journal, 151,* 181–185.

Petrides, M., & Milner, B. (1982). Deficits on subject-ordered tasks after frontal- and temporal-lobe lesions in man. *Neuropsychologia, 20,* 249–262.

Pick, A. (1903). On reduplicative paramnesia. *Brain, 26,* 260–267.

Raven, J.C., Court, J.H., & Raven, J. (1977). *Coloured progressive matrices.* London: H.K. Lewis.

Reitan, R.M. (1958). Validity of the trail-making test as an indication of organic brain damage. *Perceptual and Motor Skills, 8,* 271–276.

Ruff, R.L., & Volpe, B.T. (1981). Environmental reduplication associated with right frontal and parietal lobe injury. *Journal of Neurology, Neurosurgery, and Psychiatry, 44,* 382–386.

Semmes, J., Weinstein, S., Ghent, L., & Teuber, H.-L. (1963). Correlates of impaired orientation in personal and extrapersonal space. *Brain, 86,* 747–772.

Shallice, T. (1982). Specific impairments of planning. *Philosophical Transactions of the Royal Society of London, B 298,* 199–209.

Shallice, T., & Burgess, P.W. (1991). Deficits in strategy application following frontal lobe damage in man. *Brain, 114,* 727–741.

Shallice, T., Burgess, P.W., & Frith, C. (1991). Can the neuropsychological case-study approach be applied to schizophrenia? *Psychological Medicine, 21,* 661–673.

Shallice, T., Burgess, P.W., Schon, F., & Baxter, D.M. (1989). The origins of utilisation behaviour. *Brain, 112,* 1587–1598.

Shallice, T., & Evans, M.E. (1978). The involvement of the frontal lobes in cognitive estimation. *Cortex, 14,* 294–303.

Shapiro, D.E., Alexander, M.P., Gardner, H., & Mercer, B. (1981). Mechanisms of confabulation. *Neurology, 31,* 1070–76.

Shraberg, D., & Weitzel, W.D. (1979). Prosopagnosia and Capgras syndrome. *Journal of Clinical Psychiatry, 40,* 313–316.

Signer, S.F. (1992). Capgras symptom and delusions of reduplication in neurologic disorders. *Neuropsychiatry, Neuropsychology, and Behavioral Neurology, 5,* 138–143.

Staton, R.D., Brumback, R.A., & Wilson, H. (1982). Reduplicative paramnesia: A disconnection syndrome of memory. *Cortex, 18,* 23–36.

Stone, C.P., & Wechsler, D. (1946). *Wechsler memory scale form II.* New York: The Psychological Corporation.

Stuss, D.T., Alexander, M.P., Lieberman, A., & Levine, H. (1978). An extraordinary form of confabulation. *Neurology, New York, 28,* 1166–1172.

Synodinou, C., Christodoulou, G.N., & Tzavaras, A. (1977). Capgras syndrome and prosopagnosia. *British Journal of Psychiatry, 132,* 413–416.

Taylor, E.M. (1958). *Psychological appraisal of children with cerebral deficits.* Cambridge, Mass.: Harvard University Press.

Turkat, I.D., & Behner, G.W. (1989). Behaviour therapy in the rehabilitation of brain-injured individuals. *Brain Injury, 3*(1), 101–102.

Walter-Ryan, W.G. (1986). Capgras syndrome and misidentification. *American Journal of Psychiatry, 143,* 126.

Warrington, E.K. (1982). Neuropsychological studies of object recognition. *Philosophical Transactions of the Royal Society of London, B 298,* 15–33.

Warrington, E.K. (1984). *Recognition memory test.* Windsor, UK: NFER-Nelson.

Warrington, E.K. (1985). Agnosia: The impairment of object recognition. In P.J. Vinken, G.W. Bruyn, & H.L. Klawans (Eds.), *Handbook of clinical neurology* (Vol. 45). Amsterdam: Elsevier.

Warrington, E.K (1986). Visual deficits associated with occipital lobe lesions in man. *Experimental Brain Research Supplementum, 11,* 247–261.

Warrington, E.K., & James, M. (1967). Tachistoscopic number estimation in patients with unilateral cerebral lesions. *Journal of Neurology, Neurosurgery, and Psychiatry, 30,* 468–474.

Warrington, E.K., & James, M. (1988). Visual apperceptive agnosia: A clinico-anatomical study of three cases. *Cortex, 24,* 13–32.

Warrington, E.K., & McCarthy, R.A. (1988). The fractionation of retrograde amnesia. *Brain and Cognition, 7,* 184–200.

Warrington, E.K., & Taylor, A.M. (1973). The contribution of the right parietal lobe to object recognition. *Cortex, 9,* 152–164.

Warrington, E.K., & Weiskrantz, L. (1968). New method of testing long-term retention with special reference to amnesic patients. *Nature, 217* (5132), 972–974.

Warrington, E.K., & Weiskrantz, L. (1970). Amnesia: Consolidation or retrieval? *Nature, 228,* 628–630.

Warrington, E.K., & Weiskrantz, L. (1974). The effect of prior learning on subsequent retention in amnesic patients. *Neuropsychologia, 12,* 419–428.

Wechsler, D. (1945). A standardized memory scale for clinical use. *Journal of Psychology, 19,* 87–95.

Wechsler, D. (1955). *The Wechsler adult intelligence scale.* New York: The Psychological Corporation.

Weinstein, E.A. (1969). Patterns of reduplication in organic brain disease. In G.W. Bruyn & P.J. Vinken (Eds.), Handbook of clinical neurology (Vol. 3, pp. 251–257). Amsterdam: Elsevier.

Weinstein, E.A., Kahn, R.L., & Sugarman, L.A. (1952). Phenomenon of reduplication. *Archives of Neurology and Psychiatry, 67,* 808–815.

Whiteley, A.M., & Warrington, E.K. (1977). Prosopagnosia: A clinical, psychological and anatomical study of three patients. *Journal of Neurology, Neurosurgery and Psychiatry, 40,* 395–403.

Whitty, C.W.M., & Zangwill, O.L. (1966). *Amnesia.* London: Butterworth.

Yap, P.M. (1965a). Koro—A culture-bound depersonalization syndrome. *British Journal of Psychiatry*, *111*, 43–50.
Yap, P.M. (1965b). Koro in a Briton. *British Journal of Psychiatry*, *111*, 774–775.
Young, A.W., & De Haan, E.H.F. (1988). Boundaries of covert recognition in prosopagnosia. *Cognitive Neuropsychology*, *5*, 317–336.
Young, A.W., Robertson, I.H., Hellawell, D.J., de Pauw, K.W., & Pentland, B. (1992). Cotard delusion after brain injury. *Psychological Medicine*, *22*, 799–804.

5

Raymond: A Study of an Adult with Asperger Syndrome

Hadyn D. Ellis
School of Psychology, University of Wales College of Cardiff, Cardiff, UK

Kate M. Leafhead
MRC Applied Psychology Unit, Cambridge, UK

Testing was interrupted while Kate went to fetch coffee but the video recorder remained on and Raymond's behaviour was inadvertently recorded. He closed his eyes, grimaced horribly, yawned, and then began scratching his forearm quite vigorously while laughing to himself. During the entire period he was alone, Raymond continued these and other odd behaviours, only stopping when Kate returned. Such observations are not uncommon when dealing with people with severe learning disabilities but Raymond has a verbal IQ of 125; he reads the *Guardian* each day; has a deep interest in current affairs; and loves classical music. But in other ways he is definitely quite odd.

Raymond was referred to us by a clinical neuropsychologist who suspected prosopagnosia because he seemed to be completely unable to recognise his colleagues at the hospital where he worked in sheltered employment. Along with the referral there were some adventitious medical notes that referred to a febrile illness when Raymond was three years old and two later periods of psychiatric illness. At some stage Raymond received a tentative label of schizophrenia and neurological damage was also suspected, but these were substantiated neither by any principled diagnoses nor detailed testing.

BACKGROUND

Raymond, now in his late 30s, is a gentle man who is usually shabbily dressed and is not always particular about personal hygiene. This is doubtless partly due to his economic circumstances but mostly reflects not so much carelessness about his appearance as an almost complete lack of social awareness; an inability effectively to monitor the effect his appearance and behaviour have upon others.

When Raymond looks at you you can have the impression that his gaze is fixed at some point behind your head but this can be misleading: While appearing not to be reading your features he occasionally says something that indicates he has picked up some nuance in your facial expression. He is in many ways sensitive yet at the same time he is liable to stand too close or casually pick his nose or even break wind, seemingly oblivious to your presence. We shall detail Raymond's lack of social judgement later on. For the moment it is sufficient to note that all of the characteristics we have mentioned are part of a clinical pattern. Equally significant is Raymond's voice or, more precisely, the lack of prosody in it which, together with its soft, high pitched tone, make him sound quite as odd as he looks.

Raymond, then, is an intelligent man with a slightly strange appearance and a peculiar voice who lacks social skills. He also quickly strikes you as physically clumsy and lacking in energy. Less obvious are his relative inability to recognise people and his attentional style which at the same time is both distractable and limited.

Raymond reports that his early developmental milestones were normal: According to him he walked and said his first words by 12 months. He has a vivid first memory. At the age of two he remembers urging his mother to allow him to get out of his pram. Shortly after that Raymond developed pneumonia and, as a result of the accompanying fever, he may have suffered some neurological damage: Again his medical notes are less than clear. Raymond dates his "little problems" from that time. For him these centre almost exclusively on his lack of motor skills, though he is aware of his inability to learn new routes and sometimes refers to an emotional instability that in the past led to violent outbursts of temper and bouts of frustrated head banging—all admitted with disarming candour. His lack of insight to his essential problems, however, is quite striking. Although, when pressed to acknowledge his manifold problems Raymond is unable or unwilling to do so, he cannot be said to be anasognosic: We have never confronted him with his behaviour in order to elicit his reactions, not only because it could be unethical but, given our experience, we feel it would also be fruitless. It is interesting to note that, when describing being constantly teased by his childhood peers, Raymond attributes this to the fact that they were simply capitalising upon his tendency to react emotionally rather than his being victimised because he was so different from them.

ASPERGER SYNDROME

Although no such diagnosis was ever made for Raymond his signs and symptoms readily fit into the high-functioning autistic pattern called Asperger syndrome (Frith, 1991). Asperger published a paper in 1944 in which he described cases of what he termed "autistic psychopathy" but which now carry the diagnosis, "Asperger syndrome". The children were verbally fluent, socially inept, egocentric, gauche and stilted in the way they spoke and acted. Many were obsessive collectors of all sorts of objects and others displayed attention deficits and specific learning disabilities. In short they had much in common with the syndrome of autism independently described a year earlier by Kanner (1943), except that Asperger's cases were typically of normal intelligence (if lacking common-sense) whose symptoms were frequently not spotted until age two or three years and whose language skills, unlike those of autistic children, are normal and even (superficially) superior. This is not the place to pursue the significance of the differences between autism and Asperger syndrome; they may be part of the same spectrum but there are sufficient differences between them to warrant their separate labels (see Gillberg, 1992; van Krevelen, 1971; Wing, 1991).

Estimates of the incidence of Asperger vary between two and three per 10,000, with boys possibly outnumbering girls (Gillberg, 1992).

Various check-lists for diagnosing Asperger syndrome exist but the one by Gillberg (1992) shown in Table 5.1 is sufficiently representative to indicate the range of symptoms required to satisfy the classification. Table 5.1 also shows those that Raymond unequivocally displays.

- He shows a lack of appreciation of social cues and inappropriate behaviour.
- He has a strong, almost obsessional, interest in cricket—though whether this is any more all-absorbing than for other cricket fans is debatable.
- He has well-defined living and route-finding routines.
- Although he has superficially perfect expressive language, he shows odd prosody and often speaks in a formal, pedantic way.
- He is clumsy and displays decidedly odd gaze behaviour.
- He is clumsy to the point of being handicapped in the execution of most motor skills.

Raymond grew up as an obviously odd child who was poor at games and cruelly teased by peers. At various times labels as diverse as spastic, brain-damaged, and schizophrenic were offered by bewildered medical practitioners who were confronted by a clumsy, intelligent child who could be

TABLE 5.1
Raymond's Check-list on Gillberg's (1992) Diagnostic Criteria for Asperger Syndrome

	Raymond
1. *Severe impairment in reciprocal social interaction* (at least two of the following)	
(a) inability to interact with peers	?
(b) lack of desire to interact with peers	
(c) lack of appreciation of social cues	√
(d) socially and emotionally inappropriate behaviour	√
2. *All-absorbing narrow interest* (at least one of the following)	
(a) exclusion of other activities	√
(b) repetitive adherence	√
(c) more rote than meaning	
3. *Imposition of routines and interests* (at least one of the following)	
(a) on self, in aspects of life	√
(b) on others	
4. *Speech and language problems* (at least three of the following)	
(a) delayed development	√
(b) superficially perfect expressive language	√
(c) formal, pedantic language	√
(d) odd prosody, peculiar voice characteristics	
(e) impairment of comprehension including misinterpretations of literal/ implied meanings	
5. *Non-verbal communication problems* (at least one of the following)	
(a) limited use of gestures	
(b) clumsy/gauche body language	√
(c) limited facial expression	
(d) inappropriate expression	√
(e) peculiar, stiff gaze	
6. *Motor clumsiness:* poor performance on nondevelopmental examination	√

easily roused to tantrum and failed to fit into conventional schools. Indeed, he was sent away to a child psychiatric unit and later to a school for maladjusted boys. None of these establishments seems to have provided the necessary support for Raymond—any more than did adult training centres where attempts to teach him industrial skills served simply to point up his motor disabilities and failed completely to capitalise on his undoubted intellectual qualities. The appropriate label of Asperger syndrome, however, was not universally available in the 1950s when correct diagnosis may have been of some benefit for Raymond, if only to ensure apposite education as well as sympathetic support.

As we have noted, when Raymond is asked about his condition he shows a surprising lack of insight. His "little difficulties", as he calls them, seem to him to centre exclusively on his lack of motor abilities and his emotional instability. Only when pressed does Raymond volunteer other examples of how he is different, and even then it is obvious that he is almost totally unaware of just how different he is. He talks about "friends" but it is doubtful if these are any more than acquaintances. Why should this be? What prevents someone like Raymond from forming close relationships? And why does someone of such intelligence lack insight into the disabilities that are so obvious to others?

Social Judgement

A clue to essential problems of those with Asperger syndrome was offered by Margaret Dewey (1991) whose son, Jack, displayed many of the social characteristics that we have described in Raymond. She developed a series of eight social vignettes that each require a few decisions about people's behaviour. One of Dewey's scenarios is given below. At each choice point one is asked to judge the preceding behaviour using the scale:

A = Fairly normal behaviour in that situation.
B = Rather strange behaviour in that situation.
C = Very eccentric behaviour in that situation.
D = Shocking behaviour in that situation.

Story no. 1. In the supermarket

The market where Robert always shopped had a small sign in the door which read BARE FEET PROHIBITED IN THIS STORE BY STATE LAW. One summer day Robert saw a pretty girl enter the store without shoes. She seemed about his age, twenty, with long hair and an old-fashioned dress reaching to her ankles. Robert wanted to warn her about the sign but he was afraid to speak to her. Unpleasant things happened if he tried to talk to strange girls. Finally he decided he might be able to shield her feet from being seen by the manager. *He pushed his cart close behind hers down aisle after aisle.* ( ) Once or twice the girl looked back at him with a cross expression. *Suddenly she wheeled into the quick-check lane with twelve items in her basket although the sign said* FOR TEN OR FEWER ITEMS. ( ) Robert was more upset than ever. He thought this pretty girl was tempting fate by breaking another rule. When the check-out clerk let her through without comment, Robert finally relaxed. Just then, the barefoot girl turned and said to him, *"I don't know why you are following me, but buzz off or I'll call the police!"* (   )

Raymond's decisions at each of the three choice points are revealing. Like the high-functioning autistic adults reported by Dewey (1991), Raymond displayed an obvious inability to weigh up a social dilemma or action and decide a reasonable grade of response. For the first decision his response was quite different from that supplied by most of the seven age-matched controls we tested. Raymond thought it normal for Robert to protect the girl by pushing his shopping trolley close behind her; the controls thought this behaviour to be strange. On the other hand, Raymond thought that the act of going to the quick check-out with more than 10 items to be rather strange, whereas the majority of controls thought it normal. Finally, Raymond thought the girl's final words to Robert were shocking which sharply contrasts with the controls, all of whom thought it normal. Raymond's responses reveal a mixture of ignorance of social conventions and an over-dependence upon stated rules, such as the strictness on the number of items in a shopping basket allowed at the express check-out. In other words, he seems unable to judge each situation in a balanced way and, when a rule is contravened, finds the behaviour unusual. His responses to situations in the other seven scenarios were often similarly at variance with those offered by control subjects. From this simple test it is clear that Raymond has a distinct problem in social judgement. Younger people with Asperger syndrome have also been shown to have very similar difficulties (Ellis, Ellis, Fraser, & Deb, 1994).

Theory of Mind

Happé (1991) has analysed a small number of autobiographical information provided by high-functioning autistic/Asperger syndrome adults. She cites the case of Dr Temple Grandin, a successful animal scientist, who functions well in many situations but responds quite oddly in others. Dr Grandin, for example, sometimes writes in a way that presupposes knowledge that the reader could not possibly possess. This can be interpreted as a sort of advanced problem of theory of mind, quite different in many ways but essentially similar to those evinced by autistic children who fail to solve the Sally–Anne problem (Baron-Cohen, Leslie, & Frith, 1985) in which two dolls, Sally and Anne, act out a scene: Sally puts a marble in a basket before leaving the room and Anne moves it to a box. The question is where will Sally look for it when she returns? Autistic children are likely to say "In the box."

Raymond too shows he is quite capable of understanding such simple problems but we were interested when he volunteered that his poor performance at chess was probably due to his failing to consider what his opponent may be thinking. Accordingly, though perfectly able to plan ahead his own moves, by ignoring his opponent's strategy he cheerfully acknowledges that he is doomed to lose. When asked if he thought this failure to consider the thoughts and motives of chess opponents was a more general trait, Raymond frankly admitted that he rarely bothered to imagine what others were thinking. It is worth recording that over a two-year period of testing involving more than half-a-dozen sessions, Raymond only infrequently enquired about the many psychological tests he carried out and our reasons for administering them. He quite passively submitted to a variety of unusual procedures but rarely asked their purpose nor showed any real interest in the results, other than wanting bland assurances that he was "doing all right". It was obvious that Raymond disliked failing on any task but he gave us the impression that this was due to his desire to please, rather than because of any wish to succeed.

Cognitive Functioning

Over an extended period we were able to examine Raymond's cognitive and perceptual abilities using a wide range of tests. His recorded Wechsler Adult Intelligence Scale (WAIS) verbal IQ was 125 and his WAIS performance IQ was 74, which immediately suggests a gross division in his abilities that could be pathological in origin. We concentrated on exploring his disabilities. Here we shall simply summarise a selection of the data we have collected.

Face Processing. As we mentioned earlier, we first began to test Raymond because of his alleged problems in recognising people and we quickly established a profound problem, little short of classical prosopagnosia (Bodamer, 1947; Ellis & Florence, 1990). When shown a series of 50 faces, half famous and half unknown, and simply asked to say whether each was familiar or unfamiliar, Raymond scored 27 correct. In other words, his performance was more or less at chance level (25/50). When given 50 names to classify, however, his score was perfect. Raymond does reveal some face recognition, however. On another recognition test in which famous faces of high and low familiarity were employed, he named 12/20 of the highly familiar faces and 2/20 of the low familiar faces. When this test was repeated one month later, however, he could not name any of the highly familiar faces. This variability is admittedly extreme even for him but we often noted that his performance altered according to the time of day or his level of alertness.

Most people are better at recognising distinctive compared with typical faces (Bruce & Valentine, 1986; Light, Kayra-Stuart, & Hollander, 1979).

Raymond, too, revealed a similar advantage in naming distinctive famous faces (30% correct) compared with typical ones (10% correct). For controls the percentages were 91% and 56% respectively.

Raymond's poor performance on face recognition tasks is extreme but studies of other Asperger cases reveal similar, if less dramatic, difficulties (Ellis et al., 1994).

Picture Processing. Although Raymond's visual acuity, as measured by contrast sensitivity, was found to be in the normal range, he has trouble in simple discriminations, such as distinguishing male from female faces when hair cues are obliterated. Given 44 photographs to classify by gender Raymond scored 36 which is well below that managed by controls (42.5).

Raymond has problems, too, in recognising objects from photographs, scoring 23/90 in a simple picture naming task.

Not surprisingly, Raymond is poor at recognising pictures of famous buildings (9/20); and when shown 50 unfamiliar houses each later paired with another for recognition he scored significantly lower than controls (34 compared with 41.67 out of 50).

Rey–Osterrieth Complex Figure. Raymond has a generally poor visual memory—confirmed by his performance on the Rivermead Behavioural Memory Test (Wilson, Cockburn, & Baddeley, 1985)—and this was further explored by us when we gave him the Rey–Osterrieth Complex Figures Test (Lezak, 1983). This figure is a complex, meaningless geometric construction which is often used as a diagnostic test for right hemisphere dysfunction. Raymond failed to copy the figure in a normal way: He appeared unable to organise the elements into a whole and his ability to recall the figure from memory was typical of a neurologically impaired individual. Figure 5.1 illustrates Raymond's problems.

Voice Recognition. Unlike prosopagnosic patients, who usually have their voice recognition preserved, Raymond is relatively poor at identifying famous people from their voices. When given 38 extracts of famous voices he correctly named just four: The average for control subjects was 19.57— significantly much higher.

Musical Recognition. In contrast to his inability to recognise voices, Raymond was significantly superior to seven matched controls in his ability to identify 23 musical extracts and their composers: He scored 28 to their average of 20.57. His ability here is doubtless facilitated by an interest in music but, given his profound disabilities in other domains where daily opportunities for practice exist, it is unlikely that this alone

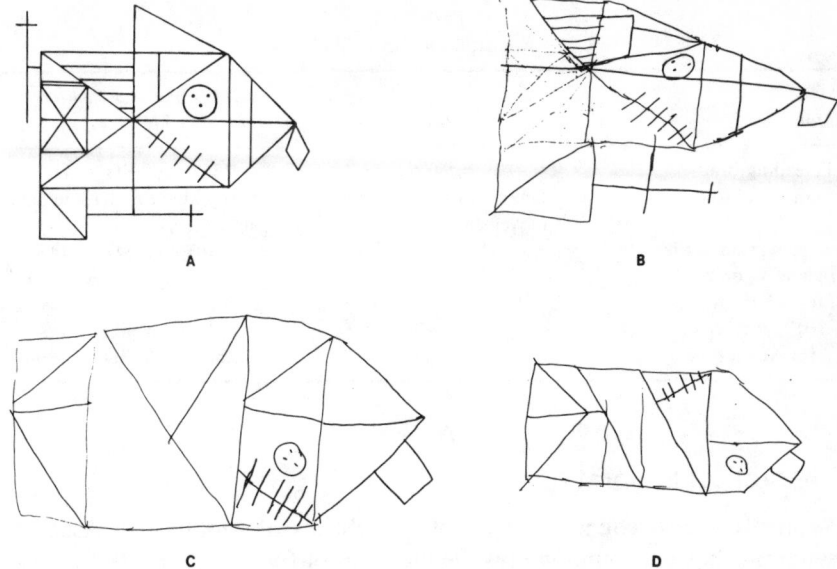

FIG. 5.1. Rey–Osterrieth figure.

A, original figure; B, Raymond's attempt at copying it; C, Raymond's immediate reproduction; D, Raymond's reproduction after a short interval. His performance is consistent with that of a person with right hemisphere damage.

can account for his skill. (Indeed, he has an even greater interest in cricket but proved almost as poor at identifying the faces of Glamorgan CC and Gloucestershire CC cricketers, whom he sees regularly, as he is at identifying others.)

Motor Skills. One of the principal features of Asperger syndrome is clumsiness. As we noted earlier, Raymond has obvious signs of motor difficulties. His gait is ungainly and he signs his name slowly and writes with obvious difficulty. In order to analyse Raymond's difficulties more formally we gave him four simple motor tests: threading beads; the Luria hand test (rapidly alternating open and closed hands, with each hand doing the opposite to the other); balancing on one leg; and a bimanual co-ordination task using "Etch-a-Sketch" to draw diagonal lines. Table 5.2 summarises Raymond's data compared with the mean results from four matched controls. On each test and every measure Raymond's performance was inferior.

Similar tests of motor skills given to a group of younger Asperger syndrome subjects by Helen Gunter of Cardiff University revealed a similar pattern of results.

TABLE 5.2
Raymond's Motor Skills

Motor Skills	Raymond	Age-matured Controls (N = 4)
Threading beads	60 sec.	35.00 sec. (SD = 11.7)
Luria hand test	Unable to alternate hand movements quickly	Easily able to alternate hand movements
Balancing on left leg	2 sec.	108 sec. (SD = 40.8)
Balancing on right leg	6 sec.	117.5 sec. (SD = 25.4)
Etch-a-Sketch		
(i) Mean errors	1.86mm	1.38mm (SD = 1.5)
(ii) Mean time	27.3 sec.	20.08 sec. (SD = 4.5)

Theoretical Integration

What the social, cognitive and motor problems of people with Asperger syndrome have in common must be the focus of future research. Of course, these apparently disparate signs may not be directly connected, but that would not be a parsimonious stand and, instead, an attempt should first be made to integrate all of the various manifestations of the syndrome by seeking some common causal mechanism.

There are numerous candidates for explaining part of the Asperger syndrome pattern. Tantam (1992), for example, has suggested that the entire autistic spectrum may arise from degrees of inappropriate eye contact during social interaction which leads to a failure both to learn rules of interpersonal engagement and to note from the direction of another's gaze where useful information can be found. Although this seems to us at best a limited theory (it fails to account for all the cognitive or any of the motor problems of people diagnosed with Asperger syndrome), we remind the reader that Raymond's eye gaze behaviour is unusual: He rarely engages one in direct eye contact and often seems to be focusing at a point behind one. Moreover, when we checked his ability to detect the direction of eye gaze we found his ability severely below normal.

We used a test developed by David Perrett at St Andrews University and modified by Andy Young of the MRC Applied Psychology Unit, Cambridge. It involves presentation of 18 pairs of colour photographs of a man's face, in one of which he is looking directly at the camera and in the other his gaze is aimed 5°, 10°, or 20° away (see Fig. 5.2). Raymond made eight errors on this test (i.e. he was almost at chance level). Interestingly, there was no logical pattern to his errors: He was as likely to make errors on the 20° deviation as the 5° deviation.

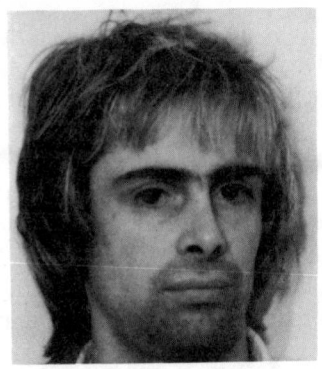 

FIG. 5.2.   An example of the gaze task.

The subject is required to choose in which of the two photographs the model appears to be looking directly at him. The task was devised by Dr Perrett (St Andrews University) and modified by Dr Young (MRC Applied Psychology Unit, Cambridge).

As we have indicated, however, Tantam's theory cannot account for all the signs of Asperger syndrome. Similarly, it is difficult to see how another popular approach to autism in general, the "theory of mind" approach (Leslie & Frith, 1990) can do so either. As we reported, Raymond does show some high-level failures, not so much of understanding what other people know but more in bothering to consider what they may be thinking. However, while it is possible to adapt the theory of mind approach to explain the poor social judgements of people with Asperger syndrome (Ellis et al., 1994), it cannot account for the data on their motor problems.

One theoretical avenue, though, seems to offer some possibility of embracing all the major signs of Asperger syndrome—or at least of accounting for what may turn out to be a significant sub-group of people. This approach has been developed by Byron Rourke and his colleagues at Windsor University, Ontario, Canada. Rourke for some years has been conducting research into what he terms non-verbal learning disorder syndrome (NLD; see Rourke, 1987).

The NLD pattern is complex: It involves tactile and motor deficiencies but is most marked by certain cognitive disorders including poor arithmetic and non-verbal problem solving. The signs also include odd voice prosody, abnormal social judgements, and a reliance upon language for relating to others and relieving anxiety. In short, Raymond fits the NLD syndrome as readily as he does the diagnostic criteria for Asperger syndrome. Rourke (1987) acknowledges the similarity between NLD syndrome and Asperger syndrome and, doubtless, would apply his theory of the former to both. In a review by Semrud-Clikeman and Hynd (1990) the NLD syndrome and attendant problems, including social ones, are well explored.

According to Rourke (1987) the fundamental problem lies in a central neurodevelopmental disorder arising from destruction or dysfunction in white matter and a consequent impact particularly on right hemisphere functioning because it, more than the left, requires intermodal integration across long communication pathways. This is not the place to offer a detailed account and considered analysis of Rourke's ideas. It is sufficient to note that they have not only a superficial plausibility for explaining Asperger syndrome but that Raymond's signs are particularly well accounted for by it.

When we tested Raymond's right hemisphere functioning by rapidly presenting pairs of faces randomly in the left or right visual fields we found it abnormal: His ability to decide whether they were same or different was particularly slow when they occurred on the left. Stimuli falling left of a fixation point are immediately relayed to the right cerebral hemisphere, which contains the centres involved in face processing (Sergent & Signoret, 1992). If Raymond has impaired right hemisphere processing, of course, such a result would be predicted—as, indeed, would his other face-related problems, including poor gaze perception. In the same experiment some pairs of faces were shown bilaterally, thus requiring interhemispheric transfer of information for a decision to be made. Raymond was significantly slower than controls in this condition, which is consistent with Rourke's (1987) suggestion that problems in white matter functioning, presumably including the corpus callosum, may be indicated.

Although Rourke's approach has merit, alternatives exist and will continue to be advanced. These may, for example, include an analysis of some if not all the signs of Asperger syndrome in terms of pre-frontal lobe dysfunctioning as a contributor to, say, problems of social judgement. A different type of approach may be to consider all of the syndrome's manifestations in terms of a functional deficit, such as a general problem in using feedback, of any description, to modify actions and behaviours. The field is relatively new and at this stage we should be open to as wide a range of theoretical explanations as possible.

OVERVIEW

Raymond's behaviour, then, is typical of someone with Asperger syndrome (Frith, 1991). His life illustrates the problems—cognitive, physical, social and emotional—that people with this diagnosis experience. Most of the relatively scant literature on Asperger syndrome concerns children, but it is clear that there is a need more fully to understand and appreciate the difficulties of adults, once they decide, or through circumstances are forced, to live independently.

When we had almost completed our investigations of Raymond we were apprised of a very similar case examined by a clinical psychologist named

Ilse Kracke. She has reported a 19 year old (HD) referred to her because of his difficulties in finding a job (Kracke, 1994). Like Raymond, HD proved to have an unusually poor memory for faces—performing virtually at the level of prosopagnosic patients and even demonstrating uncertainty about his own image in a mirror. HD's father and grandmother also related having difficulties in face recognition, suggesting a familial element to the problem.

Kracke's (1994) description of HD's social difficulties—his isolation, poor social judgement, and lack of concern for others ("an autistic-like indifference", according to one teacher), together with his precocious language development, clumsiness, unusual speech, rigid dress performance that owes little to the prevailing weather, and his emotional instability—are all reminiscent of Raymond. Together their histories make compelling reading and the similarities of their stories, along with those of other adults described by Dewey (1991), suggest that a systematic study of adults with Asperger syndrome is long overdue. Such an analysis may help in the development of appropriate remedial and counselling strategies to enable them to live happier lives and work in a more productive manner.

ACKNOWLEDGEMENTS

We are grateful to Dr Pat McKenna, Rookwood Hospital, Cardiff for referring Raymond to us, and to Dr Andy Young, MRC Applied Psychology Unit, Cambridge for suggesting he may fit the Asperger syndrome diagnosis. Collaboration with Professor Bill Fraser and Dr Shoumitro Deb, University of Wales College of Medicine on other cases of Asperger syndrome has greatly influenced our thinking.

REFERENCES

Asperger, H. (1944) Die "Autistischen Psychopathen" im Kindesalter. *Archiv für Psychiatrie und Nervenkrankheiten, 117,* 76–136.

Baron-Cohen, S. , Leslie, A.M., & Frith, U. (1985). Does the autistic child have a "theory of mind"? *Cognition, 21,* 37–46.

Bodamer, J. (1947). Die Prosop-Agnosie (Die Agnosie des Physiognomieerkennens). *Archiv für Psychiatrie und Zeitschrift für Neurologie und Psychiatrie, 179,* 6–53.

Bruce, V., & Valentine, T. (1986). Identity priming in the recognition of familiar faces. *British Journal of Psychology, 76,* 373–386.

Dewey, M. (1991). Living with Asperger's syndrome. In U. Frith (Ed.), *Autism and Asperger syndrome.* Cambridge, UK: Cambridge University Press.

Ellis, H.D., Ellis, D.M., Fraser, W.I., & Deb, S. (1994). A preliminary study of right hemisphere cognitive deficits and impaired social judgments among young people with Asperger syndrome. *European Child and Adolescent Psychiatry, 3,* 255–266.

Ellis, H.D., & Florence, M. (1990). Bodamer's (1947) paper on prosopagnosia. *Cognitive Neuropsychology, 7,* 81–105.

Frith, U. (Ed.), (1991). *Autism and Asperger syndrome.* Cambridge, UK: Cambridge University Press.

Gillberg, C.L. (1992). Autism and autistic-like conditions: Subclasses among disorders of empathy. *Journal of Child Psychology and Psychiatry, 33*, 813–842.

Happé, F.G.E. (1991). The autobiographical writings of three Asperger syndrome adults: Problems of interpretation and implications for theory. In U. Frith (Ed.), *Autism and Asperger syndrome*. Cambridge, UK: Cambridge University Press.

Kanner, L. (1943). Autistic disturbances of affective contact. *Nervous Child, 2*, 217–250.

Kracke, I. (1994). Developmental prosopagnosia in Asperger's syndrome: Presentation and discussion of an individual case. *Developmental Medicine and Child Neurology, 36*, 873–886.

Leslie, A.M., & Frith, U. (1990). Prospects for a cognitive neuropsychology of autism: Hobson's choice. *Psychological Review, 97*, 122–131.

Lezak, M.D. (1983). *Neuropsychological assessment* (2nd ed.). New York: Oxford University Press.

Light, L.L., Kayra-Stuart, F., & Hollander, S. (1979). Recognition memory for typical and unusual faces. *British Journal of Experimental Psychology, 5*, 212–228.

Rourke, B.P. (1987). Syndrome of nonverbal learning disabilities: The final common pathway of white-matter disease/dysfunction? *Clinical Neuropsychologist, 1*, 209–234.

Semrud-Clikeman, M., & Hynd, G.W. (1990). Right hemispheric dysfunction in non-verbal learning disabilities: Social, academic, and adaptive functioning in adults and children. *Psychological Bulletin, 107*, 196–209.

Sergent, J., & Signoret, J.-L. (1992). Varieties of functional deficits in prosopagnosia. *Cerebral Cortex, 2*, 375–388.

Tantam, D. (1992). Characterizing the fundamental social handicap in autism. *Acta Paedopsychiatrica, 55*, 83–91.

Van Krevelen, D.A. (1971). Early infantile autism and autistic psychopathy. *Journal of Autism and Childhood Schizophrenia, 1*, 82–86.

Wilson, B.A., Cockburn, J., & Baddeley, A. (1985). *The Rivermead behavioural memory test.* Reading, UK: Thames Valley Test Company.

Wing, L. (1991). The relationships between Asperger's syndrome and Kanner's autism. In U. Frith (Ed.), *Autism and Asperger syndrome*. Cambridge, UK: Cambridge University Press.

Section C

WHO AM I?

The concept of a unitary, stable, and enduring self is usually accepted without much question in modern societies (at least by the mythical "person-in-the-street"). None the less, there have been philosophies, psychologies, and religions in which it was argued that the person and the individual mind were not what they seemed. For David Hume, the mind "is nothing but a heap or collection of different perceptions"; B.F. Skinner admits "the uniqueness of the individual", but only as a particular assembly of changeable habits; and, for the Buddha, "this bundle of elements is void of Self". Scholars who, on the contrary, do believe in selves have disagreed about how many such entities can be associated with a single body. From Arthur Wigan to Joseph Bogen, the notion that each cerebral hemisphere might contain its own independent mind has appeared plausible to at least some members of the neuroscience community.

Although the views of such advanced, not to say enlightened, thinkers should certainly give one pause, most of us manage quite nicely with the view that "I" is somewhat more than the first person singular of a linguistic system. The thoughts and actions of this ego should "make sense" to others and, paradoxically, to itself (thereby denying the initial premise that the self is unitary). But what if someone's behaviour seems quite inexplicable in terms of the usual beliefs, purposes, and goals that guide our lives?

The "strangeness" of *dementia praecox* (now known as schizophrenia) is shown purportedly by our inability to empathise (as opposed to sympathise) with what the patient is experiencing, thinking, or feeling; on meeting a schizophrenic patient, people often report a "*praecox* feeling" of an unbridgeable gulf and this feeling has often been regarded as almost a defining characteristic of the condition. And yet there is a well-known countertradition within personality theory that regards schizotypy (or "psychoticism") as a continuum, where the difference between the sane and the mad is quantitative rather than qualitative.

Irrespective of that particular controversy, the chapters by McKay, McKenna, and Laws, and by David, Kemp, Smith, and Fahy, provide pointers towards how we might eventually come to understand patients who show different forms of severe fragmentation of the self: in "classical" schizophrenia where a previously cohesive personality seems to have dissolved into a condition where there is "no private self"; and in multiple personality disorder where there seems to be fractionation of the personality into "many public selves".

However uncanny these conditions are, it must be even more alien to "normal" rationality to believe that one is dead—the Cotard delusion described in the chapter by Young and Leafhead. If we accept Descartes' argument that "I think, therefore I am" ("*cogito ergo sum*"), what must a patient experience in order to infer that he or she is not?

A Cartesian might also argue, "I will, therefore I do". But in this case our philosopher would be puzzled by the "neurological" condition of alien hand, described in Parkin's chapter. If "my" hand engages in apparently purposive action, but not under the control of "my" will, we see yet another form of fragmentation of the self, a form that must surely perplex the patient as much as it does the examiner.

6

Severe Schizophrenia: What Is It Like?

A. Paula McKay, Peter J. McKenna, and Keith Laws
Fulbourn Hospital, Cambridge, and Department of Experimental Psychology, University of Cambridge, Cambridge, UK

When psychologists, or other clinicians who are not closely involved with psychiatry, think about schizophrenia, what thoughts go through their minds? Almost certainly, they will know that the disorder is not in any sense a split or dual personality, but that it was originally so named to denote a fragmentation of mental functioning which was believed to be the common denominator of its many and varied symptoms. They will probably also be aware that schizophrenia is a serious—perhaps the most serious—psychiatric disorder, in which the prospects for recovery are not good. This will likely lead on to a recollection that the cause or causes of schizophrenia are not well understood, and that there has been a longstanding dispute about whether the disorder i essentially the result of some kind of disturbance of brain function, or whether it is better understood psychodynamically, as a pattern of maladaptive behaviour arising from intolerable inner conflicts or disordered family relationships. From their reading of journals, they cannot have failed to notice that currently the biological school of thought is dominant, and that a substantial literature on the structural and/or functional cerebral basis of the disorder is building up. Finally, like most people, they will be aware that medication is the mainstay of treatment for schizophrenia and that in most cases this is less than satisfactory. There may be some hazy awareness of recent claims for advances in drug therapy, although like everything else in schizophrenia research, there is some dispute about this.

The psychiatric literature is full of descriptions of schizophrenia, but these convey little of the everyday clinical realities of the disorder. By means of an account of a particularly severe and intractable case, this chapter will try to give an impression of what schizophrenia is like for the clinicians who have to deal with it, and also, taking advantage of the fact that the patient ultimately became able to recount her experiences quite rationally, to some extent what it is like for the patient. The case description will be followed by a brief resumé of current thinking on the nature of schizophrenia, what underlies its symptoms, and the state of the art in the treatment of the disorder.

LAURA: A PATIENT WITH SEVERE, CHRONIC, AND TREATMENT-RESISTANT SCHIZOPHRENIA

Laura is a 28-year-old woman. She was born and grew up in North America, the elder of two daughters of a cardiologist father and a librarian mother. There is no history of mental illness in Laura's family, except that her maternal grandmother stopped eating and became rambling in speech in the few months before her death (in all probability this reflected senile dementia). However, her father is alleged by her mother to have been an alcoholic who may also have abused drugs and certainly led a dissolute life, being absent from the home for long periods, ostensibly at conferences, before eventually deserting his family altogether.

Laura was a healthy child, with normal developmental milestones. The family moved a number of times with her father's work, and her parents separated when she was 13 years old; after this she and her sister remained with their mother but saw their father regularly. At school, Laura was considered to be of above average ability in some classes, and of average ability or below in others, but without showing particular learning difficulties. Throughout her childhood and early teenage years she made friends easily and was described as "quite extrovert". According to her mother, however, she was affected by the stressful relationship between her parents. Apart from a period of having nightmares at around six years of age, which settled over a few months, she showed no obvious behavioural or psychiatric problems during childhood. In her teens, though, she truanted from school. There is no history of alcohol or drug misuse (the latter is extremely common in urban Americans of her age group).

Laura first became psychiatrically ill at the age of 16. At this time, her family and friends noticed that her behaviour was gradually becoming more and more strange. She would spend hours pacing back and forth, had a distracted air, and sometimes could be caught talking to herself. Later she started tearing up her clothes, and on one occasion she had to be prevented from jumping out of an upper storey window. She was admitted to a psychiatric hospital for several months, and received treatment with drugs and psychotherapy. On discharge from hospital, she was described as being "more or less normal".

After a few months, Laura's condition deteriorated. She started failing to turn up to school and running away when she did attend. This and a return of her other symptoms led to a further admission, following which she also made a good recovery. Over the next 12 years, she spent several long spells in hospital; typically these lasted 12–18 months, and the longest period of time between admissions was nine months. When ill, her mother and sister described Laura's behaviour as varying from extreme overactivity to near stupor. She would be rambling and incoherent in her speech, and at times slept all day and was awake all night. She also indulged in bizarre behaviours such as locking herself in the bathroom and cutting holes in her mother's and sister's clothes. Even at her best, between bouts of illness, she was described as being given to making biting personal comments and having an unpredictable "Jekyll and Hyde" tendency. A lot of the time she was obsessed with cleanliness. She also exhibited minor peculiarities of movement and speech, for example making animal noises or holding her fingers to her mouth and blowing on them. She did not mix much outside her family and was shy in the company of strangers. She would go shopping with her sister or mother, and did simple tasks in the home, but would get rather mixed up if she attempted more complex procedures such as cooking a full meal.

Prior to her most recent admission to hospital Laura was living with her mother and sister in Belgium. During this period her interest in her usual activities waned and she began spending much of her time smoking and sitting in front of the television, seemingly without caring what programme was on. She also made no attempt to learn to speak French. Gradually, her behaviour again became increasingly strange, with the re-emergence of some of the peculiarities she had shown before, such as talking to herself, both in her normal voice and in other affected voices. She would spend hours cleaning in the house, but in an abnormal way, for example cleaning one carpet tile over and over but leaving the rest of the carpet. At times she seemed distressed and tearful but seemed unable to say what was troubling her—when she did try to explain what she said made little sense.

Eventually, Laura was admitted to hospital in Belgium. By this time she was very psychotic. Against a background of being generally withdrawn and uncommunicative, she had virtually daily bouts of behavioural disturbance, ranging from a restless agitation to singing, screaming, sexual disinhibition, and occasionally violence. She often required physical restraint; this may have included a straitjacket (these are still in use in America and many other countries, although not in Britain).

During this time she was subjected to a regime of drug treatment which was aimed both at controlling her disturbed behaviour and also treating her underlying illness. The mainstay of this was neuroleptic drugs (anti-psychotics, major tranquillisers). These have a definite therapeutic effect on the symptoms of schizophrenia, but the effect is often limited and the dose has to be progressively increased according to clinical judgement—there are no laboratory tests to tell when the optimum dosage has been reached. Neuroleptic drugs are also sedative; this is particularly so when they are first given and this aspect of their effect tends to wear off with continued treatment. Other sedative drugs, notably benzodiazepines and barbiturates, are therefore often also needed to control disturbed behaviour. An idea of Laura's lack of progress and the difficulties in management that she presented during this admission can be gained from Table 6.1.

After nine months her family moved to Britain (a move which was at least partly in order to gain further and hopefully more successful treatment). Laura travelled with her mother and sister and was admitted to hospital immediately after she arrived in the country. At this time, she was thin, but general physical and neurological examination was normal. Her behaviour was severely disturbed. She seemed distressed and frightened, and would run about the ward in a chaotic fashion. At other times she would adopt bizarre postures for long periods, for example kneeling with her arms crossed, or repeating a sequence of movements many times. Sometimes these ritual sequences would involve the inappropriate repetition of a normal action—on one occasion she was noted to spend hours wiping the top of a bedside locker. She often made grimacing movements of her face. She was incontinent of urine at times, but would also use the bathroom normally, sometimes on the same day. On a number of occasions she was found trying to drink her own urine and eat her own faeces. Once, she left the hospital, gained entry to a house in the vicinity through the French windows, and smashed up the living-room furnishings.

Rapport with nursing staff, who were with her constantly, and with medical staff, who interviewed her several times a day, was poor. Generally, she made little eye contact—sometimes she assiduously avoided this for hours—but on occasion she would stare intently at the other person. She might shrink back or even run out of the room when approached by staff. At other times she would sit quietly, seeming to understand that the staff were not threatening, and even seem to be listening to the nurse or doctor speaking to her; but then she would suddenly start screaming or hit out.

Her objective emotional state ("affect") was abnormal, varying from marked perplexity to fatuousness and giggling; sometimes she would seem very frightened, but soon afterwards could be overfamiliar or sexually disinhibited. She often showed so-called incongruity of affect, laughing when discussing distressing topics such as suicide.

Speech was difficult to follow much of the time. The connections between sentences or clauses were often tenuous, tangential, or even unintelligible

TABLE 6.1
Laura's Progress on Conventional Treatment in Belgium

Date	Clinical Notes	Treatment
5/5/91	Admitted to hospital. Agitated and disorganised. Showing incoherence of speech mannerisms, stereotypies, paranoid delusions, sexual preoccupations, hallucinations. Started on oral neuroleptics.	Haloperidol 10mg/day
28/5/91	No improvement.	Haloperidol 20mg/day
29/5/91 –3/6/91	Some improvement with less agitation and disorganisation.	Haloperidol 20mg/day
4/6/91	Relapses. Severe agitation which requires physical restraints. Refuses to eat.	Haloperidol 20mg/day
6/6/91	Oral neuroleptics increased.	Haloperidol 30mg/day
7/6/91 –18/6/91	Continues to worsen. Second neuroleptic added.	Haloperidol 30mg/day Chlorpromazine 300mg/day
19/6/91 –20/8/91	Progressive decrease in agitation, disorganisation, and auditory hallucinations. Calm, mute, isolated, socially withdrawn most of the time. Runs away from the unit frequently.	Haloperidol 30mg/day Chlorpromazine 300mg/day
21/8/91	Relapses and presents symptoms similar to those at admission.	Haloperidol 30mg/day Chlorpromazine 300 mg/day
23/9/91	Depot neuroleptic medication added.	Haloperidol 30mg/day Chlorpromazine 300mg/day Haloperidol decanoate 200mg/4 weeks
24/9/91 –10/10/91	Severity of symptoms increases. Aggressive, agitated, and highly disorganised.	Haloperidol 30mg/day Chlorpromazine 300 mg/day Haloperidol decanoate 200mg/4 weeks
11/10/91	Depot neuroleptic medication doubled.	Haloperidol 30mg/day Chlorpromazine 300mg/day Haloperidol decanoate 200mg/2 weeks
28/10/91	Euphoric, playful, disinhibited, aggressive, singing and screaming. Because this suggests a manic phase, carbamazepine added.	Haloperidol 30mg/day Chlorpromazine 300 mg/day Haloperidol decanoate 200mg/2 weeks Carbamazepine 600mg/day
10/12/91	Calmer, not aggressive or agitated. Manic symptoms no longer present. Schizophrenic symptoms still present.	Haloperidol 30mg/day Chlorpromazine 300mg/day Haloperidol decanoate 200mg/2 weeks Carbamazepine 600mg/day
30/12/91	Depot neuroleptic increased.	Haloperidol 30mg/day Chlorpromazine 300mg/day Haloperidol decanoate 250mg/2 weeks Carbamazepine 600mg/day
15/1/92	Again agitated, aggressive, and violent. Oral haloperidol increased.	Haloperidol 45mg/day Chlorpromazine 300mg/day Haloperidol decanoate 200mg/2 weeks Carbamazepine 600mg/day

(formal thought disorder), and she coined new words (neologisms). The content of her speech was also abnormal, with delusions whose themes revolved around sex, religion, and a patient she had known in America whom she believed was trying to rape her. She also believed the ward staff were plotting to harm her and this accounted for some of her attacks on them (persecutory delusions). She would point to a book or magazine article, saying that it was written about her (delusions of reference). She also experienced hallucinations virtually continuously: She heard voices talking to her and commenting on her thoughts or actions. When she heard birdsong, she experienced a voice superimposed on the sounds giving her messages. She could often be heard replying to her voices or shouting at them. Sometimes, she obeyed commands given to her by the voices, for example telling her to pass urine where she was standing. She also saw flames and smelt smoke in the room; on numerous occasions she reported complex visual experiences such as seeing her own face on the body of another person, or parts of her own body from a distance or in a distorted way.

Laura also experienced a number of so-called first rank symptoms of schizophrenia, i.e. symptoms that are more or less diagnostic of the disorder. One of these was thought insertion—she felt that thoughts which were not her own, which she attributed to "the vibrations in the air", were being projected into her mind. Less often, she felt her own thoughts being taken out of her head (thought withdrawal). She worried that other people could hear her thoughts (thought broadcasting). Another first rank symptom was passivity experiences: She believed that her actions were controlled by an external force which, for example, forced her to pace up and down for long periods despite not wishing to do so.

Many aspects of Laura's presentation at this time are illustrated in a transcribed videotaped interview which was made on a day in May, 1992 when she was relatively calm and co-operative.

I   I would like to thank you for agreeing to do this today after all the false alarms we've had so far, it is very good of you to agree to do it.

L   [Smiles] Shit happens...

I   I'll start off by...

L   ...and then you die.

I   Shall we go on with the questions Laura?

L   So quit bringing me to the gynaecologist and looking through my hymen and see if you can try and tear it out and make me a slut.

I   Laura, are you able to think clearly or do you find there is any interference with your thoughts?

L   Sometimes.

I   Sometimes you find there is interference with your thoughts?

L   Sometimes I can think clearly. But very, very, very, very, very, very rarely.

I   OK. Do you find it difficult to think clearly most of the time?

L   [Takes time appearing to consider this] All of my viciousness is taken away off all of my boyfriends. I have to watch it on TV. *Home and Away* [a popular soap opera]—that show's the worst show ever on TV. They're always fussing and fighting and everybody's wearing sluts' clothes. I don't watch the show but I get the gist of it. It worries me because I think they are talking to me sometimes but I am not actually in there with them.

I   You think some of the people on the show are talking to you? What sort of things do you think they are saying to you?

L   They are harming my life.

I   They are harming your life. In what sort of way?

L   They are taking my boyfriends from me.

I   The characters on the TV programme are taking your boyfriends. Is that what you're saying?

L   What?

I   How are the people on the television taking your boyfriends away from you?

L   They flirt. Even the commercials flirt. Nothing but flirtation on TV these days, nothing but sex on TV these days. It is worse than it was when I was younger, much worse. All I'm watching them do now is brush their hair. They do that in the shampoo commercials [laughs].

I   Do you find that the television interferes with your thoughts in some way?

L   No.

I   No. OK. Are thoughts put into your head which you know are not your own sometimes?

L   Let's get back to...

I   Are you trying to concentrate on the television question?

L   Yes. Could you ask me the question again?

I   Are thoughts put into your head which you know are not your own?

L   Yes.

I   How do you know they are not your own?

L   They tell me how to put on clothes. They check my bath water for me, with this hand [gestures].

I   Who checks your bath water?

L   Whatever her name happens to be, whatever I choose her name to be, she does it for me.

Shortly after admission to hospital Laura was transferred to a ward specialising in the treatment of schizophrenia. At this point she was on a coc ail of drugs including neuroleptics (haloperidol and chlorpromazine), sedatives (benzodiazepines and barbiturates), and carbamazepine (an anti-epileptic drug which has also been found to be useful in manic-depressive psychosis and which is also commonly used in schizophrenia although there is no evidence to suggest that it is effective). The first decision made was to simplify her antipsychotic medication and gradually increase the dose of one drug. Accordingly, the chlorpromazine was stopped, the carbamazepine was tapered off, and the dose of oral and depot haloperidol was increased. Her condition continued much the same, although she now showed periods lasting up to 48 hours of relative lucidity and calmness, to the extent she was able to go out on a day trip with the ward. However, she continued to be sporadically disturbed and violent and most of the time she required continuous one-to-one nursing. Somewhat later lithium was added: This is a drug for the control of manic-depressive psychosis, but (unlike carbama-zepine) there is considerable evidence that it may also exert a modest therapeutic effect in schizophrenia.

As she became more communicative, it became possible to gain some limited idea of Laura's own subjective view of her condition, in particular her insight—for example, whether she believed she was suffering from an illness and how she reconciled her beliefs about being the victim of wrongdoing, being in danger of rape, etc. with being in hospital receiving treatment. A series of questions about these matters was put to her at a time when she was more coherent than in the first interview, but by no means well. At the time of this interview (July, 1992), Laura had been on clozapine for some weeks. Her responses are shown here.

I   Do you think you are ill, suffering from an illness?
L   Hanging around Christine [a fellow patient who frequently comments on the fact she has a diagnosis of schizophrenia], I think I have got some kind of a name tag on me—schizophrenia or something.
I   What is schizophrenia then?
L   I don't know.
I   Do you think that you suffer from it?
L   I think I just suffer from things that bother me—like trying to figure out who my mother is. I just think I am in here because doctors need money. That's what I think sometimes, anyway. I can't find the reasons why I am sitting in here. I think this place is unfair.

I   These experiences you have like voices, like there is a conspiracy to harm you, what do you think they are?

L   I think it is hypnotism. I also think the cigarettes have medication in them too.

I   Where do the voices come from?

L   Other people—other people around here are talking. I don't know how to explain it. Some people don't make a lot of sense when they are sick.

I   If I put it to you that you are ill and that the voices are a symptom of illness, that is schizophrenia, would you agree or disagree?

L   I would say that you must be wrong, partially wrong maybe.

I   Could they be symptoms?

L   Well hallucinating does not come from nothing. So maybe the voices don't as well. When people go around seeing frogs on the floor that aren't there, that is an illness.

I   Are your voices and hallucinations an illness?

L   Myself, I don't think so.

I   Why not?

L   I am not smart enough to figure that out. If you want to find an illness I guess you can find one. The voices I have sometimes are voices of people I used to know.

I   If you are not ill, why are you in hospital?

L   I don't know.

I   Is it the right place for you to be?

L   No.

I   Where should you be?

L   I should be living on welfare in New Orleans. I would like to live in California with my uncle.

I   Does everyone have experiences like voices and thinking people are out to harm them?

L   Yeah [nods thoughtfully].

I   Are you just like everyone else?

L   Yes.

I   No different?

L   Maybe. There are not many black Americans in this hospital.

After several weeks in hospital in England, it was clear that Laura had made only minor progress and there seemed to be little prospect of further improvement. At this stage treatment with ECT (electro-convulsive therapy, shock treatment) was reluctantly considered. This is acknowledged by psychiatrists to be a crude and even barbaric treatment, and one whose mode of action is unknown; nevertheless, a considerable body of research has confirmed both that is extremely effective in some severe depressive states and that it has no long-term ill effects. Although ECT is not routinely used in schizophrenia, there is evidence from controlled trials that it can sometimes be of value when orthodox treatment fails; clinical impression also suggests that it is most likely to be effective when catatonic features (i.e. peculiar and repetitive motor phenomena usually associated with stupor or excitement) are a prominent component of the presentation, as they were in Laura's case.

Until a few years ago, ECT would have been the only treatment option for patients like Laura. However, in 1990 a new neuroleptic drug, clozapine, was introduced in Britain and many other countries. This drug has been shown to be effective in a third or more of patients in whom conventional treatment has failed. Unfortunately, clozapine triggers a serious white blood cell abnormality in around 5% of cases; the only way it can be used with safety is to monitor the blood with weekly tests and to stop the drug (permanently) if signs of abnormality start to appear.

Laura was started on clozapine towards the end of May, 1992. In August, most of her other medication was stopped. A summary of her progress on this drug is given in Table 6.2.

TABLE 6.2
Laura's Progress on Clozapine

Date	Clinical Notes	Treatment
22/5/92	Relatively settled. No serious outbursts. Easily distracted. Clozapine started.	Clozapine 50mg/day Lithium 800mg/day Sodium amytal (for sedation)
27/5/92	Thought-disordered, but generally more settled. Says her auditory hallucinations have decreased.	Clozapine 100mg/day Lithium 800mg/day Sodium amytal (regularly)
1/6/92	Generally more appropriate, no posturing. Remains somewhat paranoid. Auditory hallucinations less pronounced. At times extreme thought disorder containing neologisms.	Clozapine 150mg/day Lithium 800mg/day Sodium amytal (regularly)
3/6/92	Attempted to bite a member of staff. Required sedation.	Clozapine 200mg/day Lithium 800mg/day Sodium amytal (regularly)
8/6/92	More settled, but still unpredictable	Clozapine 250mg/day Lithium 800mg/day Sodium amytal (regularly)
12/6/92	Mental state deteriorated over last 24 hours. More bizarre content of speech. Posturing more. Tried to set off the fire alarm twice.	Clozapine 250mg/day Lithium 800mg/day Sodium amytal (regularly)
21/6/92	Generally much better. Behaviour settled. Only voicing abnormal ideas occasionally. Still shows numerous instances of catatonic perseveration.	Clozapine 300mg/day Lithium 800mg/day Sodium amytal (regularly)

(Continued)

TABLE 6.2

(Continued)

Date	Clinical Notes	Treatment
29/6/92	Rather sullen, co-operative, dressed. Speech not spontaneous, but replies sometimes inappropriate: "Who's Henry the Fifth?" No auditory hallucinations.	Clozapine 300mg/day Lithium 800mg/day Sodium amytal (regularly)
2/7/92	Mental state more unsettled last 24 hours. Had auditory hallucinations yesterday telling her to set off the fire alarm.	Clozapine 300mg/day Lithium 800mg/day Sodium amytal (regularly)
6/7/92	Became more bizarre. More auditorily hallucinated. Up since 4AM today, disorganised, restless— walked off ward this AM. Confused, perplexed, "Why is everyone in the world ill?"	Clozapine 350mg/day Lithium 800mg/day Sodium amytal (regularly)
10/7/92	Beserk behaviour this evening. Writing on walls, posturing, kneeling on floor, praying, trying to bite staff.	Clozapine 350mg/day Lithium 800mg/day Sodium amytal (regularly)
16/7/92	No untoward incidents for the last five days. Remains quite psychotic, but no physical attacks.	Clozapine 400mg/day Lithium 800mg/day Sodium amytal (as required)
20/7/92	Voicing more lucid thoughts about her future. Smiling at times—appropriately. Says she is feeling a little better. Still preoccupied by auditory hallucinations.	Clozapine 450mg/day Lithium 800mg/day Sodium amytal (as required)
24/7/92	More settled. Able to hold short conversations. Concentration impaired—seemingly interrupted by auditory hallucinations.	Clozapine 500mg/day Lithium 800mg/day Sodium amytal (as required)
31/7/92	Settled behaviour has continued. Rather sleepy. Nods her head when asked if she is feeling better.	Clozapine 500mg/day Lithium 800mg/day Sodium amytal (as required)
12/8/92	Well-kempt, smiling. Negotiating sensibly with staff. Wrote a letter to her father. Some evidence of thought disorder and perseveration.	Clozapine 500mg/day Sodium amytal (as required)
17/8/92	Remains well. Ready to go on leave.	Clozapine 500mg/day
7/9/92	Reports of worsening after leave at home. Has been posturing again.	Clozapine 500mg/day
19/9/92	Says leave went well. Went to see a play with mother and sister. Looks well, smiles and speaks appropriately with concern for her future. No evidence of psychosis. However, asked to be referred to a gynaecologist to see if her hymen is ruptured.	Clozapine 550mg/day
12/10/92	Enjoyed weekend leave. No evidence of psychosis. Worries about her future—resettlement and career.	Clozapine 550mg/day
19/10/92	Not yet fully recovered. Quiet and brooding at times.	Clozapine 600mg/day
26/10/92	Remains well. No further questions about her hymen.	Clozapine 600mg/day
2/11/92	Remains well.	Clozapine 600mg/day
9/11/92	Well.	Clozapine 600mg/day

Essentially, over a period of five months and in a rather erratic fashion with several setbacks, Laura made a complete recovery. For some further period of time she continued to experience fleeting abnormal exeriences such as seeing flames, or seeing her body with someone else's face superimposed on it, but eventually these ceased altogether. Also, after periods of home leave which were emotionally stressful, she would often seem more withdrawn, and there would be a minor return of such behaviour as blowing on her fingertips. At one point she had a spell of depression lasting a few weeks; this resolved spontaneously. An idea of her general status and insight into her illness at this point can be gained from another vidoetaped interview that was made around this time (March, 1993).

I   Can you remember anything about those first few weeks in hospital, what you were like?

L   I was frightened of everything, except it never happened.

I   What sort of things?

L   Well. Um, I was afraid that my sister would take my boyfriend if I had one.

I   What made you think of that?

L   I don't know. It was probably to do with when I was sick.

I   What do you think about that idea now? Is that something your sister would do?

L   No.

I   What other ideas did you have that were unusual?

L   I thought I was going to be raped and I couldn't get out of it.

I   By anyone in particular?

L   No. Actually, there was this man who lives in New Orleans and he seemed awfully sick at the time, and I didn't know if I could get along with him. We were in the car and this man came around, and I have always been afraid of seeing him. And I guess the feelings just built up and then the next thing I knew I was thinking he was going to come and get me.

I   Was this when you were in England?

L   No, when I was in Belgium.

I   When the man was probably still in America. Does that seem realistic now? Is it possible that man could have known where you were?

L   No.

I   It was just an idea that you suddenly had about having seen that man?

L   I also used to think that I was Mary, mother of Jesus. I used to think I was in Princeton.

I   Do you know what made you think that?

L   I don't know. I think I was getting sick at this point. What I mean is ... because ... I don't know ... I think I got a card or something and, um, I didn't know whether it was my card or a card someone left in my room. There was a picture of Mary holding the baby and I used to always look at that picture. Then I noticed that there was something on her face that looked sad or something, I don't know. So I was thinking that she was giving up her job as Mary, as it was too much work or something, and she was giving it to me, or something like that.

I   So when you saw the card you thought you were Mary? You said something about being at Princeton College?

L   I don't know. I can't remember any details on that one [laughs].

I   That's all right. All these ideas, the ones you are laughing about, do they now seem a bit silly? Is there anything which you still worry a little bit about, you wonder about that worries you?

L   Maybe that man.

I   How realistic do you think that is?

L   Very unrealistic and I don't know why I do.

I   He's still in America. Would he know where you were?

L   No. I doubt it, no.

I   But you have a bit of a doubt about him.

L   I don't know why. Maybe. That is what you call paranoia, isn't it?

I   I was wondering, when you first came in to hospital, as well as these peculiar ideas, whether you sometimes heard voices at times. Do you remember anything about those?

L   I used to think that God was talking to me sometimes.

I   How did you know it was God?

L   I don't know.

I   OK. What sort of things did it say?

L   Well, when I believed I was Mary, I thought that God was ... that people would ask me questions and ask me to pray for them or whatever. And I would ask God, and God would tell me, and I would tell the people.

I   Are you a religious person?

L   No.

I   Did you hear any other voices or was it just the voice of God?

L   I used to hear voices from the TV set as if the TV set was talking to me. The people on the TV set were talking to me.

I   What sort of things were they saying?

L   Well, at one point I thought I was dead and I was in Heaven. And I was with my husband and we were watching TV, and what was on

the TV was the past life that we had. And it was kinda like we had
been having in Heaven the kinda life we were going to have. And I
can remember the TV show I thought I was on—I think it was *Home
and Away.*

I   So you were watching TV, but at the time you thought you were in
Heaven with your husband and the TV programme was telling you
about Heaven. Did that seem strange at the time?

L   No.

I   What does it sound like now?

L   I'd like to know where I get these ideas from.

I   Have you had any of these ideas or heard voices in the last few
months? Any worrying times when you feel uncertain about
things?

L   No.

While she was in hospital, psychological testing was carried out on Laura
as part of a number of research projects she agreed to take part in.
During the time she was ill she was of course unable to co-operate with
any sort of demanding examination. It should also be pointed out that,
since there is essentially no understanding of the psychological abnormalities that underlie any schizophrenic symptoms (see later), there were no
tests she could be given to illuminate particular aspects of her mental
state. After recovery, however, a battery of more or less standard
neuropsychological tests was administered. The findings are summarised
in Table 6.3. Her level of IQ functioning before she became ill was
estimated using the National Adult Reading Test (a test of reading
ability which is relatively resistant to intellectual decline); this yielded
an IQ of 108. Her current IQ measured using the Wechsler Adult
Intelligence Scale (WAIS) was 94 (verbal 96, performance 91). Thus, there
is an apparent decline of 14 points—not great, but approaching the
threshold level of 15 points usually taken as indicative of significant
intellectual decline.

On a variety of perceptual tests including identification of objects, faces,
and facial expression, Laura's performance was within normal limits. On a
test of her ability to recognise objects photographed from unusual views,
she correctly identified 18 out of 20; this was poor (most normal
individuals score 19 or 20), but the degree of impairment was obviously
minimal. Language function was assessed using a selection of tests of
semantic and syntactic function. Her performance was intact on almost all
of these, but her score on one semantic test, naming objects from pictures,
was at the lower limit of the normal range, and unexpectedly low for
someone of her IQ.

TABLE 6.3
Laura's Performance on a Battery of Neuropsychological Tests

Test	Score	Normal Range	Comment
General intellectual function			
Estimated premorbid IQ (NART)[1]	108		
Current IQ			
Verbal IQ	96		
Performance IQ	91		
Full scale IQ	94		
Perception			
Unusual views[2]	18/20	19.8 ± 0.57	Minimally poor performance
Benton face matching[3]	47/54	41–54	Normal
Ordering faces by age	23/24	22.8 ± 1.23	Normal
Matching faces across age	19/20	18.1 ± 1.44	Normal
Forced choice judging anger	13/14	13.2 ± 0.92	Normal
Language			
Graded Naming Test[4]	13/30	22.5 ± 4.3	At lower limit of normal range. Lower than expected for IQ
Modified Token Test[5]	34/36	27–36	Normal
Pyramids and Palm Trees Test[6]	50/54	51 ± 1	Normal
Short-term memory			
Forward Digit span	7	7 ± 2	Normal
Backward digit span	6	5 ± 2	Normal
Corsi block span	4	1 or 2 less than digit span	Low, but within normal range
Long-term memory			
RBMT screening score[7]	5	7–12	In moderately impaired range
Wechsler logical memory	10/50	26 ± 8	Impaired
Wechsler paired associates	10.5/24	20.6 ± 3.0	Impaired
easy	7.5/12		
hard	3/12		
Wechsler visual reproduction	32/41	32.5 ± 5.3	Normal
RMT word recognition[8]	48/50	47.6 ± 2.7	Normal (chance level 25)
RMT face recognition[8]	36/50	44.1 ± 3.2	Impaired (chance level 25)
Executive function			
Modified Wisconsin Card Sort[9] (categories achieved)	6/6	4–6	Normal
Verbal fluency (animals/1 minute)	16	14–36	Low normal
Cognitive Estimates Test[10]	12	0–13 (error score)	Just within normal range; gave some very extreme responses

[1] Nelson (1982); [2] Warrington and Taylor (1973); [3] Benton, Hamsher, Varney, and Spreen (1978); [4] McKenna and Warrington (1983); [5] De Renzi and Faglioni (1978); [6] Howard and Patterson (1992); [7] Wilson, Cockburn, and Baddeley (1985); [8] Warrington (1984); [9] Nelson (1976); [10] Shallice and Evans (1978).

However, there was evidence of memory impairment. On a clinically oriented test designed to pick up "everyday" memory difficulties (the Rivermead Behavioural Memory Test) Laura achieved a screening score of 5 out of a maximum of 12—in the moderately impaired range. Further testing revealed a distinctive pattern of impairment: Her scores on a variety of short-term memory tasks were all within normal limits. Thus, her forward digit span was 7 (average or above average). Her backward digit span, a task thought to place more demands on the central executive component of working memory, was superior at 6. Her score on Corsi blocks (a non-verbal equivalent of digit span) was, at 4, within the normal range of performance, if slightly on the low side (generally scores are one or two below that of forward digit span).

On the other hand, Laura's long-term memory showed clear evidence of deficits. Her performance on the Logical Memory subtest of the Wechsler Memory Scale, which assesses recall of stories, was 10, more than two standard deviations below the normal range for 35–44 year olds. Similarly, on the Paired Associates subtest, where subjects have to learn to associate a series of words with cue words, her performance was very poor—she showed difficulty with the "hard" pairs (for example, *cloud—nail*), but also more surprisingly on the "easy" pairs where there is an obvious relationship between the words (for example, *ear—ring*) On a widely used test of recognition memory, Warrington's Recognition Memory Test, she showed normal word recognition but very poor performance on the face recognition component of the test. However, on a test of test of recall of visual material she was normal, scoring 32 out of a maximum of 41.

Laura's performance on "executive" tests—a variety of quite different tasks all of which probe high-level decision-making functions and which tend to be affected in patients with frontal lobe lesions—revealed a mixed picture. On the Wisconsin Card Sorting Test, where subjects have to classify cards with different designs according to rules which are changed from time to time, she was able to modify her strategy without any difficulty and achieved the maximum score. Her performance on verbal fluency, the ability to name as many different items as possible in a category such as animals over a minute, was, at 16, in the normal range, although at the lower end of this given that some people are able to produce 30 or more. Another frontal/executive test is the Cognitive Estimates Test; in this the subject has to make an educated guess in response to questions to which he or she is unlikely to know the exact answer (the more extreme the answer, the higher the score). Laura's score on this test was 12, just below the fifth percentile cutoff of 13. Even so, she gave some exceptionally extreme answers, estimating the length of an average man's spine as 15 feet and the population of Britain as 100,000 (and that of the USA as 5 million).

Laura remained a hospital in-patient for several months more, while paperwork to do with immigration and social security was sorted out. In November, 1993, after two and a half years of continuous hospitalisation, she was able to move into a "halfway house" hostel in the community. Since then, she has remained free of all symptoms and has appeared normal in every way, beyond perhaps a very slight tendency to taciturnity. She also complains of memory difficulties, and staff at the hostel where she lives have noticed that her concentration is sometimes not all that it should be. Recently, she has begun work in the hospital shop and has built up a circle of friends, including a boyfriend.

DISCUSSION

Schizophrenia as a Clinical Concept

The disease category of schizophrenia was originated by Emil Kraepelin at the end of the last century and developed by a contemporary, Eugen Bleuler (see Cutting & Shepherd, 1987). They argued that several seemingly quite different forms of insanity—catatonia, hebephrenia, and certain paranoid states—should all be considered to be the manifestations of a single disorder. This was on the grounds that, first, no sharp lines of demarcation appeared to exist between any of the presentations—in other words intermediate forms were regularly encountered—and, second, that common to all of them was a tendency to pursue a downhill course ending in permanent, often severe, disability.

Despite numerous challenges, alternative proposals, and attempts at overthrow, schizophrenia has survived as a clinical concept to the present day. Perhaps the strongest evidence in favour of its existence comes from a number of reliability and validity studies that were carried out in the 1960s and 1970s. The best known of these was a worldwide survey of 1200 patients, the International Pilot Study of Schizophrenia (World Health Organisation, 1973, 1979), which demonstrated (1) that the disorder can be found across many different cultures; (2) that clinicians are (or at least can be trained to be) consistent with each other in the way they make the diagnosis; (3) that the process of diagnosis follows sensible rules which, when simulated by a computer program, reliably agree with clinical diagnosis; and (4) that, on a variety of measures of outcome, schizophrenia behaves quite differently from other psychiatric disorders. For these reasons schizophrenia is now accepted as a valid clincal entity by most psychiatrists, although some psychologists continue to challenge this view (see Bentall, 1990, and McKenna, 1994, for opposing views on this debate).

The boundaries of schizophrenia are somewhat less well defined than its existence. There has been a longstanding controversy as to whether its "cross-sectional" presentation can be separated absolutely from the other main form of psychotic illness, manic-depressive psychosis; this remains, to date, unresolved (see Kerr & McClelland, 1991). Clinicians are also unhappy about attaching the label of schizophrenia to patients who develop florid symptoms and then go on to make a full recovery without any residual signs of illness. Conversely, when, as occasionally happens, patients present solely with a schizophrenia-like social withdrawal and occupational decline but without any accompanying delusions or hallucinations, it is notoriously difficult to be sure that the diagnosis really is schizophrenia.

Accepting that schizophrenia exists, many suspect that the disorder will ultimately be found to consist of several related forms of illness, or that it will turn out to have a number of different underlying causes. So far, however, no one has managed to come up with a successful way of subdividing the disorder, although there have been some notable attempts (e.g. Crow, 1980; Langfeldt, 1960; Murray, Lewis, & Reveley, 1985). The only subdivision within schizophrenia that has been supported by evidence is the so-called positive:negative dichotomy: Every study that has examined the statistical interassociations among schizophrenic symptoms has found that they cluster into two different groups; on the one hand, positive or florid symptoms like delusions, hallucinations, and incoherence of speech (formal thought disorder); and on the other, negative or deficit symptoms such as lack of motivation, poverty of speech, and emotional unresponsiveness (Andreasen, 1985). Positive symptoms tend to wax and wane and may remit completely; negative symptoms evolve inexorably over time and account for much of the chronic disability associated with schizophrenia.

Laura fits the stereotype of schizophrenia in many ways, although some aspects of her case illustrate the problems in classification that have been encountered. She developed a florid psychotic illness in early adult life. This has pursued a relapsing and remitting, and overall worsening, course. When ill she has shown many positive symptoms including persecutory delusions, auditory hallucinations, and formal thought disorder. One complicating factor in Laura's case is that catatonic symptoms have been a prominent feature of her illness. Catatonic schizophrenia has, for unknown reasons, become rare in Western countries; nevertheless, while unusual, such symptoms are by no means unheard of in schizophrenia. Another complicating factor has been the presence at times of "manic" symptoms—overactivity, elated mood, and disinhibited behaviour—which prompted at one point the use of carbamazepine in her treatment. This would lead some psychiatrists to consider a diagnosis of "schizoaffective" psychosis, rather than straightforward schizophrenia, in her case. Others, though, would argue that she has never fulfilled the diagnostic requirements for this disorder, of demonstrating the full syndrome of mania or depression simultaneously with schizophrenic symptoms.

Most problematic of all for the diagnosis of schizophrenia in Laura has been the fact that, despite severe and protacted illness, she has always shown good recovery between episodes. She does not, therefore, conform to the typical picture of chronic schizophrenia with a presentation characterised mainly by negative symptoms. However, it is well recognised that the degree of deterioration in schizophrenia can range from the very severe, requiring institutional care, to the subtle and difficult to detect. In fact, there are clear hints in Laura's case of an enduring decline in functioning (at least until she was treated with clozapine), as evidenced by her failure to observe social niceties, her difficulties with cooking, her shyness in company in contrast to her earlier extroverted nature, and perhaps even the fact that she made no attempt to learn to speak the local language when she lived in Belgium.

The Cause of Schizophrenia

Kraepelin (1913/1919) originally believed that schizophrenia was an organic disease of the brain. He set up the first family heredity investigations into the disorder and he also inspired a number of neuropathologists to take an interest in examining the post-mortem brains of his patients. (One of these was Alzheimer, who discovered his eponymous disease while working in Kraepelin's department.)

Bleuler (1911/1950) was at best lukewarm about biological factors in the causation of schizophrenia, and invoked ideas from the newly established discipline of psychoanalysis to try and explain symptoms such as delusions and hallucinations. Over the next 50 years, elaborate psychodynamic theories flourished. One school of thought, following orthodox Freudian principles, emphasised the role of early development, unconscious conflicts, and regression to an earlier stage of personality organisation in the face of stress. Another focused on the role of the family, viewing schizophrenia as a way of thinking, behaving and interpreting experience which was rooted in an abnormal parent–child relationship. Eventually, though, an increasing body of empirical findings demonstrated beyond reasonable doubt, (1) that stress plays at most a minor role in the genesis of schizophrenia (Day, 1981); and (2) that the parents of schizophrenic patients do not show any great abnormalities in their behaviour towards their children or in their style of communication with them (Hirsch & Leff, 1975). Neither approach is entirely devoid of experimental support, however. Relatives of patients with schizophrenia show an increased range of various kinds of psychiatric disability, which is currently thought to reflect the operation of hereditary factors (e.g. Prescott & Gottesman, 1993). Research into the role of intrafamilial stress is also alive and well in studies of expressed emotion in the relatives of patients with schizophrenia—there is good evidence that high levels of this play a significant role in precipitating relapse in established illness (e.g. Leff & Vaughn, 1985).

The biological hypothesis of schizophrenia derives from two simple observations. The first is the tendency of the disorder to cluster in families, a tendency which, after prolonged and painstaking investigation, was finally shown to reflect a genetic mechanism (see Gottesman, 1991). The second was the introduction of chlorpromazine in 1952, by a French surgeon who discovered, quite by chance, that an antihistamine drug, chlorpromazine, had unusual tranquillising properties. After it was tried on a small series of psychotic patients, chlorpromazine went on to revolutionise the treatment of schizophrenia, among other things enabling thousands of previously permanently institutionalised patients to leave hospital. The fact that a chemical compound proved to be of more value than any other form of treatment in schizophrenia provided powerful support for the idea that its ultimate cause is biological rather than psychological.

Research into the biological basis of schizophrenia has been dominated for the last 30 years by the dopamine hypothesis, that schizophrenia is due to a functional excess of dopamine in some parts of the brain. This theory sprang directly from the uncovering of the mode of action of neuroleptic drugs—blockade of dopamine receptors—coupled with the complementary finding that dopamine-stimulating drugs like amphetamine have the ability to induce states resembling schizophrenia. However, a search for direct evidence of increased dopamine in schizophrenic post-mortem brains had little success, and it became clear that a decisive test of the dopamine hypothesis would require measurement of dopamine receptors during life, in patients who had never been exposed to neuroleptic treatment. Recently, this has been achieved by combining functional brain imaging with injection of radioactively labelled neuroleptic drugs. At present, the results of the two best studies of this type (Farde, Wiesel, Stone-Elander, Halldin, Nordstrom, & Hall, 1987; Wong, Wagner, Tune, Dannals, Pearlson, & Links, 1986) are contradictory. It is now assumed by most in the field that some other neurotransmitter abnormality is more central to schizophrenia, possibly one that interacts with dopamine.

A rather later development has been the application of brain-imaging techniques to schizophrenia. The first CT scan study of the disorder (Johnstone, Crow, Frith, Husband, & Kreel, 1976) suggested that the lateral ventricles of the cerebral hemispheres were enlarged—a sign of a subcortical brain damage, which could be the result of a degenerative process or of trauma early in life. Approximately 50 further studies (see Lewis, 1990; Van Horn & McManus, 1992) have in the main confirmed this, although it is now accepted that the enlargement is subtle and not usually detectable by visual inspection of scans. Latterly, the considerably more sensitive structural imaging technique of magnetic resonance imaging, which allows visualisation of grey and white matter and measurement of discrete cortical and subcortical structures, has been applied to schizophrenia. The findings are conflicting, but the most consistent of them point to possible reductions in the size of the temporal lobes, particularly the subcortical temporal structures of the hippocampus and amygdala (see Chua & McKenna, 1995).

Functional imaging of the brain is also possible, yielding a "snapshot" of the metabolic activity of different cortical regions. Initially, a number of studies suggested that there was "hypofrontality" in schizophrenia, in other words a relative lowering of the activity of the prefrontal cortex compared to that of normal individuals at rest. This finding has subsequently turned out to be far from robust and there have in fact been many more negative than positive findings (see Chua & McKenna, 1995 for a review). It may be that hypofrontality is selectively associated with the presence of negative symptoms (e.g. Wolkin, Sanfilipo, Wolf, Angrist, Brodie, & Rotrosen, 1992) or that hypofrontality may only become apparent when the schizophrenic prefrontal cortex is challenged by performance of an executive task (Weinberger, Berman, & Zec, 1986). Alternatively, schizophrenia may be characterised by an altogether more complicated pattern of functional imaging abnormality (Frith, Friston, Herold, Liddle, & Frackowiak, 1995; Liddle, Friston, Frith, Hirsch, Jones, & Frackowiak, 1992).

It is evident that, while examination of brain structure and function in schizophrenia is of considerable theoretical interest, any abnormalities are subtle to the point of testing the limits of current techniques. A corollary of this conclusion is that brain imaging is of little practical usefulness in the disorder. This is why Laura, like the vast majority of patients diagnosed as suffering from schizophrenia, has never undergone CT scanning or functional imaging, although both techniques are freely available and relatively inexpensive.

The Psychology of Schizophrenia

The overriding goal of psychological research in schizophrenia has always been to identify the psychological disturbance or disturbances which give rise to its trademark symptoms, particularly positive symptoms. Historically, the most important theory of this type has been a general one: the proposal of a defect in selective attention developed by McGhie (1969), Frith (1979), and others. Of the huge amount of perceptual information which continually impinges on the senses, only a very small amount normally enters conscious awareness at any given moment. If the mechanism underlying this "filtering" process were to break down, the resulting overload of information would certainly give rise to sensory and cognitive abnormalities, and it is easy to imagine that these might take the form of delusions, hallucinations, and formal thought disorder.

Unfortunately for the selective attention theory, its most obvious prediction, that schizophrenic patients will be more vulnerable than normal to the effects of distraction on cognitive performance, has never received any convincing experimental support. In particular, a series of distraction studies employing the dichotic listening task—in which a message such as a series of numbers is delivered through headphones to one ear, while a different message is delivered to the other ear—singularly failed to provide any strong evidence of impairment in acutely ill patients, i.e. those with prominent positive symptoms (see Cutting, 1985; McKenna, 1994). Accordingly, the selective attentional theory of schizophrenia has been abandoned by Frith and by most other psychologists, although some continue to cling on to it (e.g. Spring, Weinstein, Freeman, & Thompson, 1991) while others have resurrected it with modifications (e.g. Gray et al., 1992; Andreasen, Arndt, Swayze, Cizadlo, Flaum, & O'Leary, 1994).

In the wake of the failure of the selective attentional account of schizophrenia, a number of theories have been developed which focus on specific symptoms, including delusions (see Garety & Hemsley, 1994; Oltmanns & Maher, 1988), hallucinations (see Slade & Bentall, 1988), and formal thought disorder (see Chapman & Chapman, 1973; Rochester & Martin, 1979). Although it is fair to say that some of these theories have attracted some experimental support, it is sadly also true that they all face theoretical difficulties, or have not been adequately tested, or are plagued by non-replication of findings. At the present time there is no widely accepted psychological explanation of any schizophrenic symptom.

Proceeding alongside, and for much of the time entirely separately from, the cognitive psychological approach, there has been another line of experimental psychological investigation in schizophrenia. This has been the neuropsychological approach, characterised by attempts to establish whether and to what extent patients with the disorder show deficits in cognitive function similar to those seen in different forms of brain damage. For decades, it has been known that schizophrenic patients as a group perform more poorly than normal individuals on virtually any task that is set them (Chapman & Chapman, 1973). A substantial body of literature (reviewed by Payne, 1973) also documented beyond any reasonable doubt that IQ in schizophrenia is significantly lower than the population average of 100, and that this is at least partly due to a decline from a previously normal level of functioning rather than lifelong poor performance. Additionally, in a review of studies applying various neuropsychological tests to different groups of psychiatric patients, Heaton, Baade, and Johnson (1978) found, rather to their surprise, that groups of acute, mixed, and chronically hospitalised schizophrenic patients were progressively more difficult to distinguish from patients with organic brain disease. The obvious interpretation of these findings—that schizophrenia is associated with a tendency to develop intellectual deterioration—was for a long time discounted in favour of the view that the deficits were due to poor co-operation, lack of motivation, distraction by psychotic experiences, and so on. Later, after neuroleptic drug treatment was introduced, this was also invoked as a factor, quite uncritically in view of a substantial body of evidence which indicated that these drugs if anything improve cognitive test performance in schizophrenic patients (e.g. King, 1990).

In recent years, and at least partly as a result of the accumulating evidence for biological brain abnormality in schizophrenia, there has been a re-evaluation of these findings. Studies comparing current IQ with estimated premorbid levels using the National Adult Reading Test (NART) have clearly established (or rather re-established) that schizophrenic patients undergo a decline (Frith, Leary, Cahill, & Johnstone, 1991; Nelson, Pantelis, Carruthers, Speller, Baxendale, & Barnes, 1990). Among chronically hospitalised patients, poor performance on simple tests of cognitive function has also been found to be prevalent (Owens & Johnstone, 1980). Perhaps most crucially, it has been documented that some of this latter group of patients show the phenomenon of age disorientation, underestimating their age by a margin of five years or more. Age disorientation cannot easily be attributed to treatment, or to lifelong low intelligence, and it is closely associated with the presence of other, typically widespread and severe, neuropsychological deficits (Buhrich, Crow, Johnstone, & Owens, 1988; Liddle & Crow, 1984).

In the large group of schizophrenic patients who do not show any great degree of overall intellectual impairment—beyond, say, a decline in IQ—there is evidence for the presence of more circumscribed deficits. Impairments in executive function have been found in a number of group studies (e.g. Liddle & Morris, 1991) and have been shown in a single case study to be sometimes present in the absence of any overall intellectual impairment (Shallice, Burgess, & Frith, 1991). Similar disproportionate deficits have also been demonstrated in memory (McKenna, Tamlyn, Lund, Mortimer, Hammond, & Baddeley, 1990; Tamlyn, McKenna, Mortimer, Lund, Hammond, & Baddeley, 1992). When memory impairment is encountered in relatively pure form in schizophrenia, it seems to resemble the pattern seen in the classical amnesic syndrome (e.g. Baddeley, 1990): impairment in long-term memory is coupled with sparing of short-term and procedural memory (Clare, McKenna, Mortimer, & Baddeley, 1993; Tamlyn et al., 1992). But the picture differs from the typical amnesic syndrome pattern in at least one respect—semantic memory is affected to a degree greater than the relatively modest impairments seen in such neurological patients.

Laura's case provides an unprecedented opportunity to examine the question of neuropsychological impairment in schizophrenia without the potentially confounding effects of withdrawal, poor motivation, distraction by psychotic symptom symptoms, etc. on performance. In many ways she conforms to the typical pattern: There is some evidence of overall intellectual impairment in the shape of a borderline significant IQ decline. This might also account for the patchy, minor impairments on tests of perception and language. Over and above this, however, is evidence of a specific deficit in memory. This affects both recall and recognition, but spares short-term memory. There are also hints of poor executive performance, but these deficits do not show up very clearly in Laura's particular case.

The Treatment of Schizophrenia

After the discovery of chlorpromazine's effectiveness, many drugs with similar pharmacological actions were developed. Currently, some 30 or more compounds are in use, and many more are known but have not been developed commercially. Initial research into neuroleptic drugs established their mechanism of action and gave rise to the dopamine hypothesis of schizophrenia, as described previously. Another early goal of research in this area was to ascertain whether neuroleptic drugs had a specific effect on the core symptoms of schizophrenia, or whether their effects were merely due to their sedative or tranquillising properties. Numerous well-controlled studies (see Davis, 1985) have supported the clinical impression that the drugs specifically alleviate delusions, hallucinations, and other positive symptoms, and there are some indications of a lesser effect on negative symptoms. However, these studies have also made it clear that the response to treatment is less than satisfactory: At least 25% of schizophrenic patients will show no or only a minimal response to treatment and, in the majority, treatment does not bring about anything like a complete recovery.

A third goal of research in the treatment of schizophrenia has therefore been to develop better drugs. So far, clozapine is the only drug which shows convincing evidence of therapeutic superiority. This drug was one of the earliest drugs to be developed, but its use was abandoned in most countries after an unacceptably high incidence of a serious white cell disorder (which led to a number of deaths) was reported. By this time, though, many clinicians had been impressed with clozapine's exceptional therapeutic effects and also its lack of the usual side-effects on motor function (these include Parkinsonism—a reversible syndrome of slowness, stiffness and tremor—and tardive dyskinesia—involuntary movements affecting the face and body which are permanent in most cases). Clinical trials continued to be carried out in the USA under carefully controlled conditions, and these established that the risk of fatality could be kept acceptably low by weekly white blood cell counts. This research culminated in a large study by Kane, Honingfeld, Singer, and Meltzer (1988) which established once and for all that clozapine is more effective than chlorpromazine (and hence all other neuroleptics), producing significant improvement in 30% of otherwise treatment-resistant patients.

In approximately 10% of cases the response to clozapine is dramatic, with highly symptomatic patients who were previously completely refractory to treatment making excellent recoveries on the drug. Laura is such a case, and others are beginning to be documented (including one whose story has been made into a film starring Diana Ross). Clozapine has, justifiably, been hailed as the first significant advance in the treatment of schizophrenia since the discovery of chlorpromazine. But perhaps more significantly, it may also have provided a starting point for the development of still better drugs. It may even turn out to be the key which finally unlocks the neurochemical abnormality that is believed to underlie at least some aspects of the disorder.

ACKNOWLEDGEMENTS

The authors would like to thank Alan Baddeley for his suggestions about the content of this chapter, and also for his comments on the manuscript.

REFERENCES

Andreasen, N.C. (1985). Positive vs. negative schizophrenia: A critical evaluation. *Schizophrenia Bulletin, 11*, 380–389.

Andreasen, N.C., Arndt, S., Swayze, V.W., Cizadlo, T., Flaum, M., & O'Leary, D.S. (1994). Thalamic abnormalities in schizophrenia visualized through magnetic resonance imaging. *Science, 266*, 294–298.

Baddeley, A. (1990). *Human memory: Theory and practice.* Hove, UK: Laurence Erlbaum Associates Ltd.

Bentall, R.P. (1990). The syndromes and symptoms of psychosis. In R.P. Bentall (Ed.), *Reconstructing schizophrenia* (pp. 23–60). London: Routledge.

Benton, A.L., Hamsher, K. de S., Varney, N.R., & Spreen, O. (1978). *Facial recognition.* New York: Oxford University Press.

Bleuler, E. (1950). *Dementia praecox or the group of schizophrenias* (J. Zinkin, Trans.). New York: International Universities Press. (Original work published 1911).

Buhrich, N., Crow, T.J., Johnstone, E.C., & Owens, D.G.C. (1988). Age disorientation in chronic schizophrenia is not associated with pre-morbid intellectual impairment or past physical treatments. *British Journal of Psychiatry, 152*, 466–469.

Chapman, L.J., & Chapman, J.P. (1973). *Disordered thought in schizophrenia.* New York: Appleton-Century-Crofts.

Chua, S.E., & McKenna, P.J. (1995). Schizophrenia—a brain disease? A critical review of structural and functional cerebral abnormality in the disorder. *British Journal of Psychiatry, 166*, 563–582.

Clare, L., McKenna, R.J., Mortimer, A.M., & Baddeley, A.D. (1993). Memory in schizophrenia: What is impaired and what is preserved? *Neuropsychologia, 31*, 1225–1241.

Crow, T.J. (1980). Molecular pathology of schizophrenia: More than one disease process? *British Medical Journal, 280*, 66–68.

Cutting, J. (1985). *The psychology of schizophrenia*. Edinburgh: Churchill Livingstone.

Cutting, J., & Shepherd, M. (1987). *The clinical roots of the schizophrenia concept*. Cambridge, UK: Cambridge University Press.

Davis, J.M. (1985). Antipsychotic drugs. In H.I. Kaplan & B.J. Sadock (Eds.), *Comprehensive textbook of psychiatry* (pp. 1481–1512). Baltimore: Williams & Wilkins.

Day, R. (1981). Life events and schizophrenia: The "triggering" hypothesis. *Acta Psychiatrica Scandinavica, 64*, 97–122.

De Renzi, E., & Faglioni, P. (1978). Normative data and screening power of a shortened version of the token test. *Cortex, 14*, 41–49.

Farde, L., Wiesel, F.-A., Stone-Elander, S., Halldin, C., Nordstrom, A.-L., & Hall, H. (1987). D2 dopamine receptors in neuroleptic-naive schizophrenic patients: A positron emission tomography study with [^{11}C] raclopride. *Archives of General Psychiatry, 47*, 213–219.

Frith, C.D. (1979). Consciousness, information processing and schizophrenia. *British Journal of Psychiatry, 134*, 225–235.

Frith, C.D., Friston, K.J., Herold, S., Liddle, P.F., & Frackowiak, R.J. (1995). Regional brain activity in chronic schizophrenic patients during performance of a verbal fluency task: Evidence for a failure of inhibition in left superior temporal cortex. *British Journal of Psychiatry, 167*, 343–349.

Frith, C.D., Leary, J., Cahill, C., & Johnstone, E.C. (1991). IV. Performance on psychological tests: Demographic and clinical correlates of the tests. *British Journal of Psychiatry, 159* (Suppl. 13), 26–29.

Garety, P.A., & Hemsley D.R. (1994). Delusions: Investigations into the psychology of delusional reasoning. *Maudsley Monographs, 36*. Oxford: Oxford University Press.

Gottesman, I.I. (1991). *Schizophrenia genesis: The origins of madness*. New York: Freeman.

Gray, J.A., Rawlins, J.N.P., Hemsley, D.R., & Smith, A.D. (1991). The neuropsychology of schizophrenia. *Behavioral and Brain Sciences, 14*, 1–84.

Heaton, R.K., Baade, L.E., & Johnson, K.L. (1978). Neuropsychological test results associated with psychiatric disorders in adults. *Psychological Bulletin, 85*, 141–162.

Hirsch, S.R., & Leff, J.P. (1975). Abnormalities in parents of schizophrenics. *Maudsley Monographs, 22*. London: Oxford University Press.

Howard, D., & Patterson, K.E. (1992). *The pyramids and palm trees test*. Thames Valley Test Co., Bury St Edmunds, Suffolk, IP28 6EL.

Johnstone, E.C., Crow, T.J., Frith, C.D., Husband, J., & Kreel, L. (1976). Cerebral ventricular size and cognitive impairment in chronic schizophrenia. *Lancet, 2*, 924–926.

Kane, J.M., Honingfeld, G., Singer, J., & Meltzer, H. (1988). Clozapine for the treatment resistant schizophrenic. *Archives of General Psychiatry, 45*, 789–796.

Kerr, A., & McClelland, H. (Eds.). (1991). *Concepts of mental disorder: A continuing debate*. London: Gaskell/Royal College of Psychiatrists.

King, D.J. (1990). The effect of neuroleptics on cognitive and psychomotor function. *British Journal of Psychiatry, 157*, 799–811.

Kraepelin, E. (1919). *Dementia praecox and paraphrenia* (R.M. Barclay, Trans.). Edinburgh: Livingstone. (Original work published 1913).

Langfeldt, G. (1960). Diagnosis and prognosis in schizophrenia. *Proceedings of the Royal Society of Medicine, 53*, 1047–1051.

Leff, J., & Vaughn, C. (1985). *Expressed emotion in families: Its significance for mental illness*. London: Guildford Press.

Lewis, S.W. (1990). Computerised tomography in schizophrenia 15 years on. *British Journal of Psychiatry, 157* (Suppl. 9), 16–24.

Liddle, P.F., & Crow, T.J. (1984). Age disorientation in chronic schizophrenia is associated with global intellectual impairment. *British Journal of Psychiatry, 144*, 193–199.

Liddle, P.F., Friston, K.J., Frith, C.D., Hirsch, S.R., Jones, T., & Frackowiak, R.S.J. (1992). Patterns of cerebral blood flow in schizophrenia. *British Journal of Psychiatry, 160*, 179–186.

Liddle, P.F., & Morris, D.L. (1991). Schizophrenic symptoms and frontal lobe performance. *British Journal of Psychiatry, 158*, 340–345.

McGhie, A. (1969). *Pathology of attention*. Harmondsworth, UK: Penguin.

McKenna, P.J. (1994). *Schizophrenia and related syndromes*. Oxford: Oxford University Press.

McKenna, P.J., Tamlyn, D., Lund, C.E., Mortimer, A.M., Hammond, S., & Baddeley, A.D. (1990). Amnesic syndrome in schizophrenia. *Psychological Medicine, 20*, 967–972.

McKenna, P., & Warrington, E.K. (1983). *The graded naming test*. Windsor, UK: NFER-Nelson.

Murray, R.M., Lewis, S.W., & Reveley, A.M. (1985). Towards an aetiological classification of schizophrenia. *Lancet, i*, 1023–1026.

Nelson, H.E. (1976). A modified card sorting test sensitive to frontal lobe defects. *Cortex, 12*, 313–324.

Nelson, H.E. (1982). *The national adult reading test (NART)*. Windsor, UK: NFER-Nelson.

Nelson, H.E., Pantelis, C., Carruthers, K., Speller, J., Baxendale, S., & Barnes, T.R.E. (1990). Cognitive functioning and symptomatology in chronic schizophrenia. *Psychological Medicine, 20*, 357–365.

Oltmanns, T.F., & Maher, B.A. (Eds.), (1988). *Delusional beliefs*. New York: Wiley.

Owens, D.G.C., & Johnstone, E.C. (1980). The disabilities of chronic schizophrenia—their nature and the factors contributing to their development. *British Journal of Psychiatry, 136*, 384–393.

Payne, R.W. (1973). Cognitive abnormalities. In H.J. Eysenck (Ed.), *Handbook of abnormal psychology* (pp. 420–483). London: Pitman.

Prescott, C.A., & Gottesman, I.I. (1993). Genetically mediated vulnerability to schizophrenia. *Psychiatric Clinics of North America, 16*, 245–268.

Rochester, S., & Martin, J.R. (1979). *Crazy talk: A study of the discourse of schizophrenic speakers*. New York: Plenum.

Shallice, T., Burgess, P.W., & Frith, C.D. (1991). Can the neuropsychological case-study approach be applied to schizophrenia? *Psychological Medicine, 21*, 661–673.

Shallice, T., & Evans, M.E. (1978). The role of the frontal lobes in cognitive estimation. *Cortex, 14*, 294–303.

Slade, P.D., & Bentall, R.P. (1988). *Sensory deception: A scientific analysis of hallucination*. London: Croom Helm.

Spring, B., Weinstein, L., Freeman, R., & Thompson, S. (1991). Selective attention in schizophrenia. In S.R. Steinhauer, J.H. Gruzelier, & J. Zubin (Eds.), *Handbook of schizophrenia, Vol. 5: Neuropsychology, psychophysiology and information processing* (pp. 371–396). Amsterdam: Elsevier.

Tamlyn, D., McKenna, P.J., Mortimer, A.M., Lund, C.E., Hammond, S., & Baddeley, A.D. (1992). Memory impairment in schizophrenia: Its extent, affiliations and neuropsychological character. *Psychological Medicine, 22*, 101–115.

Van Horn, J.D., & McManus, I.C. (1992). Ventricular enlargement in schizophrenia: A meta-analysis of the ventricle:brain ratio (VBR). *British Journal of Psychiatry, 160*, 687–697.

Warrington, E.K. (1984). *Recognition memory test*. Windsor, UK: NFER-Nelson.

Warrington, E.K., & Taylor, A.M. (1973). The contribution of the right parietal lobe to object recognition. *Cortex, 9*, 152–164.

Weinberger, D.R., Berman, K.F., & Zec, R.F. (1986). Physiological dysfunction of dorsolateral prefrontal cortex in schizophrenia. *Archives of General Psychiatry, 43*, 114–135.

Wilson, B.A., Cockburn, J.M., & Baddeley, A.D. (1985). *The Rivermead behavioural memory test*. Thames Valley Test Co., Bury St Edmunds, Suffolk, IP28 6EL.

Wolkin, A., Sanfilipo, M., Wolf, A.P., Angrist, B., Brodie, J.D., & Rotrosen, J. (1992). Negative symptoms and hypofrontality in schizophrenia. *Archives of General Psychiatry, 49*, 959–965.

Wong, D.F., Wagner, H.N., Tune, L.E., Dannals, R.F., Pearlson, G.D., & Links, J.M. (1986). Positron emission tomography reveals elevated D2 dopamine receptors in drug-naive schizophrenics. *Science, 234,* 1558–1563.

World Health Organization (1973). *Report of the international pilot study of schizophrenia.* Geneva: World Health Organization.

World Health Organization (1979). *Schizophrenia: An international follow-up study.* Geneva: Wiley.

7

Split Minds: Multiple Personality and Schizophrenia

Anthony David
Department of Psychological Medicine, Institute of Psychiatry, London, UK

Roisin Kemp
Department of Psychological Medicine, Institute of Psychiatry, UK

Ladé Smith and Thomas Fahy
Maudsley Hospital, London, UK

Psychiatrists spend much of their time and energy trying to convince members of the public and lay media that schizophrenia has nothing to do with "split-personality", Dr Jekyll and Mr Hyde, or any other popular misconception. The term "schizophrenia" was coined by Swiss psychiatrist Eugen Bleuler (Bleuler, 1911/1950) to denote a splitting of psychic functions, for example the separation of thought and affect, and the loosening of associations between thoughts. In descriptive terms, schizophrenia may be seen as more of a disintegration than mere splitting. The disintegration occurs at all levels of cognitive function but, uniquely amongst neuropsychological disorders, its most obvious effects are at the highest, supra-modal, integrative levels of cognition.

A conspicuous feature of this disintegration concerns the individual's identity. Who a person is (and is not) is central to schizophrenic psychopathology (David & Appleby, 1992; Fabrega, 1989; Sims, 1990). This may be manifest in the characteristic symptoms such as certain kinds of auditory-verbal hallucinations (AVHs), thought alienation, and passivity experiences, symptoms identified by German psychiatrist Kurt Schneider (1959), which have come to be known as (Schneider's) First Rank Symptoms of schizophrenia (FRS). AVHs or hearing voices, often commenting on the individual and their actions with a third person form of address, may be the consequence of a person's failure to recognise the self-origin of inner speech and so he or she attributes it to someone else (David, 1994a, 1994b; David & Lucas, 1993; Frith, 1987). Thought

insertion, withdrawal and broadcast, are highl'
and involve the experience—somewhere bet
belief—that one's thoughts arise from or are
agent, or are somehow "available" to the ea:
feeling that private internal mental events r
strikes at the heart of the integrity of th'
therefore I am", becomes, "I am not sure '
I be sure of who I am?"

Passivity refers to sensations, movements,
individual experiences "passively", that is to
responsible for them. Over and above these specᴄᴍᴄ
volition and action, language and perception, that occur in sᴏᴍᴇ,
(Table 7.1), there is bound to be disruption of the sense of self which
depends on these subordinate functions. The hierarchy of psychological
functions put forward in Table 7.1 is arbitrary but assumes that sensori-
motor functions are simpler and involve less integrated cerebral activity
than the functions which support representations such as language and
identity.

There have been many attempts to bring together these abnormal
features under a single explanatory framework. In ego psychology and
psychoanalysis notions such as "ego boundaries" enjoyed a vogue.
Schizophrenics were viewed as having abnormally permeable psychic
boundaries leading to confusion as to where they began and ended and
where others began. Such physical metaphors remain rather appealing but
lack explanatory power. They also bring with them a further element of
confusion, perhaps another boundary, namely the distinction between the
physical and psychological self. Other accounts have arisen from existential
philosophy, an articulate and influential example of which is R.D. Laing's
The Divided Self (1961).

In neuropsychology, disorders of body image or schema have attracted
much attention. The physical body is represented in the mind in a way which
differs from a veridical reproduction. The right cerebral hemisphere is
"dominant" for the control of attention to the body image so that
disturbances more often involve the left side of the body. Sensory
representation of the homunculus reflects the density and sensitivity of
sense organs. The body image in psychiatry consists of a further order of
abstraction in which the body schema is distorted through the lens of affect,
values, and culture (Rix & Snaith, 1988; but see Cutting, 1989 and Silva,
Leong, & Luong, 1989 for intermediate cases). The size of the nose, sexual
organs, and desire for slimness, for example seem to occupy disproportionate space (Krasucki, Kemp, & David, 1995). A prime example of a
breach between the physical–psychological boundary is passivity, when
thoughts become sensations.

TABLE 7.1
A Hierarchical Scheme for Representing Psychological Functions and Psychiatric Disorders

Hierarchy of Psychological Functions	Disturbance of Body Image	Disorder	Neurological Basis	Influence of Culture
Sensory-motor	Phantom limb	Epilepsy	Strong ↕	Low ↕
Vigilance	Hemi-inattention	Schizophrenia		
Attention	Anosognosia			
Memory				
Language				
Perception	?Unilateral somatic delusions	Manic depression		
Action				
Imagery				
Volition	Dysmorphophobia	Hysterical conversion		
Planning	Transsexualism			
Beliefs	Anorexia nervosa }	Multiple personality disorder	↕ Weak	↕ High
Sense of self	Cosmetic Surgery }			

Note: Horizontal mapping of items in the Table is not intended.

125

Personal identity is frequently disturbed in schizophrenia. This may shade into physical identity, with some patients claiming to be of a different ethnicity, gender, or age than they manifestly are (Chapman, Chapman, & Raulin, 1978; Cutting, 1990). Early symptoms include the feeling that one is different or altered in some as yet indefinable way (Cutting & Dunne, 1989; Laing, 1961). In other cases, patients may believe that they are someone else, either known or unknown, famous or infamous. Rarely, they may come to believe that they are several people. Such a case will be described. Before doing so, we will return to the other disorder of identity alluded to in the introduction—split- or multiple personality disorder (MPD).

MULTIPLE PERSONALITY DISORDER

MPD is a controversial diagnosis, especially outside the USA. It attracts strong and polarised opinions, being the subject of tabloid scandals as well as erudite reviews (Piper, 1994; Spanos, 1994). In Britain, the diagnosis of MPD is rarely made, with most psychiatrists sceptical of its existence. In fact, MPD is rarely seen in the UK, except in attenuated and transient forms (Fahy, Abas, & Brown, 1989), leading many critics to suggest that the disorder is largely iatrogenic (Fahy, 1988; Merskey, 1992). Prior to 1957, very few diagnoses of MPD were made (Goff & Simms, 1993) but the publicity given to Thigpen and Cleckley's case (1957) of Eve White in a book and later on film, made the American medical profession and public aware of MPD. With the reporting of several other famous cases, e.g. 'Sybil" (Schreiber, 1973) and "Billy Milligan" (Keyes, 1981), came a "sanctioning" of MPD by the general public and the media alike.

Since the 1960s, the number of cases of MPD has increased by thousands. Ross (1991) believes that MPD may affect up to 1% of the adult population of North America. This is equivalent to the generally quoted prevalence of schizophrenia, and MPD researchers feel that often cases of schizophrenia are in fact misdiagnosed cases of MPD (Kluft, 1987; Ross, Miller, Reagor, Bjornson, Fraser, & Anderson, 1990) and vice versa. Some researchers feel that the increase in prevalence is because of the increased reporting of the problem, or more likely altered diagnostic practices among some psychiatrists combined with cultural factors such as lay beliefs about personality, selfhood, and mental illness.

The Diagnosis of MPD

An early graphic description of MPD comes from the "transition" or "switch" from one personality to another in the case of Eve White (Thigpen & Cleckley, 1957). The witnessing of a spontaneous switch is unusual. More often MPD is diagnosed after a prolonged period of psychotherapy, usually involving hypnosis. Cases appear to cluster around interested clinicians (see Spanos, 1994, for review). Because of this, MPD has become associated with the controversy over the so-called False Memory Syndrome and false allegations of satanic, ritual, or other forms of sexual abuse and even with abduction by aliens. The purpose of this article is not to recapitulate these arguments but to consider what the syndrome tells us about the social and cognitive structure of the self. In this we follow the lead taken by Humphrey and Dennett (1989) in their admirably un-partisan foray into this area. The contrast between the pathology of the self and personal identity in schizophrenia and that of MPD is used to add a theoretical framework upon which to base this consideration.

Psychiatric diagnosis is always a matter of clinical judgement based on symptoms, signs, and the history—much of which is based on the patient's subjective report. Nevertheless, operationalisation of diagnostic criteria is the first step in attaining reliability and validity of a diagnosis. According to the *Diagnostic and Statistical Manual of Mental Disorders* of the American Psychiatric Association (1994), MPD, now called "Dissociative Identity Disorder", is defined as the existence within the person of two or more distinct identities or personality states. At least two of these identities or states recurrently take control of the person's behaviour. Early descriptions (Ellenberger, 1970) assumed that distinct personalities could, apparently, occur simultaneously, but the classical type consisted of successive and mutually amnesic alters, although the pattern of amnesia could be one-way.

Over the years, researchers have assimilated a number of features that patients who are eventually given the diagnosis of MPD have presented with at some time (Putnam, Guroff, Silberman, Barban, & Post, 1986). These "associated features" are supposed to alert the clinician to the possible diagnosis of MPD. In 1987, Kluft claimed that first rank symptoms (FRS) are highly indicative of MPD, a view supported by Ross et al. (1990). It is hard to convey just how heretical these claims are, given the status of FRS in psychiatric nosology. In fact, close scrutiny of the examples given by Kluft (1987) shows that the supposed FRS would not satisfy accepted definitions (Wing, Cooper, & Sartorius, 1974), but are rather statements to the effect that it is "as if" thoughts were being inserted or withdrawn. The claim is further undermined by the report that MPD patients frequently have on average 3.6 FRS rather than the usual one or two in schizophrenia (Jablensky, Sartorius, Ernberg, Anker, Korten, & Cooper, 1992). Nevertheless, despite the inaccurate and loose application of FRS to MPD by Kluft and Ross, these authors have highlighted a basic similarity common to both syndromes—an insecure sense of self.

We describe two case histories—the first, of a patient with schizophrenia, and the second, of one with MPD—each of whom has severe disturbances of the sense of self.[1]

CASE HISTORY I

Kate is a 48-year-old single unemployed woman, who was admitted after being found at home in a state of marked neglect and isolation, living in squalid conditions and complaining that her neighbours were persecuting her. This was the latest of approximately annual psychiatric admissions, spanning 20 years, many being similar to this. She had been given a diagnosis of schizophrenia on most of these occasions and treated with neuroleptics but with little success and poor compliance on discharge.

There is no known family history of psychiatric illness, and Kate has little contact with her relatives. Her mother is an elderly woman who occasionally sends Kate clothes but has not seen her for 10 years. Her father died 16 years ago and Kate remembered him as a kind and gentle man. She has one older sister who is married with children, but they have had no contact for many years.

Kate has no details of her birth and could remember nothing of her childhood except the name of the comprehensive school she attended. She gives no history of sexual abuse. After leaving school she left England to work abroad for a year. On her return she did some restaurant work before going to art school in her mid-20s. She planned to become an art teacher but never completed the course. It was around this time that she began her patient career instead.

Kate has no partner; she remembered two sexual relationships, one in her late teens, the other in her early 20s. She currently lives alone in a low-rise council block. She has no contact with her relatives, and no friends to speak of. She is on Income Support and spends much of her time alone at home. She smokes 20 cigarettes a day and rarely takes alcohol; she does not use illegal drugs. She does not take any prescribed medication, unless compelled to do so under a Section of the Mental Health Act.

On examination, she was a plump, hirsute Caucasian woman with staring eyes and a fixed facial expression. Whilst on the ward she was frequently heard conversing loudly "to herself". Her speech was of normal rate and form, although there was a lack of prosody. She was not subjectively depressed nor elated, but had a flattened affect. She denied any suicidal ideation.

---

[1] Since this article was written, a more systematic study of the distinction between MPD and schizophrenia has been published (Steinberg, Cicchetti, Buchanan, Rakfeldt, & Rounsaville, 1994). We hope that the more descriptive approach taken here will complement that work.

Kate believed that people on her housing estate were persecuting her and when questioned about why she was talking to herself, she revealed that she was talking to "Lucinda". Lucinda was described as a young woman in her mid-20s, who was not dissimilar to Kate, and was "very pleasant and interesting to talk to". Lucinda often talked about other people and commented on what they were doing. Kate also felt that Lucinda knew her (Kate's) thoughts. She believed that Lucinda had the use of her body and when that happens, Kate "blacks out".

Later, Kate admitted that there were a number of others as well as Lucinda. Most important was "Crunchy (The Teeth)", who is depressive, has suicidal thoughts, and is awake at night when the patient is asleep and can take her body to the balcony to throw it off. Crunchy can talk through Kate's teeth. Kate also mentioned "Brenda, Breath of Life", who speaks with a breathy voice and whom the patient hears "through her throat". There were three others: Mother Earth (not described), Snotty Nose, and Face and Body, the latter two residing in their respective regions of the body. The patient had not interacted with these characters, but she could feel their presence within her.

Although Kate found Crunchy's suicidal thoughts distressing, on the whole she quite enjoyed conversing with the others, particularly Lucinda.

Standard clinical examination revealed the patient to be alert and orientated. She appeared to be of average intelligence. She felt that she did not have a psychiatric illness, and was adamant that there was nothing wrong with her. Kate occasionally wondered whether she had Multiple Personality Disorder. She had seen such people on the TV but had found them "histrionic and peculiar" in that they seemed to produce many different personalities.

To any British psychiatrist, this woman appears to have a schizophrenic illness. She has a number of Schneiderian FRS:

- commenting auditory hallucinations
- delusions of external control and bodily influence
- possible thought interference

Her other schizophrenic symptoms include:

- flattened affect
- social withdrawal
- prodrome of poor social functioning

In America, however, there is a possibility that this woman would be given a diagnosis of Multiple Personality Disorder. In Kate's case, it would be difficult to ascertain if different personalities were really present within her, but researchers in America recognise that this is a difficulty with many patients who may have MPD. According to Kluft (1991), Kate could been seen to have features of four of his 20 sub-types.

Conconscious MPD. Kate is aware of all her "alters" and does not demonstrate any clear memory gaps, although interestingly she could remember little of her childhood.

Private Secret MPD. Kate only divulged that she was talking with "other people" some time after being on the ward.

Ostensible—Imaginary MPD. Kate described Lucinda as pleasant and friendly with whom she liked to chat.

Covert MPD. Kate feels that Lucinda and Crunchy can influence her as in covert MPD.

Psychological Testing

An estimate of premorbid IQ was obtained using the National Adult Reading Test (NART; Nelson, 1982); IQ = 103 (average); the Cognitive Estimates, a test of logical inference which requires the subject to solve simple questions based on general knowledge, was given and Kate scored 4 (range 0–30, higher score = poorer performance; Shallice & Evans, 1978). She guessed the oldest person in Britain to be 120 years, the population of Britain to be 17 million, the height of the Post Office Tower as 900 feet and said there were no camels in Holland! Kate scored 8 on the Dissociative Experiences Questionnaire (DES; Bernstein & Putnam, 1986); a score of 30 is usually taken as the cut-off for MPD. This questionnaire examines a range of often transient phenomena including the lapses of memory, "visions", and the feeling that a person is separate from their own body.

Autobiographical Memory

Kate scored 12/27 (44%) on the autobiographical incidents section of the Autobiographical Memory Interview (AMI; Kopelman, Wilson, & Baddeley, 1989), 4/9 for each time period. Regarding personal semantic memory, she scored as follows:

Background	11/23
Childhood	9/21
Early adult	9/21
Recent	13.5/21
Total	43.5/86 (50.6%)

These data indicate that Kate's ability to recall information about her self and life is in the amnesic range. Her performance is as bad as the worst of the five cases of delusions studied by Baddeley, Thornton, Chua, and McKenna (in press), who, incidently believed he was "full of angels".

In order to explore Kate's self concept, a semi-structured interview based on the five categories of self proposed by Neisser (1988) was performed on two separate occasions three months apart. Responses were remarkably consistent.

1. Ecological Self. Based on perceptual information, the self as embedded/located in the environment.

Description of her physical appearance:
Height, 5 feet 6 inches, brown eyes, hair long, "blondish" on the top, size shoes $5\frac{1}{2}$, weight: used to be $9\frac{1}{2}$ stones, now $10\frac{1}{2}$–11 stones, type of complexion; "nice complexion". At one point, described herself as having "different right and left sides"; however, at a second interview three months later, could not comment on this. Similarly described herself earlier as having difficulty moving around, lack of co-ordination due to being "sticky", whereas three months later denied any such difficulty.

Has a favourite perfume "Chanel", though not known to take particular care of personal hygiene. Has favourite food, "Hamburger or egg and chips". Enjoys watching TV, especially soaps or detective series and "dancing in her room".

Comment: The patient seems to have a rather flattering view of her appearance and a quite youthful self-image. She contradicts herself at different times about her physical attributes but not her persona, or likes/dislikes.

2. Interpersonal Self. Based on affective atunement; the self that is established by these interactions; attributing mental states to others; the nature and quality of transactions with others.

Questions were based on exploration of family history; talking to others; experience of friendships; perceiving others' intentions, etc.

Spoke of difficulty relating to others; "I don't get much feedback". Likes "all sorts of people". However, this direction of questioning quickly induced a tirade of delusional thinking with marked persecutory content, and revealing passivity experiences: "A job has been done on me for black girls ... black girls are jealous of me ... this guy threatened to stab me ... gave me an injection to duff me up etc..."

The predominant themes were:

Sexual: "X duffed me up ... put pains in my vagina... The black girls wanted to get me pregnant, make me put on weight ... give me a still-born baby ... Crunchy told me (through my teeth) she was lonely at night ... she wanted to give me a baby..."

Somatic: "X duffed up my circulation when I was in hospital... I have pressure and pains in my head... They've duffed up my eyesight ... etc."

Relationships: "I don't like it by myself, I would love to have made friends, have a boyfriend... I love Crunchy very much... I love them all. I think I'll get them friends for nighttime... They tell me they love me... I love my mother and my sister very much, even though they left me... The nurses are very nice people... I've been busy in my flat with God knows what ... didn't have much time to feel lonely..."

Comment: The patient quickly develops a persecutory stance in her relationships with others. Her affect can be quite warm, but does not tolerate much interaction before becoming anxious and over aroused. This tendency is less pronounced when she is taking neuroleptic medication.

3. Extended Self.   Autobiographical memory.

"I think there's nothing much to remember, because I don't have relationships with people." Could come up with only a few memories spontaneously. Remembers sitting under a banana tree on her 21st birthday on holiday abroad. When questioned systematically about her background and upbringing, could only come up with a couple of childhood memories, e.g. sitting with her sister doing homework, their mother looking on in silence; throwing her teddy-bear up in the air; learning to ride a bicycle. "I don't really remember my childhood at all, my parents never spoke to me..." Remembers more of her teen years ... liking certain pop songs, recalls going dancing, doing the twist.

When prompted, Kate listed jobs she had held, but could not say much else about her work experience, the people she met, etc. Worked in a variety of casual jobs: as a croupier in a casino, a telephonist, a waitress, a factory packer. Her fondest memory was of her time on a kibbutz; remembers the lemon groves. However, even this memory was described with some delusional flavour; "I remember sitting on the grass with some girls, a girl put a dry bit of glass on my leg ... she was communicating with me..."

4. Private Self. Beliefs, subjective ideas; sense of knowing what it is to have certain feelings.

"I don't have values, just confidence in myself... I think I could be very happy if I got serums for my health and strength... I've no nostalgia for the past... What's precious to me? I love people... I don't have any problem making friends... Life is wonderful if you've got friends... It's terrible to be lonely, that's what makes people suicidal... I sometimes feel frightened in my flat because of the old codger who lives down the corridor ... and the children throw stones at me. The best feeling is looking good, and feeling good with nice clothes... I'd like the homeless housed and the starving fed, but I've no interest in politics or religion or current affairs... I've been shut off from the world ... should go out, get a boy friend ... etc."

Comment on 3 and 4: Kate is aware of large lacunae in her autobiographical memory ("I can't remember details... I've been preoccupied with God knows what for 12 years"). She is unable to elaborate on memories of specific events or periods in her life, and she also suggests that, although apparently having lived in a variety of diverse situations, there was little emotional impact, because she didn't interact with people. She has an idea that her life is just about to begin now, that she's entering a new phase in her life where she expects to have more interaction with people and her environment. Privately, Kate's descriptions reveal considerable pathos and loneliness.

5. Conceptual Self. Self-concept, role, ideas about body, thoughts and feelings.

Kate views herself as: "Intelligent, sexy, friendly, open, good, honest, level in moods...". Doesn't see herself as at all eccentric, or imagine that others might view her so... "I haven't had any relationships to find out what I'm like exactly... I blank out to Crunchy, Lucinda, Brenda the Breath of Life, Snotty Nose, and Face & Body. Lucinda speaks in my mouth, Crunchy through my teeth. They share the same body as me, but they are different human beings... But they are also similar to me, not completely different. Their thoughts are different to mine, though. I don't talk to them. I must be made unconscious when Crunchy comes into existence... They know about each other... They are walking miracles... I love them all equally... Lucinda talks nearly all day non-stop for about two years now, it's great company...

Crunchy was raped by a black man and made us pregnant... Brenda talks through my breath, she's suffocating at the moment because there's a job being done on us... Snotty Nose only said a few words, about a year ago. Face and Body spoke to me, she said 'I love you', I called her Face and Body, she's not the most interesting... I'm not a multiple personality disorder... I saw it on the TV. There was this person rolling about on the floor ... about 18 or 20 personalities. We're not like that, we're highly intelligent, don't bother anyone ... they keep me company. I'm not schizophrenic. Schizophrenia means suffering from delusions; I've never had delusions, there's nothing wrong with me. I don't need drugs, my problems will be solved when I get a housing transfer."

Comment: Questions explicitly about self-concept bring out the "other personalities" and Kate's relationship to them. The private and extended selves seem rather sketchy in contrast to the delusional conceptual self. Note that a separate stream of delusions is accessed through questions on interpersonal relations in the real world. Her lack of insight (David, 1990), that is awareness that she has an illness, an ability to relabel her experiences as abnormal, and an acknowledgement of the need for treatment, seems total.

The ecological self reveals a bland and happy person frozen in time, at variance with the self as seen by others. Her extended self seems discontinuous; her autobiography is patchy and incomplete, as deficient as someone with a traditional amnesic syndrome. It may therefore be understandable that this combination of deficits in Kate's self-knowledge (or "poor self-elaboration"; De Bonis, De Boeck, Lida-Pulik, Bazin, Masure, & Feline, 1994) combined with an empty, lonely existence could lead to gaps being filled by other people or bits of people.

CASE HISTORY II

Patricia was referred to one of us (TF) by an American psychotherapist. The patient had decided to return to the UK and both she and her therapist were anxious that someone acquainted with MPD should take over her care.

Patricia was a 41-year-old woman who described herself as a freelance poet. She was married and had three children. She was diagnosed as having MPD five years previously whilst living in New York, and it was alleged that she was a victim of satanic and ritual abuse at the hands of her father on the basis of a dream interpretation, although she appeared to be on good terms with him. She had numerous alters who could be aggregated into clusters (see Fig. 7.1). The alters were of a variety of ages and could be of either sex.

Her early life by all accounts was unremarkable. Her mother was a housewife and her father a carpenter. She had a twin sister who has no psychiatric problems. She was an above average student and left school at 16 to go to bible college. This was rather traumatic and she developed symptoms of anorexia nervosa and depression which responded to antidepressant medication. On leaving college she undertook various jobs including care assistant in an old people's home but found regular employment stressful and again suffered a recurrence of her psychiatric symptoms, which on this occasion responded to prayer. She then met her husband, through the church, and they spent much of their time engaged in church activities.

Five years ago they went to the US to work for a religious organisation. After less than a year, Patricia became depressed, cut her wrists and experienced fainting attacks, leading to admission to a psychiatric hospital. She began intensive personal psychotherapy through a Christian organisation. Eighteen months into the therapy, the therapist believed he had uncovered repressed memories of sexual abuse and that her family were members of a satanic cult. Shortly after this, she was diagnosed as suffering from MPD. Subsequently, her other personalities multiplied and she became deeply involved with MPD therapy groups, eventually counselling other patients with MPD. Two years later, her husband and children returned to the UK but Patricia stayed, on the advice of her psychotherapist.

On interview Patricia was a smartly dressed and highly articulate woman. She was able to describe her symptoms clearly and with a normal affective range, but when emotive topics were broached she would begin to dissociate, that is, she would stare blankly, become flushed and visibly restless. If encouraged, this would give way to an alternate personality who might ask to reveal "itself", adopt a new posture, give a different name, talk in a different voice, and proffer a different history. The scenario was highly reminiscent of Thigpen and Cleckley's description of Eve (1957). The alters were most often children, or adults with a violent or sexually active disposition. Similarly, if encouraged not to dissociate, the preferred strategy, she could, with some effort, return to her original state of mind. She described seeing and talking to her alternates and listening to their advice. She had no FRS.

Going through the mental state examination revealed considerable regret at past losses and a sense of isolation. She had few social supports or contacts outside the world of MPD and at times could see little future. When describing her disorder she would sometimes state that the alters were other people within her which, by emerging, could relieve themselves of the

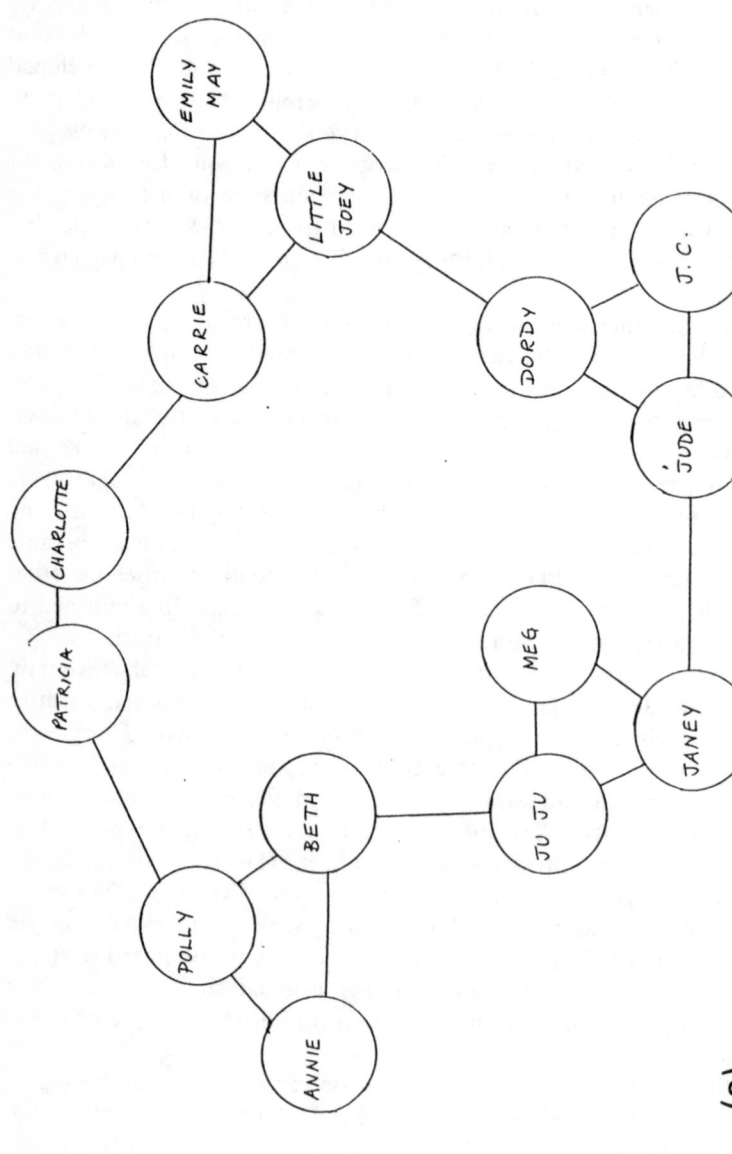

(a)

FIG. 7.1. "Maps" drawn by multiple personality disorder patient, Patricia, of her alters: (a) 1990; (b) 1992; (c) 1993.

She had additional maps of intervening periods and kept these together in a file. It appears that certain personalities occupied a central position in her mind and these in turn have given rise to subsidiary personalities (as indicated by the connecting lines).

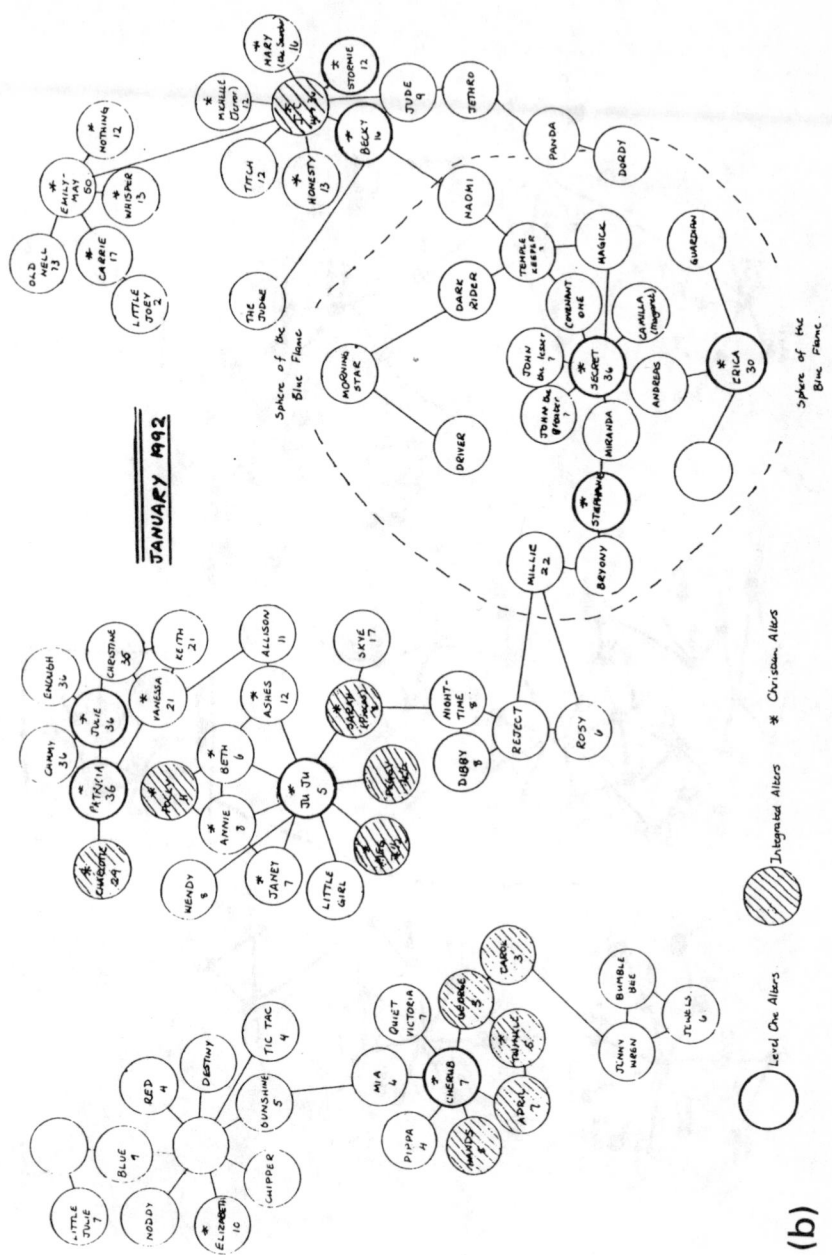

JANUARY 1992

(b)

137

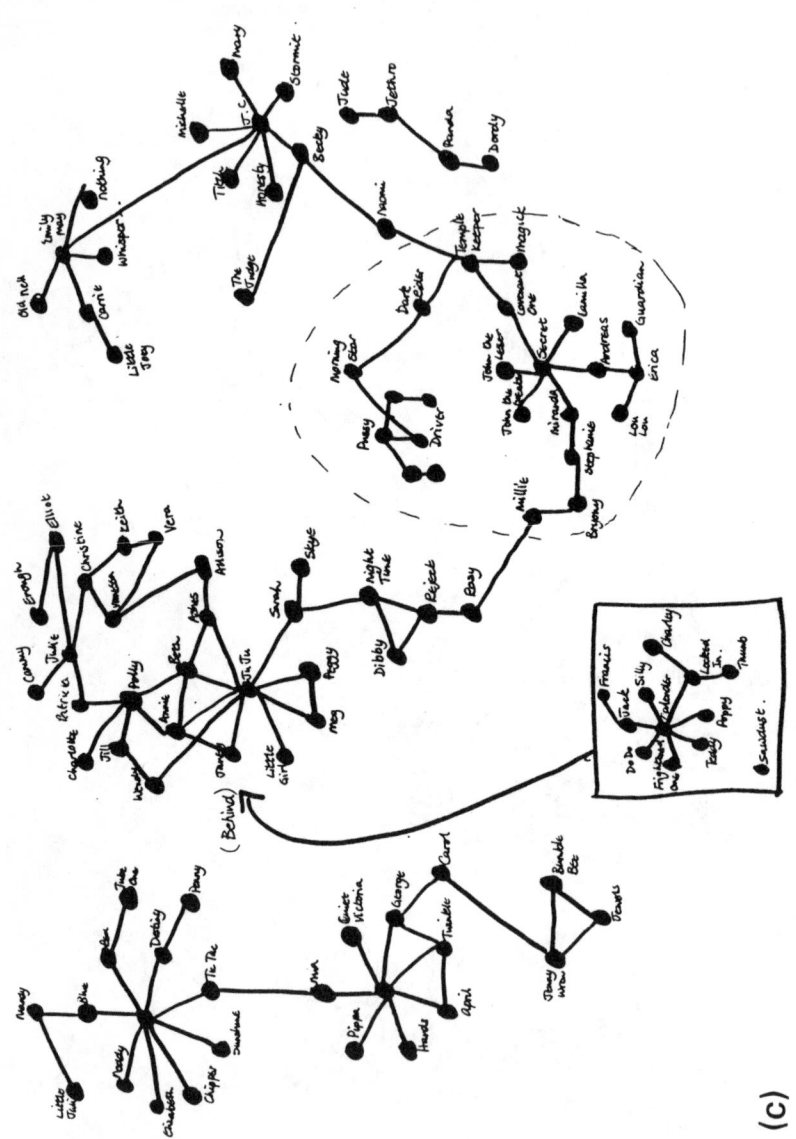

(c)

138

burden of their own distress, and so express feelings, sentiments, and memories which she herself had no access to but which, while hidden, were undermining her happiness and equanimity. On other occasions she could accept, at least for the sake of argument, that the alters were "parts of herself". Discussions such as these stirred up obvious dissonance in the patient and she would often end up confused as to who "she" really was. However, there was never any suggestion or spontaneous report of disembodied auditory-verbal hallucinations and ideas about other persons or beings inhabiting her body. She was "co-conscious" of some of her alters but not others. When these others spoke or acted, Patricia would claim to have been unaware of it and not responsible.

Sessions were often followed by phone calls or correspondence, sometimes in different handwriting and signed by alternate personalities.

Despite her discomfort she accepted a "contract" for her continued treatment, which de-emphasised MPD and concentrated instead on practical help and rebuilding a support network.

Self-report Scales

The DES and Beck Depression Inventory were used (Beck, Ward, Mendelson, Mock, & Erbaugh, 1961). The latter is a self-report scale covering most of the common "cognitive" symptoms of depression such as feelings of guilt, hopelessness and suicidal ideation (higher score = worse depression). Her initial score was 13 (mild depression below clinical cut-off), and 2 after treatment; DES score was high at 42.

Comment

In many ways, Patricia is a classical MPD patient. At no time was a diagnosis of schizophrenia even remotely considered. The major difference between Kate and Patricia was that Kate described someone (or something) that acted upon her that was not a part of her (self) but resided inside her (body). Indeed, it was as though parts of her body were disintegrated from her self. In contrast, Patricia's true, everyday self seemed to recede and her body and voice, still intact, would become the vehicle for another "person". As has been noted before, the personalities of the MPD patient are rather uni-dimensional and tend to have a few obvious attributes. Such attributes tend to be at variance with the "host" individual—that is, childlike as opposed to adult, male not female, violent as opposed to peaceful, and sexually active against sexually inhibited. The complexity of the alters diminishes further as their number increases. Patricia illustrated the multiplication and branching of her personality with diagrams (see Fig. 7.1). It would be hard to conceive of a single mind capable of sustaining dozens of other minds, lives, and relationships, leaving aside the question of whether or not such a feat was intended. Like Kate, Patricia had long periods of unity, although each would have said that the others were still there, "in the background". When acting under the influence of an alter, both would disclaim that the act arose within them. However, in the case of Patricia, the action could be purposeful and coherent, but, to the casual observer, inconsistent or out of character. With Kate, such alien actions (forced upon her by Crunchy) or speeches (produced by Lucinda) were sporadic and would not have been noticed by an observer as unusual. It is only when the characteristic third person address was used—for example, "He thinks you're a nutter and wants to lock you up" (Kate, apparently "talking to herself" but evidently being spoken to by Lucinda following an interview with the psychiatrist)—that the abnormality was detected. (Interestingly, such a statement would be quite typical as an hallucinated utterance reported by a schizophrenic, but heard only by the patient.)

SCHIZOPHRENIA, MULTIPLE PERSONALITIES, SOCIETY, AND CULTURE

The influence of societal norms for acceptable behaviour are much clearer for MPD than schizophrenia. What better way to escape opprobrium than to blame the deed on someone else? Indeed legal defences have been based on these grounds (Lewis & Bard, 1991). Less sinister and uncontroversial are the different presentations of self we all make in everyday life, as described by sociologist, Erving Goffman (1959), or "multiple enactments" outlined by social psychologist, Nicholas Spanos (1994). (See also Banaji & Prentice, 1994 for a review of this field in general.) Indeed, a person presenting a single unvarying persona for all occasions would stand out as being selfish, insensitive, and rigid.

Compare this to the situation in most schizophrenics. Violent acts may be attributed to hallucinated voices issuing commands, the voices themselves are frequently abusive in a way that leads us to suspect that the individual's unpalatable private opinions are being expressed undercover, or "projected" onto the hallucination (Nayani & David, 1996). This has a longer history as the basis for a legal defence and is enshrined in the McNaughton Rules, popularly known as "the insanity defence". However, the schizophrenic patient seldom seems to gain materially from the fragmentation of self, inherent in symptoms of passivity and hallucinations. Certainly, Kate has derived no benefit—if Lucinda expresses ideas Kate has tried to banish, they do not remain banished for long. Overall, Kate has become preoccupied with her "personalities" at the expense of all other human contact except the unwelcome attention of psychiatric services. Talking to yourself (or someone inside you) is the layperson's idea of madness; Kate is known in her neighbourhood as a mad woman and is shown nothing but hostility and taunts. For Patricia, her disorder was the key to a degree of celebrity, the source of a ready-made peer group and even a career. Ultimately, it too was an obstacle to leading a fulfilling life for her and her family.

As early as 1970, Ellenberger noted the possible cultural aspects of MPD. He noted that the first reports of MPD emerged in the 19th century, not long after reports of possession began to decrease. There are at least two types of possession syndrome—lucid and somnambulistic. In lucid possession the subject feels within him- or herself two souls striving against each other. In somnambulistic possession the subject loses consciousness of his or her own self while an intruder takes possession of his or her body and acts and speaks with an individuality of which the subject knows nothing. Possession usually leads to some kind of resolution of a problem—often with the intervention of a healer. Some authors have argued that the possession syndrome and MPD may represent parallel dissociative disorders with similar aetiologies (Adityanjee, Raju, & Khandelwal, 1989; Wijesinghe, Dissanayake, & Mendis, 1976).

How different is the situation in schizophrenia (Table 7.2). First of all, schizophrenia appears to occur with remarkable consistency throughout the developed and less developed world (Jablensky et al., 1992). Of course some schizophrenic patients may also complain of possession (or MPD), but the phenomena are clearly distinct. The ownership of individual actions, thoughts, and inner speeches is disrupted in schizophrenia, not all actions together. Few FRS are the rule, not many. The dominant feeling is that control has been usurped; this comes before the suspicion that there is a usurper. When another thing or individual is held responsible, as in the case of Kate, and begins to attract personal characteristics, these remain fragmentary. They are part selves, part bodies.

What Do MPD and Schizophrenia Tell Us About the Cognitive Structure of the Self?

The symptoms of schizophrenia are consistent with a multi-modular cognitive system, with monitors and feedback loops, which ceases to run smoothly thus exposing its component parts. The unity of conscious experience is widely regarded as an illusion. Neurological "experiments" such as the split-brain and blindsight expose this illusion (David, 1989; Sperry, 1984). The notion of modularity (Fodor, 1983) explicitly rejects it. Psychopathological states cast a different light on the problem. Hysterical fugues or amnesias, and pseudo-hallucinations; conversion disorders such as paralysis, anaesthesia, and loss of consciousness (pseudo-seizures); altered states of awareness, such as depersonalisation; and finally MPD—all are regarded as "dissociative" (after Janet, 1911 and Prince, 1908), meaning some sort of separation of consciousness and perception. These states are

TABLE 7.2
Comparison of Features of Multiple Personality Disorder and Schizophrenia

Feature	Multiple Personality Disorder	Schizophrenia
Gender	F > > M	F = M
World-wide prevalence	Massive variation	remarkable consistency
Incidence over last 30 years	↑↑↑	= or ↓
Relationship to first rank symptoms	dubious	specific but not invariable
Character of auditory hallucinations	2nd person; accompanied by "vision" of speaker	2nd or 3rd person; disembodied, auditory modality
Evidence of altered cerebral structure	−	+ +
Evidence of altered cerebral function	−/+	+
Hereditary	−	+ +
Hypnotisability	+ + +	−
Response to neuroleptic drugs	−	+ +
Influence of culture	largely determined by culture	moderately shaped by it
Influence of suggestion and therapist	+ + +	−
Alters may exist outside subject	−	+
Alters may inhabit parts of body	−	+
Disrupted early life	+ + +	+/−
Subjects' perceived need for treatment	+ +	+/−
Increasing complexity of phenomenology with time	+ +	−
Understandable reaction to life circumstances	+	−
Action not perceived as volitional	+	+ +
Relationship to possession states	+ +	+ +
First convincing description in last century	+	+
Complexity of alters/aliens, etc.	+ + (tend to be stereotypes)	+/− (tend to be fragmentary)
Spectrum of severity	+	+
Nature of experience	Single self taken over by distinct personalities	Fragmented self inhabited or influenced by different selves
Underlying psychopathology	"Dissociation" and neurosis	"Psychosis"

seen as being outside the patient's total control and are not consciously motivated, although supposedly unconscious motives may be discerned. They reveal, above all, not so much the true disunity of consciousness but lay views about the body's operation and the structure of consciousness. The pattern of paralysis and anaesthesia does not respect neurological innervation—whole limbs tend to be affected with sharp cut-offs between the affected and unaffected parts. Hysterical amnesia affects the most salient personal knowledge (name, age, address) because it signifies the person's conflict, yet this information is so deeply embedded that it is rarely affected by neurological amnesia.

So too with MPD. The illusion of unity of consciousness is not exposed in MPD but is repeated over and over again. One illusory consciousness gives way (or joins) another. Each is a coherent autonomous homunculus. It is like an illiterate forger passing off dud bank notes of different denominations but always with the word "pound" mis-spelled. But why do this? As alluded to earlier, we all have the capacity to be (slightly) different people in different circumstances. We are all prey to changes of mood, and perhaps shameful desires. We are used to dissembling. Such skills are necessary to function in a complex society with rules, etiquette and myriad expectations. It seems likely that this familiar *modus operandi* is exaggerated in MPD as a means of dealing with social and interpersonal conflict. What begins as a temporary adaptation becomes fossilised and embellished with additional ingredients provided by popular views of personality and psychoanalysis, and the widespread and unregulated practice of psychotherapy in America. Wider cultural influences such as the emphasis placed on individuality and self-knowledge in American society (Baumeister, 1987), so alien to Eastern societies (Varela, Thompson, & Rosch, 1991) may play a part. Also, the uneasy mixture of secularism and "fundamentalist" traditional religious values has destabilised notions of good and evil. Should sexual and violent thoughts be owned—to use the telling jargon of psychotherapy—or ascribed to forces beyond our control, such as our rearing, the devil, or mental illness?

Neuropsychological disorders which demonstrate dissociations of deficits are valuable in revealing dissociations—in the statistical sense—of functions. Neurological dysfunction may of course coincide with psychological dysfunction, complicating any simplistic organic–functional dichotomy (Ahern, Herring, Tackenberg, Seeger, Oommen, & Labiner; David & Bone, 1985; Rosenstein, 1994). However, psychotic disorders such as schizophrenia are more "neurological"; they are more often associated with abnormalities of brain structure, they occur in all cultures with a relatively stable prevalence, and respond predictably to pharmacological agents. They are less a reflection of prevailing attitudes and culturally specific preoccupations than hysterical and neurotic disorders. When looked at in this way, that is, the cognitive neuropsychiatric approach (David, 1993), they reveal the separability of otherwise opaque cognitive structures, often those which ultimately make us feel human.

REFERENCES

Adityanjee, Raju, G.S.P., & Khandelwal, S.K. (1989). Current status of multiple personality disorder in India. *American Journal of Psychiatry, 146,* 1607–1610.

Ahern, G.L., Herring, A.M., Tackenberg, J., Seeger, J.F., Oommen, K.J., & Labiner, D.M. (1993). The association of multiple personality and temporolimbic epilepsy: Intracarotid amobarbital test observations. *Archives of Neurology, 50,* 1020–1025

American Psychiatric Association (1994). *Diagnostic and statistical manual of mental disorders, DSM-IV* (2nd ed.). Washington, DC: American Psychiatric Association.

Baddeley, A., Thornton, A., Chua, S.E., & McKenna, P. (in press). Delusions and construction of autobiographical memory. In D. Rubin (Ed.), *Autobiographical memory* (2nd ed.). Cambridge: Cambridge University Press.

Banaji, M.R., & Prentice, D.A. (1994). The self in social contexts. *Annual Review of Psychology, 45,* 297–332.

Baumeister, R.F. (1987). How the self became a problem: A psychological review of historical research. *Journal of Personality and Social Psychology, 52,* 163–176

Beck, A.T., Ward, C.H., Mendelson, M., Mock, J., & Erbaugh, J. (1961). An inventory for measuring depression. *Archives of General Psychiatry, 4,* 561–571.

Bernstein, E.M., & Putnam, F.W. (1986). Development, reliability and validity of a dissociation scale. *Journal of Nervous and Mental Disease, 174,* 727–735.

Bleuler, P.E. (1950). *Dementia praecox and the group of schizophrenias* (Trans.). New York: International University Press. (Original work published 1911.)

Chapman, L.J., Chapman, J.P., & Raulin, M.L. (1978). Body image aberration in schizophrenia. *Journal of Abnormal Psychology, 87,* 399–407.

Cutting, J. (1989). Body image disorders: Comparison between unilateral hemisphere damage and schizophrenia. *Behavioural Neurology, 2,* 201–210.

Cutting, J. (1990). *The right cerebral hemisphere and psychiatric disorders.* Oxford: Oxford University Press.

Cutting, J., & Dunne, F. (1989). Subjective experience of schizophrenia. *Schizophrenia Bulletin, 15,* 217–231.

David, A.S. (1989). The split brain syndrome. *British Journal of Psychiatry, 154,* 422–425.

David, A.S. (1990). Insight and psychosis. *British Journal of Psychiatry, 156,* 798–808.

David, A.S. (1993). Cognitive neuropsychiatry? *Psychological Medicine, 23,* 1–5.

David, A.S. (1994a). The neuropsychological origins of auditory hallucinations. In A.S. David & J.C. Cutting (Eds.), *The neuropsychology of schizophrenia.* Hove, UK: Lawrence Erlbaum Associates Ltd.

David, A.S. (1994b). Thought echo reflects the activity of the phonological loop. *British Journal of Clinical Psychology, 33,* 81–83.

David, A.S., & Appleby, L. (1992). Diagnostic criteria in schizophrenia: Accentuate the positive. *Schizophrenia Bulletin, 18,* 551–557.

David, A.S., & Bone, I. (1985). Hysterical paralysis following status epilepticus: Case report and review of the concept. *Journal of Nervous and Mental Disease, 173,* 437–441.

David, A.S., & Lucas, P.A. (1993). Auditory-verbal hallucinations and the phonological loop: A cognitive neuropsychological study. *British Journal of Clinical Psychology, 32,* 431–441.

De Bonis, M., De Boeck, P., Lida-Pulik, H., Bazin, N., Masure, M.-C., & Feline, A. (1994). Person identification and self-concept in the delusional misidentification syndrome. *Psychopathology, 27,* 48–57.

Ellenberger, H. (1970). *The discovery of the unconscious.* New York: Basic Books.

Fabrega, H. (1989). The self and schizophrenia: A cultural perspective. *Schizophrenia Bulletin, 15,* 277–290.

Fahy, T.A. (1988). The diagnosis of multiple personality disorder: A critical review. *British Journal of Psychiatry, 153,* 597–606.

Fahy, T.A., Abas, M., & Brown J.C. (1989). Multiple personality: A symptom of psychiatric disorder. *British Journal of Psychiatry, 154,* 99–101.

Fodor, J.A. (1983). *The modularity of mind.* Cambridge, Mass.: MIT Press.

Frith, C.D. (1987). The positive and negative symptoms of schizophrenia reflect impairments in the perception and initiation of action. *Psychological Medicine, 17,* 631–648.

Goff, D.C., & Simms, C.A. (1993). Has multiple personality disorder remained consistent over time? A comparison of past and recent cases. *Journal of Nervous and Mental Disease, 181,* 595–600.

Goffman, E. (1959). *The presentation of self in everyday life.* New York: Doubleday.

Humphrey, N., & Dennett, D.C. (1989). Speaking for ourselves: An assessment of multiple personality disorder. *Raritan,* 68–98.

Jablensky, A., Sartorius, N., Ernberg, G., Anker, M., Korten, A., & Cooper, J.E. (1992). Schizophrenia: Manifestations, incidence and course in different cultures. A World Health Organization Ten-Country Study. *Psychological Medicine* (Monograph Suppl. 20).

Janet, P. (1911). *L'État Mental des Hystériques.* Paris, France: Alcan.

Keyes, D. (1981). *The minds of Billy Milligan.* New York: Random House.

Kluft, R.P. (1987). First-rank symptoms as a diagnostic clue to multiple personality disorder. *American Journal of Psychiatry, 144,* 293–298.

Kluft, R.P. (1991). Clinical presentations of multiple personality disorder. *Psychiatric Clinics of North America, 14,* 605–629.

Kopelman, M.D., Wilson, B.A., & Baddeley, A.D. (1989). The autobiographical memory interview: A new assessment of autobiographical and personal semantic memory in amnesic patients. *Journal of Experimental and Clinical Neuropsychology, 11,* 724–744.

Krasucki, C., Kemp, R., & David, A. (1995). A case study of female genital self-mutilation in schizophrenia. *British Journal of Medical Psychology, 68,* 179–186.

Laing, R.D. (1961). *The divided self.* Harmondsworth, UK: Penguin Books.

Lewis, D.O., & Bard, J. (1991). Multiple personality and forensic issues. *Psychiatric Clinics of North America, 14,* 741–756.

Merskey, H. (1992). The manufacture of personalities: The production of multiple personality disorder. *British Journal of Psychiatry, 160,* 327–340.

Nayani, T., & David, A.S. (1995). The auditory hallucination: A phenomenological survey. *Psychological Medicine, 26,* 177–189.

Neisser, U. (1988). Five kinds of self-knowledge. *Philosophical Psychology, 1*(1), 35–59.

Nelson, H.E. (1982). *National adult reading test (NART):* Test Manual. Windsor, UK: NFER-Nelson.

Piper, A. (1994). Multiple personality disorder: A review. *British Journal of Psychiatry, 164,* 600–612.

Prince, M. (1908). *The dissociation of a personality* (2nd ed.). London: Longmans Green.

Putnam, F.W., Guroff, J.J., Silberman, E.K., Barban, L., & Post, R.M. (1986). The clinical phenomenology of multiple personality disorder: A review of 100 recent cases. *Journal of Clinical Psychiatry, 47,* 285–293.

Rix, K.J.B., & Snaith, R.P. (Eds.). (1988). The psychopathology of body image. *British Journal of Psychiatry, 153* (Suppl. 2).

Rosenstein, L.D. (1994). Potential neuropsychologic and neurophysiologic correlates of multiple personality disorder. *Neuropsychiatry, Neuropsychology, and Behavioral Neurology, 7,* 215–229.

Ross, C.A. (1991). Epidemiology of multiple personality disorder. *Psychiatric Clinics of North America, 14*, 503–517.

Ross, C.A., Miller, S.D., Reagor, P., Bjornson, L., Fraser, G.A., & Anderson, G. (1990). Schneiderian symptoms in multiple personality disorder and schizophrenia. *Comprehensive Psychiatry, 31*, 111–118.

Schneider, K. (1959). *Clinical psychopathology* (M.W. Hamilton, Trans.). London: Grune & Stratton. (Original work published 1959).

Schreiber, F.R. (1973). *Sybil.* Chicago, Ill.: Henry Regnery.

Shallice, T., & Evans, M.E. (1978). The involvement of frontal lobes in cognitive estimation. *Cortex, 14*, 294–303.

Silva J.A., Leong, G.B., & Luong, M.T. (1989). Split body and self: An unusual case of misidentification. *Canadian Journal of Psychiatry, 34*, 728–730.

Sims, A. (1990). *Symptoms in the mind.* London: Bailliere Tindall.

Spanos, N.P. (1994). Multiple identity enactments and multiple personality disorder: A sociocognitive perspective. *Psychological Bulletin, 116*, 143–165.

Sperry, R.W. (1984). Consciousness, personal identity and the divided brain. *Neuropsychologia, 17*, 153–166.

Steinberg, M., Cicchetti, D., Buchanan, J., Rakfeldt, J., & Rounsaville, B. (1994). Distinguishing between multiple personality disorder (dissociative identity disorder) and schizophrenia using the structured clinical interview for DSM-IV dissociative disorders. *Journal of Nervous and Mental Disease, 182*, 495–502.

Thigpen, C.H., & Cleckley, H.M. (1957). *The three faces of Eve.* New York: Fawcett.

Varela, F.J., Thompson, E., & Rosch, E. (1991). *The embodied mind: Cognitive science and human experience.* Cambridge, Mass.: MIT Press.

Wijesinghe, C.P., Dissanayake, S.A.W., & Mendis, N. (1976). Possession trance in a semiurban community in Sri Lanka. *Australian and New Zealand Journal of Psychiatry, 11*, 93–100.

Wing, J.K., Cooper, J.E., & Sartorius, N. (1974). *The measurement and classification of psychiatric symptoms.* Cambridge, UK: Cambridge University Press.

8 Betwixt Life and Death: Case Studies of the Cotard Delusion

Andrew W. Young
MRC Applied Psychology Unit, Cambridge, UK

Kate M. Leafhead
Department of Psychology, University of Durham, Durham, UK

> *And now I see with eye serene,*
> *The very pulse of the machine;*
> *A being breathing thoughtful breath,*
> *A traveller betwixt life and death*
> William Wordsworth, *She was a Phantom of Delight* (1807)

In the 17th century, Descartes, seeking a firm basis for his philosophy, wanted to ground his views in what was indisputably real. To this end, he invented the method known as Cartesian doubt, in which he resolved to make himself question everything that could possibly be doubted, to see what was left. He began with sense data; could he doubt that he was sitting by the fire in his dressing gown? Yes, he decided, because he could dream he was dressed and by the fire when he was actually naked in bed. By gradual elimination, Descartes arrived at the view that what he could not doubt was his own existence, expressed in the famous argument, *cogito ergo sum*:

> While I wanted to think everything false, it must necessarily be that I who thought was something; and remarking that this truth, *I think, therefore I am*, was so solid and so certain that all the most extravagant suppositions of the sceptics were incapable of upsetting it, I judged that I could receive it without scruple as the first principle of the philosophy that I sought.
> Russell (1961, p. 547)

Yet there are people who doubt their own existence. Though able to walk and talk, they maintain that they do not exist, or that they are dead. Stolk

(1984) gave an example of what he called psychotic depression, in which an 18-year-old youth suddenly realised that the world had changed. He was convinced that he had died, which he found both strange and terrifying. He felt his insides were rotting and that nothing was functioning. He also thought that his mother, uncle, and aunt had died and, although still walking about, they were actually doubles or had risen from the dead. He asked Dr Stolk whether he (Stolk) had ever experienced being dead. He was very anxious and repeatedly tried to commit suicide. He recovered after a few weeks and was profoundly puzzled by his experiences.

Stolk (1984) commented that this psychotic experience may reflect the emotional changes that can occur in severe depression, when some people remark that they can't experience anything any more, as if their emotional life has been paralysed. They make comments to the effect that "I was living dead."

Of course, the notion of the living dead has had a powerful appeal down the centuries, and still exercises the imaginations of people drawn to horror movies and science fiction. But the claim that they are dead made by these depressed patients can be more than a metaphor. In the 18th century, Bonnet had described the case of an elderly lady who probably suffered a stroke (Förstl & Beats, 1992). When she recovered the ability to speak, she demanded to be dressed in a shroud and placed in a coffin, saying that she was already dead. The attempts of her daughter and servants to talk her out of this delusion only made her agitated and annoyed that they would not offer her this last service. Finally, they began to dress her in her shroud and lay her out, to calm her down. The old lady supervised this activity carefully, checking the arrangement of the shroud and the whiteness of the linen. When she fell asleep, she was undressed and put into bed, but on awakening still insisted that she was dead and should be buried. This delusional belief lasted a long time.

The classic reports were by the French psychiatrist, Cotard, who described cases of nihilistic delusions (*le délire de négation*) in which everything could seem so unreal that some of the patients thought they had died (Cotard, 1880, 1882, 1884). This was recognised as of sufficient importance to justify a monograph by Séglas (1897), who adopted Regis's suggestion that it should be known by the eponym "Cotard's syndrome". This has largely replaced Cotard's own use of *le délire de négation* in the modern research literature.

For Cotard, the central feature of these cases was nihilistic delusions. In their milder form, they were characterised by self-deprecation and feelings of despair, and in their most extreme form by a total denial of the self and external world. Cotard therefore believed the delusions could be partial or total, allowing for a continuum of severity with patients falling anywhere in between these two extremes during the course of their illness. For example, some of his patients began by voicing self-deprecatory notions about being responsible for the suffering of others and expressing feelings of guilt and shame. Later, they might start to voice the belief that parts of their bodies were rotting away. Later still, they could claim to be dead and that the world no longer existed or, paradoxically, express feelings of immortality. Cotard also noted that suicidal ideation was frequently present.

The important thing to note is that the common theme is one of negation. While Cotard allowed, indeed insisted upon, the variability of nihilistic delusions, he viewed as essential the presence of negativism and self-accusatory depressive delusions.

The wider implications of such delusions have not gone unremarked. For Enoch and Trethowan (1991, p. 163), "Cotard's syndrome has a complex psychopathology of its own and one which brings us face to face with the very meaning of existence itself." Returning to Descartes, we can see that these delusions are interesting with respect to his question of what it means to say that one exists. At first sight, the patients are bad philosophers, because even though they say that they are dead or do not exist, they maintain that they can think. This looks like *cogito* without *ergo sum*. However, the contradiction may be more apparent than real. What the patients often give as evidence of their non-existence or death is that they don't have proper feelings. But according to Russell (1961), this is actually close to what Descartes had intended, that is, *cogito* should be interpreted not just as "I think" but as "I think and feel":

> "Thinking" is used by Descartes in a very wide sense. A thing that thinks, he says, is one that doubts, understands, conceives, affirms, denies, wills, imagines, and feels
>
> Russell (1961, p. 548)

SYMPTOMS AND SYNDROMES

Over the years, the term "Cotard's syndrome" has become almost synonymous with one of the most striking features found in the nihilistic delusions he described; the belief that one is dead. Cotard himself, however, viewed this belief as present in some severe cases, but not as an essential defining feature. Yet for Enoch and Trethowan (1991, p. 162) "Cotard's syndrome is a rare condition of which the central symptom is a nihilistic delusion which, in its complete form, leads the patient to deny his own existence and that of the external world."

The idea of psychiatric syndromes derives its power from the fact that a basic requirement is an agreed and reliable way of classifying the phenomena encountered. Psychiatrists therefore tend to look for syndromes which are defined by clusters of co-occurring symptoms. Their hope is, of course, that such syndromes will often prove diagnostic of underlying mental illnesses, by analogy with the value of symptom clusters in diagnosing physical illnesses.

However, despite its widespread use in diagnosis, the usefulness of the syndrome concept in psychopathological research has been the subject of much debate in recent years (Costello, 1992). For research purposes, there are many different possible classification systems one might adopt, and these exist at different levels of generality. Rather than starting by trying to relate observations to a wide-ranging but necessarily abstract overall theory, a useful strategy may instead be to try to understand in detail a particular, relatively tightly defined phenomenon, and then see whether one's explanation can be broadened to encompass other observations. This is what we do here, by examining in detail the delusional belief that one is dead.

Similar lines of reasoning have led some authors to propose that research into symptoms is in general likely to prove more informative than is research into syndromes (Costello, 1992). Whilst we are sympathetic to this position, our own view is that what is best depends largely on what one wants to achieve. We accept that syndromes can often have diagnostic usefulness, and that broadly based groupings of cases are needed to support certain types of inference. However, we think that research into the value of explanations involving psychological factors needs to be directed at deficits defined at the same level of generality as the psychological theory employed. Since we are interested in developing and applying specific, detailed psychological models, we have preferred to concentrate on understanding particular symptoms. Here, then, our interest is in understanding psychological factors that can underlie the delusional belief that one is dead, and we use the term "Cotard delusion" as a convenient shorthand for this belief.

Interestingly, when he introduced the eponym, Séglas (1897) did not consider the delusion of being dead to be a syndrome as such, but rather a symptom which could be found in a variety of disorders. This is our own preference. However, the issue of whether the Cotard delusion can be considered to be a distinct syndrome, a symptom arising in a number of mental disorders, or a subtype of depression remains unresolved (Enoch & Trethowan, 1991).

A simple way of looking at the usefulness of the syndrome concept in such cases is to ask which features commonly or necessarily co-occur. To this end, we looked again at the cases in Cotard's (1880, 1882) original reports.

ANALYSIS OF COTARD'S CASE REPORTS

In considering the value of the concept of Cotard's syndrome, we felt that a systematic analysis of Cotard's original case reports was warranted. We have already noted that Cotard allowed for a degree of variability in his cases in terms of symptoms and severity, while noting their common features of the presence of self-accusatory depressive delusions and negativism. However, we were interested in the extent to which these and other features were universally present.

Cotard's first description of nihilistic delusions was presented in a paper read to the Société Médico-Psychologique on 28th June, 1880 (Cotard, 1880). In this paper, Cotard described a single case with key features of what would come to be known as Cotard's syndrome. His patient, Mlle X, denied the existence of God, the devil, and of many parts of her body, and said that she no longer needed to eat. Later, she believed that she was eternally damned because of her failings, and that this was justified punishment, but felt that she could no longer die a natural death, and made repeated suicide attempts. In this report, Cotard (1880) used the phrase "*délire de négation*", but more as a descriptive remark than a name for the problem.

Later, Cotard (1882) presented an extensive case series, in which he divided his cases into three categories. The first category (cases 1–8) involved the purest form in that the patients were not suffering from any other kind of delusion. The second category, represented by a single case (case 9), showed nihilistic delusions as part of a more general debilitating illness. In Cotard's third category (cases 10–11) there were concurrent nihilistic and persecutory delusions. Cotard viewed these as mixed cases, and claimed that patients with these additional delusions of persecution showed several features which differed from those patients with purely nihilistic delusions; for example, they thought of themselves as being possessed rather than damned. In terms of the putative Cotard syndrome, cases 1–8 from this series are the most important, since these were thought to be relatively pure.

To make our analysis as neutral as possible, we began simply by listing all features or symptoms from Cotard's (1882) paper. This list included any symptoms Cotard mentioned in discussion, as well as those from the case reports themselves. In all, this yielded some 31 symptoms, which are listed in Table 8.1. We then scrutinised Cotard's (1882) reports for his eight relatively pure cases, noting which of these symptoms was mentioned for each. Each of the individual symptoms noted for Cotard's eight pure cases is marked in Table 8.1. Note that some of these symptoms did not arise in any of these pure cases; this is usually because the symptoms were noted only in the other cases in Cotard's (1882) report.

As Table 8.1 shows, there is no single symptom which was noted for all eight of Cotard's (1882) pure cases. The most common symptom, though, was self-accusatory depressive delusions (7/8 cases). Also common was repetition of words or phrases (6/8 cases), which may relate to the patients consistently returning to the theme of their delusions. Resistant insanity was also noted in six cases (Cotard used this term to describe a general resistance in patients to any form of personal care, such as getting out of bed in the

TABLE 8.1
List of Symptoms Noted by Cotard (1882), and their Occurrence in his Pure Cases

Symptoms	Case 1	2	3	4	5	6	7	8
General nihilistic delusions								
Negation of others			√	√	√			√
Negation of environment				√	√			
Self-nihilistic delusions								
Negation of self, including denial of whole body	√				√	√	√	√
Belief that one is dead	√							
Immortality/inability to die					√	√		
Self-deprecatory delusions								
Self-accusatory delusions		√	√	√	√	√	√	√
Feelings of guilt	√	√	√			√	√	
Imaginary terrors or fears				√		√		
Belief that one is damned	√				√		√	
Bodily delusions								
Hypochondriacal delusions	√	√				√	√	
Denial of parts of body	√					√	√	√
Putrefaction of body parts							√	
Belief that body smells foul		√						
Changes in body parts	√							√
Metamorphosis					√			
Perceptual abnormalities								
Auditory hallucinations			√	√				
Visual hallucinations	√			√				√
Olfactory hallucinations								
Gustatory hallucinations								
Visual illusions								√
Hyperaesthesia								
Anaesthesia								
Behavioural manifestations								
Suicide attempts/thoughts	√		√		√		√	√
Violence	√							√
Refusal to eat		√	√	√	√			√
Retention of urine and faeces	√				√			
Muscular rigidity	√							
Immobility	√	√	√			√		
Mutism		√	√			√		
Repetition of words/phrases	√	√		√	√		√	√
Resistant insanity	√	√	√	√	√			√

mornings, washing, and so on, and a resistance to any form of help), but this is perhaps unsurprising as it is largely indexed by the patients acting on their delusions. Suicidal thoughts or attempts were fairly common (5/8), but violence directed at others was relatively unusual (2/8 cases, both of whom were also violent towards themselves). Feelings of guilt, negation of self, and denial of bodily parts were each also present in more than half the cases.

Strikingly, although variants of the theme that one was damned, lacking a body, or non-existent were noted fairly commonly, only one of the patients from these eight pure cases voiced the belief that she was herself dead. If we broaden our perspective momentarily to include all the case histories in Cotard's (1882) report, the claim that they had died was mentioned for only 2/11 patients. Whilst saying that one does not exist is in many ways similar to saying that one is dead, for reasons we discuss later we think that the specific claim ("I am dead") is best seen as the individual's attempt to explain to him- or herself what has happened. There will naturally be many different versions of these explanations ("I am dead", "I am damned", "My body has disintegrated", etc.).

For further analysis, the 31 symptoms listed in Table 8.1 were grouped into categories involving six types of symptom. Four of these symptom categories relate to different types of delusional belief, and the other two involve perceptual abnormalities and behavioural manifestations respectively. The first category includes general nihilistic delusions, such as denial of other people's existence or the existence of the external world. The second category involves self-nihilistic delusions, including the superficially paradoxical stance of maintaining that one is immortal or unable to die, while also voicing the belief that one does not exist. Our third grouping, self-deprecatory delusions, includes patients who accuse themselves of having been responsible for crimes they did not commit, world-wide accidents, or famine; guilt, both generalised and specifically emanating from these supposed wrong-doings; imaginary fears related to the supposed wrong-doings and resulting guilt; and, finally, another self-accusatory, guilt-based delusion—the belief that one is damned. The fourth category is bodily delusions, including hypochondriacal delusions, denial of bodily parts, changes in body parts (such as believing that one's head has become hollow), and metamorphosis (believing that one has been transformed into, for example, an animal). A fifth group, perceptual abnormalities, includes hallucinations and gross sensory changes. Finally, in a sixth grouping, we have listed all behavioural manifestations noted by Cotard. These often seem to derive from patients acting on their delusions (e.g. refusing to eat, move, or defecate, on the grounds that they are dead).

Table 8.2 presents a broad analysis, looking only at whether patients show at least one symptom within each of these six groupings (i.e. we consider only whether each patient shows any one of the symptoms

TABLE 8.2
Symptoms Noted for Cotard's (1882) Pure Cases According to Symptom Group

Symptom Group	Case							
	1	2	3	4	5	6	7	8
General nihilistic delusions			√	√	√			√
Self-nihilistic delusions	√				√	√	√	√
Self-deprecatory delusions	√	√	√	√	√	√	√	√
Bodily delusions	√	√			√	√	√	√
Perceptual abnormalities	√		√	√				√
Behavioural manifestations	√	√	√	√	√	√	√	√

belonging to a particular group). As we can see in Table 8.2, there were two symptom groups for which all eight patients experienced at least one symptom; these involve self-deprecatory delusions (group 3) and delusion-related behaviour (group 6). Bodily delusions were shown by 6/8 patients, self-nihilistic delusions by 5/8, and general nihilistic delusions and perceptual abnormalities were each noted in 4/8 cases.

To summarise, there is no specific symptom shown by every one of Cotard's pure cases, and no universally present symptom complex. However, there is a clear pattern in that all of his patients suffered from self-deprecatory delusions, and all showed some form of delusion-related behaviour. Bodily delusions were common but not universal.

This pattern confirms Cotard's original conception of negativistic delusions; *le délire de négation*. However, other symptoms did not inevitably co-occur. It seems to us this gives grounds for arguing that the term "Cotard's syndrome" should be used cautiously; at best, it represents an idealised pattern which in practice is not found even in pure cases. This is consistent with our view that in research we need to investigate such cases in terms of the presence and absence of individual symptoms.

With this in mind, we turn to three cases we have investigated: WI, JK, and KH. We present case histories for each, concentrating wherever possible on details of the patients' accounts of their experiences, and including some information which was not in previously published descriptions.

CASE WI

WI was a 28-year-old man injured in 1989 in a motorcycle accident in the Algerian desert (Young, Robertson, Hellawell, de Pauw, & Pentland, 1992). He was initially comatose, and was transferred by air ambulance to a hospital in Edinburgh. Subsequent assessment revealed a post-traumatic amnesia of three to four weeks duration. Computerised tomography (CT) scans showed contusions affecting temporo-parietal areas of the right cerebral hemisphere and some bilateral frontal lobe damage. At follow-up in 1991, some dilation of the ventricular system was evident on CT and magnetic resonance imaging (MRI) scans, and single photon emission computed tomography (SPECT) showed reduced tracer uptake in the right temporal lobe and adjacent parietal regions.

WI was discharged to outpatient care in January, 1990. Shortly afterwards, his family arranged for him to travel abroad for a period of convalescence. He was referred for ophthalmological assessment upon his return because of a persistent description of visual difficulties. Formal visual field testing in September 1990 demonstrated a left hemianopia with some central field sparing.

For some months after his accident, WI was convinced that he was dead, and experienced difficulties in recognising familiar faces, buildings, and places, as well as feelings of derealisation. The feeling of being dead gradually resolved, but subjective problems in recognising people and feelings of unreality and difficulties in deciding whether events around him were real or just imagined persisted for some time.

Specific complaints made by WI included a lack of familiarity of things he saw, especially buildings and people's faces. For example, he described walking down Lothian Road in Edinburgh, which he knew well: "I didn't recognise the whole, i.e. Lothian Road, and although I knew that the ABC cinema was on the right hand side I did not recognise any of the individual buildings; I thought well maybe they've knocked down the buildings that I used to know and put up new buildings."

These symptoms occurred in the context of more general feelings of unreality and being dead. In January, 1990, after his discharge from hospital in Edinburgh, his mother took him to South Africa. He was convinced that he had been taken to hell (which was confirmed by the heat), and that he had died of septicaemia (which had been a risk early in his recovery), or perhaps from AIDS (he had read a story in *The Scotsman* about someone with AIDS who died from septicaemia), or from an overdose of a yellow fever injection. He thought that he had "borrowed my mother's spirit to show me around hell", and that she was asleep in Scotland.

When first seen for neuropsychological investigation in May, 1990, WI still thought he might be dead, although he was no longer fully convinced of it (he gave a rating of 9 for his degree of belief in his being dead, using a 10-point scale where 0 represented not believing it at all and 10 represented total belief). He continued to fail to recognise some faces and buildings and had feelings of unreality and difficulties in deciding whether events around him were real or just imagined, but all these experiences had become less severe. Formal testing revealed general face-processing difficulties; these involved impairments in the recognition of familiar faces, recognition of facial expressions, matching of unfamiliar faces, and memory for faces.

To explore WI's knowledge of whether other people were alive or dead, he was given a simplified version of Kapur's Dead or Alive Test (Kapur, Young, Bateman, & Kennedy, 1989). The names of 30 famous people were presented, 10 of whom were alive at the time of testing, with the remaining 20 having died between 1960 and 1989. In each case, WI was asked whether the person was alive or dead. For those he thought had died, he was also asked to give the year in which they died (scored as correct if it belonged to the appropriate decade) and whether they were killed or died of natural causes. Table 8.3 shows the performance of WI and eight control subjects matched for age and education (mean age 28 years, SD 2.92 years). For all parts of the test, WI scored as well as the controls. Hence, it is clear that his delusional belief in his own death had not affected WI's general knowledge of whether other people were alive or dead, and was not accompanied by any retrograde amnesia.

Because nihilistic delusions often occur in the setting of a depressive illness, WI was asked to complete the Hospital Anxiety and Depression (HAD) depression scale, a self-assessment instrument developed for detecting depression and anxiety in patients attending general medical clinics (Zigmond & Snaith, 1983). It did seem that for WI the delusion of being dead resolved in parallel with depression. In August, 1990, WI's score of 10 on the HAD scale lay at the upper end of the borderline range, whereas his score of 2 on the anxiety scale was normal. A month later his condition had improved considerably and his depression score dropped to 2.

CASE JK

A 29-year-old woman, JK, was hospitalised five times in four years with episodes of psychotic depression (Young, Leafhead, & Szulecka, 1994). She responded well to electro-convulsive therapy (ECT), but on three occasions developed spells of elated mood following treatment. Her electroencephalogram (EEG) was normal, but a CT scan showed prominent cortical sulci.

TABLE 8.3
Performance of WI on a Simplified Version of Kapur's
Dead or Alive Test

	WI	Controls*	
		Mean	SD
Dead or alive (max = 30)	25	26.00	2.20
Killed or natural causes (max = 20)	16	15.88	2.59
Decade of demise (max = 20)	10	10.38	3.11

* N = 8; control subjects matched for age and education.

When she was most ill, JK claimed that she was dead. She also denied the existence of her mother, and believed that her (JK's) body was going to explode. On one occasion JK described herself as consisting of mere fresh air and on another she said that she was "just a voice and if that goes I won't be anything ... if my voice goes I will be lost and I won't know where I have gone". JK tried to cut her wrists with a pair of bathroom scissors, but her mother stopped her. She said that if no one could help her, she wanted to be put out of her misery.

Earlier during the year, a close friend of the family died; JK described him as having been "like a second father" to her. JK had suffered a previous episode of depression a few years before, following the death of her father from cancer. She was then admitted to hospital where she believed she "died partially" and "never really recovered".

Like Cotard's patients, JK experienced self-deprecatory delusions. She thought that she had perpetrated some act for which people were suffering, although she could not specify the nature of his act. She believed that she was responsible for bad weather and accidents world-wide because she could predict their occurrence. She was worried that she had done things for which her mother would get into trouble but, again, could not specify the nature of these wrong-doings. She felt particularly guilty about having claimed social security benefits (to which she was fully entitled) on the grounds that she was dead while she was claiming. JK was extremely worried about getting into trouble about this and no amount of reassurance would convince her that she had done nothing wrong.

JK felt frightened, confused, and guilty. At times she said that she was not human and even asked her mother if she had really given birth to her. She complained about feelings of derealisation, saying that although she could see people, objects, and her surroundings, "nothing feels real". She felt that she saw people and objects as outlines or shadows only, while remaining able somehow to perceive their features.

As was found for WI, formal testing showed that JK experienced general face-processing difficulties, with impaired recognition of familiar faces and facial expressions, and poor ability to match or remember unfamiliar faces.

JK's unusual experiences were not confined to vision; she explained that when she went to bed at night she did not feel comfortable, owing to the fact that her body felt strange. Her subjective experience of eating was similarly unreal; she felt as though she were 'just placing food in the atmosphere", rather than into her body. She would not eat, get up in the morning, bath, dress, etc., without being coerced. She reported being scared to do these things. She was similarly scared of urinating and defecating, saying "I don't know if my bowels work."

We wanted to know whether the fact that JK had thoughts and feelings (however abnormal) struck her as being inconsistent with her belief that she was dead. We therefore asked her, during the period when she claimed to be dead, whether she could feel her heart beat, whether she could feel hot or cold, and whether she could feel when her bladder was full. She said she could. We suggested that such feelings surely represented evidence that she was not dead, but alive. JK said that since she had such feelings even though she was dead, they clearly did not represent evidence that she was alive. She said she recognised that this was a difficult concept for us to grasp and one which was equally difficult for her to explain, partly because the experience was unique to her and partly because she did not fully understand it herself.

We then asked JK whether she thought we would be able to feel our hearts beat, to feel hunger, and so on if we were dead. JK said that we wouldn't, and repeated that this experience was unique to her; no one else had ever experienced what she was going through. However, she eventually agreed that it "might be possible". Hence, JK recognised the logical inconsistency between someone's being dead and yet remaining able to feel and think, but thought that she was none the less in this state. JK found this conversation very unsettling, possibly because it had presented a challenge to her delusional belief system.

Later in the course of her illness, JK no longer believed she was dead, but was frightened to go to sleep at night in case she died during her sleep. She felt that her father and the recently deceased family friend were willing her to join them, and she was frightened of experiencing death again. At the beginning of her illness, JK had denied the existence of her mother. Once she no longer believed she was dead, she voiced beliefs that her mother and brother had changed and were no longer the people they were before.

JK was by now able to talk about what she had felt at the time when she believed she was dead. She claimed that she had still been able to feel her heart beat and that her sense of hearing, smell, and taste had all been relatively normal. She said, however, that her vision and her sense of touch had been unusual; "things just didn't feel right". These unusual feelings remained long after the delusion had remitted.

When JK began to recover, she seemed to be aware of a distinction between reality and delusion. This distinction became rather blurred, however, when she discussed how she perceived and interpreted her experiences while suffering the Cotard delusion and how she viewed them once she had stopped believing she was dead. JK showed only superficial appreciation of the fact that when she was floridly ill she had been, in fact, deluded. After her Cotard delusion had resolved, we held a further conversation with JK about what it means to be dead. She said that "when you're dead, you're dead—that's it", but when questioned again about possible bodily sensations after death, she now believed that because it had happened to her it must be possible to feel one's heart beat. Such views reinforced the impression that her understanding of having been deluded was still not complete. It transpired that she was in a dilemma: "I want to understand what's happened, but I'm scared of what the truth is. Either none of this has happened and I am mad or all of it has happened and I did die. Either way I can't win. I don't want to know which one it is. I'm scared of finding out."

JK scored very highly on a scale of Magical Ideation (Eckblad & Chapman, 1983), on which high scores have also been found for people with other types of delusion (Kaney & Bentall, 1989). In this test 30 statements are presented for the person to agree or disagree with. These statements include "I have had the momentary feeling that I might not be human" and "I think I could learn to read others' minds if I wanted to". JK answered in the affirmative to these and other similar questions, scoring 17 out of a possible 30. This is a very high score; the average magical ideation score for Eckblad and Chapman's (1983) subjects was less than 3. Note, though, that JK did not score 30/30. That is to say, she was not simply going along with any idea put to her, but carefully considered the relevance of each statement to her.

One of us visited JK about a year and a half later. She was now attending a day centre four days a week and receiving reduced medication with a view to cessation of drug treatment altogether. When asked if she could now account for her beliefs at the time she was ill, she said "It was just me that changed."

When JK was questioned about her views on what happens when you die, these had altered radically from some 18 months previously. She now held the sorts of views which many religious people hold. She said she believed in a heaven, where she believed she would "meet Dad again", although she was not sure about the existence of a hell. She also believed reincarnation was possible, but was not sure what form it would take.

When asked about whether she could make predictions about events, JK said she could. These predictions, however, turned out to be the sorts of predictions made by people every day. For example, she referred to her prediction that the collieries would close. Many people in Britain predicted the same; the difference seems to be that while JK believed this is a fairly unusual thing to be able to do, most of us accept such predictions to be part of everyday life. When asked about more fantastic predictions, however, JK laughed. Without reminding her that when she was ill she had told us that she could predict the weather, we asked her if she felt this was something she could do. She laughed and said "Oh blimey no, I couldn't do something like that!"

JK completed the Magical Ideation Scale again, to see whether her altered views would be reflected in her score. She scored 10/30 on this occasion, which is less than on the previous testing, but still higher than the norm, indicating that JK still held some unusual beliefs. For example, she agreed with the statement "Some people can make me aware of them just by thinking about me", believed that numbers like 7 and 13 had special powers, and disagreed with the statement "I have never doubted that my dreams are the product of my own mind".

Like WI, JK's delusion of being dead resolved in parallel with her depression. Her HAD depression score (Zigmond & Snaith, 1983) was 17 when she was first seen, and this reduced to 0 on long-term follow-up. Her anxiety also reduced, from a score of 15 to 6 (which is within the normal range) at long-term follow-up.

CASE KH

KH was a 35-year-old unemployed man who lived on his own, separated from his wife. He was admitted to hospital with presenting symptoms of severe depression (Wright, Young, & Hellawell, 1993). Prior to admission, KH had suffered mood-incongruent persecutory delusions (believing his family were plotting to harm him) and episodes of confusion in which he was disorientated in time and place.

On admission, KH was anxious and agitated. He appeared perplexed and stated everything seemed distant to him. He was verbally hostile and lacked insight, saying he did not know why he was in hospital. He was fully conscious and alert, and at this time was fully oriented. Physical and neurological examinations revealed no obvious abnormalities.

KH underwent routine venepuncture, after which he left the ward and was later returned by his family, extremely agitated and stating that he was dead. He claimed that he had no blood in him; his family had sent for an ambulance when, to prove that he had no blood, he stabbed himself in the arm with a kitchen knife and threatened to cut off his thumb.

KH's delusion of being dead lasted for several days, but resolved on treatment with chlorpromazine. When more settled he gave a history of olfactory hallucinations, believing that he could smell tinned peaches prior to admission, and stated his belief that he was dead was a result of him "feeling nothing inside". When readmitted after stabbing himself he also failed to recognise familiar people and his surroundings, which he later felt had increased his certainty in his demise.

The history from the family revealed that KH had been increasingly depressed and withdrawn over the three months prior to admission. There was no personal or family history of mental or neurological disorder, and no history of drug abuse, although he drank to moderate excess (consuming 10–12 units of alcohol three–four times per week).

An EEG two weeks after admission supported the clinical suspicion of complex partial seizures of temporal lobe origin. CT without contrast was normal. Routine haematological, biochemical, and serological examinations showed no abnormality.

At this time, KH was also given neuropsychological tests of face processing. He was now able to recognise familiar faces, match pictures of unfamiliar faces, and recognise facial expressions of emotion, although he was very slow and hesitant at this. On a test of recognition memory for words and faces (Warrington, 1984), however, KH showed normal recognition memory for words (44/50 correct) but impaired recognition memory for faces (33/50 correct).

This is KH's account of his experiences when he thought that he had died:

I woke up at about 4 o'clock in the morning, and I knew that I had to get up, so I went downstairs and put the gas fire on. I could smell a funny smell, like tinned peaches, it was everywhere. I had a cup of tea and then I turned the fire off and went back up to bed, but I had to get up again—I felt light-headed and like I was floating. It didn't seem real. I phoned my ex-wife and we talked about it and sorted it out. I started hallucinating—I saw my wife's face, my mother-in-law and my eldest son's faces like squares down the side of the windows. They brought me in to hospital and when I woke up my mum and dad were here saying I was in hospital, but I didn't believe it because there were no white coats. And then my mother-in-law and my wife came and I thought that it must be heaven or hell, and I thought it was hell because there was all these people I'd said awful things to. At first, I wouldn't eat—I was saying it was false food and when I tried to drink it tasted horrible, so I wouldn't drink for two days. Then they were trying to keep me in, locked in so it seemed like I couldn't get out so I thought I must be dead.

One day I went out for a walk, right round town and ended up at my mother-in-law's and said to her "I'm dead" and started stabbing at my arm to try and get some blood out. It wouldn't bleed so I was saying "Look, I must be dead—there's no blood". They brought me back into hospital and I didn't know where it was—I didn't recognise anybody and they said I'd been here but I was very confused. All these people kept visiting me and it was like walking on air—it didn't feel real. After a while I realised that I was in hospital and I wasn't dead—the doctors know what's wrong with me and I respond well to the drugs.

KH settled well on low dose haloperidol and carbamazepine and was discharged home. However, the next month he was readmitted following an overdose, which seemed to be a response to lowered mood and anxiety. When his mood lifted he was again discharged, only to be readmitted some three months later with paranoid delusions that white cars were following him, that people in general were out to harm him, that the television and radio were talking about him, and that his father had been replaced by an impostor. He also believed that ward staff previously well known to him from previous admissions had been replaced by "dummies" that were out to get him, and that some of the staff were in fact members of the police who were in disguise. He claimed once again to be able to smell tinned peaches, and described people laughing aloud in his ear.

On this admission KH was severely agitated and tried to hang himself, and he was therefore detained under the Mental Health Act. There was no sign of any prolonged prodrome of lowered mood, and no evidence of the Cotard delusion. A repeat EEG was similar to the previous recording, with maximal sharp activity over the anterior temporal and frontal regions.

PROMINENT CLINICAL FEATURES

The cases described above, and especially JK, show obvious similarities to Cotard's patients. If we felt able to accept the idea of Cotard's syndrome, then JK would be a textbook case, and KH came close to this. However, WI only showed some of the features of the putative Cotard syndrome; self-nihilistic delusions, perceptual abnormalities, and somewhat limited bodily delusions. Yet all three patients, JK, KH, and WI, were at one time or another convinced they had died.

Again, then, it is clear that the syndrome concept is not very helpful. Even WI, who only showed part of the syndrome, was convinced he had died. Similarly, comparison of these three cases demonstrates that believing oneself to be dead is not simply a symptom found in the most severe cases; WI thought he was dead even though his associated symptoms were much less severe than those noted for JK.

However, this is not to say that there are no underlying similarities between these cases. On the contrary, we are very struck by the consistent combination of depressed mood, abnormal feelings, depersonalisation and derealisation, and evidence of face-processing impairments, which we will now seek to explain.

Face-processing Impairments, and the Link to the Right Hemisphere

The presence of face-processing impairments was a serendipitous finding which initially resulted from formal testing of WI because he complained of problems in recognising buildings and people's faces. Use of the same tests with JK and KH also revealed impairments of face processing, and especially memory for faces.

Memory for faces was tested with Warrington's (1984) Recognition Memory Test. This involves the presentation of 50 photographs of faces of unfamiliar people for three seconds each, whilst the person being tested performs an orienting task of deciding whether each face is "pleasant" or "unpleasant". Recognition memory for the faces is then assessed immediately, by working through a booklet of 50 pairs of face photographs. One member of each pair is a face from the original series; the task is to choose this face. An equivalent test using printed words as stimuli is also available. However, data concerning WI's recognition memory for words are not presented here, because he was given the two parts of the test at very different dates.

Table 8.4 summarises the performance of WI (Young et al., 1992), JK (Young et al., 1994), and KH (Wright et al., 1993) on recognition memory for faces and words. Their performances are expressed as a raw score for the number of items correct on each task, and converted to a z-score representing the number of standard deviations that this lies below the mean for Warrington's (1984) age-matched controls. In addition, mean scores for groups of brain-injured patients with right hemisphere lesions ($n = 134$) and left hemisphere lesions ($n = 145$) reported by Warrington (1984) are shown for comparison.

As Table 8.4 shows, severe impairments of recognition memory for faces were found in all three of our cases. These impairments led to scores which were even below the mean for patients with right hemisphere brain injuries. In marked contrast, recognition memory for words remained entirely normal for JK and KH, for whom faces and words were tested in the same session. For WI, this face-recognition impairment occurred in the context of

TABLE 8.4

Performance of WI (Young et al., 1992), JK (Young et al., 1994), and KH (Wright et al., 1993) on Warrington's (1984) Recognition Memory Test

	Faces		Words	
	Accuracy	*z*	*Accuracy*	*z*
WI	28	4.41***		
JK	35	2.45**	45	0.21
KH	33	2.99**	44	0.40
Right hemisphere lesions	39.7		44.6	
Left hemisphere lesions	41.8		39.9	

Mean scores for Warrington's (1984) groups of brain-injured patients with right hemisphere lesions ($n = 134$) and left hemisphere lesions ($n = 145$) are shown for comparison. Accuracy score out of maximum possible of 50 correct, z = number of SDs below control mean; asterisked scores are significantly below the control mean: ** $z > 2.33$, $P < 0.01$; *** $z > 3.10$, $P < 0.001$.

well-preserved knowledge of other people and, interestingly, he showed no confusion about whether famous people were alive or dead, or when and how they had died.

These findings of defective memory for faces point to a link between the Cotard delusion and right hemisphere disease. This seems obvious enough for WI, who had suffered right brain injury, but even when there was little other evidence of asymmetric organic impairment, as with JK, there was a pattern of impaired recognition memory for faces and normal recognition memory for words.

We must ask whether these impairments found on neuropsychological tests of face processing were coincidental, or played some form of causal role in the creation of the delusion. It seems to us unlikely that they were a sufficient cause of the Cotard delusion. Many people with brain injuries can perform just as badly on tests of face processing without thinking that they are dead. Moreover, face-processing impairments were found even when our Cotard delusion patients were no longer fully convinced by their delusional beliefs.

However, the fact that the face-processing impairments are not in themselves sufficient to cause the delusions does not imply that they are irrelevant. Instead, we think that recognition failures and the consequent lack of familiarity of seen things could certainly have contributed to the delusion by heightening feelings of unreality. This leads us to consider further the roles of abnormal feelings, depersonalisation, and derealisation.

Abnormal Feelings, Depersonalisation, and Derealisation

Feelings of lack of emotional responsiveness, unreality of events, detachment from the world, strangeness, and unfamiliarity were prominent clinical features in our cases, and they frequently crop up in other reports of the delusion of being dead or preoccupation with death (Drake, 1988; Greenberg, Hochberg, & Murray, 1984; Joseph & O'Leary, 1986). Even so, we think that their significance is often underestimated.

Enoch and Trethowan (1991) argued that depersonalisation ("I feel as if I am dead") needs to be distinguished from the Cotard delusion ("I am dead"), but we think there is a marked overlap between these phenomena. Our cases did not show such a clear qualitative difference, but rather a progression from a delusional conviction of their own deceasedness to greater insight as the condition resolved. All three patients alluded to their feelings of depersonalisation and derealisation as contributing substantially to their belief that they had died.

Whilst we therefore do not agree with Enoch and Trethowan's (1991) sharp demarcation of depersonalisation from the Cotard delusion, it is again clear that abnormal feelings, depersonalisation, and derealisation cannot in themselves be a sufficient cause of the Cotard delusion. As we noted with face-processing impairments, a lack of emotional responsiveness and feelings of depersonalisation and derealisation are experienced by many people who do not then draw the conclusion that they have died. A full explanation must, at a minimum, involve some further factor. We therefore turn to consider the role of depressed mood, and offer an account in terms of attribution theory.

AN ATTRIBUTION HYPOTHESIS

Modern accounts of depression owe much to Beck's insight that severe depressive reactions often occur in people who already have a negative cognitive set, consisting of negative views of themselves, the external world, and the future (Beck, 1967, 1989). According to Beck, memories of previous negative events are coded as schemas that are activated when similar events are subsequently experienced, and that influence the way these later events are interpreted. Depressive schemas tend to view the self as defective, the external world as composed of insuperable difficulties, and the future as hopeless. The activation of such schemas is thought to be automatic, and often non-conscious in the sense that we no longer remember where they've come from. Beck argues that such schemas lead depressed people to perpetuate their negative thoughts in various ways, including making arbitrary inferences on the basis of insufficient evidence (for example, thinking you are a failure because your cooker broke on the day you invited friends for dinner) and selective abstraction from one of many elements in a complex picture (for example, thinking that your employers went bankrupt because you personally did not work hard enough).

Studies of depressed people have shown that they do indeed tend to attribute the cause of negative events to themselves, instead of elsewhere. This holds even for purely hypothetical events. For example, if given the statement "You go out on a date and it goes badly", and asked what might cause such a thing if it were to happen to you, depressed people are likely to offer reasons which involve blaming themselves (Peterson, Semmel, von Baeyer, Abramson, Metalsky, & Seligman, 1982).

Ever since the original reports, the presence of severe depression has been consistently found in patients with the Cotard delusion. Moreover, we noted that the most common symptom for Cotard's pure cases was self-accusatory depressive delusions. Although correlations do not always imply direct causation, the impression that depression plays an important role in the Cotard delusion is strengthened by the observation that for all three of our cases, the delusion of being dead resolved in line with improvements in the patient's depressed mood.

Now we are able to put together the different contributory components of face-processing impairments, abnormal feelings, derealisation, and depressed mood. The simplest way of making this link is to conclude that the delusion of being dead is a misinterpretation of abnormal perceptual experiences in which things seem strange and unfamiliar. Their depressed mood leads the patients to exaggerate the negative effects of these perceptual changes whilst correctly attributing the changes to themselves.

This hypothesis fits exactly our sense of the patients' struggling to come to terms with and understand powerfully anomalous experiences, so strikingly conveyed in their descriptions of what happened. What they say does not seem to us thought disordered, illogical, or otherwise devoid of content, and their accounts were far from arbitrary; they contain several highly consistent details. Moreover, for all three of our cases, the delusion that they had died was only held with full conviction for a while, and then replaced by other attempts to explain what had happened to them. Certainly, it can be argued that even so it represented an extravagant and unlikely hypothesis, but it is none the less one which is consistent with other features noted in depressive delusions.

Our view, then, is that the Cotard delusion represents a depressed person's attempt to account for abnormal perceptual experiences. It follows that the delusion is based on an unfortunate interaction between different contributory factors. One set of factors creates the abnormal perceptual experiences, which are characterised by lack of emotional responses and feelings of emptiness, and derealisation. The other factors result in a misinterpretation of these perceptual changes, in which the patients' depressed moods lead them correctly to attribute the changes to themselves, but to exaggerate their consequences. It is also apparent that at the time that they were deluded, our patients were willing to entertain more unrealistic hypotheses than they would normally; for example, JK's score on the Magical Ideation Scale (Eckblad & Chapman, 1983) became less abnormal as her delusions resolved. From this perspective, the appropriate research agenda therefore involves identifying the roles of these various contributory factors, not looking for *the* cause of the Cotard delusion.

An obvious corollary of this hypothesis is that, if the Cotard delusion results from an interaction of different factors, it is likely to be modified or dropped if there is a change in any of the contributory components. We have used this to explore the link between the Cotard delusion and delusional misidentification; in particular, the Capgras delusion.

The Capgras delusion involves the belief that one's close relatives have been replaced by impostors (Capgras & Reboul-Lachaux, 1923). At first sight, this seems to have little to do with the Cotard delusion, except that they both involve bizarre claims about existence (for self or others). On closer examination, however, there are other parallels. Both delusions can be produced by broadly similar types of brain injury. For example, for WI, the Cotard delusion followed contusions affecting temporo-parietal areas of the right cerebral hemisphere and some bilateral frontal lobe damage (Young et al., 1992). A similar pattern has been associated with the Capgras delusion (Alexander, Stuss, & Benson, 1979; Lewis, 1987), and right hemisphere dysfunction has been shown even in cases of Capgras delusion without readily demonstrable brain injury (Ellis, de Pauw, Christodoulou, Papageorgiou, Milne, & Joseph, 1993).

There are also similarities in the cognitive difficulties experienced. Difficulties in face processing and feelings of derealisation are often noted in Capgras cases (Christodoulou, 1977; Young, Reid, Wright, & Hellawell, 1993). Furthermore, the fact that people experiencing the Cotard delusion often report that they must be dead because they "feel nothing inside" provides a parallel with a widely hypothesised lack of affective reactions in Capgras cases (Anderson, 1988; Ellis & Young, 1990; Lewis, 1987). Young et al. (1992) therefore suggested that the underlying pathophysiology and neuropsychology of the Cotard and Capgras delusions may be related.

This suggestion of a link between the Capgras and Cotard delusions is also strengthened by the fact that cases of coexistent or sequential Capgras and Cotard delusions have been described (Bleeker & Sno, 1983; Enoch & Trethowan, 1991; Förstl, Almeida, & Iacoponi, 1991; Joseph, 1986; Kim, 1991). Recall that Stolk's (1984) patient not only thought that he had died, but that his mother, uncle, and aunt were doubles or had risen from the dead. In our present cases, both JK and KH showed symptoms involving delusional misidentification. JK thought that her mother and brother had changed and were no longer the people they were before. KH thought that his father had been replaced by an impostor, that ward staff had been replaced by dummies, and that some of the staff were disguised members of the police force. For both JK and KH, delusional misidentifications occurred after they were no longer convinced they were dead.

A clue to how this could happen comes from studies which have shown that while depressed people tend to attribute negative events to internal causes, people with persecutory delusions attribute them to external causes (Candido & Romney, 1990; Kaney & Bentall, 1989). The relevance of this is that it is quite common for delusional misidentification to arise in a context of persecutory delusions and suspiciousness (Fleminger, 1992; Fleminger & Burns, 1993), and this was certainly a prominent feature for KH when he experienced the Capgras delusion. The persecutory delusions and suspiciousness that are often noted in Capgras cases may therefore contribute to the patients mistaking a change in themselves for a change in others ("they must be impostors"), whereas people who are depressed exaggerate the negative effects of a similar change whilst correctly attributing it to themselves ("I must be dead"). Although the Capgras and Cotard delusions are phenomenally distinct, we thus think that they represent patients' attempts to make sense of fundamentally similar experiences.

This attributional account of the Capgras and Cotard delusions also helps us to understand delusion-related violence. In the Capgras cases, the altered perception is externalised. So too is violence; some patients suffering from the Capgras delusion threaten or actually harm the supposed impostors (de Pauw & Szulecka, 1988; Silva, Leong, & Weinstock, 1992). In the Cotard delusion, on the other hand, where an internal attribution is made for the perceptual anomaly, violence is directed toward the self.

At first sight it appears paradoxical that people who say they are dead should try to kill themselves. The resolution to this paradox is that, as we have shown, Cotard delusion patients believe that though they are dead, they are in a unique situation of still having thoughts and feelings. Suicide may therefore represent an attempt to end their discomfort. Additionally, some patients suffering from the Cotard delusion may indulge in forms of self-injurious behaviour which are not suicide attempts. For example, KH cut his arm not in order to kill himself, but to prove that he had no blood in his veins.

TRIBUTE

Cotard died from diphtheria at the untimely age of 49, after nursing one of his children to recovery. Although now best known for his papers on nihilistic delusions, the collected works published after his death show that he had wide-ranging interests in brain disease and mental illness (Cotard, 1891).

Here, we have set out an approach to the Cotard delusion which treats it as representing the patient's attempt to make sense of abnormal perceptual experiences in which things seem strange and unfamiliar. This approach puts the patients' accounts of their experiences back into a prominent position among the facts needing explanation, but it can also deal with more objective data and incorporate otherwise puzzling anomalies, such as the link to delusional misidentification.

We see this as an extension of Cotard's own line of reasoning, since we find that his original conception of *le délire de négation* fits our observations better and has greater explanatory and heuristic value than the more widely adopted idea of the Cotard syndrome. We are enormously impressed that many of the points we have made were already made or anticipated by Cotard (1882), though they seem to have been long-forgotten in the research literature. Cotard (1880) commented that there was a kind of logic to the delusions, and in 1884 he also noted the presence of a loss of visual imagery in some of his patients (Cotard, 1884). Loss of visual imagery is a frequent concomitant of visual recognition impairments, and Cotard's mentor, Charcot, had recently described such a case (Charcot & Bernard, 1883; Young & van de Wal, 1996). Considering this to be more than a coincidence, Cotard (1884) suggested that the delusions reflected a misinterpretation of this change. Even the combination of the specific delusions of being dead oneself and having one's relatives replaced by impostors is hinted at in his reports. As well as experiencing nihilistic delusions, case 4 in Cotard's (1882) series had claimed that her daughter was a devil in disguise, and didn't recognise her husband and children when they visited (though Cotard implied that she may not have recognised her husband and children because she no longer believed in their existence).

Most impressive of all, Cotard's (1882) classic paper ends with a very thorough table listing the parallels and differences between delusions of negation and delusions of persecution. This table gives a version of the attribution hypothesis, in which Cotard points out that in delusions of persecution "Le malade s'en prend au monde extérieur", whereas in delusions of negation "Le malade s'accuse lui-même". More than a hundred years later, we can only endorse this insight, which we consider central to understanding these delusions.

ACKNOWLEDGEMENTS

We gratefully acknowledge the support provided by a grant from the EJLB Foundation (AY) and an MRC Research Studentship (KL).

REFERENCES

Alexander, M.P., Stuss, D.T., & Benson, D.F. (1979). Capgras syndrome: A reduplicative phenomenon. *Neurology, 29*, 334–339.

Anderson, D.N. (1988). The delusion of inanimate doubles: Implications for understanding the Capgras phenomenon. *British Journal of Psychiatry, 153*, 694–699.

Beck, A.T. (1967). *Depression: Clinical, experimental, and theoretical aspects.* New York: Harper & Row.

Beck, A.T. (1989). *Cognitive therapy and the emotional disorders.* Harmondsworth, UK: Penguin.

Bleeker, J.A.C., & Sno, H. (1983). Het syndroom van Cotard: een herwaardering aan de hand van twee patienten met een onsterfelijkheidswaan. *Tijdschrift voor Psychiatrie, 25*, 665–675.

Candido, C.L., & Romney, D.M. (1990). Attributional style in paranoid vs. depressed patients. *British Journal of Medical Psychology, 63*, 355–363.

Capgras, J., & Reboul-Lachaux, J. (1923). L'illusion des "sosies" dans un délire systématisé chronique. *Bulletin de la Société Clinique de Médicine Mentale, 11*, 6–16.

Charcot, J.-M., & Bernard, D. (1883). Un cas de suppression brusque et isolée de la vision mentale des signes et des objets (formes et couleurs). *Le Progrès Médical, 11*, 568–571.

Christodoulou, G.N. (1977). The syndrome of Capgras. *British Journal of Psychiatry, 130*, 556–564.

Costello, C.G. (1992). Research on symptoms versus research on syndromes: Arguments in favour of allocating more research time to the study of symptoms. *British Journal of Psychiatry*, *160*, 304–308.

Cotard, J. (1880). Du délire hypocondriaque dans une forme grave de la mélancolie anxieuse. *Annales Médico-Psychologiques*, *38*, 168–170.

Cotard, J. (1882). Du délire des négations. *Archives de Neurologie*, *4*, 152–170, 282–295.

Cotard, J. (1884). Perte de la vision mentale dans la mélancolie anxieuse. *Archives de Neurologie*, *7*, 289–295.

Cotard, J. (1891). *Études sur les maladies cérébrales et mentales* (Ed. by J. Falret). Paris, France: Baillière.

de Pauw, K.W., & Szulecka, T.K. (1988). Dangerous delusions: Violence and the misidentification syndromes. *British Journal of Psychiatry*, *152*, 91–97.

Drake, M.E.J. (1988). Cotard's syndrome and temporal lobe epilepsy. *Psychiatric Journal of the University of Ottawa*, *13*, 36–39.

Eckblad, M., & Chapman, L.J. (1983). Magical ideation as an indicator of schizotypy. *Journal of Consulting and Clinical Psychology*, *51*, 215–225.

Ellis, H.D., de Pauw, K.W., Christodoulou, G.N., Papageorgiou, L., Milne, A.B., & Joseph, A.B. (1993). Responses to facial and non-facial stimuli presented tachistoscopically in either or both visual fields by patients with the Capgras delusion and paranoid schizophrenics. *Journal of Neurology, Neurosurgery, and Psychiatry*, *56*, 215–219.

Ellis, E.D., & Young, A.W. (1990). Accounting for delusional misidentifications. *British Journal of Psychiatry*, *157*, 239–248.

Enoch, M.D., & Trethowan, W.H. (1991). *Uncommon psychiatric syndromes* (3rd ed.). Oxford: Butterworth-Heinemann.

Fleminger, S. (1992). Seeing is believing: The role of "preconscious" perceptual processing in delusional misidentification. *British Journal of Psychiatry*, *160*, 293–303.

Fleminger, S., & Burns, A. (1993). The delusional misidentification syndromes in patients with and without evidence of organic cerebral disorder: A structured review of case reports. *Biological Psychiatry*, *33*, 22–32.

Förstl, H., Almeida, O.P., & Iacoponi, E. (1991). Capgras delusion in the elderly: The evidence for a possible organic origin. *International Journal of Geriatric Psychiatry*, *6*, 845–852.

Förstl, H., & Beats, B. (1992). Charles Bonnet's description of Cotard's delusion and reduplicative paramnesia in an elderly patient (1788). *British Journal of Psychiatry*, *160*, 416–418.

Greenberg, D.B., Hochberg, F.H., & Murray, G.B. (1984). The theme of death in complex partial seizures. *American Journal of Psychiatry*, *141*, 1587–1589.

Joseph, A.B. (1986). Cotard's syndrome with coexistent Capgras' syndrome, syndrome of subjective doubles, and palinopsia. *Journal of Clinical Psychiatry*, *47*, 605–606.

Joseph, A.B., & O'Leary, D.H. (1986). Brain atrophy and interhemispheric fissure enlargement in Cotard's syndrome. *Journal of Clinical Psychiatry*, *47*, 518–520.

Kaney, S., & Bentall, R.P. (1989). Persecutory delusions and attributional style. *British Journal of Medical Psychology*, *62*, 191–198.

Kapur, N., Young, A.W., Bateman, D., & Kennedy, P. (1989). Focal retrograde amnesia: A long-term clinical and neuropsychological follow-up. *Cortex*, *25*, 387–402.

Kim, E. (1991). A post-ictal variant of Capgras' syndrome in a patient with a frontal meningioma. *Psychosomatics*, *32*, 448–451.

Lewis, S.W. (1987). Brain imaging in a case of Capgras' syndrome. *British Journal of Psychiatry*, *150*, 117–121.

Peterson, C., Semmel, A., von Baeyer, C., Abramson, L.Y., Metalsky, G.I., & Seligman, M.E.P. (1982). The Attributional Style Questionnaire. *Cognitive Therapy and Research*, *6*, 287–300.

Russell, B. (1961). *History of western philosophy and its connection with political and social circumstances from the earliest times to the present day* (2nd ed.). London: George Allen & Unwin.

Séglas, J. (1897). *Le délire des négations: Séméiologie et diagnostic.* Paris, France: Masson, Gauthier-Villars.

Silva, J.A., Leong, G.B., & Weinstock, R. (1992). The dangerousness of persons with misidentification syndromes. *Bulletin of the American Academy of Psychiatry Law, 20,* 77–86.

Stolk, P.J. (1984). *Psychiatrische verkenningen.* Amsterdam: De Arbeiderspers.

Warrington, E.K. (1984). *Recognition memory test.* Windsor, UK: NFER-Nelson.

Wright, S., Young, A.W., & Hellawell, D.J. (1993). Sequential Cotard and Capgras delusions. *British Journal of Clinical Psychology, 32,* 345–349.

Young, A.W., Leafhead, K.M., & Szulecka, T.K. (1994). The Capgras and Cotard delusions. *Psychopathology, 27,* 226–231.

Young, A.W., Reid, I., Wright, S., & Hellawell, D.J. (1993). Face-processing impairments and the Capgras delusion. *British Journal of Psychiatry, 162,* 695–698.

Young, A.W., Robertson, I.H., Hellawell, D.J., de Pauw, K.W., & Pentland, B. (1992). Cotard delusion after brain injury. *Psychological Medicine, 22,* 799–804.

Young, A.W., & van de Wal, C. (1996). Charcot's case of impaired imagery. In C. Code, C.-W. Wallesch, A.R. Lecours, & Y. Joanette (Eds.), *Classic cases in neuropsychology.* Hove, UK: Psychology Press.

Zigmond, A.S., & Snaith, R.P. (1983). The Hospital Anxiety and Depression scale. *Acta Psychiatrica Scandinavica, 67,* 361–370.

9

The Alien Hand

Alan J. Parkin
Experimental Psychology, University of Sussex, Brighton, UK

Within neuropsychology there can be no doubt that the alien hand constitutes one of the most bizarre phenomena one can encounter. First formally described by Brion and Jedynak (1972; although see the early report of Goldstein, 1908) the alien hand represents a psychomotor disorder in which the actions of one hand appear to act independently of the patient's will. Often the actions appear to be "anarchic" in that they deliberately counteract the actions of the other hand. In the most extreme cases the patient denies ownership of the hand responsible for the disruptive behaviour but, more often, the patient is aware that the hand is theirs in an absolute sense, but that they have no control over it.[1] For the patient this can be a frightening condition which is very difficult to adjust to mentally. In one recent case the patient was afraid to go to sleep in case his alien hand strangled him (Leiguardia, Starkstein, Nogues, Berthier, & Arbelaiz, 1993). For the neuropsychologist the condition is relatively easy to characterise, but its explanation, in both psychological and physiological terms, continues to present an important challenge.

---

[1] Terminologically it can be argued that the term "alien hand sign" should be restricted to instances where there is a genuine belief that the hand does not belong to the patient and that less severe forms should be considered as "inter manual conflict". However, the literature reveals no easy means of distinguishing these conditions. Patients may, for example, know it is their hand but abdicate any responsibility for it—believing it to have a mind of its own. For the purposes of this chapter, therefore, alien hand sign will be used to describe any condition in which one hand appears to act involuntarily and in a generally anarchic manner.

In this chapter I will first describe a case of alien hand which I was able to study in some detail (see Parkin & Barry, 1991) and then, on the basis of these observations and those from the literature, consider interpretation of the phenomenon at both a physiological and psychological level.

THE CASE OF MP

I first met MP, a right-handed woman in her early 40s, when visiting her in a rehabilitation centre. She was recovering from an operation to repair a ruptured aneurysm of the anterior communicating artery. This is a relatively common neurological emergency which can give rise to a range of impairments, most notably an impairment of memory. This arises because the aneurysm commonly causes infarction in various frontal lobe and basal ganglia structures now thought to be implicated in the more executive aspects of memory performance (Parkin, Yeomans, & Bindschaedler, 1994; see also Parkin & Leng, 1993 for a review). However, a far less common outcome of this disorder, and one central to understanding MP's difficulties, is damage to the corpus callosum.

On immediate recovery MP was entirely mute but she regained speech after a couple of weeks. When she became mobile it was noticeable that she had problems with the initiation of movement. She was unable to turn right and had to navigate by continually turning left. She also had problems initiating movement at certain times. Thus when confronted with the lift door opening she could not walk out. Intellectually she had undergone considerable decline. Estimates indicated a premorbid IQ of 116 which had been reduced to 85, with impairments particularly evident on measures of non-verbal performance. She also demonstrated problems on frontal lobe tests, showing reduced word fluency and a complete inability to do the Wisconsin Card Sorting Test (Nelson, 1976). The inflexibility of thought revealed on this test was also evident in her attitude to more general matters.

While the above difficulties were central to understanding her problems, one particular symptom, a florid alien hand, stood out as needing particular attention and explanation. I first saw it for myself when watching her in the swimming pool. She was swimming up and down quite normally, got out of the pool, dried herself, and then handed the towel to an assistant. At this point trouble started because her left hand reached out and tried to grab the towel back from the assistant. A tug-of-war continued between the two hands until finally the assistant pulled the towel away. This turned out to be one of many instances in which the left hand had behaved mischievously.

Other examples of this behaviour included the left hand closing doors and drawers as soon as the right hand had opened them; the left hand undoing buttons that had just been done up (although interestingly never the reverse); the left hand removing pieces that the right hand had just placed in a collage; the left hand removing items that the right hand had just packed (left unaided MP took several hours to pack a suitcase), and so on. Her husband reported instances of conflicting emotion between the hands. Thus she would pull him towards her with her right hand while the left hand simultaneously tried to push him away. When testing her on a task in which she was performing badly I noticed that the left hand was picking up each stimulus card and banging it hard on the table. I asked her if she would like to stop but she said that she was more than happy to continue.

On occasions the left hand caused mayhem by appearing to try and co-operate. In living skills MP was making good progress with an omelette when the left hand "helped out" by throwing a couple of additional uncracked eggs, an unpeeled onion, and a salt cellar into the frying pan. In another episode, involving tea making, the left hand sprayed other patients with tea from a large teapot. There were also times when the left hand deliberately stopped the right hand carrying out a task. In one instance I asked her to put her right hand through a small hole. Nothing happened and then she said "I can't, the other one's holding it." I looked over and saw the left hand firmly gripping the right hand at the wrist. The degree of disruption by MP's left hand was so great that the staff had no option but to tie it to her belt.

Over the ensuing months MP's deficits ameliorated and within two years she was able to live independently with her family. She still had a range of problems including poor memory and some difficulties with planning. On going to bed, for example, she often spent a long time sitting in the armchair while she tried to work out the order in which she should do things before going upstairs. As for her problematic left hand, difficulties still remained. Shopping, especially for items that involved a lot of choice, was very difficult. In one instance involving shoes, the left and right hands kept selecting different shoes to the point where she felt that only buying all the shoes in her size would solve the problem. Choosing a TV channel was difficult because no sooner had the right hand selected one station the left hand would press another button. The dishwasher was also problematic because as the right hand selected a programme button the left hand would select another. A process of sometimes frantic re-selection would go on until finally she would press the right button and run away from the machine before the left hand stepped in again. It was noticeable, however, that much of the behaviour had subsided. She no longer reported that the left hand was about to undo her clothes, something that was quite common in the early stages, and open–shut type incidents were rare. Explaining this she said that she had learned to become aware of when trouble might arise and had thus been able to develop coping strategies.

Subjectively, she described her alien hand experience as like having "two naughty children inside head who are always arguing". When describing the actions of the left hand she invariably described it as "it" and never attributed the hand's actions to herself. She often complained that she had no feeling, numbness, in her left hand and arm although there was no neurological evidence for this. It was remarkable that she seemed relatively unconcerned about the activities of her left arm even when its activities caused disaster. Often she would greet the antics of her left hand with laughter, but most commonly with resignation.

NEUROPSYCHOLOGICAL INVESTIGATION

Because aneurysms are repaired using metal clips it is not possible to undertake MRI neuroimaging post-operatively, but a CT scan performed a few days after the operation indicated that there had been marked damage to the anterior part of the corpus callosum (genu) as well as damage to the frontal lobes. This indicated that neuropsychological test performance should concentrate on tests of higher mental function and to look for evidence of hemispheric disconnection. I have already commented on MP's impaired intellectual functions and here will concentrate on evidence for disconnection using the criteria first formalised by Geschwind and Kaplan (1962).

The first deficit suspected was asterognosis—an inability to identify items by touch. MP was presented with 10 objects to her left hand and 10 to her right hand. Only one error occurred with presentation to the right hand. With her left hand she identified only one object correctly, a metal knife (she identified this on two more occasions but failed to identify a plastic knife). Her errors never resembled the object she was holding (e.g. tobacco pipe → "tennis ball"). Analysis of video film showed that manipulations of her left hand were extremely detailed even though, subjectively, she would sometimes ask whether anything was in her hand at all. Consistent with these findings she also showed finger agnosia. This was shown by touching each of her fingers individually while her eyes were closed and asking her to say which one had been touched. The fingers of the right hand were identified perfectly but, even though she responded immediately to her left hand being touched, she failed to identify the correct finger on any occasion.

Apraxia of the left hand was also very marked. She was asked to perform six verbal commands using her left hand. Each command contained two elements (e.g. pick up the white triangle and move it so that it is next to the blue square). MP performed only one of these correctly even though she was always able to perform the first component accurately. In contrast she had no difficulty performing this task with her right hand.

MP found it extremely difficult to write with her left hand. She could produce her name after a great effort but little else. MP's attempt to draw a face left-handed "was not very good" (Fig. 9.1). MP wrote normally with her right hand and was able to draw two-dimensional shapes and a clock without difficulty (Fig. 9.2). However, drawing in three dimensions caused much more difficulty. She has problems drawing a cube (even after several years) and her response to the command "Draw a face" resulted in a somewhat impressionistic attempt which lacked depth (Fig. 9.3).

INTERPRETATION

At one level, MP's case is relatively straightforward to interpret. Following the classic study by Liepmann (1908), a disconnection account of astereognosis, agraphia, and apraxia of the left hand proposes that these deficits all stem from an inability of right hemisphere sensory and motor processes to communicate with left hemisphere language areas (Geschwind & Kaplan, 1962). Astereognosis arises from failed right to left transmission of sensory information, and agraphia from an inability to pass information about graphic motor movements from left to right. Apraxia is explained by arguing that disconnection prevents the transmission of verbally determined arm movements. The fact that MP was able to follow some verbal commands most probably indicates the elementary verbal processing known to be possible in the right hemisphere (Beeman & Friedman, 1994). Finally, her failure to draw in three dimensions with the right hand suggests

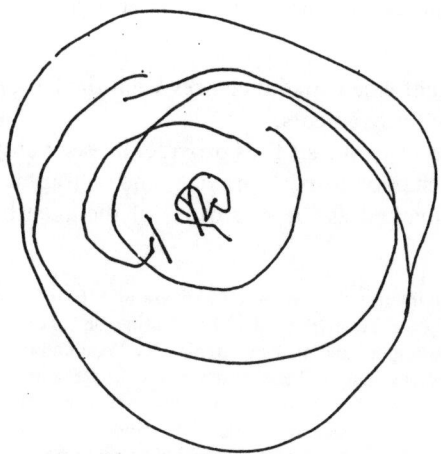

FIG. 9.1.   MP's attempt to draw a face left-handed.

FIG. 9.2.   MP's right-handed drawings of a clock and other two-dimensional shapes.

disconnection of right-sided spatial centres from the left hemisphere centres controlling her hand movements.[2]

The disconnection hypothesis thus provides a reasonably clear account of MP's left-sided astereognosis, apraxia, and agraphia. However, can disconnection be invoked as the sole cause of the alien hand? Perhaps the

---

[2] One observation of interest arose when we were asking MP to do the blocks design of the Wechsler Adult Intelligence Scale (Wechsler, 1984) using only her left hand. Under these conditions she viewed her right hand as the anarchic one: "You know I can feel my right hand wanted to step in and mess things up." Blocks design is considered to rely on right hemisphere spatial abilities. This observation suggests that somehow MP was aware that her left hand was better at this task and that, for once, it was the right hand that was causing a problem. This suggests that the "anarchic" quality may interact with the hemispheric specialisation of any task being performed.

FIG. 9.3.   MP's right-handed drawing of a three-dimensional face.

simplest explanation of alien hand is that the right hemisphere becomes freed from domination by the left hemisphere and decides to make its own way in the world. However, as we shall see, there are problems with this account. Not least in the explanation of why the right hemisphere so often appears to behave in an anarchic unhelpful way. Is it really the case that our non-dominant hemisphere builds up an alternative view of the world and our actions in it? Is it really the case, as with the patient reported by Akelaitis (1944), that the removal of a cigarette from the man's mouth by the left hand indicates an anti-smoking viewpoint in the right hemisphere?

ANATOMICAL CONSIDERATIONS

Our discussion of the points must properly begin with consideration of neuroanatomical matters. Explaining alien hand behaviour in terms of hemispheric disconnection alone is difficult because this, unlike the classic triad of disconnection symptoms, is a lasting feature only of split-brain patients who have cortical damage in addition to callosal disconnection. Reviewing the literature, Della Sala, Marchetti, and Spinnler (1991) have proposed that two forms of alien hand need to be distinguished: an acute form, which arises solely from callosal damage and subsides fairly rapidly, and a chronic form, which arises from damage to both the anterior corpus callosum (genu) and the mesial frontal cortex. In the chronic form it is reasonably clear that the critical mesial frontal structure involved is the supplementary motor area (SMA). The acute form is attributed to temporary disturbance to mesio-frontal structures that might arise by, for example, retraction of the hemispheres during surgery. Some recent studies of chronic alien hand provide good support for this theory. Della Sala et al. (1991) themselves describe the relatively rarer instance of right-sided alien hand arising in a right-handed person where there was both callosal damage and a lesion affecting the left mesio-frontal cortex due to a ruptured anterior communicating artery aneurysm. Trojano, Crisci, Lanzillo, Elefante, and Caruso (1993) describe a man with a right mesio-frontal lesion and anterior callosal damage in which many aspects of alien hand behaviour were present 11 months after a right anterior cerebral artery ischemia. Other earlier studies (see Parkin & Barry, 1991, for a review) also suggest that alien hand depends on a conjoint lesion of the anterior corpus callosum and the mesio-frontal cortex. My own case, MP, is also consistent with this position in that she had a right-sided frontal lesion in addition to anterior callosal damage. Moreover, the movement disorders she experienced are consistent with damage to SMA.

There are claims that the alien hand can arise without callosal involvement. Both Goldberg, Mayer, and Toglia (1981) and McNabb, Carroll, and Mastaglia (1988) have argued that mesio-frontal damage alone can account for the alien hand. Unfortunately, neither of these studies provides convincing evidence that callosal damage is not implicated. However, the series of alien hand patients reported by Leiguardia et al. (1993) does suggest that callosal damage may not be necessary. These patients suffered from intermittent "paroxysmal" alien hand behaviour which was attributed to ictal mechanisms. All patients had mesio-frontal or temporo-parietal lesions and the side of the lesion coincided with which hand exhibited alien hand behaviour. No evidence of callosal disconnection was evident.

The neuroanatomical evidence minimally indicates that mesio-frontal damage to the contralateral hemisphere is required for the chronic alien hand. Moreover, it would appear that the critical structure within this region is the SMA. The weight of evidence also favours an additional involvement of anterior callosal interruption although, as we have seen, this is by no means certain.

PSYCHOLOGICAL ACCOUNT

It thus seems certain that chronic alien hand depends critically on some disruption of the mesio-frontal structures, specifically the SMA, involved in the planning of movement with, additionally, some lack of inter-hemispheric connection. These anatomical facts place an important theoretical constraint on our interpretations in that the deficit must be explained in terms of deficient planning of movement as opposed to more fanciful notions of an anarchic other self. Within this framework can we now produce some explanation of why the alien hand manifests itself in the way it does?

In my interactions with MP I was struck by how relatively infrequent alien hand incidents were. I viewed with some trepidation her offer to pick me up at the station but was surprised by a smooth driving performance. Similarly, during my first meal with her, I half expected her aberrant left hand to start flicking peas at unsuspecting patients. This never happened, and it soon became apparent that alien hand behaviour was almost always restricted to two types of situation:

Category A. Tasks in which only one hand could be employed to achieve the goal and where there was a range of responses possible. Thus, the problems frequently occurred on tasks involving opening versus shutting, go versus no go, do up versus undo, pull up versus pull down, select A versus B, etc.

Category B. Tasks in which there are a number of components to performance but where these components are not overlearned procedures. An example of this is making a meal in contrast with eating one in which more routine motor acts need to be performed.

Physiological studies of the SMA indicate that it is bilaterally active even though only one hand may be employed in planning and carrying out a given task (Tanji & Kurata, 1982)—this suggests that the SMA is operating at the highest conceptual level of response planning. Under normal circumstances one can assume that any movements planned in the hemisphere ipsilateral to the activated hand are suppressed either through some direct action within the hemisphere or inter-hemispherically via the callosal pathway. However, if this suppression mechanism goes wrong, as might be the case with alien hand, then it is possible for the other hand to become active and attempt to participate.

If we accept this explanation then the apparently "anarchic" behaviour of the alien hand has a less sinister origin. If a task has only a simple goal, e.g. "open", any attempt by the alien hand to contribute positively is prevented because the right hand is already achieving that goal. However, unsuppressed and with the need to do something within that domain, the next best movement, "close", is initiated. We can interpret the persistent reselection of TV channels, choosing different shoes, pulling down trousers just pulled up, and so on as manifestations of the alien hand's inadequate attempt to make a positive contribution to the overall goal. Even the restriction of the right hand by the left (mentioned previously) can be seen as the only option if the left hand wants to pursue the goal.

While I feel that the above explanation offers a plausible explanation of much of what we see in alien hand behaviour, I do not believe that it is in any sense comprehensive. One case in point is the aberrant behaviour of the alien hand when MP attempted to make tea or omelettes. Here the alien hand produced responses of the right type but considerably ill formulated. Thus, it is not just the lack of suppression that accounts for failure; there may also be deficient planning of these unwanted movements as well. Failure to observe alien hand behaviour in routine tasks such as swimming and eating might arise because these tasks are represented at a procedural level, highly automated, and thus subject to very little higher level planning.

The pattern of impairment in MP is highly characteristic of alien hand cases in general in that the majority of aberrant behaviour takes place in Category A situations. However, not all alien hand behaviour can be accounted for like this. Why for example, did MP's alien hand always want to undo her blouse? Similarly, why did the alien hand of Case 1 reported by Leiguardia et al. (1993) grab his trouser leg repeatedly? The most likely possibility is that alien hand is not due to a single deficit but arises from various impairments that are present in different degrees. One potential complication, also associated with frontal damage, is "utilisation behaviour" (L'Hermitte, 1983), in which the hand can spontaneously and involuntarily manipulate nearby objects. Case 1 of Goldberg et al. (1981, p. 684) provides a good example of this possibility: "In the fifth week after onset [of alien hand], the patient began to walk alone. The right arm would, however, tend spontaneously to reach out and grasp objects (e.g. door knobs) that she passed, thus interfering greatly with her progression."

A final point concerns the patients' subjective interpretation of alien hand. While it is clear that some patients do regard the experience as genuinely frightening, the majority, like MP, appear to accept it as a major nuisance. The extent to which patients are depersonalised from the hand appears to vary greatly, as does their ability to cope with the bizarre activity. MP, like many patients, regards her alien hand as "it" but does not deny that it is part of her. In more extreme cases patients deny the hand is theirs and suggest that it is under the control of someone else. Thus, they shout commands and exclamations as the hand goes out of control. In some extreme cases the patient adopts a personality for the hand. Patient 6 of Doody and Jankovic (1992), for example, believed that her left hand was a baby called Joseph and that actions to other parts of her body, such as nipple pinching, were a result of feeding. Variations in the subjective interpretation of alien hand are almost certainly due to the additional damage suffered by the patients.

One interesting point is that depersonalisation from the actions of the alien hand are just as common when the lesion is in the dominant hemisphere and it is the right hand committing the aberrant acts. A feeling of "alienness" is not, therefore, associated with non-verbal expression. Thus, as with other disorders, such as neglect, in which denial plays a variable part, there is no easy explanation as to what this critical additional deficit is.

REFERENCES

Akelaitis, A.J. (1944). Studies on the corpus callosum IV: Diagnostic dyspraxia in epileptics following partial and complete section of the corpus callosum. *American Journal of Psychiatry, 101*, 594–599.

Beeman, M., & Friedman, R.B. (1994). Summation priming and coarse semantic coding in the right hemisphere. *Journal of Cognitive Neuroscience, 6*, 26–45.

Brion, S., & Jednyak, C.P. (1972). Troubles du transfert hemispherique. A propos de trois observations du tumeurs du corps calleux: Le e de la main etrangere. *Revenue Neurologique Paris, 126*, 257–266.

Della Sala, S., Marchetti, C., & Spinnler, H. (1991). Right-sided anarchic (alien) hand: A longitudinal study. *Neuropsychologia, 29*, 1113–1127.

Doody, R.S., & Jankovic, J. (1992). The alien hand and related signs *Journal of Neurology, Neurosurgery, and Psychiatry, 55*, 806–810.

Geschwind, N., & Kaplan, E. (1962). A human cerebral disconnection syndrome. *Neurology, 12*, 675–685.

Goldberg, M.D., Meyer, N.H., & Toglia, J.U. (1981). Medial frontal cortex infarction and the alien hand. *Archives of Neurology, 38*, 683–686.

Goldstein, K. (1908). Zuh Lehre der motorischen Apraxia. *J fur Psychologie und Neurologie, 11*, 169–187.

Leiguardia, R., Starkstein, S., Nogues, M., Berthier, M., & Arbelaiz, R. (1993). Paroxysmal alien hand syndrome. *Journal of Neurology, Neurosurgery, and Psychiatry, 56*, 788–792.

L'Hermitte, F. (1983). "Utilization behaviour" and its relation to the frontal lobes. *Brain, 106*, 237–255.

Liepmann, H. (1908). *Drei Aufsatz aus dem Apraxiegebeit* (Vol. 1). Berlin: Karger.

McNabb, A.W., Carroll, W.M., & Mastaglia, F. (1988). "Alien hand" and loss of bimanual coordination after dominant anterior cerebral artery territory infarction. *Journal of Neurology, Neurosurgery, and Psychiatry, 51*, 218–222.

Nelson, W.E. (1976). A modified card sorting test sensitive to frontal lobe deficits. *Cortex, 12*, 313–324.

Parkin, A.J., & Barry, C. (1991). Alien hand and other cognitive deficits following ruptured aneurysm of the anterior communicating artery. *Behavioural Neurology, 4*, 167–179.

Parkin, A.J., & Leng, N.R.C. (1993). *Neuropsychology of the amnesic syndrome.* Hove, UK: Lawrence Erlbaum Associates Ltd.

Parkin, A.J., Yeomans, J., & Bindschaedler, C. (1994). Further characterisation of the executive memory impairment following frontal lobe lesions. *Brain and Cognition, 26*, 23–42.

Tanji, J., & Kurata, K. (1982). Comparison of movement-related activity in two cortical motor areas of primates. *Journal of Neurophysiology, 48*, 633–653.

Trojano, L., Crisci, C., Lanzillo, B., Elefante, R., & Caruso, G. (1993). How many alien hand syndromes? Follow up of a case. *Neurology, 43*, 2710–2712.

Wechsler, D. (1984). *Wechsler Adult Intelligence Scale revised.* New York: Psychological Corporation.

Section D

WHERE WAS I?

That disorientation is disconcerting is no doubt a truism. We all like to know where we are (and where we stand), both literally and metaphorically. Waking or dreaming, the childhood experience of being lost is extremely frightening. Likewise, the Proustian experience of waking in a strange room and not knowing (for a few moments at least) either where we are or how we got there continues to afflict most normal adults who travel beyond their own backyards.

For the most part, of course, we do not have difficulties with orientation: The smooth working of topographic memory and autobiographical memory suffice for us to keep our place within the structure of the world. After brain damage, however, the patient may be acutely disoriented for person, place, and time. Chronically, the patient may suffer from a variety of topographical amnesias or agnosias in which familiar places are no longer recognised; or the patient may suffer from a profound retrograde memory disorder that removes a substantial part of his or her autobiography.

More puzzling are the neurological (and functional) disorders that seem to have "psychiatric" overtones: *déjà vu*, reduplication of place, and amnesic fugues. In these conditions, the primary symptom might serve to provoke in the patient a more generalised sense of being "out of touch" with lived reality. The explanation of *déjà vu*, for example, is not only a problem for the examining scientist: The patient too will need a "story" about how this (rationally impossible) state of affairs has come about.

In the first chapter in this section, Luzzatti and Verga consider the reduplicative paramnesias for place that are parallel (perhaps) to the duplication of persons seen in the Capgras delusion. If I simply don't know where I am, I can always ask someone else and believe their answer. But how will my life be changed if I am systematically misinformed (by myself) about where I am?

Even worse, one might think, is the condition of the patient described in the chapter by Della Sala, Freschi, Luccelli, Muggia, and Spinnler. In this case, organic brain damage has produced a remarkably selective retrograde loss of autobiographical memory. It is the extreme example of starting a new life. But how can one interpret one's present and plan one's future without knowing who you were and hence who you are (insofar as experience has determined identity)? As Leibniz once remarked, what is the point of reincarnation if you can't remember your previous life?

10 Reduplicative Paramnesia for Places with Preserved Memory

Claudio Luzzatti
Istituto di Psicologia della Facoltà Medica, Università di Milano, Italy

Ruggero Verga
SRRF, Ospedale di Rho-Passirana, Milano, Italy

INTRODUCTION

The term "reduplicative paramnesia" (RP) was introduced by Arnold Pick in 1903 to describe a clinical condition in which a patient states that there are two (or more) places with almost identical attributes, although only one exists in reality. Pick described this disorder in a patient with a degenerative disease of the brain, interpreting it as the result of a mild memory disorder. Using his own words, it "is characterised in that a *continuous* series of events in the patient's remembrance subsequently fall into manifold occurrences; the isolated events, though they remain pretty clearly in his memory, are impressed on him as repetitions thereof" (p. 263).

Pick observed that the reduplication occurred after an interruption in "awake consciousness". He explained this symptom as the result of a memory disorder and suggested that the patient, while aware of the similarity of salient aspects of places and events before and after the interruption, was unaware of the continuity of events during the interruption, and, therefore, believed the events were duplicated. It is a disorder of the *Bekanntheitsqualität* (Volkelt, 1901, quoted by Pick, 1903), the sense of familiarity: a new experience of a fact or person that is already known is considered as a "new" experience, even though the subject may spontaneously recognise it as identical, instead of a repetition of a previous experience (see Pick, 1903, p. 267).

Since Pick's observations, a few other cases have been described where the belief that a place had been duplicated occurred in association with a brain lesion.

187

Whereas in Pick's original case descriptions the delusional symptomatology only concerned *reduplication* of places, a similar condition has since been described for persons: Capgras and Reboul-Lachaux (1923) described the delusional belief that a person close to the patient has been *replaced* by a "double". Capgras syndrome has traditionally considered a functional disturbance associated with paranoid psychotic states, but recently several cases have also been attributed to organic diseases (Alexander, Stuss, & Benson, 1979; see Ellis & de Pauw, 1993 for a review).

Different neuropsychological explanations have been offered to account for delusional misidentifications. Organic interpretations have suggested a relation with some memory deficit or an attentional disorder. Some authors, however, have explained RP on the basis of a motivational psychodynamic process (Weinstein, Kahn, & Sugarman, 1952). Different explanations do not seem however to be mutually exclusive, if one considers that features of RP may differ from one patient to another.

Analysis of the clinical features of the about 20 neurological cases described in the literature (see Luzzatti et al., in preparation for a review), showed that some patients have delusional signs which only involve spatial knowledge (e.g. Benson, Gardner, & Meadows, 1976), whereas in other cases the reduplication also involves the identity of relatives (e.g. Alexander et al., 1979). Finally, other neuropsychological deficits, such as memory or visual perceptive disorders, do not seem to be either necessary, or sufficient. Some cases have no apparent associated cognitive disorder, whereas others have an obvious neuropsychological correlate. But in these last cases the interaction of delusional symptoms with the other neuropsychological deficits seems to be very loose, so that "frontal", memory, perceptual, and/ or attentional disorders may be present or absent.

Furthermore, when considering the qualitative aspects of cases with some typical elements of RP the features of the delusion seem to differ. For instance, in his 1903 paper, Pick discusses two patients who in fact showed different symptoms. The first patient "asserted that there were two clinics exactly alike in which he had been, two professors of the same name were at the head of these clinics, etc." In this case Pick emphasised that there were identical groups of memories. The second case was a 67-year-old woman admitted to the Neurology Department of Prague University with a progressive, presumably degenerative, brain disease. RP seemed to manifest here with slightly different features. After a convulsive attack, followed by a loss of consciousness, the patient started claiming she was no longer in the Prague clinic, but that she had been moved together with the entire hospital, as well as physicians, nurses, and patients, to K, her birthplace, a little town in the vicinity of Prague. She insisted that she had been in the clinic in Prague for five months, and that she had left there the day before: "this is a clinic, too, exactly like the one in Prague". She thought that "today's clinic" was perhaps an annex of the Prague one, that the same professor was attending at both clinics, and the assistants from the "town clinic" would come to the one in K. Interrogated by Pick whether there were actually two professors of the same name, this patient answered, unlike the previous case, that he was the same.

Thus, both cases involved a reduplication of memories, but with a different sort of delusion: In one case the reduplicated world had the features of a parallel double world, while in the second case, instead of a true double, the old world undergoes a displacement from one place to another.

A third type of place delusion was described by Paterson and Zangwill (1944). Case 1 is a 22-year-old man who suffered a severe traumatic head injury; he was in coma for three days and gradually regained consciousness. During the next two weeks he was confused and disoriented. He also had a left hemianopia with major involvement of the inferior quadrant, and left visual, somato-sensory, and motor neglect. The patient transferred the hospital where he had been admitted from close to Edinburgh in Scotland, to Grimsby, Lincolnshire, where he lived with his wife. On some occasions, he accepted that he was in Scotland, but he claimed that Grimsby and therefore his own house (or maybe vice versa, his house and therefore Grimsby) were only a few blocks from the hospital. Thus, we have here a third type of RP delusion, that is neither a "double" nor a dislocation, but seems to be a topographic displacement of the hospital from its true location (Scotland) to a more familiar spot (Lincolnshire).

Paterson and Zangwill underlined the fact that the patient had a partial knowledge of reality: When asked which town the present hospital was in, he replied "Grimsby", adding "I call it Grimsby and you call it Scotland"; or: "It is Scotland on the map but it is Grimsby nearer home." About a week later, however, the patient started acknowledging he was now in Scotland, about 300 miles from Grimsby, but he then started claiming that he had been in another hospital, before his present admission. This previous hospital was certainly located in Grimsby, but it had the same name as the present one in Scotland, and the same doctors were responsible for him.

Paterson and Zangwill consider the RP symptom as a kind of orienting disorder ("Yet it is by no means an uncommon reaction in patients recovering their orientation after a severe head-injury"). They identify three major types of rationalisation put forward by the patients to resolve their orienting disorder: (1) *verbal identification*, when a patient asserts that a given place called A is also known as B, e.g. a patient, believing himself to be in an Irish village called Ballykinder, remarked that "it is spelt 'Edinburgh' here"; (2) *spatial displacement*, when a patient asserts that A and B, though in fact many miles apart, are contiguous; (3) *reduplicative paramnesia* (narrow sense), when a patient argues that he is now in A—the "true" locality—but was shortly before at place B—the content of his disorientation. Such a distinction seems in fact to correspond to different possible features of reduplicative delusion for places.

Weinstein (1969) tried to unify under the heading of RP all the different forms of delusion connected with reduplication of space, persons, time, and parts of one's own body, in a more organic system of symptoms. He tends, however, to a motivational explanation, or at least to a motivational component of the disorder. In this context, one should remember that Weinstein and Kahn (1955) had already suggested a motivational explanation also for unilateral neglect.

Since then, about 15 other cases of RP have been described. The best analyses (as regards the amount of detail in the case description and attempt to explain the disorder) are by Benson et al. (1976) and by Alexander et al. (1979).

Benson et al. (1976) described three patients who suffered serious head trauma producing a period of coma, followed by prolonged amnesia. Like Pick's second case, all three patients dislocated the hospital to their own community. None of the patients had memory or learning disorders. The authors underlined two important features of the syndrome: (1) the reduplicative symptoms were limited to the location of the hospital; and (2) the patients ignored the overwhelming evidence that their belief was incorrect. The authors explained RP as the result of a bilateral frontal plus right parietal lesion, causing an inability to resolve conflicting conditions (frontal damage) associated with a disorder of visuo-spatial orientation (right parietal damage) and a previous memory disorder.

The case described by Alexander et al. (1979) is a 44-year-old man recovering from a severe head injury. He developed a prolonged RP associated with Capgras' syndrome; he believed his wife and five children had been replaced by nearly identical substitutes and they were living in a house just like the one he had lived in previously. The patient presented bilateral frontal and right hemisphere pathology, i.e. the pathological substrate found in the majority of the neuropsychological cases of RP. In view of this same lesion site, the authors consider Capgras' syndrome too as a form of RP. In addition to the delusional symptoms for persons and places, the patient had frontal symptomatology, a mild memory impairment and a mild disorder of his visuo-spatial functions. This relation had also been found in the five cases of RP described by Weinstein et al. (1952), where the reduplication for persons was always associated with reduplication for place.

More recently, Ellis and Young (1990) gave a cognitive interpretation of Capgras syndrome. They suggest two distinct routes to facial recognition, one for the actual identification of a face, one to give its emotional significance. Prosopagnosia results from a disruption of the first route, whereas Capgras syndrome is a "mirror image" of prosopagnosia: Thus, patients have an intact primary route to face recognition but have a disconnection along—or damage within—the route that gives the face its emotional significance. Ellis and Young (1990, p. 244) suggest a similar explanation of delusions for space, like reduplicative paramnesia. "Places, objects, etc. are not affectively neutral and so the absence of an emotionally charged input could produce the feeling of recognition, but it not being quite right. Again this would be particularly true for those places and objects with which the patient is most familiar."

Overall we have to conclude that the nature of delusion and reduplication symptoms following a brain lesion is far from being fully explained and many issues remain unresolved.

We present here a further case of a patient suffering severe reduplicative paramnesia resulting from a surgically evacuated subdural haematoma. The patient was interviewed from February to April 1993, eight to ten months after the onset of the disorders. His accounts of delusion were tape-recorded and transcribed. This chapter describes the semiology of RP and discusses the major aspects of the disorder, especially the relation with (1) other symptoms of delusion (Capgras syndrome, etc.); (2) a neurological or neurosurgical disease that generated a previous period of coma; (3) a previous or present memory disorder; and (4) with minor visuo-perceptive symptoms. We will finally discuss the different aspects of our patient's delusional beliefs, especially in consideration of his critical behaviour and awareness of the absurdity of his statements.

CASE DESCRIPTION

Clinical History

MC was a 64-year-old Italian man with a degree in engineering. He is married and has two daughters. He emigrated and lived for about 20 years in Belo Horizonte, Brazil. In April, 1992 the patient fell accidentally in his house, suffering a traumatic head injury, without any overt neurological or neuropsychological sequelae. Only about three months later, during a visit to his relatives in Italy, some mild cognitive deficits appeared, together with inertia and mild left hemiparesis. On 7th July, 1992 a CT scan showed a large right isodense fronto-temporo-parietal subdural haematoma which was surgically evacuated. The post-operative evolution was complicated by a relapse of the subdural blood layer. After the second operation, the patient was unconscious for about 10 days. At the end of September, 1992, the patient was admitted to the Rehabilitation Unit of the Passirana Hospital in Rho, a town on the northern outskirts of Milan. The patient had severe left hemiplegia and left hemianaesthesia. Perimetry indicated a left lateral hemianopia with macular sparing and only partial involvement of the inferior quadrant.

MC did not show any language disorder but he had severe left visual neglect. He also showed a spatial disorientation with the features of a reduplicative paramnesia (RP). MC believed he had been admitted to a Brazilian hospital. He had a period of retrograde amnesia for about three months before the surgical treatment, but he did not show any learning disorder. In spite of that, he denied any evidence of being in an Italian hospital. As a consequence of the continuous arguments with his relatives and the rehabilitation staff, the patient finally accepted that the hospital was located in the Milan area. Subsequently, however, he started claiming there were two cities of Milan, the true city in Italy ("Milan-Milan"; "Milan-city"), where he had spent the earlier part of his life and where his daughters still live, and a Milan in Brazil, which had previously been called Belo Horizonte but, for reasons he could not understand, everybody now called Milan ("Milan-Belo-Horizonte"; "Milan-in-Brazil"). When confronted with the overt discrepancies of that belief, the patient recognised its absurdity, but insisted that, even if hard to believe, there was no other possible explanation.

MC received daily treatment during the next four months for his left hemiplegia and for his neglect syndrome. Reduplicative symptoms lasted throughout these months, and no changes were apparent in the extent of the delusion. During the same period he never had other delusional symptoms, either for persons or for objects.

In May 1993, the patient went back to Belo Horizonte in Brazil. Once there, he did not show any further delusional belief, whereas the visual neglect persisted unchanged over the subsequent months.

Neuropsychological Evaluation
(February–March, 1993)

Language was examined by the Italian version of the Aachen Aphasia Test (AAT; Luzzatti, Willmes, & De Bleser, 1991). MC's spontaneous output was fluent, with no articulation disorder. Conversation was possible on any topic of everyday life, without any help. There were no abnormal automatised elements or any kind of perseverative verbal behaviour, or phonological, lexical-semantic, or syntactic disorders. On the AAT subtests there was a mild deficit for the Token Test, as well as for the Written Language, Naming, and Comprehension tasks. The abnormal performance in these subtests was, however, due to the severe left visual neglect. In the Written Language subtest, the pathological performance only involved the subtest "reading aloud of words and sentences", where MC consistently neglected the left side of the stimuli. The large majority of his errors in the Confrontation Naming and Comprehension tasks were also due to incomplete exploration of the left side of the pictorial material.

MC was tested on the Spinnler and Tognoni (1987) Neuropsychological Test Battery.

Attention. The patient was quite quick in crossing out the appropriate digits from a 10 × 11 matrix. There were only two false alarms, but many omissions on the left side of the matrix. After adjustment for age and educational level he obtained a score of 10.5/60 (< 5th percentile range of the normal distribution).

Memory. MC had a verbal short-term memory span of 5 (⩾ 50th percentile). Verbal learning was in the normal range: The patient learned a list of 10 words after 13 repetitions and retained 7/10 words after five minutes. The standard task for visual-spatial short-term memory (Corsi Test) could not be administered because of the severe visual neglect.

Intelligence. Abridged Raven Matrices (1938: A–D) were severely impaired. MC achieved a score of 8/48 (< 5th percentile); after presentation of the multiple-choice alternatives in a vertical modality his performance improved to 18/48 (but still < 5th percentile). Using this procedure, the score for the A series increased from 5/12 to 11/12, but performance was still severely hindered by his left neglect. Weigl's Sorting Test, a task for categorical intelligence whose construction principles are similar to those underlying the Wisconsin Card Sorting Test, was unimpaired (13/15 = 25–50th percentile). In the Italian version of the Wechsler Adult Intelligence Scale, he achieved an IQ of 108 (verbal IQ = 127; non-verbal IQ = 81).

Calculation. Mental calculation was in the normal range. The patient, however, had severe trouble with the spatial organisation of the written operations, especially the position of the carry-over values. In the standard task for acalculia used in our laboratory (Basso & Capitani, 1979), the patient reached a score of 49/101 (adjusted score: 45.8; cut-off score = 73).

Generative Naming. His score for category naming (animals, fruit, colours, towns) was poor (< 5th percentile), but naming by first-letter cueing (F, L, P) was not impaired (12–25th percentile).

"Frontal" Tasks. Reproduction of Rhythms was unimpaired (10/10) (Luria, 1980, p. 439). Drawing of Alternated Geometrical Elements was also normal. The patient had to copy and then draw freely a "Greek fret" generated by alternating spikes and squares (Luria, 1980, p. 424). He only made three errors in 20 + 20 alternated spikes and squares.

Luria's Conflicting Reactions Task. The task consists of two subsets. For every subset the examiner first shows a pair of different gestures. He then performs a randomised series of these two gestures; the patient has to respond to every gesture with the other element of the pair. MC's performance of this task was unimpaired (subset A, fist versus palm on the table = 23/24; subset B, 1 versus 2 knocks on the table = 24/24).

Thus, altogether, the performance of tasks considered to be most sensitive to the presence of frontal lesions was normal, without any obvious tendency to echopractic behaviour.

Unilateral Neglect. In all the crossing-out tasks MC neglected the stimuli placed in his left visual field. For those tasks that require cancelling only a specific set of items from a pool of different stimuli (Diller task: Pizzamiglio, Antonucci, Guariglia, et al., 1990, p. 43; Bell's task: Gauthier, Dehaut, & Joannette, 1989) the visual neglect was more pronounced than in non-selective crossing tasks (Albert, 1973; Bisiach, Luzzatti, & Perani, 1979).

Although the patient systematically neglected the left side of the stimuli when copying drawings, there was no clear constructional apraxia. When drawing a clock, the patient drew the hours one to seven and omitted the remainder. He drew a puppet with no left limbs or left side of the body.

When describing from memory the cathedral square in Milan (Bisiach, Capitani, Luzzatti, & Perani, 1981), MC produced four right but no left elements in the "facing the cathedral" condition, and three right but no left elements in the "cathedral-at-his-back" condition, resulting in a total score of seven right elements against no elements from the left side.

The visual neglect did not fade after vestibular stimulation with chilled water into the left ear (Cappa, Sterzi, Vallar, & Bisiach, 1987).

Topographic Representation. When we asked the patient to draw a map of Italy, he drew the East coast of the country in the centre of the page. He then spontaneously located some major Italian Cities. When asked to show the position of some other towns, all were located appropriately. The examiner then asked him to add other European countries to the map: MC showed the correct location of France, Switzerland, Austria, Germany, and Yugoslavia with no prompting.

The patient was then asked to draw a map of the world. MC started at the right margin of the sheet, where he drew the eastern coast of Asia; moving left, he drew the eastern coast of Africa. After some hesitation, he shifted resolutely to the left edge of the sheet, where he traced the Atlantic coast of Central and South America. He finally spontaneously entered the correct location of all the South American countries. Europe, North America, and Australia were omitted.

Neuroradiological Results

A CT scan showed the presence of a bilateral frontal layer of hygroma, and the aftermath of a right parieto-occipital lesion.

Reduplicative Paramnesia

The patient was interviewed for his reduplicative symptoms in March and April 1993. We report part of the translated transcripts and will use these to discuss the different considerations made in the introduction.

March 1993
Examiner   Please tell me the story of your disease.
MC(1)   We had heavy rain. A water-pipe in a downhill road exploded under the high pressure. The road asphalt was broken and everything on the surface was dragged down the hill: bicycles, cars, and so on. All the little things, and water and mud flooded into the garage of the house where I live. The following morning, I went down to take the car to drive my wife to the school where she teaches ... I slipped in the mud and bumped my head against a pillar. At first, you know, I felt a headache, and that was all. I went up, I was covered with mud, and had to change my clothes. I asked a friend if he could drive my wife to school. I then started my day as usual: I also played tennis. That's all: I cannot remember anything else. I know they brought me to a hospital. It must have been G [the daughter] who brought me here. Result: a haematoma for which I got two operations and a hole in my head that never ends. The left hand did not move and still does not move.[1]
E   Where did the accident happen?
MC(2)   In Belo Horizonte [BH]
E   And where are we now?
MC(3)   It is ... in Rho.
E   And where is Rho?

---

[1] In fact, after the trauma MC continued his normal life for two more months in Belo Horizonte (Brazil). He then came to visit his family in Italy. Here, the daughter noticed a slight weakness of his left arm and brought him to the hospital, where he was admitted about four months after the traumatic episode. The patient was at that time still completely conscious.

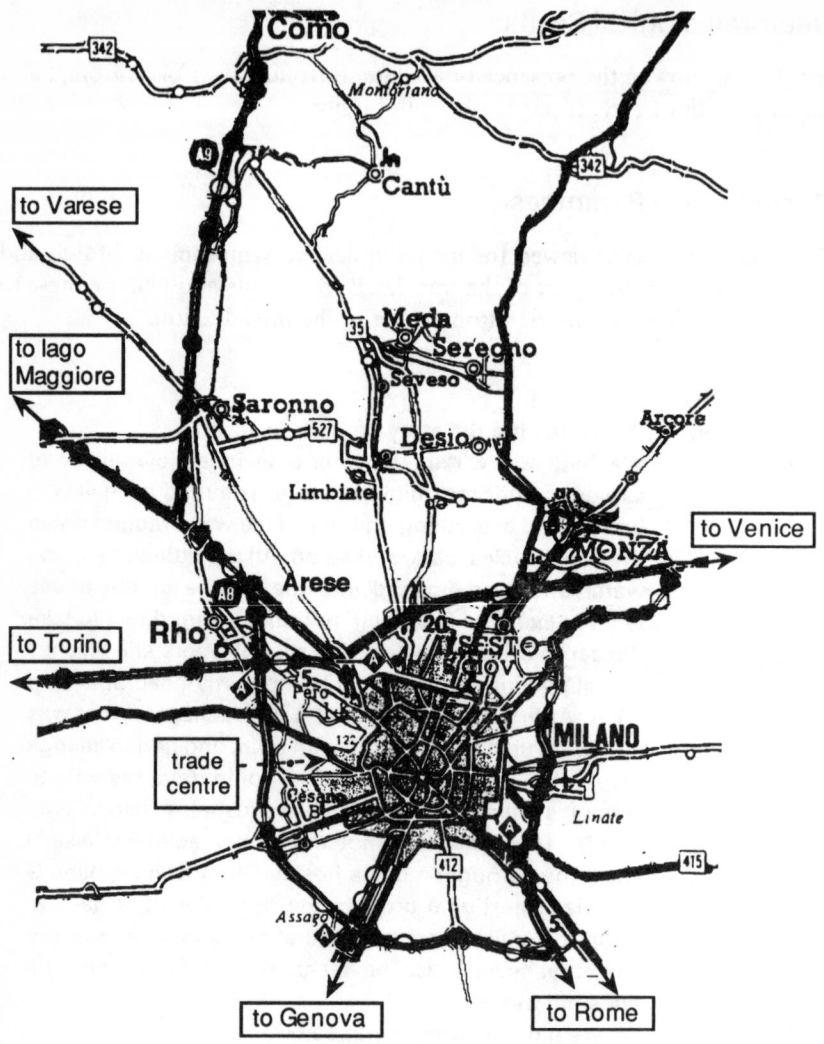

FIG. 10.1.   Map of Milan and surrounding area.

MC(4)   It is north, on the road from BH to Varese, a little away
             from the main road, on the left side. I mean, west from
             the main road [see Fig. 10.1].

E   Yes, but, I mean, in which country are we?

MC(5)   Uh, in the sense of region, I remember that before I got
             sick it was Brazil here. Now the entire zone of BH is called
             Milan. Here too, they call it Milan, and I really cannot

	understand how this works. Who was the crazy man who got this idea?
E	Could you explain that better? You know that everybody complains that it is not true!
MC(6)	Yeah, I mean, I was in BH, I went to play tennis in BH, I woke up in a hospital, the hospital of Passirana. I know it is Passirana, because they told me I was in the hospital where my daughter works. It is a suburb, of Mil- ..., no, of BH, on the road from BH to Varese. And now everybody tells me it is called Milan. OK, let's call it Milan ... The telephone, for example, is in fact Milanese: if I want to call BH I must dial the international code for Brazil, 0055, then dial the number of the Brazilian person I want to speak with. And vice versa, if they want to call me they must start by dialling the international code.
E	And don't you think this story is a bit odd?
MC(7)	Uh, I think this story is so odd that I do not want to believe it, but it is so! I did not understand how the story started, how all that has come up.
E	OK. But, all those who insist we are not in Brazil, where do they claim we are?
MC(8)	In Italy! They tell me that at the time of the disease we left Brazil, they brought me to Italy and then we went back to Brazil; then the entire affair started, of falling, of breaking my head, of coming to the hospital. I cannot remember anything at all!
E	I do not understand well: you told me you were in Brazil, then they brought you here. Did you come because of the accident, or did you come to visit your relatives?
MC(9)	No, no, because of the accident. As for me, I was in Brazil, I had the accident in Brazil. However, after I woke up, they told me I was in Italy and I think that my wife went to Italy, and she brought me back here together with G [the daughter]; but I am not sure.
E	What do you mean with "here"?
MC(10)	At the Passirana Hospital, in Rho.
E	That is in Italy or in Brazil?
MC(11)	Uh, two months ago, it was Brazil but now they call it Milan. Well, let's call it Milan!
E	What kind of money do we use here?
MC(12)	Uh, from what I hear, they are talking of Lira now. But in Brazil we had the Cruzeiro, it was a currency that was worth about one thousandth of the Italian Lira, but in the

financial page of the *Corriere della Sera*[2] that I buy and read every day, the Cruzeiro is even not listed. For this reason, I am waiting until I have some Brazilian newspaper to see briefly what it tells about this ... this story![3]

E Which newspapers can you find at the newspaper kiosk?

MC(13) The kiosk sells *Corriere della Sera, Il Giorno* ... I really do not know why they do not sell Brazilian newspapers!

E And why can you find these papers? The *Corriere della Sera* and *Il Giorno* are printed in which country?

MC(14) They are ... they must be printed here, since this affair has started: this affair called Italy. To print the *Corriere della Sera* they must use the same procedure as for Rome: it is written in Milan, and then printed simultaneously in Milan and in Rome, but also here. That's what I think happens.

E Here, what do you mean by "here"?

MC(15) I mean BH, including the whole suburb area, the town and its hinterland.

E Is there any reason why you cannot find Brazilian newspapers in the kiosk?

MC(16) ... I really do not know how this affair has happened. I'd like to read about something that created Italy and Milan, Milan by ... inside BH.

E During the weekends, you do not stay here in the hospital...?

MC(17) No, I go home to Milan: Milan, I mean, BH.

E Could you explain me what do you mean when you say "Milan, I mean, BH"?

MC(18) From here, I take the main road, then the Circular Highway that would take me to Turin or to the lakes: Maggiore, Como, Varese. I take it in the direction of Milan, until the exit "Milano–Fiera".[4] From there we drive to XXXX street, a cross road of YYYY street, which is one of the main streets of Milan, I mean, of BH.

You know, here is the centre of the city: from the centre, like in Milan, there are streets in the form of spokes, you know, leading from the centre to the old

---

[2] Major Italian newspaper, printed in Milan.

[3] cf. Paterson and Zangwill (1944, case 2): "I have not seen any newspaper which told me that Bristol isn't still there."

[4] A district in Milan which takes its name from the trade fair centre.

gates. There is Porta Venezia, Porta Romana, Porta Vigentina, Porta Genova.[5] Like we have in Italy, it is the same here too, there is Porta Romana, Porta Vigentina, Porta Ludovica.

E   Here, where?

MC(19)   Here in BH.

E   Is there here a Porta Romana and a Porta Ludovica, precisely like in Milan?

MC(2)   Porta Ludovica yes; ... well, Ludovica no, Ludovica is in Milan. In BH we do not have it: we only have Porta Romana.[6]

E   Back to our point, when you drive home, you take the highway...

MC(21)   Yeah, we drive along the Circular Highway that takes me to..., close to the "Fiera di Milano": Fiera di Milano [stress on the name of the city']..., I mean, Milan, true-Milan, right?

E   Again: when you leave the hospital for the weekend, you take the highway, you exit at the Fiera di Milano, Milan, true-Milan, and then you get to BH?

MC(22)   Yes, BH!

E   But you said you were passing close to the Fiera di Milano-Milano!

MC(23)   Uh, what a mess! I am lost.

E   Me too! Try to explain how such a thing is possible.

MC(24)   I do not know, I cannot understand. It is because I could not find anyone, until now, who could explain me the placement of the new locality called Milan; and neither could I read anything. In the *Corriere della Sera* there is not a word about it....

E   Do you watch television? Did you follow what has happened during the last few months?

MC(25)   Yes, every morning we wonder how many were sent to jail yesterday.

E   And why to jail?

MC(26)   Because of the famous rake-offs story.

E   Can you tell me something about it?

MC(27)   Uh, rake-off is when it has been decided to build some new things with the national money, such as a hospital, or a new road, and they spend the double of what it was

---

[5] The old gates on the roads out of the city to Venice, etc.
[6] Obviously wrong: there is no Porta Romana in BH.

worth, but collect for the political parties the difference that the concerns accepted to ... invoice in excess for the job they did. So, many have been jailed: some managers of ENI, some of FIAT, XXXX of YYYY, that is the holding company of FIAT in Milan, he also went to jail. And also ZZZZ, the administrative director of F. And many politicians have been impeached: AAAA—the general director of the railways— BBBB and CCCC—the big boss of the DDDD Party...

E   And do not you think it odd that the Brazilian television spends so much time broadcasting the troubles of the Italian politicians?

MC(28)   In Brazil it is the Italian television that talks about it. I never heard the Brazilian TV talking about the Italian facts...

E   And why is there an Italian TV in Brazil?

MC(19)   It is the TV people look at in Brazil now: RAI1, RAI2, RAI3. It is the Italian TV.

E   That you can see in Brazil?

MC(30)   Exact, I can see it in Brazil. I saw it and I see it now in BH...

April 1993

E   I am still not convinced with this fact that we are in Brazil. Could you explain it again?

MC(31)   I do not know; we may call my wife and she will call me an ass again!

E   Why? What does your wife tell you?

MC(32)   She says I do not want to understand. The fact is that you must explain to me how you got this idea to call Milan what previously was BH: to call it Milan ... somebody should explain to me ... I mean, let me summarise: I am in BH, I get a head trauma; I go to play tennis in BH; OK. After a while I wake up—and that happened about three months after the accident. I arrived here in coma.[7]... Well, I wake up and everybody tells me that I am not in BH, but in Milan. I want to know how this affair happened.

E   Maybe they brought you here?

MC(33)   Exact, but I cannot remember having travelled...

E   And what does your wife say about it?

---

[7] In fact not true: the subdural haematoma was diagnosed in Milan, but he arrived with no neurological or neuropsychological symptoms.

MC(34)	Uh, my wife continually tells me that we are in Milan, and that I must stop saying that we are in BH... She reproaches me that I am stubborn. Well, maybe it is true that I am stubborn. But one who was well, he wakes up in a hospital: he talks Portuguese and nurses tell him: "but what country are you from?", "what do you mean, where I come from? Aren't we in Brazil, here?" "No, we are in Italy." And I started to ... I can't make it out! I would like to read something, because when they made this definition that Rho was a district of Milan, let's call it that, something should have been written about it ... about ... that may clarify how ... and when... Nobody shows me anything.
E	Well, and Rho, where do you think it really is?
MC(35)	Rho has always been close to BH. I must say it is queer!
E	Have you seen the Duomo[8] recently?
MC(36)	No, in this ... it is not here.
E	What you do mean?
MC(37)	There is no Duomo here: BH is not Milan, it is BH. When I go home for the weekend, I go to BH that is now called Milan, that's all...

DISCUSSION

We report the case of a patient who presented with a severe orientation disorder showing the typical features of a reduplicative paramnesia (RP). The patient, an Italian man who had lived in Brazil for the last 20 years, underwent surgical evacuation of a subdural haematoma while visiting his relatives in Italy. Waking up from a coma, the patient showed delusional symptomatology: he insisted that he was in Brazil and thought that the hospital was located in Brazil instead of Milan, Italy. After a few weeks, MC eventually accepted that the hospital was located in the Milan area. Since then, however, he has insisted there are two cities of Milan, one in Italy and a second one in Brazil, and that the hospital was in the Brazilian Milan. Even in the face of compelling evidence the patient persisted with this mislocation. He was interviewed for his RP symptomatology for about two months (9–10 months post-onset).

We will now discuss the major features of RP on the basis of the observations made for our patient. Numbers in square brackets will refer to the paragraphs of the patient's transcript.

---

[8] The Milanese name for the city cathedral.

Relation to a Psychiatric Disease. As reported in the introduction, delusions are a typical symptom of a psychotic paranoid state. Yet RP has often been described as a consequence of a cerebral lesion. In some of these cases, however, the subjects also presented psychiatric and delusional episodes in their clinical history. Case 1 described by Benson et al. (1975) had a history of alcoholism; the case of Alexander et al. (1979) had developed "grandiose and paranoid delusions"; a history of alcoholism, violent behaviour and depression was also reported for the case described by Filley and Jarvis (1987). This is not the case for our patient: MC is a successful and brilliant manager of an international engineering society, and his medical history is completely clear of any psychiatric disorder.

Relation between RP and Other Symptoms of Delusion. It has been suggested that RP may appear together with other delusional symptoms, for example, with Capgras syndrome (Alexander et al., 1979; Patterson & Mack, 1985; Staton, Brumback & Wilson, 1982). This is not the case for our patient who, apart from the reduplication for space, had no trace of delusional misidentifications for relatives, or for any other object.

Relation with a Minor Visuo-Perceptive Disorder. Paterson and Zangwill (1944) consider that in RP perception would, in general, be severely restricted. The association of a perceptual disorder to apathy has also been proposed by Benson et al. (1976). A similar account was given by Alexander et al. (1979) for a traumatic head injury patient who developed complex delusional symptomatology involving both RP for places and Capgras syndrome.

Ellis and Young (1990) suggested a two-route model for face recognition that accounts for Capgras syndrome as the result of damage within the route that gives the face its emotional significance. The authors proposed this explanation for other forms of delusion, especially reduplication of places. This account, however, does not seem adequate to explain the symptoms observed in our case: first, the patient shows no delusional misidentification for relatives, but above all, his delusional misidentifications for places clearly do not result from a loss of their emotional significance.

Relation to a Memory Disorder. The interaction of a loss of consciousness and a memory disorder had already been recognised by Pick (1903) and was clearly pointed out by Alexander et al. (1979, p. 337):

> Pick observed that the reduplication occurred after an interruption in awake consciousness. He suggested that the patient had a memory disorder and, while aware of the similarity of salient aspects of events before and after the

interruption, he was unaware of the continuity of events during the interruption, and so believed the events were duplicated.

Staton et al. (1982) explained RP as a deficit in integrating newly acquired information with older memories. In fact, the majority of RP cases showed a disorder in the early stage of their disease. A problem arises if one considers that during the first hours or days after waking from coma, the large majority of traumatic head injury patients do not know where they are, are confused and confabulating, and are unaware of the continuity of events during their loss of consciousness. However, these patients accept the explanation given by their relatives and by the staff, and do not build any delusional symptomatology.

A loss of consciousness with retrograde amnesia was clearly the case for our patient [1, 6, 9, 32, 34]. However, at the time of the interviews, 8–10 months from onset, MC did not show any short-term or long-term memory disorder, either of episodic, or of biographic memory [1, 6, 12–14, 27]. As with most RP patients, MC does not accept the information given by his relatives and cannot believe their explanation [6, 11, 32, 34]. This fact seems to be in line with the conclusions developed by Paterson and Zangwill (1944), who suggested that a patient with RP puts forward many different types of rationalisation to reconcile conflicting facts in a facile and unrealistic manner. This explanation, however, is merely a description of the patients' behaviour, and is still far from an account of the mechanism underlying the disorder.

Frontal Lesions. The majority of authors agree on the presence of a *bilateral frontal* lesion, associated with a *right parietal* lesion (Alexander et al., 1979; Benson et al., 1976; Filley & Jarvis, 1987; Weinstein & Kahn, 1955). In most cases, this lesion is reflected in poor performance of the majority of so-called "frontal" tasks. The case we describe does not present clear frontal symptoms, either clinical or in specific tasks, either for verbal, or for non-verbal behaviour. The CT scan showed, however, the persistence of a bilateral frontal hygroma associated with right parieto-occipital damage. Thus, even if we could confirm the relation between RP and bilateral frontal and right parietal lesions, we did not find any association with perseverative and superficial *frontal* behaviour.

Relation to the Aetiology of the Disease. A large number of cases described in the literature are psychiatric, but the relation of RP to a neurological—more precisely, neurosurgical—disease cannot be overlooked. In a large number of cases RP follows a traumatic head injury (e.g. Benson et al., 1976; Paterson & Zangwill, 1944; Weinstein & Burnham, 1991), mostly complicated by a subdural haematoma, and followed by a period of coma (e.g. Filley & Jarvis, 1987). Other cases, however, suffered degenerative (Pick, 1903), neoplastic (Weinstein et al., 1952), or cerebro-vascular disease (Black & Kertesz, 1984; Hakim, Verma, & Greiffenstein, 1988; Patterson & Mack, 1985).

In principle, the aetiology of a focal brain injury should not primarily govern any particular pattern of cognitive disorder. However, this may actually be the case for traumatic head injury, where the pathogenesis of the disorder justifies the frequent combination of a loss of consciousness, a memory disorder, and bilateral brain lesions: a cluster of clinical variables that seem to be consistently related with RP symptoms. The presence of bilateral lesions and a memory disorder, however, cannot be taken as a rule, considering that the patients described by Black and Kertesz (1984) and by Patterson and Mack (1985) had a unilateral vascular right cerebral lesion, and there was no account of a loss of consciousness or of retrograde amnesia.

Presence of Unilateral Neglect. Besides the RP symptomatology, our patient had, as is often the case, severe long-lasting left visual neglect. The occurrence of RP with left neglect has not been stressed by any author so far, though it seems to be almost the rule (Benson et al., 1976; Kapur, Turner, & King, 1988; Black & Kertesz, 1984; Patterson & Mack, 1985). This association is obviously not mandatory, considering that unilateral neglect (ULN) cases only seldom seem to present with RP.

An aspect that is clearly shared by neglect and RP is anosognosia. It is difficult, however, to identify the possible link connecting the denial of a hemiparesis, hemianopia, or of half of one's own body and the denial of the erroneous belief characterising delusions for places. Furthermore, the denial of RP seems to show some peculiar features: MC was completely resistant to recognising and accepting cues from the external world that could direct his spatial orientation. However, when obliged to face the obvious incon-gruities, he was mostly aware of the absurdity of his delusions and spontaneously recognised the contradictions inherent in his explanations. This acknowledgement, however, lasted only a few seconds, leaving no trace of learning.

Absence of Other Cognitive Disorders. The patient had no general cognitive deficits: His verbal IQ was excellent, and the lower non-verbal IQ performance was mostly due to ULN. He was also critical and aware of most current political and economic events [6, 14, 18, 27]. This dramatically contrasts with the adamant resistance of MC to recognise the contradictions inherent in his delusion.

Different Aspects of the Symptomatology of RP. The RP symptoms presented by MC [4–5, 12, 14, 29–30, 32–34, 37] hardly correspond to the classic features of RP. In fact, he showed multiple features of delusion. He started by refusing the fact of being in an Italian hospital instead of a Brazilian one. A few weeks later he eventually accepted that the hospital was located in the periphery of Milan. Since then, however, he has claimed there are two cities of Milan, the true city in Italy and a second one, in Brazil, formerly called Belo Horizonte. Not only the Rehabilitation Unit but the entire Lombardy region was actually located in the periphery of this Brazilian City-of-Milan. With only one exception [21–22], the patient was clearly aware of the uniqueness of the hospital and made a clear distinction between the South American and the European continents. To indicate his knowledge of these distinct cities, MC speaks of a Milan-Belo Horizonte city, or Milan-in-Brazil, as opposed to a Milan-Milan or the true Milan [6, 11, 16, 21, 24].

Furthermore, one could suggest that the patient is stretched between an appropriate semantic knowledge and an erroneous spatial belief. This hypothesis could be compatible with Staton et al.'s (1982) suggestion of RP being the result of a kind of disconnection syndrome—for instance, between hemispheres. The patient's behaviour, however, is quite inconsistent and a similar hypothesis does not seem to explain all features of the patient's erroneous belief.

A possible alternative explanation of RP is that the disorder is neither an orientation nor a memory nor a perceptual disorder, but a deficit in integrating the actual perceived reality with one's own internal belief. This conflict is actually inherent in many natural conditions, for instance when waking up in a strange room, or when driving distractedly along a familiar street (Benson et al., 1976). In this circumstance, the internal belief is compared to the information acquired sensorially from the external world, and thus the internal belief adapts to the perceived reality. This integration seems to be lost in patients with RP. We suggest therefore that the disorder might be considered an adaptative rather than a reduplicative phenomenon.

An incapacity to shift from a believed to the perceived reality might be considered a kind of "perseverative" behaviour we could identify in our patient. However, as already discussed, he presented no other element of perseveration in action or in other conceptual areas.

Such an adaptative disorder, however, does not seem to completely involve the conscious experience. In fact, in some more automatised conditions, MC seemed automatically to produce the correct co-ordinates of the real spatial representation [6, 16, 17, 18]. This suggests that he has two levels of spatial belief: a deeper, more automatic one, less sensitive to RP, and a superficial one that is more overtly disrupted by the adaptative disorder. This apparent dissociation might warrant more extensive research.

ACKNOWLEDGEMENTS

We are grateful to the medical staff and the therapists of the Rehabilitation Unit of Rho-Passirana for help in the collection of neurological and neuropsychological data and to Edoardo Bisiach, Klaus Schonauer, and Marina Nespor for much advice and many suggestions on the interpretation of the patient's symptoms. We also thank Glyn Humphreys and Jane Riddoch for their comments on a preliminary version of this chapter.

REFERENCES

Albert, M.L. (1973). A simple test of visual neglect. *Neurology*, *23*, 658–664.

Alexander, M.P., Stuss, D.T., & Benson, D.F. (1979). Capgras syndrome: A reduplicative phenomenon. *Neurology*, *29*, 334–339.

Basso, A., & Capitani, E. (1979). Un test standardizzato per la diagnosi di acalculia: descrizione e valori normativi. *AP, Rivista di Applicazioni Psicologiche*, *1*, 551–568.

Benson, D.F., Gardner, H., & Meadows, J.C. (1976). Reduplicative paramnesia. *Neurology*, *26*, 147–151.

Bisiach, E., Capitani, E., Luzzatti, C., & Perani, D. (1981). Brain and conscious representation of outside reality. *Neuropsychologia*, *19*, 543–551.

Bisiach, E., Luzzatti, C., & Perani, D. (1979). Unilateral neglect, representational schema and consciousness. *Brain*, *102*, 609–618.

Black, S.E., & Kertesz, A. (1984). *A case of reduplicative paramnesia and neglect due to a right hemisphere lesion studied by nuclear magnetic resonance.* Paper presented at the 7th European Conference of the International Neuropsychological Society. Aachen, Germany.

Capgras, J., & Reboul-Lachaux, J. (1923). Illusion des "sosies" dans un delire systématisé chronique. *Bulletin de la Société Clinique de Médecine Mentale*, *11*, 6–16.

Cappa, S., Sterzi, R., Vallar, G., & Bisiach, E. (1987). Remission of neglect and anosognosia during vestibular stimulation. *Neuropsychologia*, *25*, 775–782.

Ellis, H.D., & de Pauw, K.W. (1993). The cognitive neuropsychiatric origins of the Capgras delusion. In *The neuropsychology of schizophrenia* (pp. 317–335). Hove, UK: Lawrence Erlbaum Associates Ltd.

Ellis, H.D., & Young, A.W. (1990). Accounting for delusional misidentifications. *British Journal of Psychiatry*, *157*, 239–248.

Filley, C.M., & Jarvis, P.E. (1987). Delayed reduplicative paramnesia. *Neurology*, *37*, 701–703.

Gauthier, L., Dehaut, F., & Joanette, Y. (1989). The bells test: A quantitative and qualitative test for visual neglect. *International Journal of Clinical Neuropsychology*, *11*, 49–54.

Hakim, H., Verma, N.P., & Greiffenstein, M.F. (1988). Pathogenesis of reduplicative paramnesia. *Journal of Neurology, Neurosurgery and Psychiatry*, *51*, 839–841.

Kapur, N., Turner, A., & King, C. (1988). Reduplicative paramnesia: Possible anatomical and neuropsychological mechanisms. *Journal of Neurology, Neurosurgery and Psychiatry*, *51*, 579–581.

Luria, A.R. (1980). *Higher cortical functions in man* (2nd ed.). New York: Basic Books.

Luzzatti, C., Willmes, K., & De Bleser, R. (1991). *Aachener Aphasie Test (AAT). Versione Italiana.* Firenze: Organizzazioni Speciali.

Paterson, A., & Zangwill, O.L. (1944). Recovery of spatial orientation in the post-traumatic confusional state. *Brain*, *67*, 54–68.

Patterson, M.B., & Mack, J.L. (1985). Neuropsychological analysis of a case of reduplicative paramnesia. *Journal of Clinical and Experimental Neuropsychology*, *7*, 111–121.

Pick, A. (1903). Clinical studies: 3 cases: on dreamy mental states; on the pathologically protracted duration of senses (...); on reduplicative paramnesia. *Brain*, *26*, 242–267.

Pizzamiglio, L., Antonucci, A., Guariglia, C., Judica, A., Montenero, P., Razzano, C., Foccolotti, P. (1990). *La Rieducazione dell'Eminattenzione Spaziale*. Milano: Masson.

Spinnler, H., & Tognoni, G. (1987). Standardizzazione e taratura italiana di test neuropsicologici. *Italian Journal of Neurological Sciences*, 8 (Suppl. 8), 1–120.

Staton, R.D., Brumback, R.A., & Wilson, H. (1982). Reduplicative paramnesia: A disconnection syndrome of memory. *Cortex*, *18*, 23–36.

Weinstein, E.A. (1969). Patterns of reduplication in organic brain disease. In P.J. Vinken & G.V. Bruyn (Eds.), *Handbook of clinical neurology, Vol. 3: Disorders of higher nervous activity* (pp. 351–357). Amsterdam: North-Holland.

Weinstein, E.A., & Burnham, D.L. (1991). Reduplication and the syndrome of Capgras. *Psychiatry*, *54*, 78–88.

Weinstein, E.A., & Kahn, R.L. (1955). *Denial of illness*. Springfield, Ill.: C. Thomas.

Weinstein, E.A., Kahn, R.L., & Sugarman, L.A. (1952). Phenomenon of reduplication. *Archives of Neurology and Psychiatry*, *67*, 808–814.

11

Retrograde Amnesia: No Past, New Life

Sergio Della Sala*
Department of Psychology, University of Aberdeen, Aberdeen, UK

Roberto Freschi
Reparto di Neurologia, Ospedale di Legnano, Italy

Federica Lucchelli
Reparto di Neurologia, Ospedale S Carlo Borromeo, Milan, Italy

Silvia Muggia and Hans Spinnler
Clinica Neurologica III, Ospedale S Paolo, University of Milan, Italy

INTRODUCTION

Ever since the days of horse-and-buggy practice, when a doctor had much time for speculation and reflection between his visits, the clinician has made his own peculiar approach to the truth. He carries at the back of his mind certain unsolved problems in his field of special interest, and he stumbles unexpectedly on clues to their solution, constructing his own tentative hypotheses. In that place at the back of the mind that is reserved for wonder, he should be, to the best of his ability, a pathologist, an anatomist, and a physiologist. Thus, when disease or accident presents to him the perfect experiment, he has a mind prepared and can, perhaps, ask the question and get the answer for which the problem waits, doing this before the fleeting chance is gone. Retrograde amnesia is such a problem.

Penfield and Mathieson (1974, p. 152)

In neurological parlance retrograde amnesia (RA) defines the loss of memories acquired before the occurrence of brain damage. The neuropsychological characteristics of RA have been recognised about a century ago (Abel & Colman, 1895; Charcot, 1892). In some of the cases, RA has been reported as an isolated phenomenon without anterograde (i.e. normal learning of new information) and procedural memory disorders ("pure RA"). In other instances, RA presents in a less pure form; the patients show

---

*Names are listed in alphabetical order.

a substantial RA coupled with other neuropsychological deficits, both within the memory domain (e.g. anterograde amnesic traits) or in extra-memory domains (e.g. executive disorders). The aetiology reported in these latter cases is often a well-recognised clinical entity, such as sequelae of herpetic encephalitis, cortical degenerative diseases (e.g. Alzheimer's disease), transient global amnesia, or Korsakov's amneso-confabulatory syndrome. On the contrary, the onset of pure RA is sudden and follows heterogeneous brain insults (e.g. head injury) with or without morphological or metabolic (namely positron-electron tomography—PET or single photon emission computed tomography—SPECT) evidence of a brain lesion. The pure form of RA arises also within the framework of psychiatric problems. The content of the past information not retrievable varies from one patient to the other. Most of the times patients cannot retrieve information of recent events, while some of them can no longer retrieve autobiographical, media-mediated or encyclopaedic knowledge. With a few outstanding exceptions (Abel & Colman, 1895; Lucchelli, Muggia, & Spinnler, 1995; Stracciari, Ghidoni, Guarino, Poletti, & Pazzaglia, 1994), RA does not improve over time, nor does it worsen.

Cases of isolated RA have not been disregarded by novelists, journal-ists, or by movie-makers (e.g. *Amateur* by H. Hartley, USA, 1994). Italian readers may remember the once notorious case of "Bruneri–Canella", in which the picture of a bearded man, published under the title "Who knows this man?" in popular Italian magazines in 1927, opened a sensational case. It held the newspapers for years, dividing the Italians into "Canellists" and "Brunerists". An unknown man, caught in the act of stealing, declared himself amnesic and was hospitalised in Collegno's asylum near Turin. The relatives of a certain Professor Canella, who had been missing since the war, believed they recognised him in the photograph, and a subsequent meeting with him confirmed their belief. After some initial doubts, this recognition became certain, mostly because of the insistence of Canella's wife. All inconsistencies in the man's behaviour were traced back to his amnesia, and the responsibility for proving his identity lay entirely with Mrs Canella. She eventually resumed their married life with the "forgetful man from Collegno" and had two children. However, significant evidence (e.g. the man's fingerprints) pointed in a different direction.

The claimed amnesic was not the pious and learned philosophy professor but Mario Bruneri, a Turinese typographer, long time wanted by the police for small thefts and frauds. Was memory loss but an expedient to avoid prison? A trial was started which could have been avoided but for the passionate obstinacy of Mrs Canella, persuaded that her husband had been found. The case provoked immediate literary responses: One year before the final decision of the court against Mrs Canella, Pirandello's piece about the

Bruneri–Canella story (*Come tu mi vuoi*, 1931) was played in Turin; the same story has been recently re-written from a different perspective by Sciascia (*Il teatro della memoria*, 1981). Anecdotes of similar cases fill up the news pages of several magazines and news agencies around the world (e.g. *Reuters*, 31st October, 1991; *Rockland (NY) Journal-News*, 8th September, 1991).

These intriguing stories owe their popularity to their intrinsic ambiguity: readers wonder whether they are cases of malingering, true amnesia, or psychological disturbances. It is worth noticing that the popular notion of amnesia generally refers to the inability to retrieve one's past rather than to the inability to learn new information.

Although some RA cases can be gleaned from earlier scientific literature (e.g. Abel & Colman, 1895; Schilder, 1923), only very recently have they been redrawn to the attention of the scientific world, and the problem of the interpretation of their symptoms has been reappraised by different students (De Renzi, 1994; Kapur, 1993) from different perspectives.

In this chapter we report and discuss the case of DV, a patient who suffered from pure RA following a mild head trauma. The interpretation of DV's RA—between functional and organic amnesias—remains open to debate.

As Goldberg, Antin, Bilder, Gerstman, Hughes, and Mattis (1981) pointed out, given the rarity of isolated RA, unaccompanied by a comparably severe anterograde amnesia or general arousal deficit, every case is of considerable interest. Indeed, these cases can help in throwing some light on our understanding of long-term memory, in so far as, for instance, they can help in disentangling retrograde from anterograde processes. In discussing the case of DV, we aim at adding to the debate of the possible aetiology of RA. In fact, RA has been sometimes diagnosed as "psychogenic" (Abeles & Schilder, 1935; Charcot, 1892; Janet, 1928; Russell, 1971; Schacter & Kihlstrom, 1989; Stengel, 1966); in some other instances it has been interpreted as malingering (Kopelman, 1987; Kopelman, Christensen, Puffett, & Stanhope, 1994); and in a few other cases it has been traced back to brain pathology (De Renzi, Lucchelli, Muggia, & Spinnler, 1995; Hodges & McCarthy, 1993; Kapur, Ellison, Smith, & McLellan Burrows, 1992; Markowitsch, Calabrese, Liess, Haupts, Durwen, & Gehlen, 1993).

Moreover, there is a second reason to report all possible cases of pure RA, that of emphasising the behavioural complexity which is their invariable characteristic. It is hard to believe in objective descriptions exempt from cultural biases. Neuropsychological, psychiatric, and psychodynamic aspects are all present in most histories of RA patients; each one of these possible and alternative interpretations could be privileged.

We, however, will describe DV's RA in neuropsychological terms, since this is the area we are most familiar with.

CASE REPORT

DV, an intelligent 33-year-old chemist, was hospitalised unresponsive, immediately after he fell down the stairs after lunch in his parents-in-law's home, at the beginning of December, 1993.

Neurological History

The signs of a blunt injury were clearly visible on the scalp in the posterior regions of DV's head. These signs progressively disappeared over the following few days. The period of unresponsiveness resolved in about 45 minutes. During this period vital functions were monitored, and no abnormalities were evident. DV did not show convulsions, vomiting, or perspiration, but he was ashen grey, showed ocular jerks, upward deviation of the eyes with fluttering of the eyelids, and repetitive swallow-like movements.

A diagnosis of concussion (commotio cerebri) was postulated. The neurological examination was normal. In order to find out whether the blunt head injury produced a brain lesion that could possibly be held responsible for the patient's behavioural disturbances, an extensive neuroimaging programme was carried out. Skull and brain computerised tomography (CT) scans, a magnetic resonance image (MRI), and two electroencephalograms (EEGs) did not reveal any abnormality. On three different occasions (5, 15, and 45 days after the trauma), single photon emission computed tomography (SPECT) following injection of technetium-99m HM-PAO (hexamethylpropyleneamine) was performed. This is a suitable means for visualising the regional cerebral blood flow (Sharp, Smith, Gemmel, Lyall, Evans, & Grozdanovic, 1986). In all instances a bilateral decreased uptake indicated dishomogenous hypoperfusion of both hemispheres, without any regional pattern of damage.

Given this negative data, the clinical neurologists in the ward considered the possibility of "psychogenic amnesia".

It is worth mentioning that, from the age of 17, DV had had five or six episodes that he and his relatives describe as fainting spells. These episodes were characterised by a sudden loss of strength; the patient became flabby and too feeble to stand. Consciousness was abolished abruptly, but he never hurt himself severely. The attacks lasted from a few seconds to 10 minutes. The last one occurred five months before the amnesic trauma. They occurred with no prodrome, and with no apparent triggering cause, although on two occasions they occurred immediately after a meal. Other symptoms, such as salivation, perspiration, vomiting, or cardiac abnormalities were never apparent. DV had no memory of what occurred during the attacks. He was never taken too seriously by the physicians who examined him from time to time. He was invariably dismissed from emergency wards, with no request for further investigations. Specific causes of his attacks, such as heart diseases, atonic and reflex epilepsy, or hypoglycaemia have been investigated and considered unlikely. Neurological (including repeated EEGs) and cardiological (including 24-hour electrocardiographic or ECG recordings) assessments, as well as blood-tests, failed to reveal any abnormality. It is possible that DV's fall on the staircase was due to one of these faints.

Neuropsychological History

The first neuropsychological assessment took place two weeks after the accident. DV was extensively studied over the following two months. An informal check of his RA was carried out 10 months post-onset. On this occasion his amnesia was found unchanged.

Behavioural Traits

DV's behaviour during assessment was co-operative and thoughtful. His metamemory was strikingly good. He was invariably able to tell apart spontaneously activated old memories from relearned information about his past. His very few spontaneous resurgences were akin to dreams, beclouded and somewhat indistinct. They did not trigger any contextual association. On the other hand, DV's source memory for relearned information was particularly good. His wife repeatedly emphasised his efforts in editing all relearned autobiographical information into a meaningful plot, although he did not miss an opportunity to claim that relearned notions about himself did not revive any emotion.

Immediately after regaining consciousness, DV was extremely anxious because (so he claimed) of his awareness of having lost conscious memory of his past to the point of having lost his personal identity. He seemed overtly disconcerted by the tenderness of his wife, whom he did not recognise. Likewise, he did not recognise relatives and friends. However, he did recognise his parents and a friend from his school years, although he was unable to associate any autobiographical context with these recognitions. He also claimed that he did not remember his own name, age, or address. On the other hand, he did remember few scattered details of his profession: He knew that he worked as a chemist in a firm, for instance, but could not retrieve any further information about his job. DV was well aware of his retrograde memory problems and clearly worried about them. Confabulations or hallucinations were not observed and his verbal communication was fully normal. He reported that after regaining consciousness his mind had been "completely blank" for one or two hours and this period of identity loss was accompanied by a state very similar to a fugue, which, however, at that time he kept to himself and was unapparent to everyone. Personal identity was then recovered in less than 15 minutes as far as name and age were concerned, but he could still not recall his address and most relevant autobiographical information, such as the fact that he was married.

In the following hours, DV's relatives and acquaintances were increasingly astonished by the sharp dissociation between his efficient learning (relearning) ability and his severe RA. Two parties quickly formed. One party traced the dissociation back to some form of psychogenic disorder, whilst the other one, which included DV's wife and mother, considered his RA defect as a consequence of the trauma. Doctors and nurses were also split. The negative outcome of the brain CT scan persuaded the majority to embrace the psychogenic hypothesis.

Autobiographical Memory. DV vaguely remembered having worked with his father as a young chemist, but all the details attached to the experience were fuzzy. In the first week post onset, DV relearned to recognise the members of his family. His parents, in their pedagogic drive, showed him several times large amounts of photographs taken from the family album.

DV for instance, promptly relearned he had a sister. However, he was unaware that his beloved 17-year-old sister had died five years before from long-lasting leukaemia, and was therefore surprised that his sister did not come to visit him in the hospital. The news of her death left him appalled and incredulous. He was troubled by the lack of sorrow his sister's death yielded and argued that this was due to the fact that it was a relearned notion, and "therefore" detached from any emotion.

Requested to describe his parents' dining room, DV provided vague memories, and it was clear he was reporting some features (such as the fireplaces) of the corresponding room of his parents-in-law. When DV returned to his own home, he failed to recognise his apartment as well as everything therein; even the view from the windows was unfamiliar to him. In less than 12 hours, he relearned all this visuo-spatial information.

DV almost invariably recognised himself in the photographs, even when portrayed at a much younger age or among others. With the exception of his mother and grandfather, other people were felt to be totally unknown. The context and the scenes were also not recognised, so that their general meaning remained obscure to him.

The patient remembered that his office work required computer knowledge. He confusedly remembered being on call at the time of his trauma; he knew that he was carrying a portable telephone, that he was expected to take back, but he could not remember to whom or to where. When DV returned to work, about two months following his trauma, he knew his office was on the third floor, but he was completely disorientated in the building. He failed to recognise his office, desk, and personal computer. Moreover, he could not find his folders, although he promptly recognised them and their content, being able to carry on with the work. His colleagues did not look familiar to him, and he did not remember their names nor their positions. However, he quickly relearned all the details connected with his work. His brilliant relearning was devoid of past experiences, as if DV were a new, bright employee.

The patient was also unable to retrieve memories connected with the leisure trips he had undertaken to the USA and the Grand Canyon and twice to Corsica by motorbike; he could not remember his honeymoon to the Seychelles Islands. Even the photographs of those trips did not prompt any recognition of events, places, or people. One month after his trauma, DV recognised without hesitation a friend from his school years, but was puzzled to find him much older than he expected, as if he was relying on memories dating back to his school-time, about 15 years before. These anecdotal data, while pointing to the fact that DV had some implicit knowledge of his past, are too scanty to allow us to state that, at least for some contents of his past, DV's RA was characterised by a temporal gradient. Once again, his recognition was detached from biographical information. About two months after the trauma, DV experienced a vague spontaneous memory about his military service: Even though he could not remember the exact location where he had served in the army, he correctly said that it was somewhere in the mountains and that at that time he had contracted chickenpox. When DV visited two friends in another town, whom he had not met for four years, although they were keeping in touch by telephone, he recognised and named them promptly, but again could not retrieve either their biographies or any of the experiences they had shared.

DV had forgotten almost everything about his many hobbies. He could not remember anything about football games that he used to play on Saturdays, or about cross-country motorbiking that he had been enjoying for almost 20 years. He had also lost all memories about fishing, one of his favourite sports, and musical interests (he was the promoter of a small band and was himself a guitarist).

Memory of Contemporary Events.   DV habitually read the newspaper and kept well informed about political news. After the trauma, he was unable to retrieve any notion about current political events (e.g. the hearings of the trial concerning the bribes and corruption of many eminent Italian politicians). None the less, he could tell in general terms the difference between the progressive and the conservative views on social affairs. The same inability to bring to consciousness traces of contemporary events was paramount independently of the event (e.g. crime news, cultural debates, law reports, or society gossip).

Although DV was very fond of movies, he could not remember one, nor did rewatching help him to remember. His wife, though, noted that when he saw an already known movie, he made the same comments he had made in the past. He grasped the humorous gist of a witticism only when it resorted to logical paradoxes (namely, in the case of semantic implausibilities), but not when the jest implied the knowledge of contemporary events or personalities.

DV could not reproduce nor recognise any short song he once knew, and was unable to associate popular melodies with their title, text, or author. However, two months after the trauma he could hum some popular melodies, though unable to retrieve their words.

General Knowledge. Whereas autobiographical and contemporary information was almost inaccessible to DV's consciousness, the same did not apply to most items and categories in the domain of general (i.e. encyclopaedic) knowledge. Therefore, besides the striking antero/retrograde dissociation, another dissociation appears in this patient's amnesic picture.

He failed to retrieve nearly all issues related to information learned at school, which he was unlikely to use frequently in his everyday life. His wife was mostly surprised by his inability to recall even simple notions of history and mythology, topics he had been especially interested in, but his knowledge of literature was also clearly impaired.

DV had some patchy problems with semantics. For instance, he knew what a motorbike was and recognised motorbikes in photographs, but could not report any feature (e.g. make, approximate price). It should be noted that he was very fond of motorbikes and was himself the owner of a Japanese cross-country motorbike. He knew that BMW and Honda produced cars but ignored that they also produced motorbikes. Another impaired category was fish. Living near a lake and several rivers, he had been an experienced fisherman since childhood. After his head injury, he still knew what a fish was, but he could not tell the difference, for instance, between a trout and a carp or a perch; he could not describe fishing techniques nor simple recipes for cooking different fish.

One day, while watching a ski competition on TV, he commented that, although he knew what snow was chemically and physically, he could not retrieve any feeling connected with snow except for coldness. It became apparent that he had no idea of what skiing implied, except that high boots were probably necessary; he was not able to give any account on how one reaches the height of a slope in order to ski downhill.

All the other investigated categories were shown to be well preserved: for instance, DV was flawless in listing makes, prices, and models of new and old cars; he had no problems with Italian geography; he could describe regional gastronomic specialities. He was absolutely brilliant in dealing with his professional expertise. For instance, he easily filled up Mendelejev's periodic table, he described the contributions to chemistry by Lavoisier and

Kekulé in detail and he easily defined terms of computer slang. Most of his "cognitive estimates" (an Italian adaptation of Shallice & Evans's enquiry, 1978) were correct. DV perfectly described and recognised the flag of the football club he supported, but, to his own surprise, was unable to list the players or the wins of the last few years.

Abilities Based on Procedural and Implicit Memory. Procedures and implicit retrieval were completely spared.

In the first days of his hospitalisation, DV surprised his boss (whom he did not recognise) by proving able to penetrate his portable computer secret access key in a few minutes. At home and at work he had no problems in using computers even when he decided to practise unusual routines. At the same time, he was unable to provide any information concerning his previous training experience with computers.

From the first days after his trauma, DV easily recalled telephone numbers he had frequently used, but he could not retrieve the names of the corresponding people. He relearned these associations very quickly.

DV had no difficulty in finding his way around, and on the day he was discharged from the hospital he drove his car (which he did not recognise) without any difficulty back to his home. However, when he arrived there, he did not recognise the house and had to rely on the street number he had relearned. He was able to drive to nearby cities following familiar routes, but he was surprised by the country and town sights that he felt were unfamiliar.

DV did not know whether he was a smoker or whether he was able to play chess or to play the guitar. However, once back at home, he took a pipe from his array of pipes, mixed different blends of tobacco according to his regular taste and smoked in the same style as before; he proved to have retained all procedural information about chess; finally, he played his guitar as skilfully as before. DV could fill up the tax forms correctly, although relying upon the financial information passed him by his wife. He automatically sat at his usual place at the dinner table; he found the bathroom even if its door was closed; and he found the appropriate place for the ladle in the kitchen and the drawer were the scissors were kept. On the other hand, he had no idea where his clothes or his personal computer were.

It is worth reporting two instances clearly suggesting a preserved implicit knowledge in the dearth of explicit awareness. DV was very good at remembering test words from one session to the other, including those he did not know the meaning of. In one session he had some difficulty in giving a definition of the different priests in the Catholic hierarchy and he could not provide a conclusive definition of the word "papa" (pope); its meaning was not explained to him. In a subsequent session he ran into difficulties with the word "parroco" (parish priest). While trying unsuccessfully to retrieve its meaning, he commented that the word surely had something in common with the other one ("papa") he had not identified in one of the previous sessions (and still failed to do). A further example of implicit knowledge occurred at work. His colleagues could not figure out a signature on an old document of the firm. DV easily read the signature but had to admit that he did not know who the person was (he was a chief executive for whom DV had worked in the past).

Summing up, the behavioural observations suggest the fact that (1) DV was severely impaired in recollecting autobiographical and contemporary information, (2) his general knowledge was well preserved, with a few notable exceptions, and (3) procedural and implicit memory were spared. It was also apparent that (4) DV's learning abilities were intact without any evidence of further forgetting.

Formal Neuropsychological Assessment

DV's cognitive abilities were formally assessed in three sessions from December 1993 to February 1994, one to two months after the trauma. His language was normal and informative. The range of his cognitive performances in different non-memory tests is laid out in Table 11.1.

From this table it is evident that DV's performance in a variety of non-memory cognitive tests is well within the normality range, and indeed mostly well above the median score of the normal population.

DV's performance on tests of anterograde memory, taxing both short- and long-term memory, is shown in Table 11.2. It is clear that his short-term memory and his learning and retention abilities are well within the boundaries of normality, once again being for the most part above the median score.

In contrast to his excellent learning abilities DV performed poorly on a version of the test originally devised by Kapur, Heath, Meudell, and Kennedy (1986), in which the patient is required to learn associations between famous names and activities which differ from the ones for which they are known (e.g. Bob Dylan—football player). Pure retrograde amnesics are expected to perform better than normal subjects because of the loss of interference by known, well-established associations. DV proved unable to learn any of the six "false" associations at the first trial, he learnt four of them on the second trial and only succeeded in learning all of them after the fourth presentation. This unexpected performance can be traced back to the sparing of implicit memory, which interferes with the learning process; alternatively, an *ad hoc* malingering cannot be excluded.

DV's remote memory deficit was also formally and extensively investigated. His performance in a range of tasks testing his recollection

TABLE 11.1
DV's General Cognitive Assessment

	DV's Score	Cut-off Score	Controls' Median Score
Intelligence			
Raven PM47*	32	17.5	31
(range 0–36)			
Weigl's sorting test†	12.25	4.50	10.75
(range 0–15)			
Cognitive estimates	10	na	na
(range 0–12)			
Language			
Token test	33.5	26.25	33
(range 0–36)			
Verbal fluency‡	34	16	32
(phonemic cue)			
(range 0–∞)			
Object naming test§	48	35	45
(range 0–48)			
Perception			
Judgement of line orientation¶	28	17	26
(range 0–30)			
Visual form discrimination¶	30	23	31
(range 0–32)			
Unknown face matching¶	52	38	46
(range 0–54)			

Age/education-adjusted scores; * Basso, Capitani, and Laiacona (1987); † Spinnler and Tognoni (1987); ‡ Novelli, Papagno, Capitani, Laiacona, Vallar, and Cappa (1986); § Unpublished normative data; ¶ Benton, Hamsher, Varney, and Spreen (1983); na: not available.

of famous events and famous names, and his competence in checking the familiarity and identification of faces, are set out in Table 11.3. The deficit in retrieving information learned before the injury is indisputable.

DV's knowledge of famous people and places was also assessed by means of a task in which he was required to discriminate real from invented, albeit plausible, names. Two different versions of the task were given: in one version 30 names of real people were presented one at a time intermingled with 30 false names; in another version 36 real proper names of people as well as of places, historical sites, musical bands, etc. were intermingled with 36 phonologically similar names for discrimination. In both versions, he never made an error in identifying the false names as false; on the contrary, all his errors concerned real names: he failed to recognise 17 out of 30 and 26 out of 36 items.

TABLE 11.2
DV's Anterograde Memory Performance

	DV's Score	Cut-off Score	Controls' Median Score
Digit span* (range 0–∞)	6.5	3.5	5.25
Verbal span† (range 0–∞)	4.25	3	4.50
Spatial span† (range 0–∞)	6.5	3.75	4.75
Story recall† (range 0–16)	16	4.75	13.25
Word list learning‡ (range 0–30)	16	8	17.25
Supra-span verbal learning (Buschke-Fuld)† (range 0–180)	113	36	110
Supra-span spatial learning† (range 0–29.16)	24.13	5.75	18.50

Age/education-adjusted scores; * Orsini, Grossi, Capitani, Laiacona, Papagno, and Vallar (1987); † Spinnler and Tognoni (1987); ‡ Novelli, Papagno, Capitani, Laiacona, Cappa, and Vallar (1986).

We also formally tested DV's semantic knowledge in different domains. His performance in a 10-question questionnaire about chemistry (e.g. definition of ion, isomer, aromatic compound) was perfect. He also answered flawlessly five questions on physics (e.g. description of the principle of Archimedes, of the principles of thermodynamics, the definition of force, etc.), six questions on mathematics (e.g. simple equation, definition of parabole, of hyperbole, etc.), five questions on astronomy (e.g. definition of

TABLE 11.3
DV's Retrograde Memory Performance

	DV's Score	Cut-off Score
Famous public events† (range 0–40)	10	na
Famous faces* (error score)	4.62	≤ 1.32
Familiar faces* (error score)	3.1	≤ 1.42

Age/education adjusted scores; * Faglioni, Cremonini, and De Renzi (1991); † Costa, De Renzi, and Faglioni (1989); na: not available.

axis of the earth, of eclipse, etc.), and five questions on biology (e.g. definition of photosynthesis, difference between arteries and veins, etc.). Geographic notions were well preserved: He had no difficulty in identifying 10 Italian districts, the capitals of 13 nations, the currency of eight countries. He easily defined acronyms (e.g. AIDS, Fax), neologisms (e.g. Bancomat, Italian for AutoBank), and foreign words (e.g. Walkman). On the other hand, in spite of his keen interest in mythology, when asked to provide the corresponding Greek name of six ancient Latin gods (e.g. Hermes–Mercury), he succeeded in only two instances. Even more surprising, his ability to retrieve historical information was very poor: In an easy multiple-choice questionnaire requiring him to choose the correct definition of a famous historical name (e.g. Napoleon: explorer, heretic, emperor), he scored only 3 out of 12. It is worth mentioning that his knowledge relating to famous chemists was astonishingly good.

Autobiographical memory was examined by means of a semi-structured interview prepared with the help of DV's mother and wife. Sixty-six facts of DV's personal semantic knowledge (Kopelman, Wilson, & Baddeley, 1989) and 45 autobiographical incidents were investigated, covering education, addresses, career, hobbies, military service, affective life, unusual family events (illnesses, car accidents, etc.), holidays, and leisure trips. A score ranging from 0 to 3 was given for each answer according to vividness and richness in details. A score of 0 was given for no or completely wrong answer and a score of 3 was attributed to an exhaustive answer. DV scored 67 (32%) out of a maximum score of 208 (66 × 3) on "facts" and 20 (15%) out of 135 (45 × 3) on "incidents". DV could give satisfactory answers only to questions related to his work. When retested one month later DV's scores were closely similar (65 and 19, respectively). The quality of DV's answers on the second autobiographical testing did not reveal any remarkable difference with respect to the answers he gave during the first testing session. No temporal gradient ever emerged. In agreement with the informal data, DV's autobiographical memory is clearly impaired.

He was also presented with twelve photographs, six depicting himself and familiar people and six of totally unknown people. He always recognised himself, but most of the time he failed to recognise his relatives. He never misidentified as familiar unfamiliar people. These findings tie in with those of the informal assessment.

Psychiatric History

A psychiatrist (Dr Franco Pittini, Ospedale S Paolo, Milan) evaluated the patient, by means of interviews, alone and with his wife, in several different sessions. During these interviews the patient never appeared depressed.

DV is described as an extrovert, making friends easily. On the other hand, he was rather elusive about his privacy and reluctant to share his inner life. He was quite defensive about his innermost emotions and longed to appear moral in his everyday behaviour, although he was not a religious bigot.

From the psychiatric interviews, it emerged that a few months before the trauma DV had progressively begun to show less and less interest in his young wife, whom he had known for five years. He did not share her anguish over her father's terminal cancer.

After being discharged from hospital, DV was upset by the over-protective and rather school-teacherish attitude of his wife, whom he had relearned to conceive as such, his feelings being completely blunted. Often he announced the wish of turning over a new leaf, given that he did not recall anything of his previous relationships. This intention was maintained with particular intensity in regard to his wife. It looked as if a latent marital crisis became overt after the accident. DV admitted that he did not like "going back" to his "previous" life, and even confessed that he felt the urge to hurt his wife's feelings. A few months after the onset of his amnesia, DV formally decided to divorce.

DV's wife reported that in the year immediately preceding the trauma her husband had associated himself with a group of new acquaintances of both sexes, rather heterogeneous in age, education, and social background. He used to practise with them a role-playing game in which they all dressed up as round-table knights. In response to DV's wishes, his wife never took part in these encounters. While DV was in hospital, she found at home a whole collection of pornographic magazines of sado-masochistic content. This left her appalled, given the moralistic behaviour of her husband.

DV attempted to accommodate the anxiety derived from his amnesia by enhancing the rational unconcern that had always characterised his attitude toward life. DV felt bothered by his relatives who incessantly tried to convince him to relearn his past. In fact, he claimed that he did not have any control over the veracity of the information they passed on to him and that it did not convey any feeling of intimacy whatsoever. He said "everything appears as a montage of depersonalised images". He is acutely aware that his uneasiness came from the blurring of self-identity due to his RA and the impoverishment of his emotions.

The psychiatrist confidently excluded malingering as well as multiple personality, hysteria, and psychosis. He favoured a neurological genesis of DV's cognitive deficit, although, at the end of the period of observation, he did not exclude the possibility of a "psychogenic" amnesia.

DV was also given a computerised version of the Minnesota Multiphasic Personality Inventory (Hathaway & McKinley, 1951). Accounting for the patient's amnesia, the personality scales on the whole indicated the adequacy of his reality judgements and did not reveal anxiety traits or depressive hints. The questionnaire results also suggested that DV is emotionally disturbed but does not show any tendency to lie, dissimilate, or repress information.

Re-check 10 Months After Onset. DV's RA has not substantially changed over time. His feeling of familiarity about people and places from his past gradually increased. However, this feeling was decontextualised and remained devoid of any biographical and chronological information. Moreover, these feelings never cropped up at the moment of the re-experience, but days after as in a daydream. Feelings of familiarity were never raised by false memories. None of the autobiographical events he relearned from others elicited any emotion.

It may be worth mentioning that in the last few months DV started a satisfying love story with another young man. DV asked to add this new state of affairs to his legal action to obtain divorce.

His good learning ability allowed DV to fill up all the non-autobiographical memory gaps. He is now running his professional activity as efficiently as before. He maintains that he is resigned to the loss of his past, to the point of engaging himself in building up a "new" life. He is in the process of divorcing.

DISCUSSION

As long ago as 1895, Abel and Colman described the case of a 36-year-old British railway fireman who became severely amnesic (possibly with a temporal gradient) after the feeder of an oil can entered his right cheek and pierced the base of his skull. After surgery it was quite obvious (p. 365) that "the whole of his life for twenty years before the accident was wiped out from his memory". The condition only slightly improved in the following year. The patient became also amnesic in term of ongoing information, impulsive, and had "very little control over his emotions". To our knowledge this is the first report of a long-lasting, albeit not "pure", RA.

Since then, about 20 cases of pure RA have been reported in a neuropsychological framework; surprisingly, most of them are crowded into the last few years. They have been thoroughly reviewed by De Renzi (1994) and others (Kapur, 1993; Lucchelli et al., 1995). Patient DV adds to this collection.

Our aim in reporting case DV is twofold. First, RA cases are still under-reported, at least by neurologists. In fact, they are likely to disregard apparently neurological signs and symptoms whenever the suspicion can be raised that they may be "psychogenic". The sudden onset of pure RA easily induces such a suspicion in nearly all cases. Second, we are interested in the complexity of these cases. Cultural prejudices may sometimes become radically alternative, and this state of affairs adds sensibly to the complexity of RA reports. DV's case is particularly complex. Actually, different stories could in principle be generated by resorting to different perspectives: neurological and neuropsychological (our own), or psychological, both from a psychiatric or a psychoanalytic approach. Each one would employ a different rhetorical layout with a different background of empirical knowledge and speculative beliefs. Admittedly, no argument can be cogently provided to falsify the alternative possible interpretations of DV's behavioural disorders. Thus, a psychiatrist could describe DV as a compulsive liar, who feigned in the past several pseudo-organic fainting spells and thereafter took advantage of a mild head trauma to simulate RA: the story of a conscious impostor. It could also be a story of malingering, DV's secondary gain being that of getting rid of his no longer beloved wife. This behaviour would be assimilable to a rational way of acting. A psychoanalyst could emphasise in DV's RA a means of escaping from the super-egoic constraints induced by the outer world (family, wife, society, religion): a story of an unconscious way to resolve "intra-psychic conflicts". More generally, RA can be conceived as the most extensive instance of Freud's *Verdraengung* (remotion) mechanism. Freud's speculation actually can be conceived as the only coherent view (i.e. a model *in nuce*) of psychogenic amnesia. One unconsciously forgets tokens of his past information that no longer fit into his/her present emotional economy. "Forgetting" has the same meaning as render unretrievable some specific sets of information by means of an active, albeit unconscious mechanism. Such a mechanism is by definition devoid of any neurostructural abnormality. However, the wide extent of RA losses across different knowledge systems can hardly be explained taking the vantage point of a strictly Freudian approach.

We will discuss DV's amnesia from a neurological, neuropsychological, and psychological perspective.

From a Neurological Perspective

DV's memory deficits cannot be labelled as classic "post-traumatic amnesia", in so far as DV's anterograde memory was completely spared, RA lasted too long (the follow-up presently covers nearly one year) and he did not recover (Mayes, 1988; Russell, 1971; see Levin, 1989 for a review). The duration of DV's amnesia also rules out the possibility of tracing it back to a special case of transient global amnesia (Evans, Wilson, Wraight, & Hodges, 1993). Furthermore, DV's amnesia was never global (Roman-Campos, Poser, & Wood, 1980). Following Kapur (1993), we think it worth conceiving a new neurological entity: "pure permanent RA". Its main feature is the sudden onset of a persistent memory deficit limited to the retrograde domain without other neuropsychological deficits. Different patients show different patterns of memory impairment within the retrograde domain, though almost invariably autobiographical memory is impaired and procedural memory spared. A few instances of pure permanent RA follow a surprisingly mild head injury with no neurological sequelae and with or without neuroimaging evidence of brain pathology (case MM in Lucchelli et al., 1995; Stracciari et al., 1994). Cases have been described in which no apparent trauma was reported (Andrews, Poser, & Kessler, 1982; Dalla Barba, Mantovan, & Denes, in press; De Renzi et al., in press). Other authors have linked RA to miscellaneous aetiologies (see De Renzi et al., 1995, and Kapur, 1993, for reviews).

In the case of DV, no anatomical lesion was found, even after careful scrutiny of the temporal cortices and the mesencephalon (Goldberg et al., 1981; Penfield, 1952) with 1.5mm thick MRI sections. This does not allow the straightforward anatomical interpretation put forward in other RA cases (Goldberg et al., 1981; Hodges & McCarthy, 1993; Markowitsch, Calabrese, Haupts, Durwen, Leiss, & Gehlen, 1993). The only neuroimaging technique that showed abnormalities was SPECT, which consistently revealed abnormal perfusion in the subcortical areas of both hemispheres. This pattern speaks against any definite localisation but it points toward a diffuse organic derangement. However, this has to be taken with some caution. Structural damage has a heuristic value only if it can be related to a well-agreed neuropsychological model, which, in the case of retrograde memory remains as yet unsettled. Therefore, DV's SPECT findings are inconclusive and *per se* do not add to the neurological hypothesis of his RA.

On the other hand, once the hypothesis of malingering is laid to rest, the possibility that DV's RA is functional remains open to debate. The boundaries that seem to divide the psychogenic (i.e. functional) and neurological (i.e. organic) RA are blurred, and, in our opinion, this distinction is based on a somewhat old-fashioned partition. Thus, if we were successful in detecting a sound brain lesion, we would feel authorised to label the phenomenon under observation as "organic". If we failed in our hunt for neurostructural evidence, the phenomenon would be regarded as "psychogenic" by default. According to this logic, most of the cases of transient global amnesia, for instance, ought to be considered psychogenic. However, nowadays nobody would engage in a debate about the psychogenic origin of transient global amnesia.

From a Neuropsychological Perspective

DV's RA qualifies as "pure", that is, without any anterograde or procedural component, as well as without any extra-memory cognitive defect. At variance with a few cases (e.g. Lucchelli et al., 1995, case MM), the temporal extension of DV's RA encompasses his whole past life with no temporal gradient. Given that DV's RA did not modify in the follow-up period, it can be considered permanent; no gradient emerged in the 10-month follow-up. However, it is worth remembering that very few cases have been reported in which memory was recovered, sometimes after a long interval, without any feature predicting this fortunate occurrence (Lucchelli et al., 1995, for the description of two cases and a review). The rare emergence of fragments of memories never evoked further successful recollections, nor did they spontaneously flow in dreams as reported in case MA by De Renzi et al. (1995).

RA refers to those memories currently labelled as "old" or "past traces". In this designation reference ought to be made to sets of information organised in "knowledge systems", as distinct from mere ongoing past events. A good example of these knowledge systems is Conway's (1992) conceptualisation of autobiographical memory. The neuropsychological description of RA cases will allow us to fractionate the systems responsible for holding past traces, possibly beginning to specify their architecture. In fact, across different cases RA variably encroaches upon different domains of past memories.

DV's RA involves autobiographical traces as well as knowledge of contemporary public events. A patchy involvement of a few aspects of semantic knowledge was also demonstrated. It is tempting to speculate that the building of memory archives is guided by the context within which the relevant information were acquired. Along these lines it would be possible to distinguish: (1) self-experience mediated sets of information, essentially encompassing autobiographical knowledge; (2) media-mediated sets of information, referring to contemporary and ongoing updating about politics, sports, entertainments, cultural news, and events around the world; (3) education-mediated sets of information, including most of the "general knowledge of the world" or, following De Renzi et al. (1995), "encyclopaedic knowledge"; and (4) habit-mediated sets of abilities, including both strictly procedural performances as well as automatically initiated sequences of actions (e.g. Memory Organized Packets, or MOPs, Shank, 1982).

As it is true for most of the reported cases of RA, DV is severely impaired in the self-experience and media-mediated knowledge acquired before the trauma. Within the encyclopaedic domain, only a few, well-circumscribed areas were involved (fish and motorcycles, which were related to DV's specific hobbies, and history, which had been of particular interest for DV). This pattern cannot be explained in terms of category-specific semantic impairments, but it could be interpreted as the specific involvement of areas of the encyclopaedic knowledge most strictly related to autobiographical experiences. Habit-mediated abilities remain untouched. Therefore, the features of DV's RA substantiate the hypothesis that self-experience and media-mediated information are more fragile than encyclopaedic knowledge. Encyclopaedic knowledge is constantly involved in everyday ongoing activities because of the continuous call for predictions and plausibility guesses. To an even more remarkable degree, the same holds good for habits. On the other hand, knowledge of autobiographical and contemporary events is not as necessary in coping with everyday activities. Such a difference in rehearsal might account for the difference in DV's post-traumatic retrograde memory outcome, a view already proposed for semantic amnesia by Snowden, Griffiths, and Neary (1994). However, there are other ways of conceptualising the different fragility of the previously sketched sets of long-term memory. For instance, one could trace back their different fragility to different organisational features (in this perspective, reference is made to the "knowledge systems"). Actually one could rank the knowledge systems from a looser to a tighter interconnectivity of the relevant informational nodes. The latter condition would allow an easier and quicker associative retrieval with respect to the former one whenever some piece of information had already surfaced to consciousness.

The trend of differential ranking of domain fragility, replicated in most of the reported cases of RA, suggests that it is possible to conceive a preliminary fractionation of the organisation of the memory archives. It is likely that the form of acquisition of memory traces, the organisation of their contents, and the frequency of their use all play an interactive role in bringing about differences which become apparent only when a still unsettled kind of brain insult produces the permanent and pure RA syndrome. Thus, it may become understandable why DV's cognitive estimates are much better preserved than his knowledge of the French Revolution, even if both belong to encyclopaedic knowledge.

The radical dissociation between DV's brilliant anterograde memory performances and the impaired retrograde recollection underlines once more a substantial independence between processes devoted to bringing to consciousness past traces and learning mechanisms (Mayes, 1988). The deficit cannot be attributed to a general retrieval defect, since the impairment is limited to the retrieval from the stock of traces learned and consolidated before the trauma (for a similar argument see De Renzi et al., 1995). Instead, DV's ability to retrieve information learned after the trauma is unimpaired and indeed very effective. Traditionally, anterograde and retrograde memory were said to be concurrently impaired in amnesics. The co-occurrence of the two deficits is often reported, for instance in Korsakov amnesia (see Parkin & Leng, 1993, pp. 143–147, for a brief review) and sometimes referred to as continuity hypothesis (e.g. Ryback, 1971). The dissociation shown by RA patients coupled with the opposite dissociation of preserved retrograde memory in spite of a documented anterograde deficit (Dall'Ora, Della Sala, & Spinnler, 1989; Della Sala, Laiacona, Spinnler, & Trivelli, 1992; Malamut, Graff-Radford, Chawluk, Grossman, & Gur, 1992; Syz, 1937), offers firm ground to argue for the radical distinctness of anterograde and retrograde memory mechanisms.

Easy learning is a common finding in RA patients, and in DV in particular. It appears counterintuitive, since it seems to suggest that a looser network of knowledge available to consciousness speeds up the learning process. We uphold the alternative view that ease in learning is baffling only in the case of relearning. Even if not formally verified, this is what appears to be at work in DV. It seems that most of the information is not lost: although unavailable to consciousness, it is perhaps implicitly available. We suggest that relearning of inaccessible information cannot be compared with learning from scratch.

DV's implicit access to stored information would support the interpretation of the patient deficit as an access disorder rather than a loss of stored information. This conclusion is suggested by the fact that some knowledge (e.g. the familiarity with the colleague's signature, the easy finding of the right location of a kitchen tool in his house) seems implicitly spared, in spite of an explicit dearth of information (see also Stuss & Guzman, 1988). In this framework, RA can be interpreted in terms of a rise of the threshold in the mechanism that makes stored information available to conscious processing. Therefore the genesis of RA can be thought of as the deficit of an access mechanism which in normal condition allows traces in long-term memory to be activated, so that they exceed the threshold of consciousness, thus becoming available for further process.

As said above, DV quickly relearned most of the information that he could not retrieve and this allowed him to progressively fill up most of his RA gaps. It would be expected that this should also hold good for his autobiographical deficit, the most disturbing aspect of RA. None the less, DV perceived all relearned notions about his past as extraneous, devoid of feelings, and he compared them to the notions of ancient history (e.g. the Pharaohs) one learns at school. This condition appears akin to the *jamais vu* experience which is part of some psychomotor seizures (Penfield, 1955). Given the loss of emotionally loaded memories of his past, DV felt to be a "new person" just beginning to build up a biographical self (Fitzgerald, 1991). Actually, new experiences, as distinct from relearned ones, entered his memory normally, conveying knowledge and emotion linked together. Admittedly, this particular feature of DV's relearning capabilities defies any neuropsychological interpretation. It is an issue worth being addressed in future studies of RA cases.

From a Psychological Perspective

Three hypotheses will be considered, namely that DV is a malingerer, that his pure RA is psychogenic, and that DV consciously made use of his "true" (i.e. organic) amnesia.

The possibility of malingering was eventually thought to be unlikely since we deemed it quite difficult for DV deliberately to simulate a 45-minute lasting unresponsiveness followed by permanent RA, starting from the unquestioned occipital trauma. The only gain he could possibly achieve was a divorce from his wife, but it seems implausible that, to this end, DV chose such a tortuous way. We are, however, aware that a really conclusive argument against a deliberate feigning of RA is lacking.

It was harder to reach an unanimous conclusion about the psychogenic or neurogenic nature of DV's RA. Also, the psychiatrist who followed him up modified his view over a six-month period, wavering from the confident "organic" interpretation embraced after the first sessions to an eventually doubtful psychogenic one. Three neuropsychologists, who evaluated DV's behavioural and cognitive features on three different occasions over a one-month period at the beginning of the follow-up, took note, each time after extensive discussion, of their guesses about the probability of DV's disorders being of a malingering, psychogenic, or organic nature. In spite of these discussions, there was a great inter-rater discrepancy. These arbitrarily percentualised guesses are set out in Table 11.4.

The increasing rejection of the malingering hypothesis is clearly evident. On the other hand, the overall trend for a psychogenic genesis cannot be overlooked. This diagnostic guess was based on DV's loss of self identity, coupled with drive to flee, the oft-expressed emotional flatness and the marital crisis (namely, a paradigmatic negative life event) (Abeles & Schilder, 1935; Kopelman et al., 1994; Schacter & Kihlstrom, 1989; Stengel, 1966). By the same token, however, arguments can be raised in favour of the neurogenic interpretation. DV had a substantially normal pre-morbid personality. He was never anosognosic about his RA. The course of his RA has been stable throughout almost 10 months of follow-up. Spontaneous

TABLE 11.4
Average Percentual Guesses of Three Neuropsychologists at the End of Three Different Assessment Sessions Regarding the Aetiology of DV's Amnesia

	Malingering	Psychogenic	Neurogenic
I Assessment (27/12/1993)	26	41	33
II Assessment (29/12/1993)	22	66	12
III Assessment (1/2/1994)	3	50	47

(i.e. non-relearned) islands of past memories fuzzily re-emerged from his past. DV's answers to the examiner's questions were never blatantly implausible. Finally, DV's RA extended well outside the boundaries of the autobiographical domain.

We do not conceive DV as a case of double personality similar to that reported by Franz (1933), where the patient changed personality about every decade. It was apparent that DV underwent a sort of transition to a somewhat different person, but this appears to be a direct consequence of his autobiographical amnesia, which concealed the original self. DV was well aware of this transition, which was nil for some aspects (e.g. the professional skills) and complete for others (e.g. emotion). He was also aware that turning over a new leaf and being a "new person" would be socially awkward. The awkwardness of his new self was paramount in the negotiation of his divorce, which in turn could simply be thought of as the consequence of a long-lasting marital crisis, possibly due to DV's first latent and then overt homosexuality. Alternatively, one can believe that DV made up, so to speak, a "rational" use of his organic RA to get free from his no longer satisfying marriage. In this respect, the case reported by Kopelman et al. (1994) could share some similarity with DV, in the sense of a complex interaction of different mechanisms in the genesis and maintenance of RA. Their patient was a 42-year-old American woman who, during a visit to London, underwent a psychogenic RA, lasting a few days. She surreptitiously extended in time her amnesic state and used this condition of being a brand-new person to bail out from her first, unhappy, marriage, later engaging in a new one.

Syz (1937, p. 374) maintained that:

> wherever those nervous structures which control the personality-organization are damaged, it may become particularly difficult to discriminate between alterations of function due to organic lesions and alterations due to reactive tendencies of the total organism in its adaptation to the environment. So that we may be confronted with combinations of fusions of the two types of processes which are difficult to disentangle.

We entirely agree and deem it more profitable to go beyond the cultural trap of the psychogenic versus organic alternative approach. Indeed, the study of the amnesic phenomenon *per se*, independently of its aetiology, can add to the theoretical body of knowledge proper to different cultural viewpoints.

SUMMARY

A case of pure retrograde amnesia (RA) following a mild head trauma is reported. The patient, DV, showed two dissociations: A clearcut RA was coupled with normal anterograde memory abilities, and, within the retrograde domain, procedural-implicit memory was probably normal in the face of overt amnesia for autobiographical and media-mediated information. Encyclopaedic memory was largely spared. No other neuropsychological deficit was detectable.

The description of the patient's symptoms is framed in a neuropsychological perspective, and in this context his amnesic defects are interpreted as a selective disorder of access.

The discussion also considers different frames of description and interpretation of DV's RA, namely those belonging to the realm of so-called "functional amnesias".

ACKNOWLEDGEMENTS

We are indebted to Franco Pittini, MD, for his invaluable help in pin-pointing the patient's personality, and to G.L. Spreafico, MD, who carried out the SPECT assessment. We read about the amnesics reported by newspapers in *Fortean Times* no. 61, 1992. Mrs Jo Watson amended the English. The work described in this chapter has been partially supported by a grant (no. 87.00233.04.115.12234) to HS, from the Consiglio Nazionale delle Ricerche.

REFERENCES

Abel, H.M., & Colman, W.S. (1895). A case of puncture of the base of the brain by the spout of an oil can, in which there was loss of memory of previous events. *British Medical Journal*, 356–358.

Abeles, M., & Schilder, P. (1935). Psychogenic loss of personal identity. *Archives of Neurology and Psychiatry*, *34*, 587–604.

Andrews, E., Poser, C.M., & Kessler, M. (1982). Retrograde amnesia for forty years. *Cortex*, *18*, 441–458.

Basso, A., Capitani, E., & Laiacona, M. (1987). Raven's coloured progressive matrices: Normative values on 305 adult normal controls. *Functional Neurology*, *2*, 189–194.

Benton, A.L., Hamsher, K. de S., Varney, N.R., & Spreen, O. (1983). *Contributions to neuropsychological assessment: A clinical manual*. Oxford: Oxford University Press.

Charcot, J.M. (1892). Sur un cas d'amnésie rétro-antérograde. *Revue de médecine*, *12*, 81–96.

Conway, M.A. (1992). A structural model of autobiographical memory. In M.A. Conway, D.C. Rubin, H. Spinnler, & W.A. Wagenaar (Eds.), *Theoretical perspectives on autobiographical memory* (pp. 167–193). Dordrecht: Kluwer Academic Publishers.

Costa, M., De Renzi, E., & Faglioni, P. (1989). Un questionario italiano per lo studio della memoria retrograda. *Archivio di Psicologia Neurologia e Psichiatria*, *50*, 735–755.

Dalla Barba, G., Mantovan, M.G., & Denes, G. (in press). Remembering and knowing the past: A case study of retrograde amnesia. *Cortex*.

Dall'Ora, P., Della Sala, S., & Spinnler, H. (1989). Autobiographical memory: Its impairment in amnesic syndromes. *Cortex*, *25*, 197–217.

Della Sala, S, Laiacona, M., Spinnler, H., & Trivelli, C. (1992). Is autobiographical impairment due to a deficit of recollection? An overview of studies on Alzheimer dements, frontal and global amnesic patients. In M.A. Conway, D.C. Rubin, H. Spinnler, & W.A. Wagenaar (Eds.), *Theoretical perspectives on autobiographical memory* (pp. 451–472). Dordrecht: Kluwer Academic Publishers.

De Renzi, E. (1994). *Retrograde amnesia*. Paper presented at International Neuropsychological Society Workshop, Cincinatti, Ohio, 2nd February.

De Renzi, E., Lucchelli, F., Muggia, S., & Spinnler, H. (1995). Persistent retrograde amnesia following a minor trauma. *Cortex*, *31*, 531–542.

Evans, J., Wilson, B.A., Wraight, E.P., & Hodges, J.R. (1993). Neuropsychological and SPECT scan findings during and after transient global amnesia: Evidence for the differential impairment of remote episodic memory. *Journal of Neurology, Neurosurgery and Psychiatry*, *56*, 1227–1230.

Faglioni, P., Cremonini, A., & De Renzi, E. (1991). Taratura su soggetti normali di test di facce sconosciute e familiari. *Archivio di Psicologia Neurologia e Psichiatria*, *52*, 339–350.

Fitzgerald, J.M. (1991). Autobiographical memory and conceptualization of the self. In M.A. Conway, D.C. Rubin, H. Spinnler, & W.A. Wagenaar (Eds.), *Theoretical perspectives on autobiographical memory* (pp. 99–114). Dordrecht: Kluwer Academic Publishers.

Franz, S.I. (1933). *Persons one and three: A study in multiple personalities*. New York: McGraw-Hill.

Goldberg, E., Antin, S.P., Bilder, R.M. JR, Gerstman, L.J., Hughes, J.E.O., & Mattis, S.C. (1981). Retrograde amnesia: Possible role of mesencephalic reticular activation on long-term memory. *Science*, *213*, 1392–1394.

Hathaway, S.R., & McKinley, J.C. (1951). *Manual for the Minnesota multiphasic personality inventory* (rev. ed.). New York: The Psychological Corporation.

Hodges, J.R., & McCarthy, R.A. (1993). Autobiographical amnesia resulting from bilateral paramedian thalamic infarction. *Brain*, *116*, 921–940.

Janet, P. (1928). *L'evolution de la mémoire et de la notion de temps* (p. 619). Paris, France: A. Chahine.

Kapur, N. (1993). Focal retrograde amnesia in neurological disease: A critical review. *Cortex*, *29*, 217–234.

Kapur, N., Ellison, D., Smith, L.P., & McLellan Burrows, E.H. (1992). Focal retrograde amnesia following bilateral temporal lobe pathology. *Brain*, *115*, 73–85.

Kapur, N., Heath, P., Meudell, P., & Kennedy, P. (1986). Amnesia can facilitate memory performance: Evidence from a patient with dissociated retrograde amnesia. *Neuropsychologia*, *24*, 215–222.

Kopelman, M.D. (1987). Amnesia: Organic and psychogenic. *British Journal of Psychiatry*, *150*, 428–442.

Kopelman, M.D., Christensen, H., Puffett, A., & Stanhope, N. (1994). The great escape: A neuropsychological study of psychogenic amnesia. *Neuropsychologia*, *32*, 675–691.

Kopelman, M.D., Wilson, B.A., & Baddeley, A.D. (1989). The autobiographical memory interview: A new assessment of autobiographical and personal semantic memory in amnesic patients. *Journal of Clinical and Experimental Neuropsychology*, *11*, 724–744.

Levin, H.S. (1989). Memory deficit after closed head injury. In F. Boller & J. Grafman (Eds.), *Handbook of neuropsychology* (Vol. 8, pp. 183–207). Amsterdam: Elsevier Science Publishers.

Lucchelli, F., Muggia, S., & Spinnler, H. (1995). The "petites madeleines" phenomenon in amnesic patients: Sudden recovery from retrograde amnesia. *Brain*, *118*, 167–183.

Malamut, B.L., Graff-Radford, N., Chawluk, J., Grossman, R.I., & Gur, R.C. (1992). Memory in a case of bilateral thalamic infarction. *Neurology*, *42*, 163–169.

Markowitsch, H.J., Calabrese, P., Haupts, M., Durwen, H.F., Liess, J., & Gehlen, W. (1993). Searching for the anatomical basis of retrograde amnesia. *Journal of Clinical and Experimental Neuropsychology*, *15*, 947–967.

Markowitsch, H.J., Calabrese, P., Liess, J., Haupts, M., Durwen, H.F., & Gehlen, W. (1993). Retrograde amnesia after traumatic injury of the fronto-temporal cortex. *Journal of Neurology, Neurosurgery and Psychiatry*, *56*, 988–992.

Mayes, A.R. (1988). Human organic memory disorders. Cambridge, UK: Cambridge University Press.

Novelli, G., Papagno, C., Capitani, E., Laiacona, M., Cappa, S.F., & Vallar, G. (1986). Tre test clinici di memoria verbale a lungo termine. Taratura su soggetti normali. *Archivio di Psicologia, Neurologia e Psichiatria, 2,* 278–296.

Novelli, G., Papagno, C., Capitani, E., Laiacona, M., Vallar, G., & Cappa, S.F. (1986). Tre test clinici di ricerca e produzione lessicale. Taratura su soggetti normali. *Archivio di Psicologia, Neurologia e Psichiatria, 4,* 477–506.

Orsini, A., Grossi, D., Capitani, E., Laiacona, M., Papagno, C., & Vallar, G. (1987). Verbal and spatial immediate memory span: Normative data from 1355 adults and 1112 children. *Italian Journal of Neurological Science, 8,* 539–548.

Parkin, A.J., & Leng, N.R.C. (1993). *Neuropsychology of the amnesic syndrome* (pp. 143–147). Hillsdale, NJ: Lawrence Erlbaum Associates Inc.

Penfield, W. (1952). Memory mechanisms. *Archives of Neurology and Psychiatry, 67,* 178–198.

Penfield, W. (1955). The twenty-ninth Maudsley Lecture: The role of the temporal cortex in certain psychical phenomena. *Journal of Mental Science, 101,* 451–465.

Penfield, W., & Mathieson, G. (1974). Memory, autopsy findings and comments on the role of hippocampus in experiential recall. *Archives of Neurology, 31,* 145–154.

Pirandello, L. (1992). *Come tu mi vuoi.* Milan: Mondadori.

Roman-Campos, G., Poser, C.M., & Wood, F.B. (1980). Persistent retrograde memory deficit after transient global amnesia. *Cortex, 16,* 509–518.

Russell, W.R. (1971). *The traumatic amnesias.* Oxford: Oxford University Press.

Ryback, R. (1971). The continuum and specificity of the effects of alcohol on memory. *Quarterly Journal of Studies in Alcoholism, 32,* 995–1016.

Schacter, D.L., & Kihlstrom, J.F. (1989). Functional amnesia. In F. Boller & J. Grafman (Eds.), *Handbook of neuropsychology* (Vol. 3, pp. 209–231). Amsterdam: Elsevier Science Publishers.

Schilder, P. (1923). Aufhellung der retrograden Amnesie eines wiederbelebten Erhaengten durch Hypnose. *Med Klinik, 19,* 604–606.

Sciascia, L. (1981). *Il teatro della memoria.* Torino: Einaudi.

Shallice, T., & Evans, M.E. (1978). The involvement of the frontal lobes in cognitive estimation. *Cortex, 14,* 294–303.

Shank, R.C. (1982). *Dynamic memory.* New York: Cambridge University Press.

Sharp, P.F., Smith, F.W., Gemmel, H.G., Lyall, D., Evans, N.T.S., & Grozdanovic, D. (1986). Technetium 99mTc-HMPAO stereoisomers as potential agents for imaging regional cerebral blood flow: Human volunteer studies. *Journal of Nuclear Medicine, 27,* 171–177.

Snowden, J., Griffiths, S.H., & Neary, D. (1994). Semantic dementia: Autobiographical contribution to preservation of meaning. *Cognitive Neuropsychology, 11,* 265–288.

Spinnler, H., & Tognoni, G. (1987). Taratura e standardizzazione italiana di test neuropsicologici. *Italian Journal of Neurological Sciences, 8* (Suppl. 6).

Stengel, E. (1966). Psychogenic loss of memory. In C.W.M. Whitty & O.L. Zangwill (Eds.), *Amnesia* (pp. 181–191). London: Butterworth.

Stracciari, A., Ghidoni, E., Guarino, M., Poletti, M., & Pazzaglia, P. (1994). Post-traumatic retrograde amnesia with selective impairment of autobiographical memory. *Cortex, 30,* 459–468.

Stuss, D.T., & Guzman, D.A. (1988). Severe remote memory loss with minimal anterograde amnesia: A clinical note. *Brain and Cognition, 8,* 21–30.

Syz, H. (1937). Recovery from loss of mnemonic retention after head trauma. *Journal of General Psychology, 17,* 355–387.

Section E

WHAT DO I BELIEVE?

In both the popular and the psychiatric imagination, hallucinations and delusions have usually been regarded as the very hallmark of insanity. Which is very odd.

True, hallucinations occur (by definition) in many "psychoses", but they can also occur in conditions of sensory deprivation, after ingesting certain classes of chemicals, and after relatively focal brain damage. Purely peripheral clouding of sight or impairment of hearing can often lead to visual and auditory hallucinations, respectively, in people who are mentally perfectly fit. When "psychotic" individuals suffer hallucinations, are these visions and voices qualitatively or quantitatively any different from the experiences reported by the normal subject? Are the underlying mechanisms the same? Are the overlying interpretations the same? That is, can we distinguish *medically* between hallucinations that are positively versus negatively evaluated by individuals or societies?

Similar problems arise with respect to delusions. It is easy to define a delusion as a belief that could not possibly be true and that is held for the "wrong" reasons or with too great a conviction. But caveats are immediately required. For example: "Statistics show that 55 per cent of people who buy counterfeit luxury goods think that they are genuine, even though they may have bought them more cheaply than they would have expected" (*Business Life*, November 1995). Many social and religious beliefs of one's culture are given a "medically protected" status, as indeed are the extremely odd hypotheses of the culture's theoretical physicists. Common sense and truth do not always coincide. Just as a language is a dialect with an army and a navy, so a religion is a cult that has the backing of the state. A *"folie"* can be individual or *"à deux"*, but where between three and infinity does a delusion become a cultural given? The history of science is littered with examples of people who held to a hypothesis for many years, against all the odds, and with an unshakeable conviction not shared by their colleagues. In the long run, some of these scientists turned out to be right (and others, admittedly, wrong). Is delusion the price we pay for quantum mechanics or washing one's hands after delivering a baby? According to Thomas Kuhn at least, scientific hypotheses fade away not when they are falsified but rather when their adherents die.

The two final chapters of this volume deal explicitly with cases of (pathological) hallucination and delusion in two very different types of condition: head injury (Halligan and Marshall) and schizophrenia (Cahill and Frith). In both cases, however, the authors are concerned with the question of how *particular* delusional beliefs come into being and are sustained. To what extent are they determined by false percepts and to what extent by false reasoning?

12 The Wise Prophet Makes Sure of the Event First: Hallucinations, Amnesia, and Delusions

Peter W. Halligan and John C. Marshall
University Department of Clinical Neurology, Neuropsychology Unit, Radcliffe Infirmary, Oxford, UK

INTRODUCTION

Cases of complex but encapsulated delusions secondary to visual hallucinations after brain damage (Anderson & Rizzo, 1994; Peroutka, Sohmer, Kumar, Folstein, & Robinson, 1982; Richardson, 1992; Starkstein, Robinson, & Berthier, 1992) raise a range of theoretical questions about the nature of cognitive processes involved in perception and belief construction. Previous accounts of such phenomena are rare and provide scant details about the origin, quality, and extent of the patients' beliefs (Levine & Finkelstein, 1982; Levine & Grek, 1984; Price & Mesulam, 1985). Furthermore, little has been written about how these patients behave when confronted with or challenged about the peculiarity of their beliefs.

For each individual case, we suggest that an appropriate and meaningful analysis would involve elucidating the exact nature of the relationships between the specific modular pathologies and those central processes involved in their interpretation (Malloy, Cimino, & Westlake, 1992; Young, Ellis, Szulecka, & de Pauw, 1990). This analytic approach involves the study of specific symptoms rather than traditional diagnostic categories (Altman & Jobe, 1992; Halligan, Marshall, & Ramachandran, 1994; Persons, 1986) and has proved useful in deconstructing conditions such as the misidentification syndromes (Young, Reid, Wright, & Hellawell, 1993). A related and important development is the application of cognitive neuropsychological methods to the study of such neuropsychiatric

237

phenomena (O'Carroll, 1992). This approach seeks to understand neuropsychiatric symptoms in terms of damage to normal cognitive processes.

In this chapter, we describe a delusional disorder secondary to post-traumatic hallucinations in a patient (Jim) two years after right hemispheric brain injury. Jim's visual hallucinations, which became progressively worse after the road traffic accident responsible for his brain damage, occurred in the context of left hemiparesis, sensory loss, and mild visual neglect. The subjective reality of these vivid hallucinations caused considerable distress that was associated with psychogenic seizures. The morbid content of the hallucinations, together with their temporal contiguity to closely related public events (reported in the media), convinced the patient that he possessed paranormal abilities. Specific attention is drawn to the strength of this delusional conviction, the degree of insight shown, the intactness of normal beliefs outside the affected domain, the need to attribute meaning to the hallucinations and the causal relationship between hallucinations and delusions.

CASE REPORT

Jim is a thin 63-year-old, right-handed man who never learned to read or write. Born in Ireland, Jim has worked and lived in England for the past 30 years. Married, with three grown-up sons and three grandchildren, Jim has taken several odd jobs including window cleaning and roof repairs since retiring from the local steel plant. The road traffic accident which gave rise to his head injury occurred while he was walking near his home in January 1990. He was struck by a van near a pedestrian crossing and was taken by ambulance to the local hospital. A computerised tomography (CT) scan showed a large right parietal extradural haemorrhage. In the accident he also fractured his right hip and clavicle. Transferred to the Radcliffe Infirmary (Oxford), he was operated on to remove the large haematoma. This operation involved a right parietal craniotomy with evacuation of the blood clot. After the operation, a CT scan showed that the main haematoma had been successfully removed but there were still several small haemorrhages in the right temporal and parietal lobes. Jim remembers the night of the accident, and some of the events leading up to the accident; his next memory is approximately 11 days after the accident.

When admitted to Rivermead Rehabilitation Centre (Oxford) two months later in March 1990, Jim's main problems were left-sided weakness, left visual field deficit, severe post-traumatic amnesia, left-sided visual neglect, impaired concentration and attention span. On the star cancellation task from the Behavioural Inattention Test (Halligan, Cockburn, & Wilson, 1991) he scored 11/54, indicative of severe neglect. He also showed impairments on memory (Rivermead Behavioural Memory

Test: 5/12) and orientation tasks (Hodkinson Mental Test: 2/10; Hodkinson, 1972). Spoken language and comprehension was not affected. Over the next three months, Jim succeeded in learning to walk again and became functionally independent. On the Barthel ADL (Activities of Daily Living; Wade & Collin, 1988) index his functional abilities improved from 5/20 to 17/20. When discharged in July 1990, Jim still had severe memory problems, scoring 5/12 on the Rivermead Behavioural Memory Test (Wilson, Cockburn, & Baddeley, 1985). Following discharge, Jim continued to make good progress and over the course of the following two years went on several walking holidays with his wife to Germany, Scotland, and Switzerland.

When we first saw Jim in the spring of 1990, there were no indications of any ongoing neuropsychiatric symptoms. Indeed, it was almost two years later before we discovered that Jim was experiencing visual hallucinations and that these had begun when he left Rivermead in 1990. Given the progress he had made, Jim thought it unnecessary to mention the hallucinations to his doctors or care staff. He just hoped that his "visions" would remit with time.

It was on Jim's readmission to Rivermead in September 1992, following a series of falls, that he mentioned, for the first time, that he had been experiencing visual hallucinations since leaving Rivermead two years previously. Although Jim's family doctor did not mention hallucinations, he did refer to Jim's "absence attacks" and their association with falls during the summer. Assuming an epileptic cause, a course of anti-convulsants was begun; these proved ineffective and if anything the number of falls increased. In addition, the witnessed episodes did not provide convincing evidence for real convulsive activity. Over the course of three months at Rivermead in 1992, some of these "absence attacks" were observed by care staff; in most instances, Jim was staring out of a window or at a wall. Jim himself reported that the "absence attacks" coincided with the increasingly vivid visual hallucinations he was experiencing. During these "absence attacks", Jim often manifested what care staff described as "seizure-like" behaviours including vigorous fist clenching, facial grimacing, conspicuous frowning, and occasional shouting. He would often strike the arm of his chair forcibly with his right or left clenched fist and on several occasions would end up crying. Once the "attack" was over, Jim immediately reverted to his usual self and could converse rationally. These motor behaviours varied in intensity and were, in Jim's opinion, precipitated by the content of his hallucinations.

After a severe "seizure-like" attack in November 1992, Jim was taken to the Radcliffe Infirmary for radiological and electrophysiological investigations. A repeat CT scan showed no additional changes other than a mature area of low attenuation in the right hemisphere. There was no evidence of hydrocephalus or new pathology. Anticonvulsants did not affect the hallucinations or the seizure-like activity. Epileptic discharges were thought unlikely for several reasons: (1) the presentation of the attacks was not suggestive of grand mal seizures. There was no drowsiness, confusion, or focal neurological deficits. Reflexes were normal, there was no tongue biting, incontinence, or loss of consciousness; (2) administration of anticonvulsants had little or no effect on the attacks; (3) on two separate occasions, split-screen electroencephalic telemetry using standard 10–20 scalp electrodes failed to substantiate epileptic discharges.

During this telemetry, nine "seizure-like attacks" were recorded. The attacks were not stereotyped and were usually brought on by looking out the window; they lasted between 30 seconds and 7 minutes and the clinical signs included opening and closing of the left fist, striking the side arm of the chair with his right fist, and eyebrow and forehead movements. At times, Jim's whole body would shake as if he was crying and he would then use his hanky to wipe his eyes. None of these nine "attacks" were associated with pathological epileptic changes on EEG. During the episodes, Jim was responsive to others around him and it was possible to talk him out of the attack. The EEG results found high theta and delta amplitudes in the right posterior hemisphere and polymorphic slow wave activity in the right occipital temporal lobe. The right hemisphere readings were dominated by high amplitude 1–6Hz theta/delta activity. The theta wave was mainly at 7Hz and 40–70Uv, peak to peak. Varney, Hines, Bailey and Roberts (1992) have suggested that theta bursts after closed head injury are clinically significant in that such patients commonly experience a range of symptoms similar to those seen in complex partial seizures. These include memory gaps, *déjà vu*, visual illusions, severe headaches, and "staring spells". The extensive electrophysiological investigations led to the conclusion that Jim's observed "attacks" were probably psychogenic (Boon & Williamson, 1993), precipitated by anxiety which was in turn provoked by the content of Jim's "visions". A behavioural management approach was begun, but this did not reduce the frequency or severity of the pseudo-seizures.

Neuropsychological and Psychiatric Testing

Apart from the "absence attacks", hallucinations, and psychogenic seizures, Jim appeared in good health: his left-sided weakness had improved considerably since his first admission in 1990 (motricity scores: left arm = 84%; left leg = 76%), although he still showed constructional apraxis and moderate left-sided neglect (107/146 BIT). Visual fields were now normal to confrontation, visual acuity was 6/18 right eye, 6/24 left eye and there was a full range of ocular movements. Saccades to the left were hypometric and jerky. Performance on the Barthel ADL index had improved to 18/20. Speech production and comprehension were normal.

Jim's inability to read limited the range of neuropsychological assessments attempted. Nevertheless, Jim's scores on Raven's Coloured Progressive Matrices (Raven, 1977) and the Graded Naming Test (McKenna & Warrington, 1983) indicated that he was within the dull normal range of intelligence. Although Jim's illiteracy contributed to poor performance on the standard mental orientation tests, it did not appear to affect his social interactions on the ward, where he was well liked and was often involved in helping other less mobile patients. There was no evidence of anosognosia, anosodiaphoria, visual agnosia, prosopagnosia, or optic ataxia. Prior to the accident Jim had never experienced any type of hallucination and there was no history of neurologic or psychiatric illness.

Jim was usually cheerful but would become tearful when talking about his late parents and brothers. Although he denied feeling depressed, Jim expressed specific concern about his hallucinations. There were no strong biological signs of depression; Jim was eating and sleeping well and he socialised appropriately on the ward and easily made friends with other patients. On the Hospital Anxiety and Depression (HAD) scale (Zigmond & Snaith, 1983), Jim's anxiety score revealed considerable apprehension and worry (13/21) whereas his depression score was within normal limits (7/21). Likewise on the Wakefield Depression Inventory (Snaith, Ahmed, Mehta, & Hamilton, 1971), a more general assessment of depressed mood and symptomatology, Jim scored 8/36, which is well within the normal range. On the Present State Examination (Wing, Cooper, & Sartorius, 1974), there was no evidence of formal thought disorder; he showed considerable insight into his situation, agreeing that the experiences he was describing were unusual and that nobody else but him could see the people and events involved. Although he described being able to read the thoughts of other people, there were no experiences to suggest thought broadcasting, thought insertion, or blocking.

Delusions

The first indication that Jim was harbouring delusions became evident soon after his readmission in 1992. In response to questions by an orthoptist regarding his eyesight, Jim replied that he "could see through walls like [through] a window" and that he "could see things happening elsewhere". For example, he reported that he could see what was happening to his son who was working in Germany. He also told the admitting doctor at Rivermead that he could predict the future and had feelings of déjà vu. When questioned about the source and characteristics of his visual hallucinations, Jim revealed a complex set of inter-related delusions which he seemed to have inferred from the content and temporal sequence of his hallucinations. The extent and reliability of these beliefs became clear over the course of subsequent discussions with Jim, his family, and care staff.

Hallucination Characteristics

Hallucinations are one of the traditional hallmarks of psychiatric disturbance and have "contributed a great deal to the mystery of 'madness'" (Asaad & Shapiro, 1986). Hallucinations are perceptions which occur in the absence of appropriate external stimulation; they can be found in a wide variety of clinical conditions ranging from functional psychosis to focal brain damage (Cutting, 1990; Halligan et al., 1994).

To investigate the nature of Jim's hallucinations and establish the consistency of his recollections, we saw him six times between October 1992 and February 1993. With Jim's permission, all these sessions were recorded. Throughout, he was fully co-operative and answered all our questions. Jim confirmed that the visual hallucinations began after his head injury in 1990 and typically occurred with his eyes open and when he was staring at a wall or out of a window. The hallucinations were experienced as existing in real space outside the patient's body (although they were sometimes seen as "superimposed" on an otherwise veridical percept). Furthermore, the visions were always experienced as "fixed" on the retina: "when I turn ... then they go with me ... they travel with my eyes".

The hallucinations, which occurred without warning, were fully formed, dynamic, normally shaped and coloured. Jim claimed to have no control over their frequency, content, or onset. The hallucinations were often associated with shaking and other apparently involuntary movements, but no vocalisations occurred. Although the hallucinations could extend across the whole visual field, they were typically located in the top right-hand corner of the visual field. Jim described them as more vivid and much larger than a TV screen. He found it difficult to estimate the frequency of his hallucinations but agreed that once a week was not uncommon. The content of the hallucinations was realistic, distressing, and unwelcome.

During and sometimes before these hallucinations, Jim experienced a dull pain which extended across his forehead and the top of his head. All hallucinations were associated, he said, with a build up of "heat" and throbbing inside his head. Jim described it was "... when the pain starts to die down that's when the heat starts to build up". He explained the grimacing and banging of his right fist on the chair rest or table as one way of dissipating this build-up of "heat".

Content of Hallucinations

Most of Jim's hallucinations (or "visions" as Jim preferred to call them) were distressing to him and concerned death and destruction. They divided into two main types: those relating to people from his past and those concerning public events, many of which Jim claimed had not yet taken place at the time of his hallucination. The first type included seeing the bodies of dead friends, family members and work colleagues. The second type comprised public events and included IRA bombings in Northern Ireland and London, an attempt to assassinate the prime minister John Major, and an air crash. For Jim, the most disturbing aspect of these visions was the fact that he claimed to have "seen" details of the tragedies *before* they took place.

In one of his first hallucinations, Jim claimed to have foretold the events of a bombing in Northern Ireland in some detail the day before the bombing took place. He could not remember when he had this hallucination but claimed that it produced a bemused and sceptical reaction at the day centre; subsequently Jim kept reports of the hallucinations to himself. According to Jim, the inability to be taken seriously together with the inability to forewarn or prevent harm to others exacerbated his anxiety. Discussing the event with us on 8th October, 1992, Jim reports:

I seen the yellow van ... and I told them long before it happened ... I told the wife in advance it was coming ... I said there will be a bomb blast, they blew the whole blessed lot up ... then it was on the television and she said now I can see what you mean.

From details provided by Jim, the bombing described probably refers to the murder of eight Protestant construction workers as they drove home in a transit van in Northern Ireland on 17th January, 1992.

Description of Hallucinations

To appreciate the character of the hallucinations, it is helpful to provide some of the details in Jim's own words (8th and 14th October, 1992).

Hallucinations from the Past.

E   When did these visions first occur?
Jim   They happened after the accident, I could see nothing before ...
      it was after I went home the first time [May 1990]. It happened
      one day ... that was all ... no background to it whatsoever ...
      just came out of the blue.
E   What happened?
Jim   I'll have to put it in my own words ... I went into the day care
      centre and that's when it started to show up ... there was a man

	died in that house ... but I could look at the ceiling and it would open up and I could see right through it ... I could see the gentleman the same as he was then ... with a red beard...
E	Where did you see him?
Jim	When I went out of the room into the hall and looked up the stairs... I saw a man with his back to a wall, he had a red beard, he must have been gone some fifty years.
E	Was he dead?
Jim	Yes.
E	Had he decomposed?
Jim	No.
E	Did he look normal?
Jim	Yes.
E	Was he alive?
Jim	No ... dead!

Jim knew this hallucinated man with the red beard by name; he had been a former work colleague who had died 40 years ago. Jim "saw" him several times, but did not initially mention this to anyone but his wife:

E	What did you make of it when you saw him? Did you think it was a ghost?
Jim	It's there in reality ... he looked as if he'd died standing where he was.
E	Could you touch the body?
Jim	Yes I could.
E	Could other people touch it?
Jim	I don't know ... yes they could do, if they could see it.
E	So if you could see it then you could touch it?
Jim	Yes.
E	Presumably, there are people who can't see it?
Jim	Oh God, yes.

Jim also claimed to have seen the bodies of several other former work colleagues and family members who had died over the previous 20 years. These "dead" people were seen several times at a day centre he was attending (prior to coming to Rivermead in September, 1992). Jim (who claims not to be particularly religious or superstitious) did not classify these "dead" people as "ghosts" at the time, since he felt that they were real enough to touch. He did not report actually touching any of them. The "dead people" were seen standing up, with their eyes closed, fully dressed and appeared normal. The sight of these dead people in an otherwise normal context frightened him initially. The "dead" people did not communicate with Jim nor he with them. Jim decided not to mention his experiences to others after the initial, understandably negative, reactions he received from the fellow patients and staff at the day centre.

Hallucinations from the Present. Another visual hallucination involving Jim's family and friends occurred while he was attending the funeral of his father-in-law. He told us (20th October, 1992) that he had been sufficiently concerned to consult the hospital chaplain over the matter:

E   You said you saw the chaplain this morning?
Jim   Yes ... I had to ask him some very awkward questions ... I went home last weekend to my father-in-law's funeral and the hearse came to the house and we had to walk from the house to the car... There was the coffin in the hearse and a lot of flowers ... there was a cross of flowers and it stood straight up on the coffin twice ... by itself ... the wife knew something had hit me, she knew I had seen something ... no one else saw because I asked. I asked the chaplain to see if I could get an answer to it. The way I saw it, it was my father-in-law's wife had gone about a year and it was a symbol to me that they had met in heaven.
E   Did the people you asked think it was strange that you saw this happen?
Jim   They did yes ... the chaplain couldn't give me an explanation ... I told him about me having the visions and that ... and said I'd like to get to the bottom of it and get them stopped, but he couldn't give me an explanation.

Hallucinations of the Future. Jim's most distressing visions concerned bombings which took place in London and Northern Ireland. Other visions included an airline crash and an attempted assassination of John Major. The latter refers to the mortars fired at the War Cabinet in Downing Street on 7th February, 1991. As with all his hallucinations, the descriptions were always first-person accounts of a sequence of witnessed events. Much of the details that Jim "reported" were clearly available from newspaper, radio, or TV accounts of the events (and were in some cases factually incorrect). A detailed description of one of these visions, reported to us on 8th October, 1992, is described below:

E   Tell us about your recent visions ... the last one for instance?
Jim   Last night [7th October, 1992] I was looking at the wall ... I seen the bombs getting planted in London. Two went off last night and there's one more to go. One of the bridges... I couldn't say which one... I seen them getting their stuff.

E	When you see these visions, is it like watching a TV screen?
Jim	It's stronger ... and bigger ... square, like a football field.
E	What did you see?
Jim	I saw two men walking along ... there were two behind them ... about four yards and they slowed down a pace until the two at the back of them catches up ... and there's money handed over. One man and two ladies take a steel tube and they open the door to a church and walk in ... they put the tube in ... like what tool makers use and they put it in there and carry it down the road by the side of the bridge ... and have a look around.
E	What time of day was this? Were there any other people around?
Jim	Nobody takes any notice at all ... about 4 in the afternoon ... they took the tube out and had a look around ... there was a policeman walking the other way ... but they shielded the tube and he went the other way. When they got so far along the way they were going, one in particular stepped out of line and ... okayed with the thumbs up and the message was received...
E	When is the bomb set to go off?
Jim	Maybe tomorrow when there's more people and traffic around ... the others went off in the early hours of this morning.
E	So you had this vision yesterday?
Jim	Yes.

During the week of testing, eight small bombs exploded in London, killing one man and injuring four others (Bew & Gillespie, 1993). The bombings received extensive coverage on the radio and TV.

When we saw Jim six days later (14th October) we asked him:

E	Have you seen anything recently?
Jim	Yes ... it was last night [13th October] ... I seen a bomb planted that is due to go off tonight ... in Ireland ... Belfast ... they had a job to move it into a car ... planted next to a railway bridge ... out of the car ... under the bridge ... it's in a bag ... two and one man to explode it. If it goes off it will take the bridge with it. 400 people will be killed, all coming around the shops and a lot of children. I can't notify anyone ... who is going to listen to me?

A bomb on 13th October injured five people in the West End of London. There were no bombings in Northern Ireland between 13th and 15th October but on 21st October, three bombs exploded in London; one at the Territorial Army Centre in west London, a second at the railway bridge over the North Circular Road, and a third at the railway line near Willesden in

North London. This brought the total of bombs in the previous fortnight to 13 (Bew & Gillespie, 1993).

Six days later (20th October) Jim was asked if he had experienced any more visions:

Jim	I have seen an airliner ready to drop from the sky ... it's a big plane ... British Airways ... going abroad ... it's going to happen in about four months time ... and it's like the last one that came down and demolished the two blocks of flats.
E	Did you predict that one?
Jim	Yes.
E	Did you mention it to anyone?
Jim	Yes, quite a few and they laughed at me ... they still don't know why it came down ... they will never find out.
E	Why not?
Jim	Because they don't know what they are looking for ... it's staring them in the face.
E	What do you know that they don't?
Jim	They used a different pipeline to feed the plane and that will only stand so much pressure ... they used plastic whereas they used to use copper pipes ... this was used in all the planes ... Freddie Laker never came down!

In a subsequent discussion, Jim described this "predicted" air crash in considerable detail. As far as we are aware, no British Airways plane crashed while flying abroad during this period. The accident that "demolished the two blocks of flats" probably refers to the EL-AL Jumbo Jet that crashed into the Bijlmermeer district of Amsterdam on 4th October, 1992. This crash received extensive coverage in the media.

Four months later (15th February 1993):

E	Have you had any more visions?
Jim	Yes, I'll be honest I have ... definitely ... they eased off but now they're starting to build up again ... troubles all over the world.
E	Are they always about troubles?
Jim	Yes ... I sit here and look up at the windows ... it happens.
E	If I were to pull the curtains across the windows, would you still see things?
Jim	Not as much ... I seen it in day care ... my eyes wander ... and I see ...
E	Are there any recent episodes?

Jim   Yes there is ... there is going to be two massive bombs set out in London and the police cannot do anything about it because they don't know who they are looking for ... set down to take a bridge ... a lot of people will go across and it will take a lot of people.

In December 1992, two bombs exploded in London injuring four people. During February 1993, there were four major bombings on the British mainland. Three of these bombs exploded at a gasworks in Warrington in Cheshire. On 27th February, 18 people were injured when a bomb exploded in Camden in London. Later, in March, two young boys were killed and fifty-six people injured when two bombs exploded in a shopping centre in Warrington.

Reaction and Explanation of Hallucinations

In the course of our discussions, we asked Jim for his explanation of and reactions to the hallucinations. On 8th October, 1992:

E   Why do you think you can see these "visions" and other people cannot?

Jim   Since my accident, I have got a hell of a strong eyesight power.

E   So has the accident increased your ability to see?

Jim   Yes ... other people could see this if they'd had the same ... but most people can't see.

E   Did you have these powers before the accident?

Jim   No.

E   What would you think of someone who told you these sorts of things before your accident?

Jim   I would not have believed them.

E   How would you explain it?

Jim   Well, I will be honest.... If I met a policeman I'd say to him that man is gone in the head ... I'd walk away and leave them to it.

E   Would you understand it if someone walked away from you?

Jim   Oh God yes ... because I would take the same opinion ... I put it down to the head injury.

Six days later (14th October):

E   If you heard someone describing these visions, what would you think about them?

Jim   Well ... if they were speaking to me I would think "there's something wrong with your head" ... I would think ... "why can you see things and I can't?" I have the same will power as you through life ... I'd think they were strange. How it affected *me* this way I do not know.

E   If you had the choice tomorrow not to have this power, would you take it?

Jim   Yes I would ... it gives me too much agony ... seeing things and I can do nothing about it and nobody will believe it ... I'd definitely like not to have it.

E   And you don't know why you have it?

Jim   No ... I never had it before the accident.

On 20th October:

E   Are your predictions always right?

Jim   No.

E   How do you get a prediction wrong?

Jim   I turn my head away or someone has spoken to me ... I turn my attention to something else.

When asked why he had not closed his eyes or turned his head away from the visions, Jim indicated that he was terrified of "meddling with what I saw". He felt that by interfering he could in some non-specific way bring harm to himself and his family. Furthermore, Jim indicated he had no control over the visions: They appeared to come "out of the blue". He found their content distressing and often expressed the wish not to have them. Asked if he knew of any other people with his ability, Jim said he had "asked around" but had not found any.

HALLUCINATIONS

Hallucinations are a well-recognised symptom of brain dysfunction (Anderson & Rizzo, 1994). They can occur after various types of brain damage, including tumours, strokes, epilepsy, and head injury. Neuropsychological investigations of hallucinations remain limited (O'Carroll, 1992); they are normally studied in the context of more general syndrome disorders. Although visual hallucinations are often associated with damage to the occipital lobes (Kölmel, 1985), such damage is neither necessary or sufficient to cause hallucinations (Anderson & Rizzo, 1994).

Any serious account of Jim's hallucinations must explain their cause and content. The proximal cause of Jim's visual hallucinations is presumably the cerebral contusion following the head injury sustained in 1990. Jim's wife confirmed that the reports of visions only began a few months after the head injury. The experience of visual hallucinations usually has a negative emotional impact on the subject (Slade & Bentall, 1988) but not invariably so (Miller, O'Connor, & DiPasquale, 1993). In Jim's case he was clearly distressed by the content of his hallucinations.

A major obstacle to the study of hallucinations lies in the fact that the patient's reports are objectively unverifiable: The only data about the quality and occurrence of these phenomena are the patient's first-person reports. One way to assess the phenomenological qualities of different perceptual experiences is provided by the studies of "reality monitoring", reported by Johnson and Raye (1981). "Reality monitoring" (in their sense) refers to the normal process by which perceived and imagined events are discriminated in memory. Johnson and Raye (1981) suggest that memories originating from experienced events have more contextual, perceptual, and meaningful information than memories of dreams and fantasies. In one study by Johnson, Foley, Suengas, and Raye (1988) normal subjects gave genuine events higher ratings than imagined events on characteristics such as perceptual and contextual information.

To ascertain whether Jim could discriminate between the qualitative characteristics of his memories for real events and his hallucinations, we asked him to rate two identifiable memories (one real, one hallucinatory) on the Memory Characteristics Questionnaire (Johnson et al., 1988). The test consists of 39 questions and assesses a wide range of memory characteristics (e.g. visual detail, complexity, spatial and temporal information, and feelings). The questions have been found to cluster into five major factors: clarity (e.g. degree of visual detail); sensation (e.g. modalities involved); context; thoughts and feelings (feelings at the time); and intensity (e.g. level of feeling). For most items the subject responds by checking a number on a seven-point scale which concerns the qualities of the memory. Having agreed upon a specific event (the visit by his wife at the weekend) and a specific recent hallucination (the predicted BA air crash), Jim was requested to rate his memories of the two episodes on the questionnaire: his scores on the five major factors of the MCQ are plotted in Fig. 12.1.

The shape of Jim's ratings of the hallucinated and the real event is similar, although it is interesting to note that the real event scores higher for context and thoughts/feelings. Overall then, Jim's memories of the hallucination appear to resemble memories of a real event in terms of the overall pattern of their phenomenological characteristics. This similarity did not, however, produce an impairment of reality monitoring for Jim; he knew perfectly well what was a memory of a "real" event and what was a memory of a hallucination.

Although the mechanisms of visual hallucinations are far from understood (Asaad & Shapiro, 1986), it seems reasonable to conjecture that at least some of Jim's hallucinations involved pathological activation and enhancement of stored memorial representations (Anderson & Rizzo, 1994) and that these in turn were influenced by the patient's particular interests

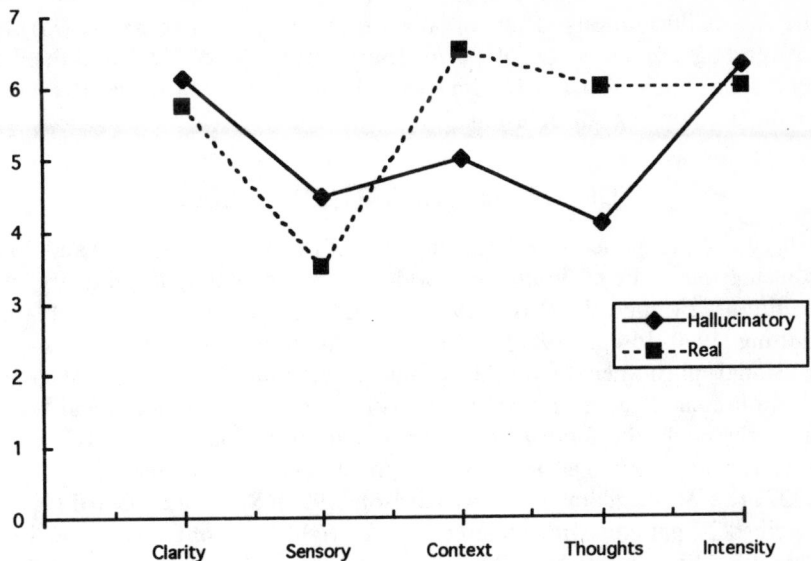

FIG. 12.1. Performance on memory characteristics questionnaire—for recall of real and hallucination memory.

and concerns. Cutting (1990) suggested that hallucinations resulting from right hemisphere lesions (and including visions of people) are typically more specific and more related to the patient's personal experience than those consequent upon left hemisphere lesions. Several authors have suggested that the content of hallucinations will often be related to the patient's personal experience (Asaad & Shapiro, 1986; Cohen, Verstichel, & Pierrot-Deseilligny, 1992). Cohen et al. (1992) suggest that patients may unconsciously hold "in mind" the idea for the hallucination. Consequently, the set of neurons underlying the stored representation concerned might be set at a "higher level of activity" and therefore would be "preferentially selected in the course of a hallucination". In Jim's case, we have converging evidence (from Jim and his family) which indicated his premorbid concerns with terrorist bombings and the death of family members and friends.

Exactly how brain damage provokes hallucinations is unknown, although a recent SPECT study by Kim, Park, Intenzo, & Zhang (1993) showed increased perfusion in both parieto-occipital lobes during hallucinations. Schultz and Melzack (1991) have suggested that "sensory deprivation" plays a role. Asaad and Shapiro (1986) propose that hallucinations secondary to acquired brain damage are qualitatively different from those found in functional psychoses. The latter, they suggest, are mediated by neurotransmitters originating in the brain stem, whereas hallucinations after organic lesions may relate (p. 1095) to "descending aminergic or other neurotransmitter tracts which influence brain stem biochemistry". In Jim's case, hallucinations provided the basis for the development of delusions.

DELUSION CHARACTERISTICS

Delusions remain one of the key symptoms of psychiatric diagnosis and, like hallucinations, can be found in a wide variety of functional and organic conditions (Maher & Ross, 1984). Yet, even within neuropsychiatry (Cutting, 1990; Joseph, 1986), there are few attempts to disentangle organic delusional phenomena from delusions in functional psychoses such as schizophrenia. The lesions typically involved in delusions after focal brain damage include the tempero-occipito or parieto-tempero cortex (Cutting, 1990; Levine & Finkelstein, 1982; Levine & Grek, 1984; Peroutka et al., 1982; Price & Mesulam, 1985; Richardson, 1992). Slater and Beard (1963) described 25 patients with unilateral left or right hemisphere epileptic foci, some of whom reported grandiose delusional beliefs, strange religious beliefs, or the ability to foretell the future, read thoughts, or see through walls.

Delusions are false beliefs held with conviction and subjective certainty, that are not usually capable of being corrected by experience or rational argument. Most of us hold some false beliefs, but in themselves these are not considered evidence of mental disturbance (Garety & Hemsley, 1994). Delusions by their very nature are "essentially private ... subjective states of mind" (Garety & Hemsley, 1994). Evidence of delusions must thus be inferred from the verbal accounts (and other behaviour) of the subject. A model of the putative processes involved in belief formation is presented in Fig. 12.2.

Until recently the content of delusions was regarded as a mere psychopathological curiosity, however Cutting (1990) has argued that the analysis of the content of delusions can be more illuminating than the more traditional and formal nosologies. There are currently several different accounts of delusion formation (Garety & Hemsley, 1994). When delusions are secondary to hallucination, it is instructive to consider Maher's account of delusion formation. Maher's theory (1974) of delusional formation argues that delusions originate from aberrant sensory experience for which the delusion offers some explanation. Cutting (1990) has similarly argued that right parietal damage facilitates delusion formation through its effect on perception. Delusions are the patient's explanation of perceptual anomalies that he or she experiences. Furthermore, the patient may arrive at an explanation by using normal cognitive mechanisms. The explanation (i.e. delusion) therefore can be derived from normal cognitive processes.

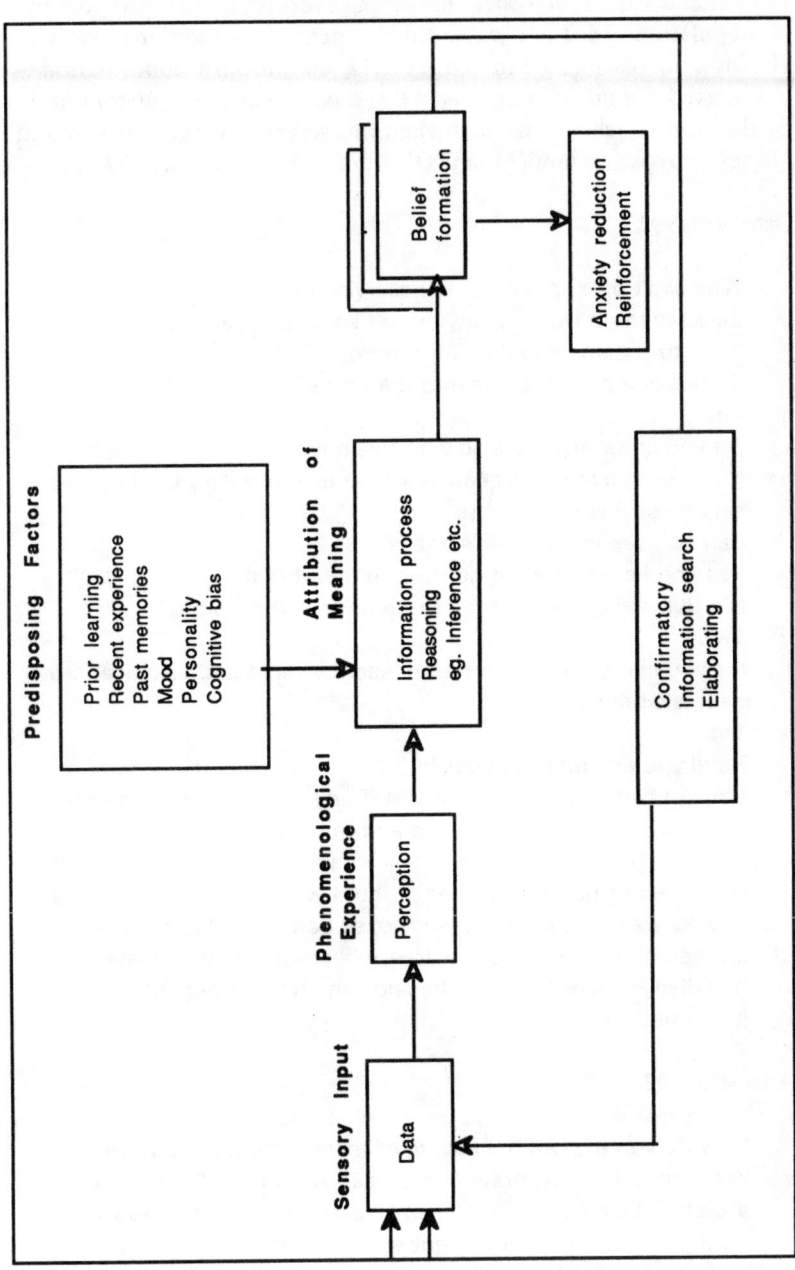

FIG. 12.2. A model of putative processes involved in the generation of normal and abnormal beliefs, (adapted from Roberts, 1992; Bentall, 1994; and Garety and Hemsley, 1994)

French (1992) suggests that normal biases in reasoning and confirmation may explain the extent of belief in the paranormal in the (supposedly) normal population. In Jim's case, faulty memory in conjunction with normal biases in reasoning—in particular a bias toward confirmation—probably played a role. It may even be the case that the "supernatural" account that Jim attaches to his hallucinations serves to reduce the fear and anxiety they provoke in him (Miller, O'Connor, & Dilasquale, 1993).

14th October, 1992:

E   Why can't other people see these visions?

Jim   Because my power ... why I don't know ... I can see more into the future than I should ... far more.

E   So this is a power to see into the future?

Jim   Yes.

E   Do you know anyone else with this power?

Jim   No ... but there was a chap in the same house [Day Centre] who said he saw similar things.

E   Can you see into people's heads?

Jim   Yes and I can see what goes on in their brain.

E   Did this ability come at the same time as the visions?

Jim   Yes.

E   So you can see into the future, see the dead and also see into people's brains?

Jim   Yes.

E   Have you any other powers?

Jim   I think I can quite safely say that if any of my sons were hurt I could look at the wall and see and tell my wife ... yes ... very clear. On the Wednesday last, my wife's dad died and she didn't tell me so as not to upset me ... but I was in the car and asked how he was ... she said he was not so bad ... but I said I saw it in a different light but I had to accept her word for it ... I knew he had died ... I saw her at his bedside and her brother didn't make it in time.

20th October, 1992:

E   How do you explain the source of these supernatural powers?

Jim   When they done my brain ... my head was drilled through to get a clot of blood removed ... my head was left open too long during the operation and I got a spider's web across the brain and now one feeds the other ... and the older I get the stronger it gets.

E	Is the spider in there as well?
Jim	No ... that's given me the power because the web feeds off the brain.
E	Why does the spider's web allow you to have these supernatural powers?
Jim	I don't know ... it's connected to the brain for an unknown reason.

We discovered that this account was derived in part from a friend who had visited Jim while he was recovering. When explicitly questioned about the feasibility of the spider's web, Jim thought it was an unlikely explanation but additional questioning revealed the absence of any alternative explanations! The character and content of the hallucinations together with his friend's suggestion had persuaded Jim about the "spider's web" theory. As in much of science, any theory is better than no theory.

Two days later (22nd October):

E	Did you know how you got these powers?
Jim	No ... and still no one can answer this ... I have a theory ... but is my theory right?
E	What is your theory?
Jim	My scalp was open for too long (in the operation) and whatever was done it was left that bit long ... and a spider's web got in it and now one feeds the other ... until that's dead I have to bear it for the rest of my life...
E	So what you are saying is that a spider crept into your brain while the operation was going on and spun a web?
Jim	Yes ... to me that's the only thing I can put it down to.
E	Did you think up the theory yourself or did you hear from someone else?
Jim	No, someone said it to me ... I think it was a friend.
E	Are you convinced by the story about the spider?
Jim	I am kind of convinced because of these visions. The more I have them the more I am convinced that one is feeding the other. I do not want my brain taken out again!

Four months later (15th February, 1993) Jim persisted with the same explanation. No better explanation had occurred to him.

E	What caused this exceptional ability?
Jim	The only thing I can put it down to ... is when I went to hospital

to get a clot of blood out of my brain ... the operation ... it's built up stronger and stronger and it will be with me until the end of my days ... it seems that when the doctors were doing the job it was in the background ... they left the brain open and a spider's web was made in the brain ... they didn't block it off, it's the spider's web that does that.

E   If I said that I had these exceptional abilities, what would you think?

Jim   No ... I'd have to find out what you had gone through.

E   If I had an accident like you?

Jim   Then I'd say it were true ... you were right to your word if there were something there in your brain.

E   Would everyone be as sympathetic?

Jim   Oh God, no!

To quantify the subjective qualities of the two main delusions reported by Jim we used the Delusional Rating Scale of Garety and Hemsley (1987). This 11-item scale assesses qualitative characteristics of belief. These characteristics include conviction, preoccupation, interference (identifiable influence on behaviour), resistance (e.g. not liking to think about the belief), dismissibility, absurdity, worry, unhappiness, reassurance, self evidentness, and pervasiveness. Scoring is on a scale from 1 to 10. Jim's two delusions were evaluated: (1) his belief in possessing supernatural powers, and (2) his belief that he had a spider's web in his head. The relative score values for each characteristic are given in Fig. 12.3. As the original scale varied the direction of the items to control for response acquiescence (Garety & Hemsley, 1994), the scale scores have been adjusted so that a score of 1 always represents the lowest degree and 10 the highest degree of the assessed characteristic.

Jim's performance on the Delusional Rating Scale reveals some interesting differences. On every characteristic save one, Jim's belief in supernatural "powers" is rated higher than his belief in the "spider's web". The degree of intensity, preoccupation, interference and pervasiveness of the former is almost twice that of the latter. Jim's belief in his supernatural abilities is "confirmed" every time a new bombing is reported in the media. But no such "independent" confirmation is available to Jim concerning the validity of the "spider's web" theory. It remains merely a theory (albeit one with no obvious competitors for Jim), that Jim needs in order to explain how he came to possess his supernatural powers.

Reaction to Delusions

Although Jim recognised that most people (including himself prior to the accident) did not have such supernatural abilities, he thought it was

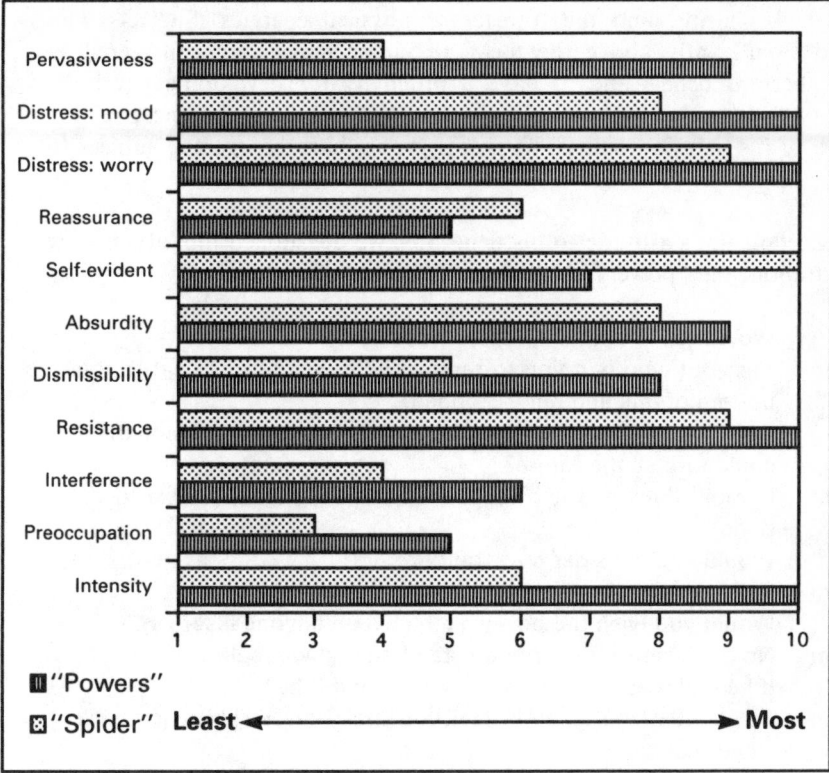

FIG. 12.3. Performance on the Delusional Rating Scale

possible for other similarly brain-damaged patients to develop these powers. This is not an unusual belief (Fenwick, Galliano, Coatte, Rippere, & Brown, 1985). Several studies have suggested that right hemisphere damage after head injury is associated with claims of paranormal abilities and mystical experiences (Geschwind, 1978; Neppe, 1980; Sensky, 1983).

Jim indicated that he had asked "no end of people" if they had experiences similar to his own, but so far had found none. To ascertain whether Jim held strange or unusual beliefs, we administered Eckblad and Chapman's (1983) Magical Ideation scale. This 30-item test was developed to measure belief in different forms of causation considered invalid by most conventional (Western) standards. The scale specifically enquires about the subject's personal beliefs rather than belief in theoretical possibility. Items have to be endorsed as true or false and they cover a range of magical causations including thought transmission, psychokinesis, precognition, astrology, spirit influence, reincarnation, the efficacy of good luck charms, and the transfer of physical energies. Subjects who scored significantly above the mean (8.56 for males) are considered to have aberrant beliefs and to have a proclivity for developing psychosis (Garety & Wessely, 1994). Jim's score of 4/30 confirms the encapsulated nature of his delusion beliefs: he is less prone than the average subject to believe in "magic" and the "supernatural"!

To ascertain Jim's attitude to his delusions, we questioned him about how he felt about the "powers" he claimed (20th October):

E   Would you want this problem resolved?
Jim   Yes! But who is going to remove it? I would like to get to the bottom of this and get it stopped.
E   What would you think if I said to you, before your accident, that I could foretell the future?
Jim   I would think it was a load of nonsense! ... impossible to be done.
E   Would you consider me strange?
Jim   Yes ... at the time, yes ... definite.
E   Would you wish the power you have on anyone else?
Jim   No ... because it's more outstanding that we realise.
E   If I could give you one wish what would it be?
Jim   To get rid of this ... and I'll tell you straight ... I'd like to get back to normal.

Delusion Formation

What is the basis for Jim's assertion of supernatural powers and how does Jim himself explain the delusions and hallucinations? If the "paranormal" is excluded, is it possible to provide an explanation for Jim's strong belief that he can see the future? Can we construct an explanatory account in terms of the neuropsychological deficits involved? Jim's wife had a simple explanation: Jim, she told us, "tended to see things on the TV which he later claimed to have predicted". It is clearly true that the content of most of his visual hallucinations was drawn from current events that were readily available to Jim from radio or TV coverage or from talking with fellow patients. Although illiterate, Jim spent a lot of his spare time in the TV lounge or chatting with other patients at the centre. Furthermore, from discussions with him and his wife, it became clear that the hallucinations were related to news items that were of particular relevance to Jim. He was much affected by the Northern Ireland troubles and had very real concerns about IRA bombings: his son was a serving officer in the Royal Air Force and was based in Germany. Members of the Armed Forces had been shot and bombed while on duty there in the recent past. (The IRA had bombed the British Army base at Rheindalen in March 1987, injuring 31 people. In 1989, two British soldiers were shot and in June 1990 an army major was shot in West Germany).

It became apparent from our interviews with Jim that the content and timing of the hallucinations were crucial in facilitating the emergence of his delusional belief in paranormal abilities. Jim claimed that many of the hallucinations depicted events that predated their actual chronological occurrence. But if Jim forgot the original sequence of events, then the following conjecture (illustrated in Fig. 12.4) seems possible.

Having heard or seen a relevant news item on the radio or TV (at T1), the details of this news item provide (much of) the content for the subsequent personalised hallucinatory episode. Given the frightening nature of the hallucinations, it might be expected that Jim would remember the content of the hallucinations perhaps more clearly than episodic memories related to the event derived from various media sources (T1). Subsequently, the events of the hallucinations (T2) are confirmed at T3 when the radio or TV over the following day(s) provides further information and follow-up stories of the news event (Loftus & Banaji, 1989). The repetition of this sequence would foster and reinforce Jim's belief (T4) in supernatural powers. For this account to go through, however, it would be necessary for Jim to show demonstrable memory impairments.

By his own admission, Jim had a poor memory, particularly for dates and times. Neuropsychological assessments at this time (October, 1992) confirmed this impairment of memory. In particular, temporal orientation was severely affected (e.g. Jim frequently confused the day, month, year, and season). When tested on the Mini-Mental State Examination (Beatty & Goodkin, 1990) on two different occasions in October 1992, Jim got the year, day, and month wrong. Tested on the Rivermead Behavioural Memory Test (Wilson et al., 1985) in October 1992, Jim scored 6/12, indicative of moderate memory impairment. In addition, there was a tendency for Jim to confabulate on some of the functional memory tasks, particularly where they related to temporal orientation. Much of Jim's confabulatory behaviour was "provoked" (Kopelman, 1987) in that it usually occurred in response to specific questions about episodic memories and orientation in time and place. He showed little evidence of confabulation when tested on questions of personal or general semantic memory (Dalla Barba, 1993).

Overall then, it is reasonable to speculate that when Jim is confronted with media confirmation (T2) following a frightening hallucination, he concludes that his familiarity with the content had been derived from the previous frightening hallucinatory experience rather than the earlier news description of the event on the TV or radio (T1).

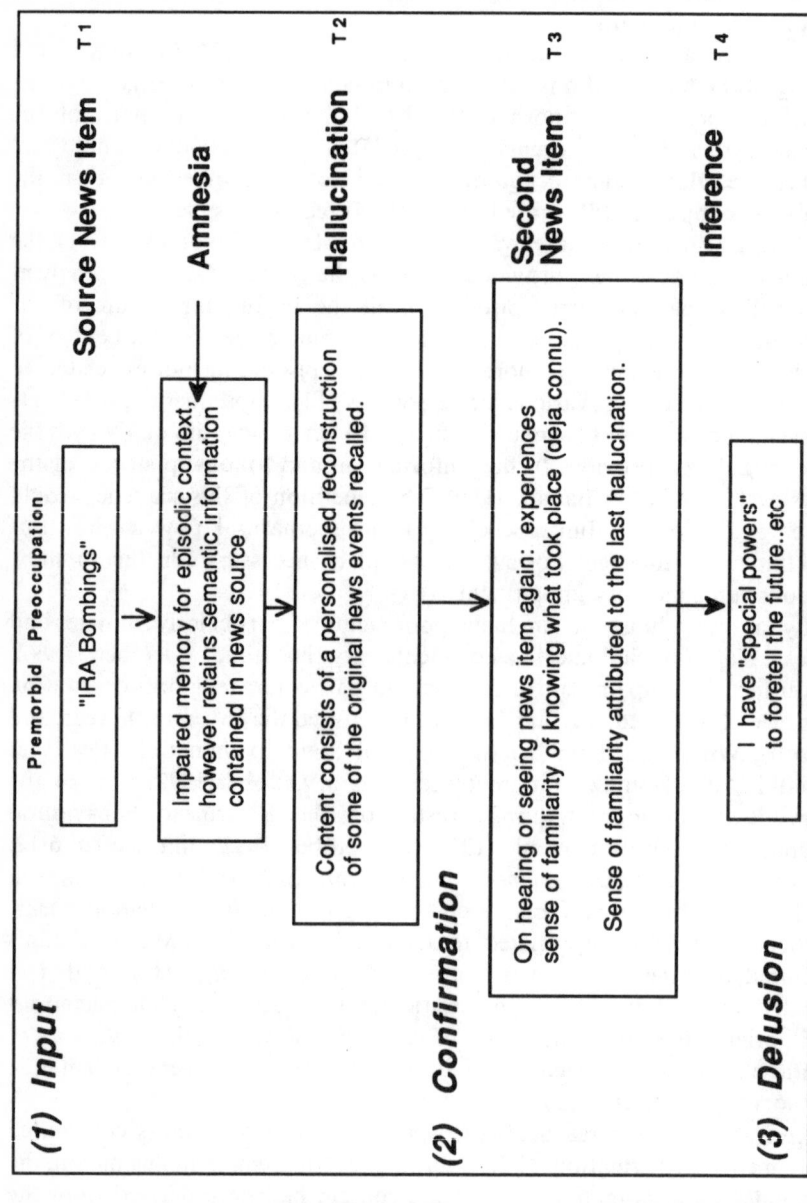

(1) Input

Premorbid   Preoccupation

Source News Item   T 1

"IRA Bombings"

Amnesia

Impaired memory for episodic context, however retains semantic information contained in news source

Hallucination   T 2

Content consists of a personalised reconstruction of some of the original news events recalled.

(2) Confirmation

Second News Item   T 3

On hearing or seeing news item again: experiences sense of familiarity of knowing what took place (deja connu).

Sense of familiarity attributed to the last hallucination.

Inference   T 4

(3) Delusion

I have "special powers" to foretell the future..etc

FIG. 12.4.   Conjectural sequence of events that gave rise to Jim's belief in possessing supernatural powers of precognition.

Can we explain Jim's belief in the "spider's web" as the source of his paranormal powers? The hallucinations were sufficiently powerful to convince Jim that what he was experiencing was supernatural and that the "visions" originated from the time of his accident. Jim's attempts to explain these extraordinary abilities thus very reasonably implicated the brain damage caused by the road traffic accident. As we saw earlier (Fenwick et al., 1985), it is not unusual for people to believe that they have special psychic powers after sustaining a head injury. Jim on the contrary was surprised to discover he had the ability to "see things" which he knew other people could not. When confronted with the need to be more specific, Jim told us of his "theory" but was unsure as to its validity. Jim's "theory" was that during the operation, he was left "unattended" with his brain "open" for longer than was necessary. He believed that during this time a spider crept into his brain and spun a web there. The web and his damaged brain now interact and "feed off" each other. This in turn provides him in some admittedly unspecified way with "the power". Until this relationship between his brain and the web is broken, Jim feels that the power will remain with him. He has no explanation as to why a spider's web should give him these abilities. Jim's position is thus not greatly different from that in which most cognitive neuroscientists find themselves.

Our discussions with Jim, and his scores on the Delusional Rating scales, showed that he did not hold the "spider's web" theory with great conviction. It is, for Jim, a less than fully convincing explanation of how "his powers" originated and how they are currently maintained. Jim's humility in this respect contrasts strongly with the belief systems of some neuroscientists.

Insight

Insight refers to awareness of one's own condition (David, Buchanan, Reed, & Almeida, 1992) but is not considered to be an "all or none" phenomenon. David (1990) has suggested that an evaluation of insight in psychiatric patients should consider three main dimensions: (1) awareness of illness; (2) the capacity to recognise psychotic experiences as abnormal; and (3) treatment compliance. The schedule for assessing these components of insight proposed by David (1990) consists of a series of questions about treatment compliance (scored 0–4); the recognition of mental disturbance (scored 0–6); and the relabelling of psychotic phenomena (scored 0–4). The schedule also includes a supplementary question of hypothetical contra-diction (0–4) where the patient is requested to indicate how they feel about people who do not believe their delusion. When this question is included the score ranges between 0 (no insight) and 18 (full insight). Jim showed considerable insight, scoring 13/18. He totally accepted and indeed requested medical treatment for his condition; and he fully acknowledged that he had a "mental problem" that was a direct result of his head injury. Although he maintained a firm belief in possessing supernatural powers, Jim was prepared to consider, in the light of other people's disbelief, that there might be something wrong with him (15th February, 1993).

E   Do you always make it known to people what you see?
Jim   Oh no! ... people would start to laugh at me ... think I was off my rocker! ... they'd think I was very, very strange.
E   You wouldn't necessarily volunteer information about the visions?
Jim   Oh God ... No! ... It's the greatest thing I ever got ... the spider's web ... to see other countries and that ... but I can't tell anyone ... I've got to bottle that as much as possible.
E   So do you like the powers you have?
Jim   God, no!

From our discussions with Jim, we gained the impression of a man struggling to contain his bizarre beliefs within the context of otherwise normal everyday beliefs. Jim always maintained that he fully understood people's scepticism about his claims. His wife, for instance—he pointed out to us—thinks that he is "talking a lot of nonsense", and he admits that before his accident he would have regarded his very own comments as very strange. When confronted with the suggestion that his powers of precognition might in fact result from radio and TV news bulletins, Jim argued that the content of his hallucinations were not at all the same as those pictures or radio reports he had seen or heard. He was also sceptical of the claims that others could possess strange powers

    The level of insight shown by Jim supports the claim of Bisiach, Rusconi, and Vallar (1991) that "an outstanding feature of delusions ... is cognitive encapsulation in the sense that outside the affected domain, the contents of the patients' thought processes may appear to be fairly normal" (p. 1029). Common examples of encapsulated "misrepresentational" delusions that follow right hemisphere brain damage include anosognosia for hemiplegia, somatoparaphrenia (Halligan, Marshall, & Wade, 1995), supernumerary phantom limb (Halligan, Marshall, & Wade, 1993), allesthesia, misoplegia, and reduplication (Critchley, 1953; Levine & Grek, 1984; Marshall, Halligan, & Wade, 1995). Jim showed no evidence of any of these conditions. There are a number of delusional states (provoked in many cases by right hemisphere pathology) that involve an interplay of modular and central systems. Examples include the reduplicative paramnesias, and metamorphopsias, Frégoli syndrome, and Cotard's syndrome. Impairment of specific modules can have the effect of misfeeding or misleading central systems which then produce confabulatory or delusory beliefs. Jim should have realised that "predicting" bombings at the height of an IRA bombing campaign does not necessarily require supernormal abilities. But he does at least have the "excuse" that he was experiencing very vivid hallucinations. What excuse can be advanced by those purportedly normal people who believe in ghosts (Gallup & Newport, 1991) or consult their horoscopes every day is less clear.

EPILOGUE

We contacted Jim on 14th June, 1995 to find out what developments had taken place since we had last seen him at Rivermead two years previously. Although he still attends a day centre twice a week, Jim felt that there had been a big improvement in his condition; the frequency of hallucinations had reduced considerably although he still reported an occasional "vision". These hallucinations were now less morbid. He had also moved from the house where he had seen many of the original hallucinations when staring out of the window. The reduction in "visions" was accompanied by a change in the delusions. When questioned about his previous belief in possessing supernatural powers, Jim said that he no longer believed he possessed such powers. In addition, he now maintained that the "spider theory" was the work of "his imagination". One can only admire Jim's scientific attitude, and his willingness to consider that some of his conjectures might be refuted (Popper, 1963).

ACKNOWLEDGEMENTS

This work was supported by the Medical Research Council (PWH and JCM). We are grateful to Dr Derick Wade for referring the patient, to Val Berry for transcribing the interviews, and to staff at Rivermead Rehabilitation Centre for their reports on the patient.

REFERENCES

Altman, E., & Jobe, T.H. (1992). Phenomenology of psychosis. *Current Opinion in Psychiatry*, *5*, 33–37.

Anderson, S.W., & Rizzo, M. (1994). Hallucinations following occipital lobe damage: The pathological activation of visual representation. *Journal of Clinical and Experimental Neuropsychology*, *16*, 651–663.

Asaad, G., & Shapiro, B. (1986). Hallucinations: Theoretical and clinical overview. *American Journal of Psychiatry*, *143*, 1088–1097.

Beatty, W.W., & Goodkin, D.E. (1990). Screening for cognitive impairment in multiple sclerosis. An evaluation of the Mini-Mental State Examination. *Archives of Neurology*, *47*, 297–301.

Bentall, R.P. (1994). Cognitive biases and abnormal beliefs: Towards a model of persecutory delusions. In A.S. David, & J.C. Cutting (Eds.), *The neuropsychology of schizophrenia* (pp. 337–360). Hove, UK: Lawrence Erlbaum Associates Ltd.

Bew, P., & Gillespie, G. (1993). *Northern Ireland: A chronology of the troubles, 1968–1993*. Dublin: Gill & Macmillan.

Bisiach, E., Rusconi, M.L., & Vallar, G. (1991). Remission of somatoparaphrenic delusion through vestibular stimulation. *Neuropsychologia, 29*, 1029–1031.

Boon, P.A., & Williamson, P.D. (1993). The diagnosis of pseudoseizures. *Clinical Neurology and Neurosurgery, 95*, 1–8.

Cohen, L., Verstichel, P., & Pierrot-Deseilligny, C. (1992). Hallucinatory vision of a familiar face following right temporal haemorrhage. *Neurology, 42*, 2052.

Critchley, M. (1953). *The parietal lobes*. London: Edward Arnold.

Cutting, J. (1990). *The right cerebral hemisphere and psychiatric disorders*. Oxford: Oxford University Press.

Dalla Barba, G. (1993). Confabulation: Knowledge and recollective experience. *Cognitive Neuropsychology, 10*, 1–20.

David, A.S. (1990). Insight and psychosis. *British Journal of Psychiatry, 156*, 798–808.

David, A.S., Buchanan, A., Reed, A., & Almeida, O. (1992). The assessment of insight in psychosis. *British Journal of Psychiatry, 161*, 599–602.

Eckblad, M., & Chapman, L.J. (1983). Magical ideation as an indicator of schizotypy. *Journal of Consulting and Clinical Psychology, 51*, 215–225.

Fenwick, P., Galliano, S., Coatte, M.A., Rippere, V., & Brown, D. (1985). "Psychic sensitivity", mystical experience, head injury and brain pathology. *British Journal of Medical Psychology, 58*, 35–44.

French, C.C. (1992). Factors underlying belief in the paranormal: Do sheep and goats think differently? *The Psychologist, 5*, 295–299.

Gallup, G.H., & Newport, F. (1991). Belief in paranormal phenomena among adult Americans. *Skeptical Inquirer, 15*, 137–146.

Garety, P.A., & Hemsley, D.R. (1987). Characteristics of delusional experience. *European Archives of Psychiatry and Neurological Science, 266*, 294–298.

Garety, P.A., & Hemsley, D.R. (1994). Delusions: Investigations into the psychology of delusional reasoning (Maudsley Monograph No. 36). Oxford: Oxford University Press.

Garety, P.A., & Wessely, S. (1994). The assessment of positive symptoms. In R.E. Barnes & H.E. Nelson (Eds.), *The assessment of psychosis: A practical handbook*. London: Chapman & Hall.

Geschwind, N. (1978). Behavioural changes in temporal lobe epilepsy. *Psychological Medicine, 9*, 217–221.

Halligan, P.W., Cockburn, J., & Wilson, B.A. (1991). The behavioural assessment of visual neglect. *Neuropsychological Rehabilitation, 1*, 5–32.

Halligan, P.W., Marshall, J.C., & Ramachandran, V.S. (1994). Ghosts in the machine: A case description of visual and haptic hallucinations after right hemisphere stroke. *Cognitive Neuropsychology, 11*, 459–477.

Halligan, P.W., Marshall, J.C., & Wade, D.T. (1993). Three arms, a case of supernumerary phantom limb after right hemisphere stroke. *Journal of Neurology, Neurosurgery and Psychiatry, 56*, 159–166.

Halligan, P.W., Marshall, J.C., & Wade, D.T. (1995). Unilateral somatoparaphrenia after right hemisphere stroke: A case description. *Cortex, 31*, 173–182.

Hodkinson, H.M. (1972). Evaluation of a mental test score for assessment of mental impairment in the elderly. *Age and Ageing, 1*, 233–238.

Johnson, M.K., Foley, M.A., Suengas, A.G., & Raye, C.L. (1988). The phenomenal characteristics of memories perceived and imagined autobiographical events. *Journal of Experimental Psychology: General, 117*, 371–376.

Johnson, M.K., & Raye, C.L. (1981). Reality monitoring. *Psychological Review, 88*, 67–85.

Joseph, R. (1986). Confabulation and delusional denial: Frontal lobe and lateralised influences. *Journal of Clinical Psychology, 42*(3), 507–520.

Kim, S.M., Park, C.H., Intenzo, C.M., & Zhang, J. (1993). Brain SPECT in a patient with post-stroke hallucination. *Clinical Nuclear Medicine, 5*, 413–416.

Kölmel, H.W. (1985). Complex visual hallucinations. *Journal of Neurology, Neurosurgery and Psychiatry, 48*, 29–38.

Kopelman, M.D. (1987). Two types of confabulation. *Journal of Neurology, Neurosurgery and Psychiatry, 50*, 1482–1487.

Levine, D.N., & Finkelstein, S. (1982). Delayed psychosis after right temporo parietal stroke or trauma: Relations to epilepsy. *Neurology, 32*, 267–273.

Levine, D.N., & Grek, A. (1984). The anatomic basis of delusions after right cerebral infarction. *Neurology, 34*, 577–582.

Loftus, E., & Banaji, M.R. (1989). Memory modification and the role of the media. In V.A. Gheorghiu, P. Netter, H.J. Eysenck, & R. Rosenthal (Eds.), *Suggestion and suggestibility: Theory and research*. London: Springer-Verlag.

Maher, B.A. (1974). Delusional thinking and perceptual disorder. *Journal of Individual Psychology, 30*, 98–113.

Maher, B., & Ross, J.S. (1984). Delusions. In H.E. Adams & P. Sutker (Eds.), *Comprehensive handbook of psychopathology*. Plenum: New York.

Malloy, P., Cimino, C., & Westlake, R. (1992). Differential diagnosis of primary and secondary Capgras delusions. *Neuropsychiatry, Neuropsychology, and Behavioural Neurology, 5*, 83–96.

Marshall, J.C., Halligan, P.W., & Wade, D.T. (1995). Reduplication of an event after head injury? A cautionary case report. *Cortex, 31*, 183–190.

McKenna, P., & Warrington, E.K. (1983). *The graded naming test*. Windsor, UK: NFER-Nelson.

Miller, L.J., O'Connor, E., & DiPasquale, T. (1993). Patients' attitudes towards hallucination. *American Journal of Psychiatry, 150*, 584–588.

Neppe, V.H. (1980). Subjective paranormal experience and temporal lobe symptomatology. *Parapsychological Journal of South Africa, 1–2*, 78–98.

O'Carroll, R. (1992). Neuropsychology of psychosis. *Current Opinion in Psychiatry, 5*, 38–44.

Peroutka, S.J., Sohmer, B.H., Kumar, A.J., Folstein, M., & Robinson, R. (1982). Hallucinations and delusions following a right temporo-parieto-occipital infarction. *Johns Hopkins Medical Journal, 151*, 181–185.

Persons, J.B. (1986). The advantages of studying psychological phenomena rather than psychiatric diagnoses. *American Psychologist, 41*, 1252–1260.

Popper, K.R. (1963). *Conjectures and refutations: The growth of scientific knowledge*. London: Routledge & Kegan Paul.

Price, B.H., & Mesulam, M. (1985). Psychiatric manifestations of right hemisphere infarctions. *Journal of Nervous and Mental Disease, 173*, 610–614.

Raven, J.C. (1977). *Manuals for Raven's progressive matrices and coloured matrices*. London: Lewis.

Richardson, J.K. (1992). Psychotic behaviour after right hemisphere cerebrovascular accident: A case report. *Archives of Physical and Medical Rehabilitation, 73*, 381–384.

Roberts, G. (1992). The origin of delusion. *British Journal of Psychiatry, 161*, 298–308.

Schultz, G., & Melzack, R. (1991). The Charles Bonnet syndrome: "Phantom visual images". *Perception, 20*, 809–825.

Sensky, T. (1983). Religiosity, mystical experience and epilepsy. In C. Rose (Ed.), *Research progress in epilepsy* (pp. 214–220). London: Pitman Medical.

Slade, P.D., & Bentall, R.P. (1988). Sensory deception: A scientific analysis of hallucination. London: Croom Helm.

Slater, E., & Beard, A.W. (1963). The schizophrenia-like psychoses of epilepsy, (i) Psychiatric aspects. *British Journal of Psychiatry, 109*, 95–150.

Snaith, R.P., Ahmed, S.N., Mehta, S., & Hamilton, M. (1971). Assessment of severity of primary depressive illness: Wakefield self assessment depression inventory. *Psychological Medicine, 1,* 143–149.

Starsktein, S.E., Robinson, R.G., & Berthier, M.L. (1992). Post-stroke hallucinatory delusional syndromes. *Neuropsychiatry, Neuropsychology and Behavioural Neurology, 5,* 114–118.

Varney, N.R., Hines, M.E., Bailey, C., & Roberts, J.R. (1992). Neuropsychiatric correlates of theta bursts in patients with closed head injury. *Brain Injury, 6,* 499–508.

Wade, D.T., & Collin, C. (1988). The Barthel ADL index: A standard measure of physical disability? *International Disability Studies, 10,* 64–67.

Wing, J.K., Cooper, J.E., & Sartorius, N. (1974). *Measurement and classification of psychiatric symptoms.* Cambridge, UK: Cambridge University Press.

Wilson, B., Cockburn, J., & Baddeley, A.D. (1985). *The Rivermead Behavioural Memory Test Manual.* Bury St Edmunds, UK: Thames Valley.

Young, A.W., Ellis, H.D., Szulecka, K., & de Pauw, K.W. (1990). Face processing impairments and delusional misidentification. *Behavioural Neurology, 3,* 153–168.

Young, A.W., Reid, I., Wright, S., & Hellawell, E.J. (1993). Face processing impairments and the Capgras delusion. *British Journal of Psychiatry, 162,* 695–698.

Zigmond, A.S., & Snaith, R.P. (1983). The hospital anxiety and depression scale. *Acta Psychiatrica Scandinavica, 67,* 362–370.

13 False Perceptions or False Beliefs? Hallucinations and Delusions in Schizophrenia

Connie Cahill and Christopher Frith
Wellcome Department of Cognitive Neurology, Institute of Neurology and Department of Psychology, University College London, UK

So it happened that witches and wizards came to live with me. They started fighting me with occultic forces... In the midst of this I decided to show them I was not afraid of them. I banged on their doors and maybe hit one of them. So the landlord and policeman came and I got locked in a cell. And here evil spirits would come near and move away.

SYMPTOMS IN THE DIAGNOSIS OF SCHIZOPHRENIA

Had Mani been the subject of such experiences in the London of the 17th century, she might well have been deemed a witch herself. Indeed, her own family, in her native Africa, have harboured such doubts about her. However, in the scientifically advanced cultures of the 1990s Mani's behaviour is considered the remit of the medical profession.

Mani was aged 31 and had been living alone in London for four years. Her introduction to psychiatry was not atypical (Johnstone, Crow, Johnson, & McMillan, 1986). Police were called to her flat to investigate a disturbance. She was found to be extremely agitated, claiming that a neighbour whom she had confronted was a demon with evil intentions towards her. As a consequence she was escorted to the local police station where she was interviewed by a police surgeon who recommended admission to a psychiatric unit. Whilst arrangements were made for her transfer Mani sang hymns and read aloud from her bible in the police cell.

On being admitted to the hospital ward, Mani was interviewed by a psychiatrist. She was noted to be well-dressed, well-mannered, and apparently well-educated; she was also found to be oriented in person, time, and place. However, she divulged that she heard voices all the time and one, a prophetess, had told her that she would be brought to a psychiatric hospital. Her neighbours she said were "satanists" who persecuted her by sending psychic messages to her, meddling with her thoughts; she claimed she could even feel evil spirits walking on her back. They were also responsible for poisoning her food and tapping her telephone. Chanting and reading aloud from the bible was her only means of combating these evil forces.

In volunteering such information Mani amply satisfied the cardinal criteria for a diagnosis of schizophrenia. However, she did not believe herself to be ill and did not therefore wish to remain in hospital or accept medication. Believing that her behaviour put her at physical risk and that she could benefit from treatment, a section of the Mental Health Act (1983) was applied, allowing care staff to detain her on the ward and administer treatment.

Attempts to control her symptoms have taken the standard route recognised by modern psychiatry in the prescription of "anti-psychotic" medication. Whilst these drugs have the power to reduce the occurrence of abnormal experiences, auditory hallucinations in particular, in a great many patients, for Mani they have been found to be of little benefit. Since she first came to the attention of the local services some four years ago she has been readmitted on five separate occasions. She is now well known to the local services as a "chronic schizophrenic". When well enough to look after herself she lives alone in a bedsit, but she maintains regular contact with the psychiatric services. She attends a day hospital, where she engages in activities such as art, discussion, and "work skill" groups. By Mani's own account, however, evil spirits and demons are always close at hand.

Schizophrenia is not an uncommon condition. The lifetime risk of developing this disorder is about 1%, a figure which varies very little around the world (World Health Organization, 1973). Table 13.1 lists the American Psychiatric Association's diagnostic criteria for schizophrenia; this classification system, known as *DSM-IIIR* (American Psychiatric Association, 1987), is the most widely used system today. Two other systems are in regular use: the *International Classification of Diseases*, known as *ICD-10* (World Health Organization, 1992), which is the system adopted by the World Health Organization and the CATEGO computerised system which is based on the Present State Examination (a standardised psychiatric interview; Wing, Cooper, & Sartorius, 1974). However, in the absence of any objective or valid theoretical bases for the psychiatric classification systems, the diagnostic criteria are necessarily almost entirely based on the elicitation, observation, or reports of abnormal experiences and behaviour.

TABLE 13.1
Summary of DSM-IIIR Criteria for a Diagnosis of Schizophrenia

Criteria	Symptoms
Must include two of	delusions
	prominent hallucinations
	incoherence or marked loosening of associations
	catatonic behaviour
	flat or grossly inappropriate affect
or	bizarre delusions
or	prominent hallucinations of a voice
The above should occur within the context of	characteristic symptoms for one week at least
	marked deterioration in everyday functioning, i.e.: in terms of self-care, work, social relations
	no major alterations in mood
	continuous signs of disturbance for at least six months
	no evidence of organic factors (e.g. head injury, drug abuse)

Table 13.2 indicates the prevalence of individual symptoms based on data acquired via the World Health Organization's collaborative study of the determinants of outcome of severe mental disorders (Sartorius, Jablensky, Korten, Ernberg, Anker, & Cooper, 1986). We should point out that while hallucinations (and delusions) are of singular importance in psychiatric diagnoses (including mood disorders and post-traumatic stress disorder), they are not by any means restricted to these disorders. In fact they have an astonishing range, being associated with conditions such as epilepsy,

TABLE 13.2
Patients Classified as CATEGO S+ (Signifies Schizophrenic Psychoses)

Symptom	Approx. %
Delusional misinterpretation and misidentification	73
Delusions of reference	63
Delusions of control	50
Non-affective verbal hallucinations (spoken to the subject)	57
Visual hallucinations	32
Thought broadcast or sharing	22
Dissociative hallucinations	15
Thought echo or commentary	10
Olfactory hallucinations and delusions	5

$N = 727$, from 12 centres in 10 countries.

SOURCE: Sartorius, Jablensky, Korten, Ernberg, Anker, & Cooper (1986, p. 922).

Alzheimer's disease, Huntington's disease, systemic lupus erythematosus, and occurring within the contexts of alcohol and drug abuse, bereavement, closed head injury, postoperative delirium, to name but a few instances (see Lishman, 1987). In this chapter we will be concerned solely with hallucinations in psychiatric illness.

Within the bounds of psychiatric diagnostic systems the variety and individuality of presentations is enormous. Many different forms of hallucination and delusion are recognised, and each person's abnormal experience reflect or is coloured by their own personality, preoccupations, life history, etc. In practice, it can on occasion be quite difficult to have confidence in one's classification of particular experiences reported by the patient. Many patients have great difficulty in providing detailed or coherent descriptions of their inner experience, and subtle differences in descriptions can be important. It is also the case that patients can describe experiences which do not fit neatly into standard symptom definitions.

In this chapter we attempt to convey some of the characteristic features as well as the complexity of psychotic symptoms as they are experienced. For the most part we focus on the experience of one patient (Mani*) in the hope that reporting a single case in detail offers a more complete understanding or feel for the way in which severe psychotic illness can be, at one and the same time, an expression and major determinant of an individual's whole experience. However, those with little or no experience in the field of psychiatry should bear in mind that Mani's story is "prototypical": It depicts many of the defining, common, shared, and recognised features of the psychotic experience whilst also expressing the personal and individual characteristics. Furthermore, in order to be able to represent a wide range of experiences we have necessarily had to present the case of someone who would be considered quite severely affected.

Our second aim, which we hope capitalises on the first, is to present an analysis of the phenomenology which will highlight key psychological processes in the psychological make-up of these phenomena. In our opinion, traditional clinical diagnostic schemes have been demonstrably lacking in furthering our understanding of psychopathy. What is required is an analysis of hallucinations and delusions in terms of psychological constructs, such as motivational, perceptual, cognitive, and emotional states and dynamics. We also present some of our own recent research findings which have been instrumental in forming our opinions and finish with some suggestions as to what form of theory of psychotic symptoms might take. But first, we will describe, and allow the individuals who report hallucinations and delusions to describe, their experiences. As Strauss (1989, p. 83) points out: "It is on those reports, for example, of delusions

---

* Identifying personal details have been altered to protect patients' anonymity.

and hallucinations that we base our notions of diagnostic categories, the diagnoses we make, and the development of aetiological formulations. Thus, patients' reports of their experiences provide the foundation for studying disorder and hence its biological, developmental and social correlates."

PHENOMENOLOGY OF HALLUCINATIONS

Slade and Bentall (1988, p. 23) provide a definition of an hallucination as follows:

> Any percept-like experience which (a) occurs in the absence of an appropriate stimulus, (b) has the full force or impact of the corresponding actual (real) perception, and (c) is not amenable to direct and voluntary control by the experiencer.

Whilst this definition is entirely accurate and sufficient for the purposes of objective identification, it fails—as perhaps all such definitions are bound to fail—to capture some of the vital aspects of hallucinations. Aggernaes (1972) attempted to elucidate some of these aspects by examining the "reality qualities" of hallucinations in a sample of chronic schizophrenic patients. Identifying the concepts of "Sensation", "Behavioural relevance", "Publicness", "Objectivity", "Existence", "Involuntarity", and "Independence", it was found that chronic schizophrenic patients rated their hallucinations (which were predominantly auditory) "positively" for all of these qualities, with the exception of the quality of "Publicness". Thus, Aggernaes' patients reported that their hallucinations did not just have "real" perceptual qualities (though they were aware that other people could not perceive these stimuli) but they also held beliefs about the source of these experiences (i.e. ascribing an existence and identity to a proposed source) and described the voices as being of personal relevance to them (i.e. the voices were experienced as meaningful in terms of their emotions, needs, actions, etc.). The positive rating of the quality of "Independence" reflects patients' experience that the voices are alien and outside their control. This quality is associated with the belief that these experiences were not the result of their being in abnormal physical or emotional states.

The following excerpt from an interview conducted with Mani illustrates some of these characteristics:

Mani   I still have the evil spirit talking to me. That's why I'm here. I still hear voices. I hear the voice of the evil spirit talking to me all the time. And I don't want to hear it; I'm tired of it. I don't want to hear it; I'm not willing.

Interviewer	Does it talk to you virtually all the time?
M	It talks to me virtually all the time, but I don't hear it with people, when I'm in company.
I	So when you're with us now you don't hear it?
M	It's listening. It's going to start telling me things when I leave this place about ... you, maybe about somebody. Sometimes it gets loud, screams at me, tells me I'm not moral, that I'm just pretending to be moral, I'm not eh ... I'm immoral. It tells me I'm amoral.
I	So when you say it screams at you, does it sound angry?
M	It sounds frustrated.
I	So does it have a high-pitched voice or ... ?
M	It gets high-pitched. Sometimes it has this high-pitched voice. It speaks to me in the voice of an African woman. Shrill. Shrill. [and] It starts singing inside me. Usually, it sings choruses from the church ... or songs from Mary's radio. And it starts to sing within me and tells me to sing to it. And I say I don't want to sing. I don't feel like singing. So I try and stop it. I try to stop my mind going along with the singing ... Or sometimes I start to sing another tune so that it doesn't control me to sing.

And of the voice of God she says:

Mani	When I first heard the voice of God ... it was just a man's voice—very deep.
Interviewer	Is it like a voice you know from your past?
M	It's not like any voice I know. It's just ... like a roar.
I	And is it loud or soft or ... ?
M	Just loud enough for me to hear.
I	Does it come through your ears like my voice, Mani?
M	Yes.
I	He doesn't talk directly into your head?
M	No, he doesn't.
I	So it sounds like my voice coming through. It sounds that real does it?
M	Yes.
I	Does it sound near or far away?
M	Far away.
I	So can it be difficult to make out?
M	No.
I	Can you pin-point where it's coming from in space? When it comes do you sometimes look around because

	it's coming from behind you? ... or do you listen over that way because it's coming from that direction?
M	It comes from above. It sounds like someone speaking actual words.
I	You appreciate all the words?
M	Yes.
I	And it's the same with the evil voice inside?
M	Yea.
I	It's not just a meaning you get?
M	It's not just the meaning I get. I pick the words. I know the words. I understand.
I	And the evil voice is different?
M	It's a man's voice but it's within me. God's voice is external.

Mani's "voices" are typical in so far as they take the form of a "voice" making suggestions or comments which the patient feels relates to them personally. The distinction between voices inside the head (known as "pseudo-hallucinations") and those externally located is also common and both types occur with equal frequency (see David, 1944). Different types of hallucinations are recognised according to their form and content. A distinction is made for instance between voices speaking in the second person ("you are sinful") and the third person ("she is dull"). These latter voices, as well as voices commenting on the patient's actions (and other symptoms including delusions of control) were identified by the German psychiatrist Kurt Schneider (1959) as symptoms of "first rank importance" in the diagnosis of schizophrenia. Schneider made no attempt to provide a theoretical basis for this cluster of symptoms. His was purely an empirical observation that such symptoms rarely occurred in association with other diagnoses.

Mrs Patel, an Indian housewife in her 60s, suffered a number of first rank symptoms. She claimed to have voices living inside her and that these voices would talk from her chest, though she heard them in her ears. She had kept them secret for a long time because they had threatened to do her harm if she reported their existence. No matter what she was doing, she said, the voices were always there. She did not always hear them, but she knew they were still with her. They spoke to her in Gujarati—her native tongue. These voices were prone to giving running commentaries on Mrs Patel's actions. Thus, whilst cooking: "chopping onions"; "let the water run"; "don't do that". Consequently, Mrs Patel gave up cooking for herself. Third-person hallucinations included the diametrically opposed "she is a good wife" and "she is a bad wife". Interestingly, Mani also reports hearing voices speak in the third person. However, when she hears "she is not your equal", "she is dirty", she frequently infers that the voices are referring to some other person. Voices also use the third person (male) referring (she believes) to her psychiatrist—"he is not a happy man"—and this extends to the third person plural—"they make love". Mani understands this as the voices "gossiping".

Probably the most distressing forms of auditory hallucination are those experienced or perceived as commands or threats. The content of commands may range from simple everyday actions, e.g. "shut the door", "stand up", to something the patient finds objectionable, e.g. "ignore him", "kick him"; in the most extreme cases the voice may go so far as to urge the patient to injure seriously or even kill themselves or someone else. Mani gave the following example of the kinds of thing the evil voice tells her to do:

> He might tell me to do unholy things. He tells me to put powder on my face instead of a moisturiser. And I actually feel a need to put powder on my face. When it tells me to do this. When I say no … I feel like putting powder on my face. It makes me feel like putting powder on my face. But I don't usually do it. I feel the need to put powder on my face … overpowering feeling to put powder on my face … It tells me not to … to do certain things. To go to parties rather than go to church. It tells me to eh … have a boyfriend, to fornicate. It would say "Mani, Mani, why don't you go to parties instead of going to church?"

For many patients who experience these kinds of voices, their subjective force and reality can be of such magnitude that the patient believes failure to comply with their commands may have serious consequences. Mani reported: "It can take control of me. If I listen to it it will control my life. I will become a witch, an occultic person." For this reason, she expends considerable energy "fighting" the "demons". In their study of the beliefs that hallucinating psychotic patients hold about their voices, Chadwick and Birchwood (1994) found that all of their patients viewed the voices as omnipotent and omniscient; furthermore, all patients also had additional beliefs about the consequences of obedience and disobedience and "without fail, voices believed to be malevolent provoked fear and were resisted while those perceived as benevolent were courted" (p. 192). One of the strategies of cognitive therapy investigated by Chadwick and Birchwood is to have patients systematically test the power of their voice by deliberately disobeying its commands. In this way patients can learn that evil consequences do not follow disobedience.

As Chadwick and Birchwood observed, voices can also be viewed as positive experiences. Such is the case for Mani in respect of the voice of God.

Mani	God left me alone for some time. He didn't speak to me or do anything to me. I didn't hear the voice of the Holy Spirit. I didn't see Jesus or anything. And eh, God left me for some time; and I prayed and prayed and prayed. I found it difficult to pray. I was worried and anxious. And God didn't speak to me for some time and later God started to speak to me again. He gives me happiness.
Interviewer	So you really wanted God to speak to you Mani?
Mani	I wanted God to speak to me, not to just leave me alone.

Visual Hallucinations

While auditory hallucinations are a common and defining feature of schizophrenia, visual hallucinations are relatively rare (see Table 13.2). This may be because the major feature of the hallucinatory experience is agency; the patient feels that another being is trying to influence their thoughts and behaviour. Such a feeling is most easily conveyed by words. It is more usual for visual hallucinations to be associated with identifiable organic pathology. Psychiatrists believe that it is particularly important that visual hallucinations are distinguished from illusions, which are (mis)interpretations of an external stimulus, and hypnagogic and hypnopompic hallucinations, which occur at the point of falling asleep and waking up respectively. Sims (1988) suggests that it is more common in schizophrenia for the patients to describe visual pseudohallucinations, i.e. they do not have the properties of real visual objects such as casting shadows and interacting with the normal gravitational environment. Rather, they are flat, static, and transparent with minimal colour. They are often associated with auditory hallucinations. "The visual experience is often inferred on the basis of the auditory hallucinations and of contemporaneous delusions" (Sims, 1988, p. 71). The visual hallucinations described by Mani take this form:

Mani	They [the pictures] come from an evil spirit. It talks to me all the time. It tells me it's a seducer. If you read the bible, the bible talks about seducing spirits and doctrines of devils. It's trying to turn me away, away from the way that I am chosen to follow.
Interviewer	To get back to the picture Mani, are there colours in it?
M	Yes there are colours in it.
I	What kinds of colours, do you know?
M	Depending on the colour that they should be.
I	The colour that they would be in reality?
M	Yes. [In the course of the interview Mani reported seeing

	a face and was in fact unable to report the colour of any part of it.]
I	Can you tell me what kind of things do you see?
M	Human beings. When he's talking to me about a human ... like, I used to know a man that I could have gone out with, that I could have married. And I still think about this man. But it's not my fault: I'm not in love with him or anything. And then this evil spirit keeps flashing pictures of the man into my mind. When it's talking to me about this man it flashes the picture of the man right before my eyes so I can see him.
I	Do you see the entire man?
M	I see eh ... I don't see him standing up. I see him sitting down, so I see this part [M indicates from waist up].
I	Is he life size? I just like he would be in real life?
M	Just like a picture. Just like a picture can capture the size of a person without being the size of that person.
I	Besides pictures of this man Mani, do you ever see any other kinds of pictures?
M	Oh I see all sorts of pictures. It also has a sense of humour. It tries to make me laugh—the evil spirit. So if it wants to, like eh ... I'm thinking about something, it can read my mind. He just flashes the face of that person into my mind, so I can see that person and put a funny look on the face, so I can laugh.
I	So is it nearly always faces you see then Mani?
M	Faces eh ... I don't think it's always faces ... it controls my mind. It doesn't allow me to think about what I want to think about. It blocks my mind; holds down my mind so I'm not able to reason.
I	What about objects ... do you ever see objects?
M	I should think so, but I can't really name you one off my head now.
I	So when this [face] is flashed in front of you Mani it doesn't affect how you see other things in the environment? You can get up and you can see the door and walk to the door...
M	Yes I can.
I	And it doesn't go away if you get up and move around.
M	It doesn't. It only goes away if the evil spirit takes it away.

Hallucinations in Other Sense Modalities

Hallucinations can occur in any of the five senses as well as in somatic sensation. Mani is extremely unusual in that she describes hallucinations in virtually every modality. The evil spirits, it seems, manage to insinuate themselves into almost every route of her conscious perception and sensation. Thus she reports: "They send smells to me. [These have been described as horrible nasty smells.] I don't believe the people are that smelly. It's just me notices. It's meant for me." Again, it is the case that these olfactory hallucinations can be associated with auditory hallucinations: "When I see a husband and wife they tell me, 'They make love and this is the smell of that love-making.'" More distressing are the haptic hallucinations, i.e. hallucinations of bodily sensation: "Sometimes, it makes love to me, moving in and out, when I'm lying in my bed."

Delusions of Control (or Passivity Experiences)

"The essence of this symptom is that the patient *experiences* his *will* as replaced by that of some force or agency" (Wing et al., 1974, p. 215; our italics). They are "those events in the realm of sensation, feeling, drive and volition which are experienced as made or influenced by others" (Sims, 1988, p. 122). In these experiences one's sense of "self" itself is disturbed: It is as if some alien being has managed to penetrate and take over aspects of one's (normally self-generated) functioning. In hallucinations at least this fundamental and primary sense of self remains intact: In hallucinations the agent or source remains external.

Although categorised as a delusion, this symptom as it is generally understood also has, it seems, a perceptual component. There is the suggestion or implication that there is a sense in which we feel our actions or thoughts are self-generated—or not—as the case may be. Indeed, it is this aspect which distinguishes this particular class of symptom from other delusions. The standard PSE question for this symptom reads "Do you *feel* under the control of some force or power other than yourself?" Thus a patient may report a (delusional) belief that other agents have the power to control his/her mind via a satellite, for example, but that belief alone does not constitute a delusion of control.

Mani describes her "possession" by the demons which she believes effectively take control of her: "It gets into my hands ... when washing my clothes. And it gets into my feet. It can influence my step. It showed me it can take control of one of my legs by making it twitch... [It] shows me that it can take control of my body. It tries to walk with me. It tells me it can make me more beautiful by making me walk in a certain way." More unusually, Mani claims that the demons can control her mood: "It puts feelings into me: joy, happiness, embarrassment, depression. It just puts it in and I feel the glow spread over me." In another form of passivity experience, the symptom of thought insertion, patients report that they feel the thoughts which occur in their heads are not actually their own. They are not experienced as thoughts communicated to them (see "telepathy" later) but it is as if another's thoughts have been engendered or inserted in them. One of our patients reported physically feeling the alien thoughts as they entered his head and claimed that he could pin-point the point of entry! Such a feeling is not simply determined by the inserted thoughts having an unusual or unexpected content.

In these experiences patients are recipients. They do not recognise these feelings as their feelings, as having an origin within themselves; they do not relate in any identifiable way to current circumstances. They are imposed upon them. In a sense, they feel as if they become vehicles for the ideas, feelings, or actions of other agents.

Hallucinations in Relation to Other Psychotic Phenomena

Apart from auditory hallucinations, persons diagnosed psychotic also report receiving communications or becoming aware of some other agent's thoughts in a variety of ways. In delusions of reference patients understand public, social, or everyday communications, behaviours, or events as having special personal significance to them. One patient reported: "They [people he identified as out to get him] do it in subtle ways of communication. This is where it goes off the rails ... to sound really weird. I started seeing my ideas in films and in print and like posters. That's not purely coincidence, that's communication. For instance, the Carling Black Label adverts—there was a whole string of them—and they all referred to me. And I can understand how you can read into it, but it's just too much of a coincidence." For many patients the communications are much more personal: "the way she handed me the change, it meant she knew I was a homosexual".

"Telepathy", i.e. people having the power to read each others thoughts, for example, is a not uncommon form of communication in patients' reports. Patients may feel that they have special powers which enable them to read others' thoughts, or that the power resides in others who use this medium to communicate with them. This notion may incur substantial delusional elaboration with the patient specifying a fantastic means of communication.

Apart from communicating to them (via hallucinations, telepathy, etc.), or taking them over (as in passivity phenomenon) patients also report many ways in which the delusional agent can affect them and influence them. It may be held to have the power to read or access the patient's mind, to stop or control the content of their thoughts, or to "withdraw" or "broadcast" their thoughts.

Roddy has been in contact with the psychiatric services for over 20 years. He lives alone and visits a day hospital twice a week. He has persistent auditory hallucinations which do not respond to treatment with antipsychotic medication. Roddy believes that a certain person whom he has met in the past and who lives some hundreds of miles from him:

> has control of my thoughts. He's a devil satanist and can broadcast [mine and his] thoughts in the atmosphere. By him thinking something he can get the voice in the atmosphere. And he can enter my mind and broadcast my thoughts too. Anybody can hear it. I can hear the broadcasting. But, mentally I throw everything back at him. I hear his voice and he hears my thoughts and that's the only way I get back at him.

This description illustrates the way in which the experiences reported can appear as a blend of a number of different psychotic phenomena.

When reporting such experiences patients may have great difficulty describing what happened in clear or definitive terms (i.e. as either a thought or a voice) or they may describe experiences which do not readily fit standard symptom descriptions or definitions. (Strauss, 1989 has suggested that there is some pressure to ignore such reports.) As an example of the former problem, Mani has reported: "They know a feeling and they send it to you, not by speech. They send it to you and you understand it, but it's not by speech." When asked if it was like telepathy, she said "Yes. But it speaks too!" An example of the latter—she has noted that "the demons have made hymns sound like the passing of wind!"

Moreover, as Chapman and Chapman (1988) and Strauss (1969) have pointed out, psychotic individuals also report experiences which appear to lie on a continuum between "normal" and "psychotic". Consider Mani's description of the evil spirit telling her to put powder on her face (mentioned previously): She apparently feels a "need", almost a compulsion, to do something which is not of her own choice or "free will" (i.e. passivity of impulse), though she resists and this feeling is not translated into action. Although this experience would undoubtedly be classed as psychotic, it seems to us to represent, in part, an intermediate state between the (normal) perception/belief of one's actions as self-generated and the (abnormal) delusion of control.

ANALYSIS OF THE PHENOMENOLOGY

The fact that the boundaries between different classes of symptoms are not clear-cut indicates that the traditional classification system is inadequate.

This is perhaps best illustrated in the apparent contradiction in the use of the term "delusion" to denote what is largely defined as a perceptual experience in "delusions of control". This throws into relief fundamental questions concerning the nature of hallucinations and delusions: Is this experience based on an abnormal percept or is it simply another mistaken belief? Is it a combination of the two? More generally, we can ask, can hallucinations and delusions be described in mutually exclusive terms? And from a theoretical cognitive perspective: What is the difference between these two states in terms of dysfunctional cognitive systems? To what extent do they involve affect and/or conation as well as perceptual or other cognitive processes?

We hope it is clear from these accounts that hallucinations as they occur in psychiatric disorders are not simply perceptual experiences, nor are they passive experiences. They are not "inert" perceptual experiences. Frequently, they reflect the personal concerns of the perceiver and they are conceived as part and parcel of a belief system. They are considered to be the manifestation of the existence of real entities who have significant and powerful relationships with the perceiver. As such they arouse emotions and influence behaviour. These features have been well-documented (see Benjamin, 1989; Chadwick & Birchwood, 1994). Thus, there exists a special relationship between the percipient and their "voices" or rather, the identified source of their abnormal and disturbing experiences. Patients can usually describe the physical characteristics of the voices, the vividness of which conveys their "reality". However, as in normal communication, it is the message and the motives, etc. of the messenger which are of primary importance. The meaning, i.e. the personal relevance of the experience is paramount; perceptual properties are secondary. Similarly, commenting on visual hallucinations, Marcia Johnson (1988, p. 39) suggests that: "Rather than having vivid *visual* experience, some of these patients seem to be having particularly compelling *interpretive* experiences (our italics)." (Might this explain the bewildering fact that congenitally deaf persons who suffer psychosis can report "voices"? See Critchley, Denmark, Warren, & Wilson, 1981.)

This analysis should sensitise us to the active, organisational (if unconscious) processes at work in the experience of hallucinations. An example of such a process is the attribution of meaning to the voice content. Typically, voices communication with few words. Most patients report hearing single words (of which the most common is a well-known four-letter expletive) or very short phrases, e.g. "don't do it", "in the bed", "nice day". Yet the perceivers frequently report they know what is meant by these minimal phrases, or why such phrases are being used. In Mani's case, when she hears the word "dance" or "run" she immediately knows this is the evil spirit trying to influence her by telling her to do something against God's will. It also happened that in the course of an interview with Mrs Patel the voices offered answers to questions put to her, as well as commenting on the immediate circumstances. When asked about where the voices came from, they suggested "from within"; and referring to the fact that the interviewer was taking copious notes (according to Mrs Patel) they said "that's enough", "that's plenty". It seemed to the interviewer as if they were anticipating Mrs Patel's own thoughts, though she did not understand the experience in this way. Mani has reported an experience which may be construed in a similar manner: 'When I am trying to summarise the bible it likes to suggest words. It suggests all the words in my mind and then I don't want to use it." Objectively, it appeared as though just as thoughts were reaching consciousness in Mani's mind they acquired the identity of "the evil spirit".

Finally, in comparing and contrasting different experiences we would suggest that psychotic experiences can be conceptualised along a belief-perceptual dimension. Experiences range from pure belief states (e.g. fantastic beliefs), to predominantly perceptual experiences (i.e. hallucinations), with intermediate states in which it seems impossible to separate our perceptual and belief components. Indeed, in their recent study of the phenomenology of delusional memories David and Howard (1994) report that the perceptual characteristics of delusional memories are stronger than those of real memories. It is as if the experience is forged at one and the same time in perception and belief. Take, for instance, the description below:

Mani	[the evil spirit] tries to match-make. It tries looking for a boyfriend for me. It tries to match-make me with a man. It makes me eh ... think of him. It puts ideas into my mind about men.
Interviewer	So you find yourself...
M	Thinking about men until it stops. It tries to make me jealous.
I	How does it do that?
M	It can make a woman look striking. I don't know what it does ... but it puts that look on a woman ... to make that person very attractive. So I would look, and maybe in church for instance, it makes the person sing beautifully.
I	And you would be jealous of that person.
M	It tries to put that jealousy within me. I don't feel jealous about the person. There's a particular girl, at the place, that he tries to make me jealous of. He tries to make her look striking. Tries to make her sing beautifully. Tries to make her do all sorts of things. And em ... I'm not jealous of the person, but he tries to make me jealous.

	Starts thoughts about that person within me; so I actually start taking notice of that person.
I	So it's really affecting your perception of that person is that right?
M	Yes.
I	It's not actually affecting that other person really?
M	No.
I	That person looks to you as being more attractive.
M	More intelligent.

TOWARDS A THEORETICAL ACCOUNT OF PSYCHOTIC PHENOMENA

The development of theory in this field has been hampered to a large extent, firstly, by the acceptance and adoption of the dominant medical framework in which individual symptoms are only important in so far as they direct one towards the ultimate goal, which is the identification of underlying disease processes; and secondly, by considering these phenomena as more or less independent entities with research following completely separate lines of enquiry.

Thus, there exists a great body of psychological research conducted on groups of patients diagnosed schizophrenic, manic-depressive, etc. However, increasingly there has been a realisation that this approach suffers from some serious pitfalls; not least of which is the fact that despite considerable advances in the reliability of current diagnostic systems their validity remains questionable (Costello, 1992). A number of researchers have presented cogent arguments in favour of a focus on "symptoms", such as hallucinations (Costello, 1970, 1992; Persons, 1986). Furthermore, Frith (1992) cited the results of Johnstone et al. (1988) as evidence of a common biological mechanism, which does not respect diagnostic boundaries, underlying positive symptoms (i.e. hallucinations and delusions). One advantage of the "symptom approach" is that our attempts at understanding these abnormal experiences may be cast in terms of some of the most powerful theoretical and experimental paradigms available in psychology today. Advances in the development of cognitive theories, particularly in the field of neuropsychology, and the growing acceptance and application of appropriate methods of investigation in these fields (the single-case study paradigm for example) provide much needed leverage in opening up this field of research. (For an example of this kind of analysis see the work of Ellis & Young, 1990 and Wright, Young, & Hellawell, 1993 in relation to Capgras syndrome.) The approach which we choose to adopt reflects these influences and developments.

A fairly extensive range of theories have been put forward to account for auditory hallucinations. In their exhaustive review, Slade and Bentall (1988) identified four classes of theory: conditioning, seepage, imagery, and inner speech. Few of these theories continue to generate research, though the results of some of the experiments they engendered may still inform our current attempts at formulating new theories. By contrast, theories regarding delusion formation are few and far between. Interestingly, the most prominent psychological theory of delusion formation (excluding psychodynamic accounts) is a perceptual one (Garety, 1991). Maher (1974, 1988) suggests that delusions are the result of an entirely normal attempt to account for abnormal perceptual experiences. Unfortunately, little by way of experimental data has been forthcoming to substantiate this claim.

Upon reviewing the psychological literature on hallucinations, Slade and Bentall (1988, p. 214) suggested that one of the more promising veins to be explored would be the role of judgement in discriminating between the real and the imaginary:

> Most theories to date have tended to focus on the sensory properties of private experiences without questioning the way in which that information is used by the individual to classify events as self-generated or originating from an external source... While it is entirely possible that the sensory properties of particular private experiences (e.g. if they happen to be especially vivid) may mislead a person into describing those events as externally caused, it is not clear that this is a necessary or sufficient condition for hallucination. Other types of information might be responsible for the individual being misled. Alternatively, the error might lie, not in the information that is available, but in the inferences that the person makes on the basis of that information.

Thus, Bentall, Baker, and Havers (1991, p. 214) conceptualised auditory hallucinations as the result of failures in "reality discrimination" (a concept borrowed from the work of Johnson & Raye, 1981), such that "internal, private events are misattributed to an external source". They then directly addressed the question of whether hallucinating schizophrenic patients do have problems in discriminating their own vocal output from that of someone else. When they asked hallucinating patients to identify the source (i.e. self, experimenter, new) of a target word presented previously, their overall level of performance was no worse than that of delusional patients. However, when they did make mistakes schizophrenic patients were more likely to disattribute self-generated responses which were of high cognitive effort to the experimenter ("Other"). Similarly, Frith, Leary, Cahill, and Johnstone (1991) asked schizophrenic patients to generate category exemplars (animals, fruit, parts of the body) and to listen to a similar number of exemplars spoken by the experimenter. Again the patients' ability to discriminate self-generated from experimenter-generated and new exemplars was tested, this time minutes later. Contrary to expectation, patients with a history of hallucinations performed just as well as other patient groups; only patients who demonstrated incoherence or incongruity of affect displayed a significantly reduced level of performance.

We believe that these experiments probably produced these negative results because the paradigms used do not have the potential for tapping into the cognitive processes underpinning auditory hallucinations. Essentially, what is being tested is source memory, i.e. discrimination of the source of past events (what Johnson, 1988, called "reality monitoring"). It is not at all clear that a deficit here would have any bearing on the individual's capacity for processing current, ongoing events—the domain in which hallucinations are located. What is required is a testing of Johnson's (1988) "reality testing" function, which refers to the discrimination of ongoing perception from ongoing imagination. Furthermore, these paradigms require the discrimination of self and other (or internally and externally) generated material; however, hallucinations (and perhaps other phenomena such as thought insertion) must surely be based on stimuli which are solely and entirely internal in origin.

In 1992 one of us (Chris Frith) formulated a cognitive model of hallucinations which has the capacity for explaining how stimuli which are internal in origin might be misclassified and misattributed to an external agent. Drawing on the notions of "corollary discharge" (Sperry, 1950) and "reafference copy" (von Holst & Mittelstaedt, 1950). These terms refer to a mechanism proposed by neurophysiologists to explain how an organism handles the perceptual consequences of its own actions. For example, when we move our eye the image of the world moves across the retina and yet we do not perceive the world as moving. A simple means of achieving this result is for a "corollary" message (or "reafference copy") to be sent to the perceptual system at the same time as the motor signal that causes the eye muscles to contract. This corollary message indicates the expected movement of the image on the retina that will be caused by the eye movement. If there is no discrepancy between the expected movement and the actual movement then there has been no movement in the outside world. This is effectively a monitoring mechanism which permits identification of self-generated stimuli. Frith suggests that the auditory hallucinations of schizophrenia arise from a failure in a self-monitoring mechanism operating within the domain of speech processing. Such a mechanism, it is argued, would make comparisons between the person's intention to generate speech (either as inner speech or as vocalisation) and the information relayed in the auditory systems (Frith, 1992).

According to this model, hallucinations are experienced as a result of a failure of the internal registration of the intention to generate inner speech. Thus, the inner speech produced is experienced as not arising from the patient's own intentions, and consequently is (mis)attributed to an external agent. This formulation essentially concurs with that of Hoffman (1986) on the point that internally generated verbalisations are classed as external in origin because they are experienced as unintended.

Frith's model also has parallels with Johnson and Raye's (1981) model of "reality testing" and "reality monitoring". Johnson and Raye suggest that memories originating from perception should have more perceptual information (e.g. colour, sound) in comparison to memories originating from thoughts, which should have information relating to cognitive operations (e.g. reflective processes, including intentional constructive and organisational processes), and these differences are held to reflect differences in perception and imagination as originally experienced. In terms of Frith's model, "corollary discharge" essentially corresponds to a cue for the "intention" component of the speech generation act; the absence of this cue resulting in the misattribution of source. This account can explain certain auditory hallucinations (failure to monitor the initiation of inner speech and thought) and passivity experiences such as delusions of control (failure to monitor intentions to act). However, it is not clear that the account can explain visual hallucinations.

An Experimental Study of Hallucinations

In order to test Frith's theory we attempted to assess "source attribution" in schizophrenic patients with different symptom profiles as close in time to the point of speech production as possible (Cahill, Silbersweig, & Frith, submitted). All our patients ($N = 20$) had satisfied DSM-IIIR criteria for a diagnosis of schizophrenia. A paradigm was developed which would enable us to challenge the attribution process, specifically by forcing patients into a relative reliance on internal cues in order to establish the source of their own speech which was presented to them instantaneously via headphones with varying degrees of pitch distortion. This was achieved through the patient wearing a throat microphone which relayed their speech through a special effect device (Yamaha SPX90).

On the basis of Frith's model, it was hypothesised that the hallucinating schizophrenic patients would be unable correctly to identify themselves as the source of the speech relayed to them.

Measures abstracted for analysis were patients' identification of the source as "self" or "other" at each of 12 levels of pitch distortion and presentation with no distortion and ratings of symptom severity on the Krawiecka scale (Krawiecka, Goldberg, & Vaughan, 1977). This scale provides a simple and clearly specified scheme for rating a series of features associated with schizophrenia such as delusions, hallucinations and poverty of speech.

Results

An intriguing pattern of results emerged. Contrary to our hypothesis, two patients who were actively hallucinated (but in whom we failed to elicit delusions) did not misidentify the source of the auditory input. Three individuals who were symptom-free at the time of testing produced a similar result; at each testing trial they identified themselves confidently as the source. However, those patients who were not hallucinated but scored positively for delusions ($n = 5$) did on occasions misattribute the source (mean number of misattributions per patient 1.4, range 0–3). This result was unexpected. Finally, by far the greatest number of misattributions occurred in the group of patients who were experiencing both hallucinations and delusions ($n = 10$; mean 6.5, range 0–13). (We should point out that this result is confounded by greater severity of delusions in this group.) Examination of correlations between the total number of "self" and "other" classifications for each patient and the Krawiecka symptom ratings revealed that misattributions (i.e. identifying source as "other") were highly and significantly correlated with the severity rating for delusions on the Krawiecka scale (Spearman's Rho 0.57, $P < 0.01$). By contrast, patients' scores on ratings of Hallucinations and the control symptom Psychomotor Retardation did not produce significant correlations (Table 13.3).

Mani's performance was typical of a patient who scored highly on both the delusion and hallucination subscales of the Krawiecka scale (Table 13.4).

These results demonstrate that, in conditions of distorted feedback of elicited vocalisations, patients who are both deluded and hallucinating will readily and spontaneously (mis)attribute the source of the stimulus to "an other". It appeared that they were more than willing to (1) override those cues which were available to them and (2) entertain the notion that some other agent might operate in this way.

Thus, the findings would appear to contradict the notion of Maher (1988) in that we have not found that patients with delusions explain abnormal

TABLE 13.3
Correlation Matrix between Symptom Ratings and
Total Number of "Other" Responses Obtained for
Each Subject

Symptom	*"Self"*	*"Other"*
Hallucinations	−0.14	0.35
Delusions	−0.58*	0.57*
Psychomotor retardation	−0.09	−0.16

$N = 20$; * $P < 0.01$ Spearman's Rho statistic.

TABLE 13.4
Sample of Mani's Responses During the Pitch Distortion Experiment

Pitch	Response
+2	"It only speaks when I speak. Sounds like the sounds a deaf person might make."
+5	"Still the same thing. Any time I try to speak it speaks with me."
−4	"The voice has changed to a masculine voice. Same as a deaf masculine voice. I think it's an evil spirit speaking when I speak."
0	"A female voice doesn't sound like me."
−3	"A masculine voice. Different people."
−6	"A different masculine voice. I think it's lower."

experiences in a normal way. Rather, they seem abnormally likely to experience events as caused by alien agencies.

Whilst we would obviously like to see these results replicated in larger samples of patients, we believe that we can trust their reliability on the grounds that they are in accordance with other findings in hallucinating and deluded patients. Mintz and Alpert (1972) demonstrated that, when required to make judgements about the content of degraded auditory stimuli, hallucinating patients were overly confident in the correctness of judgements made under conditions of low accuracy. In the visual domain, early (incorrect) perceptual hypotheses tend to be accepted (McCormick & Broekma, 1978; cited in Fleminger, 1992). And Huq, Garety, and Hemsley (1988) demonstrated deluded patients' tendency to "jump to conclusions" in the context of a probabilistic reasoning task (replicated by Garety, Hemsley, & Wessely, 1991). It seems to us plausible that each of these studies illustrates in its own way the operation of a common cognitive style (as opposed to a bias) which facilitates the acceptance of certain incorrect and inappropriate interpretations or responses.

CONCLUSIONS

Reality is not given by experience, but by judgement processes. The characteristics of mental experience that provide it with the quality of reality are similar for perception, event memories and beliefs: sensory detail; embeddedness in spatial and temporal context; embeddedness in supporting memories, knowledge and beliefs; and the absence of consciousness or memory for the cognitive operations producing the event or belief. Reality testing of on-going perception and reality monitoring of memories and beliefs are complex judgement processes that are subject to error and more difficult in some situations than others.

Johnson (1988, p. 57)

Under normal conditions our sensory system makes the distinction between those stimuli that are properly categorised and presented to consciousness as external in origin and those that are presented as the products of internal processes (e.g. images, memories, ideas). In normal circumstances these latter experiences are invariably coterminous with "the self". When I just had a thought "enter my mind" about telephoning my mother-in-law I may have briefly thought about why that particular thought should enter my head just then, but I did not question whether that thought was of me: the attribution of "I" is unconscious, automatic, "transparent".

In many of the experiences we have described in this chapter it would appear that this (unconscious) attribution process has gone awry. We have outlined a cognitive theory which models this process and we have described an experimental paradigm which would appear to have potential in tapping this process. Applying this paradigm we have demonstrated that many patients (the majority in our experiment) who are hallucinated and deluded are predisposed to locate the source of their own internally generated speech in an external agent. However, the fact that in this study two hallucinated patients in whom delusions could not be elicited did not misattribute the source suggests that such a tendency may not be the only, or most significant even, cognitive factor underlying auditory hallucinations.

Rather, the results detailed above suggest to us that the delusional state, or delusional processing style renders patients more amenable to attribution errors, which may in turn render them more susceptible to the experience of auditory hallucinations; some other processing deficit is required in order to generate auditory hallucinations. We would suggest that the "corollary discharge" deficit proposed earlier still stands as a possible candidate.

This formulation fits very well with current models of psychiatric disorders and symptoms. These models incorporate and attempt to describe the dynamic interaction of cognitive processes involved in (1) belief generation and maintenance, (2) perception, and (3) judgement processes. Thus, in his theoretical account of episodes of delusional misidentification, Fleminger (1992) proposed a "morbid cycle" of false expectations, driven by false beliefs which may result in misperceptions, which in turn reinforce those false beliefs. In essence this is a positive feedback mechanism involving belief, judgement, and perception. Misperceptions can arise as a result of poor quality data or dysfunction in any of these domains. Central to this account is the notion of perception as an active, constructive process incurring substantial preconscious processing. These preconscious processes operate in such a way as to limit hypotheses concerning the possible nature of the stimulus and consequently influence the interpretation and the perceptual experience of the stimulus (see Marcel, 1983).

On the basis of our experimental results we would like to suggest a cognitive explanation of auditory hallucinations along the lines of

Fleminger's general model. Specifically, we would like to suggest that in some schizophrenic patients who experience auditory hallucinations the (internal?) speech generation system is compromised in terms of a dysfunction in a "corollary discharge" system, which at a preconscious level leaves internally generated events unlabelled as such. This, coupled with a co-existing proclivity or propensity for (mis)attributing events to external agents results in the experience of auditory hallucinations. Moreover we believe this theoretical account can be extended to explain other symptoms. The critical factor is which sensory system develops a fault in the "corollary discharge" mechanism. A failure of the normal "corollary discharge" associated with body movement could provide the source of delusions of control (for evidence of such a dysfunction in schizophrenic patients see Frith & Done, 1989; Malenka, Angel, Hampton, & Berger, 1982; Mlaker, Jensterle, & Frith, 1994), while a dysfunction in the realm of thought might explain "telepathy", "thought broadcasting", and "thought insertion" or "thought withdrawal".

In this chapter we have tried to give a flavour of what it is like to have hallucinations and delusions. We have shown that these symptoms cannot simply be classified as false perceptions and false beliefs. Although hallucinations have a strong perceptual component, the voices are usually experienced as emanating from an external agent with specific (and usually malevolent) intentions towards the hearer. Thus, this readiness to find malevolent agents in the world seems to be a common feature of both hallucinations and delusions. In order to understand these abnormal experiences it will be necessary to develop cognitive accounts of belief formation and how this relates to perception. As in other areas of psychology, the study of the abnormal beliefs and perceptions described by psychotic patients should have a major role in the construction of such accounts.

REFERENCES

Aggernaes, A. (1972). The experienced reality of hallucinations and other psychological phenomena: An empirical analysis. *Acta Psychiatrica Scandinavica, 48*, 220–238.

American Psychiatric Association. (1987). *Diagnostic and statistical manual of mental disorders* (3rd ed., rev.). Washington, DC: American Psychiatric Association.

Benjamin, L.S. (1989). Is chronicity a function of the relationship between the person and the auditory hallucination? *Schizophrenia Bulletin, 15*, 291–310.

Bentall, R.P., Baker, G.A., & Havers, S. (1991). Reality monitoring and psychotic hallucinations. *British Journal of Clinical Psychology, 30*, 213–222.

Cahill, C., Silbersweig, D.A. & Frith, C.D. (Submitted). *Psychotic experiences induced in deluded patients using distorted auditory feedback.*

Chadwick, P., & Birchwood, M. (1994). The omnipotence of voices: A cognitive approach to auditory hallucinations. *British Journal of Psychiatry, 164*, 190–201.

Chapman, L.J., & Chapman, J.P. (1988). The genesis of delusions. In T.F. Oltmanns & B.A. Maher (Eds.), *Delusional beliefs*. New York: Wiley.

Costello, C.G. (1970). Classification and psychopathology. In C.G. Costello (Ed.), *Symptoms of psychopathology*. New York: John Wiley & Sons.

Costello, C.G. (1992). Research on symptoms versus research on syndromes: Arguments in favour of allocating more time to the study of symptoms. *British Journal of Psychiatry, 160*, 304–308.

Critchley, E.M.R., Denmark, J.C., Warren, F., & Wilson, K.A. (1981). Hallucinatory experiences in prelingually profoundly deaf schizophrenics. *British Journal of Psychiatry, 138*, 30–32.

David, A. (1994). The neuropsychological origin of auditory hallucinations. In A.S. David & J.C. Cutting (Eds.), *The neuropsychology of schizophrenia*. Hove, UK: Lawrence Erlbaum Associates Ltd.

David, A.S., & Howard R. (1994). An experimental phenomenological approach to delusional memory in schizophrenia and late paraphrenia. *Psychological Medicine, 24*, 515–524.

Ellis, H.D., & Young, A.W. (1990). Accounting for delusional misidentification. *British Journal of Psychiatry, 157*, 239–248.

Fleminger, S. (1992). Seeing is believing: The role of "preconscious" perceptual processing in delusional misidentification. *British Journal of Psychiatry, 160*, 293–303.

Frith, C.D. (1992). *The cognitive neuropsychology of schizophrenia*. Hove, UK: Lawrence Erlbaum Associates Ltd.

Frith, C.D., & Done, J.D. (1989). Experiences of alien control in schizophrenia reflect a disorder in the central monitoring of action. *Psychological Medicine, 19*, 359–363.

Frith, C.D., Leary, J., Cahill, C., & Johnstone, E.C. (1991). Performance on psychological tests: Demographic and clinical correlates of the results of these tests. *British Journal of Psychiatry, 159* (Suppl. 13), 26–29.

Garety, P. (1991). Reasoning and delusion. *British Journal of Psychiatry, 159* (Suppl. 14), 14–18.

Garety, P., Hemsley, D., & Wessely, S. (1991). Reasoning in deluded schizophrenic and paranoid patients. *Journal of Nervous and Mental Disease, 179*, 194–201.

Hoffman, R.E. (1986). Verbal hallucinations and language production processes in schizophrenia. *Behavioural & Brain Sciences, 9*, 503–548.

Holst, E., von, & Mittelstaedt, H. (1950). Das Reafferenzprinzip (Wechselwirkungen zwischen Zentralnervensystem und Peripherie). *Naturwissenschaften, 37*, 464–476.

Huq, S.F., Garety, P., & Hemsley, D.R. (1988). Probabilistic judgements in deluded and non-deluded subjects. *Quarterly Journal of Experimental Psychology: Human Learning and Memory, 40A*, 801–812.

Johnson, M.K. (1988). Discriminating the origin of information. In T.F. Oltmanns & B.A. Maher (Eds.), *Delusional beliefs*. New York: Wiley.

Johnson, M.K., & Raye, C.L. (1981). Reality monitoring. *Psychological Review, 88*, 67–85.

Johnstone, E.C., Crow, T.J., Frith, C.D., & Owens, D.G.C. (1988). The Northwick Park "functional" psychosis study: Diagnosis and treatment response. *Lancet, 322*, 119–125.

Johnstone, E.C., Crow, T.J., Johnson, A.L., & McMillan, J.F. (1986). The Northwick Park study of first episodes of schizophrenia. Vol. 1: Presentation of the illness and problems relating to admission. *British Journal of Psychiatry, 148*, 115–120.

Krawiecka, M., Goldberg, D., & Vaughan, M. (1977). A standardised psychiatric assessment for rating chronic psychotic patients. *Acta Psychiatrica Scandinavica, 55*, 299–308.

Lishman, A. (1987). *Organic psychiatry* (2nd ed.). Oxford: Blackwell Scientific Publications.

Maher, B.A. (1974). Delusional thinking and perceptual disorder. *Journal of Individual Psychology, 30*, 98–113.

Maher, B.A. (1988). Anomalous experiences and delusional thinking: The logic of explanations. In T.F. Oltmanns & B.A. Maher (Eds.), *Delusional beliefs*. New York: Wiley.

Malenka, R.C., Angel, R.W., Hampton, B., & Berger, P.A. (1982). Impaired central error correcting behaviour in schizophrenia. *Archives of General Psychiatry, 39*, 101–107.

Marcel, A. (1983). Conscious and unconscious perception: An approach to the relations between phenomenal experience and perceptual processes. *Cognitive Psychology, 15*, 238–300.

McCormick, D.J., & Broekma, V.J. (1978). Size estimation, perceptual recognition and cardiac response rate in acute paranoid and non-paranoid schizophrenics. *Journal of Abnormal Psychology, 87*, 385–398.

Mintz, S., & Alpert, M. (1972). Imagery vividness, reality testing and schizophrenic hallucinations. *Journal of Abnormal Psychology, 79*, 310–316.

Mlakar, J., Jensterle, J., & Frith, C.D. (in press). Central monitoring deficiency and schizophrenic symptoms. *Psychological Medicine.*

Persons, J.B. (1986). The advantages of studying psychological phenomena rather than psychiatric diagnoses. *American Psychologist, 41*, 1252–1260.

Sartorius, N., Jablensky, A., Korten, G., Ernberg, G., Anker, M., & Cooper, J.E. (1986). Early manifestations and first-contact incidence of schizophrenia in different cultures. *Psychological Medicine, 16*, 909–928.

Schneider, K. (1959). *Clinical psychopathology.* New York: Grune & Stratton.

Sims, A. (1988). *Symptoms in the mind: An introduction to descriptive psychopathology.* London: Baillière Tindal.

Slade, P.D., & Bentall, R.P. (1988). *Sensory deception: A scientific analysis of hallucination.* London: Croom Helm.

Sperry, R.W. (1950). Neural basis of the spontaneous optokinetic response produced by visual inversion. *Journal of Comparative and Physiological Psychology, 43*, 482–489.

Strauss, J.S. (1969). Hallucinations and delusions as points on continua function. *Archives of General Psychiatry, 21*, 581–586.

Strauss, J.S. (1989). Subjective experiences of schizophrenia. *Schizophrenia Bulletin, 15*, 179–188.

Wing, J.K., Cooper, J.E., & Sartorius, N. (1974). *The measurement and classification of psychiatric symptoms.* Cambridge, UK: Cambridge University Press.

World Health Organization. (1973). *Report of the International Pilot Study of Schizophrenia.* Cambridge, UK: Cambridge University Press.

World Health Organization. (1992). *The ICD-10 classification of mental and behavioural disorders: Clinical descriptions and diagnostic guidelines.* Geneva: World Health Organization.

Wright, S., Young, A.W., & Hellawell, D.J. (1993). Sequential Cotard and Capgras delusions. *British Journal of Clinical Psychology, 32*, 345–349.

Author Index

Abas, M. 126
Abed, R.T. 17
Abel, H.M. 209, 210, 211
Abeles, M. 211, 229
Abrams, R. 30, 31
Abramson, L.Y. 165
Adityanjee 141
Ahern, G.L. 143
Ahmed, S.N. 241
Akelaitis, A.J. 179
Albert, M.L. 194
Alderman, N. 64
Alexander, M.P. 31, 167, 188, 190,
    202–203
Almeida, O. 261
Almeida, O.P. 18, 167
Alpert, M. 287
Altman, E. 237
Anderson, D.N. 17, 22, 167
Anderson, G. 126
Anderson, S.W. 237, 249, 250
Andreasen, N.C. 112, 116
Andrews, E. 225
Angel, R.W. 289
Angelergues, R. 56

Angrist, B. 115
Anker, M. 127, 269
Antin, S.P. 211
Antonucci, A. 194
Appleby, L. 123
Arbelaiz, R. 173
Ardila, A. 31
Arndt, S. 116
Asaad, G. 242, 250, 251
Ashenhurst, E.M. 24

Baade, L.E. 116
Baddeley, A.D. 53, 86, 109, 117, 130,
    131, 221, 239
Bailey, C. 240
Baker, G.A. 283
Banaji, M.R. 140, 259
Barban, L. 127
Bard, J. 140
Barnes, T.R.E. 117
Baron-Cohen, S. 9, 84
Barry, C. 174, 180
Basso, A. 193, 219
Bateman, D. 156
Baumeister, R.F. 143

Subject Index